MW00484303

Big Business and the State

SUNY series in the Sociology of Work and Organizations

Richard H. Hall, editor

Big Business and the State

Historical Transitions and
Corporate Transformation,
1880s–1990s

HARLAND PRECHEL

STATE UNIVERSITY OF NEW YORK PRESS

Published by
State University of New York Press, Albany

© 2000 State University of New York

Printed in the United States of America

For information, address State University of New York Press,
State University Plaza, Albany, N.Y., 12246

Production by Michael Haggett
Marketing by Dana E. Yanulavich

Library of Congress Cataloging-in-Publication Data
Prechel, Harland N.
    Big business and the state : historical transitions and corporate transformation,
1880s–1990s / Harland Prechel.
        p.   cm — (SUNY series in the sociology of work and organizations)
    Includes bibliographical references and index.
    ISBN 0–7914–4593–3 (hc : alk. paper) — ISBN 0–7914–4594–1 (pbk. : alk. paper)
    1. Big business—Government policy—United States—History.   2. Industrial
policy—United States—History.   3. Corporation law—United States—History.   4.
Corporations—United States—Growth—History.   5. Industrial organization—United
States—History.   6. Capitalism—United States—History.   I. Title.   II. Series.
HD2356.U5 P73   2000
338.973'04—dc21   99-054293

10 9 8 7 6 5 4 3 2 1

To the memory of my grandfather, Louis Prechel (1893–1989),
whose personal narratives helped me to understand
class and politics in the United States.

Contents

Tables

Figures

Abbreviations

ACRS	Accelerated Cost Recovery System
AD	Antidumping
AISI	American Iron and Steel Institute
BOF	Basic Oxygen Furnace
CAD	Computer Automated Design
CAM	Computer-Aided Manufacturing
CIM	Computer-Integrated Manufacturing
CVD	Countervailing Duty
EEC	European Economic Community
EPA	Environmental Protection Agency
GATT	General Agreement on Tariffs and Trade
IPO	Initial Public Offering
ITC	International Trade Commission
MLSF	Multilayered Subsidiary Form
MDF	Multidivisional Form
NLRB	National Labor Relations Board
OPEC	Organization of Petroleum Exporting Countries
OSHA	Occupational Safety and Health Agency
PPSS	Plant Planning and Scheduling System
RA81	Economic Recovery Tax Act of 1981
RA87	Revenue Act of 1987
ROI	Return on Investment
SPC	Statistical Process Control
SQC	Statistical Quality Control
STAC	Steel Tripartite Advisory Committee
TCA	Transaction Cost Analysis
TLP	Team Leadership Program
TPM	Trigger Price Mechanism
TRA86	Tax Reform Act of 1986
USW	United Steel Workers of America
VRA	Voluntary Restraint Agreement

Acknowledgments

This book benefited substantially from financial support provided by the National Science Foundation/American Sociological Association Fund for the Advancement of the Discipline (1994), which supported my proposal, "The Multisubsidiary Form," to collect data on corporate divisions and subsidiaries. The Office of Graduate Research at Texas A&M University provided additional support to collect these data, and a faculty leave sponsored by the Office of the Provost and my department head, Dudley Poston, allowed me the time to write. I'd also like to acknowledge the late Derek Gill, my former department chair at the University of Maryland Baltimore County, who enthusiastically supported the early stages of the quantitative phase of this project. I am indebted to American Steel Corporation (a pseudonym) for providing access to their archives, and permission to conduct the many hours of interviews with their employees who provided crucial data for the case-oriented analysis. I am indebted to the Calumet Regional Library for access to their archives. I thank Glen Harrison and the Department of Economics in the International School of Business at the University of South Carolina for providing office space and other support so that I could be away from my department and concentrate on writing this manuscript during my faculty leave.

This book has also benefited from the input of several people whom I would like to thank. No doubt, I have omitted acknowledging the important contributions of some people to whom I apologize for not keeping better records. At the State University of New York Press, Nancy Ellegate was supportive from the onset and Michael Haggett provided valuable advice and answered many questions on how to sharpen the manuscript presentation. I thank Odelia Wong who helped me think about how to design the variable-oriented phase of my research. The many conversations with John Boies, my coauthor on some of the variable-oriented research that emerged from this project, helped me to think through many issues. Tim Woods, an extremely talented graduate research assistant, was directly involved in several phases of the project. I thank Tim for his assistance in data collection, data management, ideas about directions to pursue, and, most importantly, for taking the initiative on the project when other tasks drew my attention away from it. I also thank two very dedicated, bright, and conscientious undergraduate students: Laurie Reaver, a student at the University of Maryland Baltimore County, who collected much of the data on the largest one hundred industrial corporations, and Sheri Locklear, a student at Texas A&M University, who played a key role in completing the data collection on these corporations and extending the data collection to the two hundred largest industrial corporations. I also thank Derek Kalahar, Theresa Morris, and Beverly Stiles, graduate students at Texas A&M University, for their careful work on the data collection, entry, and management. Some of my ideas and material published here were drawn from my previously published articles in the American Sociological Review, Social Science Quarterly, Sociological Forum, and Sociological Inquiry.

Several colleagues provided valuable feedback and encouragement on various parts of the project. They include Howard Aldrich, Kenneth Benson, Alessandro Bonanno, Linda Brewster Stearns, Michael Burawoy, Alfred Chandler, Dan Clawson, Kevin Delaney, Frank Dobbin, Jerald Hage, Richard Hall, Kevin Leicht, Donald Light, Clarence Lo, Mark Mizruchi, Jill Quadagno, William Roy, and Donald Tomaskovic-Devey. I thank Charles Warriner who introduced me to the literature on complex organizations. Bob Antonio and Dave Willer have been supportive critics over the years, encouraging me to pursue this project as well as providing crucial feedback on it. I thank Dave for pressuring me to think about sociological issues in new ways. I thank Bob for encouraging me to take Occam's razor to the big ideas during the early phase of the project. I am also indebted to John Harms and Patrick Akard for the ongoing dialogue that began when we were in graduate school. In addition, both John and Pat read the entire manuscript and provided detailed comments that helped me to sharpen the conceptual framework. I also thank my wife, Ruth Larson, whose scholarly counsel aided me in presenting my ideas more clearly. And I thank our three-year-old daughter, Helen, who offered delightful distractions at the proper moments, making this a better book than it otherwise would have been.

Big Business and the State

CHAPTER 1

Capital Dependence, Historical Transitions, and Corporate Transformations

With the possible exception of the state, few organizations exercise more power or have more effect on individuals than the corporation. Decisions made in corporations have profound effects on the organization of work and the production and distribution of wealth and income. Further, corporations have tremendous effects on other powerful organizations including the state and quasi-state organizations such as the Federal Reserve Bank and the General Agreement on Tariffs and Trade. The corporation has achieved its current position as a powerful social actor in just over one hundred years.

My motivation to examine the modern corporation emerged, in part, from a desire to understand corporations' responses to the economic instability that emerged in the 1970s and 1980s. After my initial examination of corporate change in the contemporary period, it became apparent that responses to capitalist instability are affected by class-based politics and by institutional arrangements established during previous historical periods. As a result, the effects of capitalist instability, institutional arrangements, and social actors' motives and interests on corporate change became central themes in my analysis.

I conceptualize the corporation as a profoundly historical phenomenon and examine the micro, meso, and macro levels of the social structure to understand the emergence and development of the corporation. Managers are actively engaged in coordinating micro activities across space and time. They try to bring the activities of people in different times and places into a sequence to ensure outcomes (e.g., transforming iron ore and other raw materials into automobile fenders). Managerial activities occur at the micro level and are explicitly oriented toward and defined by the meso (i.e., corporate) and macro (e.g., political, economic) levels. However, this process is fraught with problems. Within the inherently unstable conditions of capitalist economies, the corporation attempts to maintain equilibrium with its environment by (1) structuring the managerial process so it can manufacture products that meet market demand, and (2) stabilizing markets directly through market control or indirectly through political behavior. Two interrelated questions are central to this examination of macro level structures and processes, corporations, and micro-level behaviors. How do structures and processes shape the course of action available to social actors? How do social actors shape structures and process?

To answer these questions, I investigate transformations in the corporation form from the end of the nineteenth century to the end of the twentieth century. The analysis gives particular attention to the relationship between historical transitions and the three most significant shifts in the trajectory of the corporation (i.e., 1880s–1890s, 1920s–1930s, 1980s–1990s). I illustrate how social forces in corporations' environments affect social actors' external-oriented political behavior to restructure the institutional arrangements within which corporations are embedded; these social forces also affect social actors' internal-oriented behavior to restructure the corporate form and managerial process. The particular content and form of these changes are affected by the historically specific institutional arrangements that define the parameters and options available to social actors.

Most corporations changed to the multidivisional form during the middle decades of the twentieth century, a period of economic stability and growth. In contrast, rapid change to the holding-company form in the late nineteenth century and to the multilayered subsidiary form (for more detail, see below) in the late twentieth century occurred during periods of economic instability. The holding-company form and the multilayered subsidiary form share important advantages over the multidivisional form; they provide parent companies with more self-financing capability and make them less liable for breakdowns (e.g., financial, product safety) in their corporate entities (i.e., subsidiary corporations). Changes to the nineteenth century holding-company form and to the late twentieth century multilayered subsidiary form are associated with two of the largest merger waves in the last 110 years, which contributed to the rapid increase in size and wealth of the largest parent companies.

The Framework

In this book, I examine the relationship between historical transitions and the emergence of the modern corporation and analyze its three major transformations. The analysis begins with an investigation of the effects of changing institutional arrangements (e.g., political, economic, ideological) on the emergence of the late nineteenth-century public holding company. This investigation illustrates how various social actors (e.g., capitalists, labor, farmers, state managers) engage in political behavior and effect *transitions*: stages along historical trajectories and radical shifts (Abbott 1997). I also examine the relationship between these macro-level historical transitions and meso-level corporate *transformations*, which may take the form of "deletion, replacement, redistribution, or addition of organizational activities" (Zammuto and Cameron 1985; Prechel 1991: 426). My concern is with those sharp departures from previous corporate forms and managerial processes and with the historical sequences that produce those shifts.

Politics played a central role in the historical transitions and corporate transformations in the United States from the late nineteenth century through the late twentieth century. In his analysis of the Progressive Era (1900–1916), Gabriel Kolko argued that political behavior emerged in response to economic conditions. Kolko defined *political capitalism* as "the utilization of political outlets to attain conditions of stability, predictability, and security—to attain rationalization—in the economy," which included preserving the social relations essential to capitalist society (1963:3). He pointed out that although big business does not always have a coherent conception of the relationships between their economic goals and the actions necessary to achieve those goals, they exercise power to establish state policies that facilitate rationalization of the economy. According to Kolko (1963:3), *rationalization* is "the organization of the economy and the larger political and social spheres in a manner that will allow corporations to function in a predicable and secure environment permitting reasonable profits over the long run."[1] Rationalization is not equivalent to efficiency or rational. Rationalization is a historical process that entails contradictions, irrationalities, disequilibria, and conflicts (Antonio 1979). Because capitalism is inherently unstable, its social organization is politically constructed and reconstructed. The intensity of this change varies historically as do the conflicts and contradictions that bring about the political behavior to reconstruct the social organization of capitalism in general and the corporation in particular.

Two interrelated theoretical logics are crucial to understanding the causal processes that produced the corporation and changes in it. First, the logic of capital accumulation constitutes an important causal force of corporate change because the survival of the corporation is dependent on accumulating capital. *Capital accumulation* reflects the overall financial position of the corporation; it entails the mobilization, transformation, and exploitation of inputs to increase the total capital of the corporation (Marx 1977; Sweezy 1970; Bowles and Edwards 1985; Prechel 1990:652, fn. 4). Capital accumulation is important not only because it is essential to the survival of the corporation, but also because capital-accumulation considerations constitute a crucial basis for state managers and corporate managers' decisions. Capital accumulation requires access to markets and maintenance of an adequate *liquidity position:* cash and marketable securities less any short-term borrowing to meet operating expenses. Liquidity is necessary to ensure capital for reinvestment and to reduce corporations' dependence on external capital. These variables (e.g., profit, liquidity) affect the financial strength of the corporation, the value of its stock, and, ultimately, its capacity to survive. A narrow focus on prof-its can obscure the financial strengths and weaknesses of a corporation because state business policy (e.g., tax investment credits, depreciation allowances) pro-vides corporations with substantial tax deductions that improve their liquidity po-sitions, but may lower their reported profits. High liquidity facilitates corpo-rations' capacity to accumulate capital over the long term by improving their cash flow and capacity to reinvest in technological innovations, and to merge with or acquire other corporations.

Second, corporate change is affected by the logic of power. Max Weber [1921] (1978) defined social power as the probability that actors will be able to realize their own objectives even against opposition from others. Some researchers argue that Weber's conception of behavioral power is too narrow, and call for a concep-tion of power that draws from rational choice theory and includes a conception of how rational action produces structural power: "the ability to determine the con-text within which decisions are made by affecting the consequences of one alterna-tive over another" (Roy 1997:13). There are two ways in which this dimension of power is important. It is commonly used to understand how social action affects social structure. Although I use this formulation to understand behavior at the micro level (i.e., individuals), there is a second and important dimension of struc-tural power. The rational-action assumption in structural power—social actions that set up the context for decisions—draws attention to the presence of irration-ality in historical processes. That is, an examination of structural power shows that the self-interested (i.e., rational) behavior of social actors produces social struc-tures that are frequently contradictory and irrational over the long term. Thus, a conception of structural power—based in rational-choice assumptions—is impor-tant because it shows that social actors are only *intendedly rational:* social actions may not have rational outcomes. Historical analyses of power must be sensitive to how the exercise of power produces outcomes that are both rational and irrational. Although social actors may act rationally at a particular time and place, their ac-tions are not equivalent to rationality in history. Rationality is historically contin-gent; the definition of rationality is time dependent. Also, what is rational for some social actors at one point in time may not be rational for others.

Rethinking rationalization as a historical process is important because big busi-ness does not always have a coherent conception of the relationship between their economic goals and the actions necessary to achieve those goals. Although big business frequently obtains acceptable outcomes, the resolution of class and class segment conflict may not (and often does not) produce the structure and context intended by the social actors who exercise power (Prechel 1990, 1991, 1994b). Indi-vidual rationality is bounded because social actors cannot predict the direction of capitalist development. Thus, historicizing the corporation entails developing a conceptual framework that acknowledges irrationality in historical processes. This framework explicitly acknowledges that irrationalities exist between levels of the social structures. Whereas the logic of capital accumulation is dynamic (i.e., markets change), the logic of social control used in the corporation is static (i.e., corporations develop elaborate mechanisms to ensure standardization of social action). As a result, social structures move out of equilibrium with the market in which they are embedded.

The analysis here deviates from most studies of the corporation in four fundamental ways. First, I show that rapid organizational change does occur. Much organizational research advances inertia arguments or assumes that change occurs through diffusion on a gradual or incremental basis.[2] I suggest that certain historical conditions generate rapid change. A task for historical sociology is to identify the processes that contribute to rapid social change. The comparative-historical method is employed here because it is attuned to complex social processes that are affected by many variables. Explicit within this analysis is that inertia has a stabilizing effect on social structures, but unique constellations of variables at certain historical junctures change pattern-oriented action and produce historical transitions and corporate transformations.

Second, I theorize agency. Although organizational inertia can be an important source of stability, it is important to understand the basis of that stability: structures remain stable because social actors reenact those structures. Social structures are patterns of relations "continuously enacted by actors doing things with others" (Abbott 1977:99; also see Mead 1931; Weick 1969). Even during periods of stability, the agency structure relationship is crucial to understanding social process because social action reconstitutes structure. Structures provide a memory of the past (Abbott 1997). As such, social structures provide knowledge of what is required to reenact the future in such a way that it informs social actors that have interests in retaining or changing the social structure. Reenacting the past or changing the future entails the exercise of power. Each social action "reconnects some existing structures, disconnects others, and indeed creates some structures unseen before" (Abbott 1997:99).These "structures unseen before" emerge because social actors change their behavior.

The theoretical logic developed here conceptualizes change as the outcome of social action that occurs inside and outside the corporation. Rather than assuming that managers are autonomous from capitalists, the framework here suggests that "a wide degree of control over the policies of management may rest in hands outside the enterprise, by virtue of their power over credit or financing" (Weber 1978:139–140). That is, the separation of the managerial function from the ownership function is not synonymous with the separation of ownership from control (Zeitlin 1974). Although capitalists may not be actively engaged in managing the corporation, top managers remain accountable to them. Capitalists exercise their power during historical junctures when they perceive that their interests are jeopardized (e.g., after extended periods of capital accumulation constraints and declining profits). Capitalists' mobilization focuses on two broad strategies: (1) inside restructuring (e.g., managerial process, corporate form), and (2) outside restructuring (e.g., corporations' political, economic, and ideological institutional arrangements).

Corporations are conceptualized as collectives of social actors—with differing degrees of power—that use their resources to achieve goals and agendas. Corporations must accumulate capital to survive, and top management and its board of directors are responsible for ensuring those outcomes. Top management is allocated authority and responsibility over strategic decisions to ensure that corporations achieve stated goals. Although top managers' behaviors are affected by many variables, corporations' capital accumulation goals have priority. Further, the imperatives associated with top managements' structural position have the greatest effect on their motives and behaviors. As James and Soref (1981:2–3) put it: "social structural positions and their associated imperatives have a logical causal priority over the motivations of the individuals who are selected to fill those positions." Structural imperatives create incentives for top management: low profit is the most consistent determinant for dismissing top managers (Zeitlin 1974; Berg and Zald 1978; James and Soref 1981). Corporations' structural imperatives produce behaviors that are affected by historically specific profit-making opportunities and constraints. These structural imperatives are independent of particular individuals occupying decision-making positions in corporations.

Third, the theoretical framework developed here examines the relationships among the micro, meso, and macro levels of analysis. The failure to bridge the gap among levels of analysis is characteristic of sociological theory in general (Coleman 1986; Collins 1988). As a result, social theory does little to elucidate key interactive relationships that constitute social structures (Giddens 1979). The corporation is an appropriate unit of analysis to articulate micro-meso-macro linkages because it affects, and is affected by, macro-level processes and social actions at the micro level. The micro-level link is important because without understanding the intricate and routine day-to-day organizational processes it is hard to understand how social structures are constructed or how organizations attempt to control individual behavior oriented toward some ultimate end (Stinchcombe 1990).

Fourth, the corporation is conceptualized as both a legal and an administrative entity. This is in contrast to most studies of the corporation that conceptualize the corporation as a managerial-administrative entity. This difference has important effects on research designs and findings. For example, in *Strategy and Structure* (1962) Alfred Chandler identified the managerial characteristics associated with the multidivisional form (MDF). Then, he used this definition to assign a corporate form to other corporations with these characteristics (also see Rumelt 1974; Harris 1983).[3] In contrast, the framework used here incorporates property rights, which define the legal and financial obligations between parent companies and their corporate entities. An examination of property rights directs researchers' attention toward the parent company's rights over its corporate entities, the limits of its responsibilities, and how those laws define *ownership control:* the percent of ownership necessary to control a corporate entity. This formulation captures the financial and organizational feasibility of establishing alternate forms of ownership control as corporate property rights and incentives to exercise those rights change over time.

An examination of property rights draws attention to the legal basis of the relationship among corporate entities, especially between parent companies and their *subsidiary corporations*, which are separate legal entities that are partially or wholly owned and controlled by a parent company (Prechel 1997:409). There are several implications of this form of ownership control, including the financial tools available to raise capital and the amount of capital necessary to control business entities (i.e., subsidiaries versus divisions) (Prechel 1991, 1997b). Parent companies can exercise ownership control when they own more than 50 percent of a subsidiary corporations' stock. The use of subsidiaries and divisions to organize corporate assets is historically contingent and is affected by their institutional arrangements, which include regional state (e.g., New Jersey, Delaware) laws of incorporation, federal tax laws, and corporations' capacity to raise capital from internal and external capital markets.

Although capital-dependence theory elaborated here deviates from prevailing theories of organizational change, the idea that capitalist competition is historically contingent and results in social change is not new. Marx (1977) understood capitalism as an economic system that contained contradictions that produced periodic crises requiring resolution. Schumpeter's (1964) conception of "creative destruction" viewed historical variation in the form of competition as the primary mechanism through which older forms of organization were replaced by new forms. More recently, sociologists maintain that industries develop at different times, and historical conditions shape and reshape the industry structure, the exit and entry of organizations, and the adaptive structure of firms (Stinchcombe 1965; Benson 1977; Tushman and Romanelli 1985; Prechel 1991; Roy 1991, 1997).

Historical transitions and corporate transformations are effected by the interrelated logics of power and capital accumulation, which are manifested in the behavior of corporations, classes, and class segments. The corporation is a crucial social actor in the rationalization process because it is an organizational entity that provides a basis of political and economic power. Corporate actors do not simply react to the institutional arrangements (e.g., the market, an autonomous state). Rather, corporations are political actors. Corporations are organizations through which capitalists define their interests, establish political coalitions, and pursue political behaviors to advance their agenda. Corporations, however, do not always have the power to overcome crises and contradictions in the economy. Under these historical conditions, political unity emerges within the capitalist class and class segments.

Capitalist class segments are collectives of social actors that represent the divisions that exist among business segments and conform to the relationship each branch of capital has with the economy. Class segments emerge as political actors because differential rates of capital accumulation exist within the various segments of capital (Offe 1975; Poulantzas 1978; Aglietta 1979). As a consequence of their distinct location in the social process of production, class segments have specific political economic requirements and concrete interests that may be contradictory to those of other class segments (Zeitlin, Neuman, and Ratcliff 1978; Zeitlin 1980; Prechel 1990). Because the capital-accumulation process affects them differently, capitalist class segments frequently disagree on solutions to contradictions that emerge as crises. The resolution of conflict entails the exercise of power, and the outcome of power struggles are manifested in both state and corporate policies and structures. These political behaviors include attempts to define the institutional arrangements within which corporations are embedded and in which capital accumulation occurs.

Historical Transitions

In examining social change, I address a central theoretical problem of political and historical sociology: the conditions under which classes mobilize and act on their shared interest (Tilly 1981; Staples 1987; Prechel 1990: 664). I raise three questions that are related to this theoretical problem. First, what are the bases of social action? Second, if similar historical conditions emerge at different points in time, do similar interests emerge and do groups act on those interests in similar ways? Third, to what extent do historical conditions and the social structures affect political mobilization, the capacity of social actors to exercise power, and historical transitions?

To address these questions, I use comparative-historical methods. Specifically, to analyze the relationship between historical transitions and corporate transformations, I draw from the agency-structure linkages in Max Weber's comparative-historical conception of *multicausality* where organizational, legal, ideological, and economic forces are all dominant (Kalberg 1994). Economic change, by itself, does not produce change in the social organization of capitalism. Incipient legal and ideological forms must already exist (Kalberg 1994). However, an analysis of economic transitions is crucial to understanding corporate transformations. The corporation is a profit-making entity that responds to changing economic conditions, especially during crisis periods. Therefore, an examination of corporate change must examine the historical conditions that generate an "economic ethic" or an "economic form" of action.

Weber's historically informed conception of multicausality stipulates that causal forces are historically contingent. For Weber, economic, political, legal, and cultural forces constitute the broad categories that influence social action. Weber explicitly argues that patterned action-orientations may vary in intensity.[4] The emphasis on patterned action-orientations also directs researchers' attention toward causes that are constant in one or more cases at different points in time. This is a crucial part of the historical-comparative method. I examine whether similar causes produce *turning points*—consequential shifts that redirect a process (Abbott 1997)—in the corporate form. To identify the causal forces that produce historical transitions, researchers must first identify *trajectories*—interlocked and interdependent sequences of events—(Abbott 1997) that produce patterned action-orientations. While trajectories represent stability, turning points represent change. Identifying trajectories and turning points is essential for understanding historical sequences and identifying transitions.

I employ historical case-oriented (i.e., small *n* and many variables) and variable-oriented methods (i.e., few variables and a large *n*) to examine the historical processes that produce social change. Shortcomings of variable-oriented analysis include data limitations. Quantitative data are frequently unavailable or unreliable. Thus, historical processes are difficult to quantify and mathematize.[5] Crucial variables are frequently not operationalized, which constrains theory-driven research. Also, the ahistorical assumptions in quantitative methods are not well suited to analyzing corporate change; they are constrained by assumptions of linearity and normality that cannot explain the complexities and disequilibria of social processes (Benson 1977; Heydebrand 1977; Isaac and Griffin 1989). In contrast, historical case-oriented methods make it possible to examine evidence about historical sequence and agency, and capture the complex social processes that produce motives, behaviors, and social structures (Abbott 1997; Ragin 1997; Rueschemeyer and Stephens 1997). The historical narrative here relies on case-oriented data and describes how linkages among levels of the social structure break down and how social actors mobilize politically to restructure their institutional and organizational arrangements.

Case-oriented studies have been criticized for their lack of generalizability. Although important, that argument obscures the contributions of case-oriented research. The importance of case-oriented research rests in its capacity to show whether the case is typical or atypical. That is, the value of a case is in whether it resembles or differs from prevailing conceptions of the empirical world, and why those resemblances or differences are theoretically important (Prechel 1994b:728). If case-oriented research identifies a deviation from prevailing theory, this is sufficient evidence in its own right to justify further investigations of the phenomena, which may include more theoretically restrictive variable-oriented analysis. Both methods are used here because case-oriented analyses "form the backbone of making institutions dynamic," and variable-oriented analysis "allow statements about the breath of institutional impact" (Janoski, McGill, and Tinsley 1997:262).

Capital Dependence Theory

Since the nineteenth century, researchers in the political economy tradition have argued that the availability of capital affects corporate behavior. By 1867, Karl

Marx (1977) argued that the need to generate capital internally was a driving force behind capitalists' efforts to extract labor from the labor power they purchased. In the 1920s, Max Weber (1978) maintained that decisions concerning capital are defining features of the business enterprise, and that the "autonomous action" of the corporation is dependent on availability of capital, which affects its capacity to pursue opportunities in the market. By the 1960s, John Kenneth Galbraith (1967) argued that few changes have had more effect on the "character of capitalism" than those related to the "shift in power" associated with external versus internal sources of capital (also see Berle and Means 1932; Baran and Sweezy 1966). More recently, researchers suggest that the most important decisions made by managers are those involving the firm's capital structure and who controls its financing (Mintz and Schwartz 1985; Mizruchi and Stearns 1994).

There are four primary forms of financing the corporation (Cutler, Hindess, Hirst, and Hussain 1978). First, corporations obtain financing from internal sources. This capital is the difference between the revenues from the sale of products and operating costs. Second, financing is secured from the state through, for example, tax laws that vary over time (e.g., investment tax credits). Third, corporations obtain capital from debt financing that typically takes the form of bonds or loans. The fourth source of capital is stock issuances, which is a form of self-financing. Although parent companies and their subsidiary corporations can issue stocks and bonds because they are separate legal entities, there is an important difference between these forms of financing. Whereas *stocks* are the legal capital of the business unit divided into shares and are sold, *bonds* are certificates of debt that entail interest payments and must be repaid at a designated time (Rosenberg 1978). The form of financing varies historically and corporations' capacity to use these financial tools is defined by the corporate form and its institutional arrangements.

Capital-dependence theory builds on these and other social embeddedness theories to understand the relationship between social action and emergent corporate forms (Granovetter 1993). Capital-dependence theory is a special case of resource dependence. Whereas resource dependence broadly focuses on all of the resources that are internally produced or exist in the environment that affect behavior (Pfeffer and Salanik 1978), capital-dependence theory focuses on corporations' historically contingent capital-dependent relationship to the political, economic, and ideological dimensions of their institutional environments.

To overcome historically specific capital dependencies that create barriers to profit making, big business mobilizes politically to redefine state business policy. Political solutions are the outcome of the historically specific character of the economy, the state structure, the parameters of the state's formal authority, and the network of interests both inside and outside the state (e.g., alignment of classes and class segments, maintaining stable relations with foreign nation-states) (Prechel 1990). These conditions both elicit responses and define the parameters of social actors' responses. Corporate political behavior is more pronounced when capital dependence and capital shortages constrain profit making. Under these conditions, corporations attempt to realign their internal managerial controls and external institutional arrangements.

Contingent capital-dependence theory suggests that capitalists mobilize politically in order to overcome historically specific barriers to profit making. Following this theoretical logic, I examine those social processes that emerge as contradictions among dimensions of the social structure. Resolutions of contradictions entail restructuring to ensure that the linkages between the levels of the social structure (e.g., micro, meso, macro) are organized in such a way that they facilitate profit making. Under some historical conditions capitalist class segments align their interests with other capitalists and mobilize politically to change these linkages (e.g., corporate form, state business policy). However, their political behavior is dependent on historical variations in corporations' embeddedness in their institutional environment (e.g., political, economic), and their relationship to other class segments and to the state (Prechel 1990; Akard 1992; Quadagno 1992). Conditions encompass "the structure of available alternatives as well as incentives and constraints"—intended and unintended—that result "in aggregates of individual actions or of collective decisions" (Hernes 1976: 515, 534; Prechel 1997a: 411). Although institutional arrangements (e.g., political-legal) affect corporations' capital dependence, motives, and behaviors, the specific alignment of institutional arrangements varies historically (Moore 1966), which, in turn, affects the options available to social actors. In contrast to other social actors, corporations and capitalist class segments have greater power to make their own history. The institutional arrangements that they create, however, may constrain their behavior at a future historical juncture.

Thus, understanding how corporate change occurs must include an examination of how historically specific opportunities and constraints affect decisionmakers' motives, and behaviors. The examination of historical conditions aids in identifying variation in the political-legal structure, in identifying how that variation affects capitalists' capacity to redefine and legitimate the corporation, and in identifying the degree to which the logic of capital accumulation and the logic of power are intertwined. The power of one social actor resides in its structural location in the network of power relations with other social actors engaged in related activities. There are two crucial features of these social relationships: The power of one social actor resides in the dependence of other social actors; the dependence of A upon B is the basis for B's power (Galaskiewicz 1985). However, understanding how power relationships affect behavior—whether of individuals, corporations, or classes—entails identifying social actors and the conditions within which they are willing or unwilling to "risk exclusion from valued resources" (Markovsky, Willer, and Patton 1988:232; Willer 1986). This framework directs the research toward conflicts, the resolution of those conflicts, and determines how the institutional arrangements provide some social actors with power over others.

Using this theoretical framework, I seek to explain how the exercise of power affects the institutionalization and deinstitutionalization of corporate forms and managerial processes. This is in contrast to theories that emphasize isomorphism, diffusion, and inertia. These models have been criticized for focusing "on a small amount of change that goes on within political and economic institutions" (Janoski et al. 1997), and doing little to elucidate *how* corporations change their managerial processes and forms (DiMaggio 1988; Friedland and Alford 1991; Prechel 1991; Hirsch 1997; Stinchcombe 1997).

The Empirical Focus

The empirical focus of my analysis departs from previous analyses in several ways. First, I examine change during three historical periods (i.e., 1880s–1900, 1920s–1930s, 1980s–1990s). I argue that insufficient attention is given to the emergence of the late-nineteenth-century holding company and the social forces that contributed to its rise and decline (but see Roy 1997). I also show that a corporate form similar to the nineteenth-century holding company is emerging in the late twentieth century. I also compare the conditions that effected previous corporate transformation with those effecting current corporate change. Thus, my research is a sharp departure from most analyses of the business enterprise that focus on the emergence and spread of the multidivisional form (MDF).

Second, I show that in response to a range of historical contingencies, the corporation is currently undergoing a transformation to the *multilayered subsidiary form* (MLSF): "a corporation with a hierarchy of two or more levels of subsidiary corporations with a parent company at the top of the hierarchy operating as a management company" (Prechel 1991, 1994a, 1997a: 407). Although the MLSF shares some characteristics with the nineteenth-century holding company, unlike the corporate shell of the holding-company form, many contemporary parent companies with MLSFs actively engage in the financial management of their subsidiary corporations. The MLSF also shares some characteristics of the MDF. Unlike divisions in the MDF, however, subsidiaries are legally separate from the parent company. The implications of these differences are examined in chapters 9, 10, and 11.

Third, the analysis here is a sharp departure from theories that assume the corporation represents quasi markets and that transactions in them result in efficiency (Williamson 1975, 1985). These researchers assume that politics and power do not affect decisions on how to control the managerial process. Instead, they assert that the emergent conception of control is explained by efficiency criteria. Although several researchers question efficiency assumptions, little systematic evidence exists to challenge it (but see Johnson and Kaplan 1991; Prechel 1991). Elaborating on this research, I show that by the 1920s, financial controls were set up to monitor and direct the managerial process in some of the largest industrial corporations. The historically specific form of financial control was affected by the capital-dependent and power relationships between finance capital and industrial capital. Financial control did not represent quasi markets, as efficiency arguments assert. It was unable to assess corporations' cost efficiency. In the middle decades of the twentieth century (i.e., 1930–1970s) corporations did not accurately measure their costs. Further, the formally rational controls set up by corporations created incentive structures and social actions (e.g., decisions) that undermined corporate substantive goals.

Temporality: Historicizing the Corporation

Social change—whether rapid or incremental—is irreducibly a historical question. Changes in routines, rules, and structures evolve through history-dependent processes that do not reliably or quickly reach equilibria (March and Olsen 1989). Examining historical sequences avoids over- and underestimating the effects of certain events, provides insights into the causal sequence of events, and takes into account variation of historical context. In this respect, historical methods are useful to distinguish between time-dependent and non-time-dependent effects. Although historical sequencing does not establish causation, it facilitates the identification of potential causal processes. By examining the constellations of factors (i.e., the sequence of inputs) that produce an output (e.g., state structure change, corporate-form change) the historical comparative method is sensitive to *multiple conjunctural causes*, which do not "anticipate causal uniformity across . . . cases," but expect "different combinations of causes" to produce the same outcome" (Ragin 1997:36). That is, "different causes combine in different and sometimes contradictory ways to produce roughly similar outcomes in different settings" (Ragin 1997:36). I show that corporations began changing to similar forms in the late 1880s and in the late 1980s, and the same or similar variables effected this change (e.g., market competition, availability of capital, state structures). The focus on multiple conjunctural causes entails an examination of complex interaction effects: "the magnitude of any single cause's impact depends on the presence or absence of other causal conditions" (Ragin 1997:37). Temporality is crucial to understanding change because the degree to which we can evaluate the effects of events depends on the degree to which we can grasp the temporal and spatial relationships that influence these changes.

Capital-dependence theory departs in three ways from evolutionary conceptions of change that assume a gradual evolution or diffusion of corporate structures. First, by incorporating a conception of temporality—time dependent variation in the degree of capital dependence—the theory recognizes the differential power of events in history and posits that all events do not have equal effects. Second, by acknowledging the temporal power of events in history, the theory moves beyond assumptions of historical continuity and recognizes historical ruptures. Continuity assumptions entail a "continual unfolding of the same underlying communality," which misrepresent historical processes by homogenizing the differences between space and time (Isaac and Griffin 1989:876). Third, temporality suggests that historical contingencies structure the "motives and actions" of social actors as well as their "interests and opportunities for satisfying them" (Prechel 1990:665). Complex interdependencies shape the particular pathway a process follows and "the determining force of a property or variable is not constant, but contingent on the entire situation at a given time" (Abbott 1991:22). Although past choices affect future options, multiple options are available at a particular time and these options are not predetermined. Focusing on the sequence of events allows the researcher to establish agency and connect the outcome (e.g., policies, social structures) to the social actors exercising power.

To operationalize this conception of temporality, I draw from the periodization used by social structure of accumulation (SSA) theorists (Gordon, Edwards and Reich 1982). This perspective suggest that institutional arrangements weaken under certain historical conditions (e.g., extended periods of slow economic growth), which constraints investments into innovative and productive technonlogy (Gordon 1980: 17). Drawing on long-wave theories of growth and decline (Kondratieff 1935), SSA theorists identify three distinct stages in each SSA: exploration, consolidation, and decay (Gordon et al., 1982:10–11; for a summary see Prechel 1997a:412). Whereas *decay* represents periods when institutional arrangements are incapable of ensuring a steady rate of capital accumulation, *exploration* is characterized by capitalists and state managers attempting to reestablish stable conditions for profit making. My analysis focuses on the *decay-exploration transition:* creating new institutional arrangments in response to prolonged market instability and declining profits. During decay-exploration transitions, capitalists mobilize politically and become more active in their pursuit of political solutions to economic problems. Capitalist class unity increases during these historical junctures because realigning the institutional arrangements necessary to regain stability is dependent on their collective political power (Prechel 1990). Institutionalizing *stability* entails eliminating "internecine competition and erratic fluctuations in the economy" (Kolko 1963:3) that threaten capital accumulation and a predictable rate of return on investment. Table 1.1 identifies three historical transitions and the concomitant state structures, basis of economic organization, basis of the labor and managerial processes, and corporate form.

The first decay-exploration period focuses on the formation of the modern corporation during a period of competitive capitalism (1870s–1890s). The business response to the recessions and depressions beginning in the 1870s succeeded in convincing regional state managers to provide wide-ranging property rights to

TABLE 1.1 Decay-Exploration Transitions: State Structure, Economic Organization, Management Form, and Corporate Form, 1870s–1990s

Decay-Exploration Periods	Prevailing State Structure	Prevailing Economic Organization	Scientific Management Form	Prevailing Corporate Form
1870s–1890s	Federalism: Few Federal Regulations	Competitive Capitalism	Taylorism	Holding Company
1920s–1930s	Stabilizing State: Moderate Federal Regulation and Enforcement	Oligopolistic Capitalism	Fordism	Multidivisional Form
1970s–1990	New Federalism: Reduced Federal Regulation and Enforcement	Global Capitalism	Neo-Fordism	Multilayered Subsidiary Form

business enterprises, which included limited liability. Once regional states developed business policies and enforcement structures, subsequent policies were affected by existing policies and enforcement structures defining the relationship between corporations and regional states. The public holding company emerged within these institutional arrangements.

The second decay-exploration period (1920s–1930s) is characterized by economic depression, by the movement toward oligopoly, and by state business policy that created financial disincentives for organizing corporate entities as subsidiaries. During this period, corporations began to organize their corporate entities as divisions, creating the MDF.

The third decay-exploration period is characterized by intensification of global competition (1970s-1990). In the 1970s, changing economic conditions were manifested in the corporation as high debt, capital shortages, and declining profits. Corporate restructuring strategies included mergers and acquisitions and market consolidation. During this period, the size of the largest U.S. parent companies dramatically increased (Prechel and Boies 1998a:323). These economic conditions and corporate strategies resulted in restructuring the managerial process and the corporate form (e.g., divisions as subsidiaries).

By focusing on these three periods of rapid change, I demonstrate how incompatibilities among different levels of the social structure elicit a response. I also illustrate how historical conditions (1) shape and transform state business policy, and (2) effect change in the corporate form and the managerial process. Documenting these changes entails a conception of agency and an examination of how historical conditions affect the profit-making agenda of powerful class segments, the social forces that effect change in state business policy, and how corporate structures are mediated by precise calculation, attuned—often imperfectly—to the process of capital accumulation. Conflicts and incompatibilities between these dimensions of the social structure are catalysts for change when they undermine profit-making. Explicit in this framework is that the rationalization of corporate structures and institutional arrangements is not an abstract process that evolves over time. Rather, social change is an outcome of social actors' attempts to resolve incompatibilities, crises, and constraints on their political and economic interests.

By recognizing the importance of certain events in history and examining their effects on organizational variables across time and space, this analysis suggests that transitions in the corporation emerge from *crises*: "critical points" in corporations' histories when they "must undergo reorientation and revitalization to survive" (Benson 1977; Weitzel and Jonsson 1989; Prechel 1991:426). Meso-level organizational crises are brought on by macro-level constraints on profit-making. During the three historical junctures specified here, the response contributed to the content and form of the historical transitions and corporate transformations.

Contradictions exist among different levels of the social structure. The specific form of the contradiction, however, is affected by its structural location. My study identifies two structural locations where contradictions exist. *Micro-meso contradictions* emerge when the managerial process—which structures decision making (i.e., social action)—is incompatible with corporate structures. Micro-meso contradictions typically emerge gradually and incrementally as parts of the corporation change semi-independently of other parts. In contrast, *meso-macro contradictions* exist between the corporation and its environment. Although these contradictions also emerge gradually and incrementally, they are sometimes brought on by sudden shifts in corporations' institutional arrangements (e.g., depression). Contradiction at each level may emerge independently (table 1.2). The probability of corporate transformation (i.e., rapid change) is highest, however, when contradictions at each level occur at the same historical juncture (Prechel 1991:439). The resolution of contradictions is not an uncontested process that evolves from consensus. Rather, resolution entails the exercise of power by social actors.

Irrationality in the Rationalization Process

The Inherent Irrationality of the Micro-Meso Linkage

If managers set up control systems based on perfect information and if administrative structures had the capacity to process new information and continually redefine incentive structures, it might be possible to establish control systems capable of achieving corporations' goals over time. The designers of control systems, however, do not have access to perfect information. Moreover, they are limited by bounded rationality and do not always know whether the controls they set up have the intended effect. I examine the managerial process to show how information is translated into formally rational controls, and to determine

TABLE 1.2 Contradictions and Corporate Transformation

Level of Analysis	Level of the Social Structure	Location of the Contradiction	Outcome
Micro	Decision-Making	Micro-meso Linkage	Corporate Transformation
Meso	Corporate Structure	Meso-macro Linkage	
Macro	Institutional Arrangements		

whether organizational controls produce contradictory and irrational social actions (i.e., decisions).

Central to this analysis is an examination of how information is used in the decision-making process. Max Weber maintained that rational calculation was a defining feature of the modern corporation because capitalism demands stable, strict, and intensively calculable administration. Weber argued that the demand for information and the advancement of rational calculation are historically contingent, occurring at a slower rate "in the absence of [an] objective need" (Weber 1978:106). Contemporary researchers have begun to give attention to corporate accounting and its relationship to decision making. However, their analyses are limited to corporate restructuring during the early and middle decades of the twentieth century (Chandler 1977; Johnson and Kaplan 1991; Johnson 1991; Temin 1991).

To elucidate the relationship between information and decision making, the analysis here makes the analytic distinction between capital (i.e., financial) accounting and cost accounting. This distinction is important because cost and capital accounting provide information on different phenomena. Thus, the ways in which these data are used have important effects on decision making. Inappropriate use of information derived from financial and cost accounting may increase, rather than decrease, costs.

Cost accounting is oriented toward operating costs. Cost-accounting managers (e.g., controllers) try to identify and control product costs. Calculation that takes the form of cost accounting also provides information to ensure standardization of decisions, the manufacturing process, and product quality (Prechel 1994b). In contrast to cost accounting, financial accounting provides information on corporations' financial needs. *Financial accounting* is attuned to the use and availability of capital. Financial accountants measure the financial strength of the corporation, and its capacity to finance ongoing operations and strategies from internal sources. When internal capital flow declines, financial managers seek external sources of capital.

The data derived from corporations' account-control system provide much of the information used to design the labor and managerial processes. These data were used to establish *scientific management*: controls to standardize behavior and ensure that a minimum amount of time is spent on each operation. Data are centralized and used to separate the production process into discrete work activities. After the component parts of the production process are separated, the process is reunited in an effort to create an integrated production system with an extensive division of labor. The objective of scientific management is to create a unified mode of control. Historically, the application of scientific management progressively centralizes authority using increasingly subtle and more extensive forms of control. Despite historical differences in scientific management and its capacity to achieve outcomes, it is always oriented toward control, predictability, and product standardization.

The crucial issue is whether financial and accounting controls have their intended effect. To have the intended effect, the system of control must accomplish two things. First, it must create an incentive structure that ensures social actions (e.g., decisions) contribute to corporate-unit goals. Second, it must ensure that corporate-unit goals are compatible with the corporations' ultimate substantive goal.

The Inherent Irrationality of the Meso-Macro Linkage

If capitalism were stable and predictable, linkages among levels of the social structure would not be problematic. The market, however, is dynamic, characterized by uneven development and fluctuating demand. Moreover, the rate of change is unpredictable. Thus, an incompatibility exists between the logic of the market and the logic of the administrative structure (McNeil 1978). Corporate structures are designed to make a profit at one point in time that constitute a specific means of organizing production and an overall strategy for growth. However, those formally rational structures—which are based on property rights and bureaucratic rules—may not be conducive to profit making when market conditions change. That is, whereas corporate structures are time independent (i.e., stable over time), markets are inherently unpredictable and time dependent. Thus, corporate structures—which are designed to ensure predictability—are embedded in an economy that is vulnerable to sudden shifts (e.g., recessions, depressions, globalization). As a result, incompatibilities emerge between markets and corporate structures.

However, corporations are not totally constrained by their institutional arrangements. The corporation is a power holder in its own right, and attempts to create institutional arrangements that facilitate profit making. Through coordinated political activity, large and powerful corporations pressure state managers to define business policies. Core industries[6] and class segments are particularly influential because they are the most politically unified. Moreover, they have a high degree of legitimacy; elected and appointed state managers view them as important to ensure stable economic growth because they generate a large proportion of the gross national product (O'Connor 1973; Offe 1975; Jessop 1982).

Still, this process is fraught with problems. Whereas the political-legal system that defines the relationship between the corporation and the state is relatively static, the economy may undergo rapid and unanticipated changes. During these historical junctures, the state's institutional arrangements may be incompatible with economic growth. Also, state business policy is affected by the state's own goals and agenda, which are sometimes incompatible. Proposals to establish the conditions for domestic economic growth may conflict with the state's agenda to maintain stable relations with other nation-states. These incompatibilities place limits on policy initiatives (e.g., protectionism) acceptable to domestic classes and class segments.

Thus, the responses to economic crisis are shaped by the historically specific political and economic context, the state's competing agenda, and the power of competing classes and subclass and class segments. Historical variation in capital accumulation structures the interests, motives, and actions of competing groups and the opportunities for satisfying their interests. State structures become the product of past policies that congeal and develop a network of interests inside and outside the state, which shapes the options and alternatives available (Beetham 1987; Prechel 1990). These structures affect current policy outcomes by aligning competing interests and creating consequences for policy implementation.

Thus, for legal and sociological reasons, the state is conceptualized as a complex organization. The relationships among the various supra-units in the state (i.e., judicial, executive, legislative) are defined by a single legal document (e.g., the Constitution). The various supra-units within the state exist in relationship to one another; the functions, goals, and agenda of the executive, judicial, and legislative branches have meaning in relationship to each other. Similarly, subunits (e.g., Federal Trade Commission) within the supra-units have meaning because of their relationship to the supra-units to which they are accountable (e.g., executive branch).

Summary

The conceptual framework here suggests that social actors have choices, but their choices are constrained by the historically specific form of social embeddedness within which decisions are made. When the social structure constrains decisions so that an adequate rate of capital accumulation cannot be maintained, an "economic ethic" emerges that entails both politically and economically driven social action to redefine the managerial process, corporate form, and institutional arrangements.

Although crises result from contradictions and produce changes in the social structure, historical transitions are not disconnected from the past. There is a continuity to history because decision makers are affected by existing structures. Understanding crises and their resolution requires an analysis of historical trajectories to determine how crises are shaped. Just as historical events create new op-portunities and constraints for decision making, the struggle to define the future takes place within a social structure that provides a memory of the past. This so-cial structure defines the opportunities and constraints available to the corpora-tion, which is a complex structure in the process of change whose essence is con-trol attuned to profit making. The ideology of scientific management is a central component of the control structure; it provides a memory of the past through which problems and their solutions are understood and resolved. This ideology emphasizes rational calculation, which transforms information into bureaucratic and technical controls at the point of production.

The theory and method elaborated here conceptualizes the corporation as a profoundly historical phenomenon.[7] Managers are actively engaged in coordinat-ing micro activities across space and time. They try to bring the activities of peo-ple in different times and places into a sequence to ensure outcomes. Managerial activities occur at the micro level, but are explicitly oriented toward and defined by the meso and macro levels. Within the inherently unstable conditions of capi-talist economies, the corporation attempts to maintain equilibrium with its envi-ronment by (1) structuring the mode of control so it can manufacture products that meet market demand, and (2) stabilizing markets directly through market control or indirectly through political behavior. The following chapters examine the linkages between large-scale structures and processes and micro-level behav-iors. Two interrelated questions are central to this inquiry. How do structures and processes shape the course of action available to social actors? How do social actors shape structures and process?

Part I
*Corporate Transformation
in the Late Nineteenth and
Early Twentieth Centuries*

Corporate Transformation in the Late Nineteenth and Early Twentieth Centuries

This part of the book analyzes the emergence of the modern industrial corporation in the nineteenth and early twentieth centuries. As discussed in chapter 1, capital-dependence theory suggests that corporate transformations occur in response to changing economic opportunities and constraints. The way in which the business enterprise is embedded in its institutional environment and the historical conditions of capital accumulation structure decision makers' motives and behaviors. Historically, capitalists respond to constraints by pursuing two strategies: (1) reconfiguring the business enterprise, and (2) transforming their environment. Business enterprises are embedded in and their form dependent on institutional arrangements. Also, state managers have an interest in ensuring economic stability and corporate growth because the state's legitimacy and revenues depend on it. Thus, the content of strategies for changes is affected by this two-way dependence of the corporation and the state. Chapter 2 examines the relationship among the capital dependence of regional states on business enterprises, the emergence of the late-nineteenth-century holding company, and the institutional arrangements produced by the Federalist state structure. Chapter 3 focuses on the merging of banking and industrial capital to produce finance capital, how the capital dependence of industrialists on bankers provided the latter with the capacity to influence the form of industrial organization, and how the holding-company form was used to establish monopolistic controls. Chapter 4 examines how the political-legal process redefined corporations' institutional arrangements in such a way that it lead to the demise of the holding-company form.

CHAPTER 2

The Federalist State and the Emergence of the Modern Corporation

The nineteenth-century holding company is important because it provided the legal (1) mechanism to consolidate and organize industrial capital, and (2) foundation for the modern business enterprise.[1] Two interrelated components of nineteenth-century Federalism were crucial in defining the modern corporation. Federalism provided regional states with relative autonomy over economic activity within their geographic boundaries. Federalism required regional states to generate revenues to cover their governance costs.[2]

To avoid the politically unpopular position of taxing their residents, nineteenth-century regional states established arrangements with business enterprises to raise revenues. Typically, as a result of these arrangements, regional states became dependent on revenues from business enterprises. Dependence created competition among regional states for business. A regional state could not impose strict laws on ownership or access to resources (e.g., iron ore, waterways, timber, coal) if its neighboring states had liberal resource-allocation policies (Hartz 1948; Scheiber 1975; Grandy 1993). Therefore, the most successful strategy for a regional state to attract capital was to impose few restrictions on business activity. This dimension of Federalism became increasingly important over time, resulting in political-legal changes that extended a wide range of rights to business enterprises.[3]

Eighteenth- and Nineteenth-Century Political and Economic Conditions

Weak Ties Among Business Enterprises, Ideology, and the Federalist State

In the eighteenth century the term "corporation" referred to a broad range of organizations. However, they shared one characteristic: corporations were developed to carry out activities for the public (Roy 1997). The first corporations in the colonies extended British authority through trade, education (e.g., Dartmouth College), land (e.g., The Ohio Company), and religious and military societies. The business corporation was slow to develop. The first quasi business corporation was established in 1709. The first verifiable record of a profit-seeking corporation organized under a legislative charter was the New London Society United for Trade and Commence in Connecticut (1732). Although laws defined the relationship between the state and business before the American Revolution, these regulations were narrowly defined (Thorelli 1955). Thus, most of the larger businesses that began to form after the American Revolution continued to operate as voluntary associations or partnerships. This method of organization created a problem for capitalist development: the absence of laws governing the business enterprise also provided it with few legal rights.

By the end of the eighteenth century, the corporation began to gain legal status. A corporation was defined as a *franchise* (i.e., privilege), a concept inherited from British common law under which "the very existence of the corporation was conditioned by a grant from the state" (Berle and Means 1991:120).[4] Since regional states had powers of self-governance, the regional state where the corporation was located defined the terms of the franchise. Federal laws governing the business enterprise remained largely nonexistent.

After the turn of the century, several changes including the rise of finance capital, foreign demand for goods created by the Napoleonic Wars, and the expansion of canal and rail transportation (1815–1835) contributed to the expansion of business corporations. As the number of business enterprises increased, the demand for business *charters* (i.e., certificates of incorporation) increased.[5] These charters focused on corporations' capital structure and attempted to ensure the rights of the public, creditors, and shareholders. Regional states negotiated these rights separately with each business. Frequently, corporate charters included provisions unique to the enterprise. This meant that the regional state managers examined and voted upon the powers granted to each corporation. It required a special legislative action to pass each charter. As the demand for certifications of incorporation increased, it became increasing cumbersome and time consuming to write a separate charter for each business.

To streamline operations, regional states began to establish uniform laws of incorporation. In 1811, New York passed the first law providing for the incorporation of manufacturing companies. By 1837, Connecticut and Michigan had passed similar laws and Maryland had enacted laws based on a general incorporation principle (Haney 1920; Berle and Means 1991). After regional states established general incorporation laws, elected state managers often allocated the authority to negotiate the details of the corporate charters to an appointed state manager in a government agency (e.g., the secretary of state).

Some states attempted to establish formal controls over the emerging business enterprise. However, laissez-faire ideology dominated. Few legal controls or restrictions governed business activity (Cochran and Miller 1942; Thorelli 1955). The strict application of laissez-faire ideology was a double-edged sword and created dilemmas for capitalists. Although laissez faire ideology kept state intervention in business activity to a minimum, the absence of laws governing business behavior provided business enterprises with few legal rights. If the charters did not specify an activity, it was prohibited (Berle and Means 1991). For example, the nineteenth-century regional state defined firms incorporated outside its geographic boundaries as foreign corporations. *Foreign corporations* had no legal rights in the state. This provision limited business activity to the regional state of incorporation. Also, the absence of laws governing stock ownership prohibited one corporation from owning stock in another corporation. Stock ownership in one corporation by another was explicitly prohibited in Illinois, Maryland, Massachusetts, New York, and Pennsylvania. Unless a special legislative act granted stock ownership rights to a business enterprise, it was illegal for one business to own stock in another (Bonbright and Means 1932; Eichner 1969; Hogan 1971). Together with the Federalist state structure, the laissez-faire ideology of the nineteenth-century provided few rights and little protection for business enterprises engaged in economic activity outside their regional state of incorporation.

Strategies to Overcome "Cutthroat Competition": Nineteenth-Century Market Controls

The first large factories in the United States emerged in the textile industry in the early 1800s. All or nearly all of the production process occurred within a single mill. Armory production also occurred in a self-contained unit. Consolidation was limited to these industries, however, until the 1840s and 1850s when new manufacturing technologies were implemented. Most consolidated industries, however, used batch production technologies until after the Civil War. In the late 1870s and 1880s, several industries (e.g., agricultural products) set up continuous processing technologies (Chandler 1977).[6] Higher tariffs facilitated domestic industrial expansion by providing higher profits. This capital was used to expand existing facilities or merge with other firms (Gordon et al. 1982; Eckes 1995).

The shift from labor-intensive to capital-intensive continuous production significantly increased workers' output. However, the second half of the nineteeth century was a period of economic volatility. When capitalists employed labor-intensive technologies, variable capital (i.e., labor costs) constituted a high proportion of total capital investment. To cut costs during economic downturns, capitalists would simply lay off workers. However, the transition to more capital-intensive production rendered this strategy less effective. As the proportion of

fixed capital (e.g., machinery, land, buildings) to total capital increased, the capacity to reduce costs during economic downturns decreased.[7]

Capitalists' vulnerability to economic downturns escalated after the Civil War.
Following the depression from 1873 to 1878, economic growth created new markets and businesses expanded to meet market demand. Expansion in good times
created excess-production capability in bad times. After the third major economic
depression in the late nineteenth century (i.e., 1873–1878, 1882–1885, 1893–1897),
capitalists focused on the need for economic stability. Financiers, such as Andrew
Carnegie, characterized the depression of the 1890s as a "disastrous cyclone" (in
Kirkland 1967:7).

To overcome the threat to profits created by these boom-or-bust conditions,
the largest capitalists initiated consolidation strategies to control production and
prices. A common consolidation strategy, the *pooling agreement*, typically organized by cartels in trade associations, set minimum prices and divided markets.
Several pooling agreements were set up after the prolonged crises in the 1870s.
These arrangements were most common from 1875 to 1895.[8]

Although the pooling agreement was easy to organize, capitalists' dependence
on accumulating capital led pool members to ignore it during periods of slow economic growth. To ensure an adequate rate of return during economic downturns,
pool members would frequently lower prices to capture a larger share of the market. Gaining a larger market share increased members' *capability utilization rates:*
the relationship between the actual output and the overall production capability
of the operating facilities. Capability utilization rates became more important as
the proportion of fixed capital, as percentage of total capital, increased. A higher
proportion of fixed capital required a higher utilization rate to reach the *break-
even point:* the point at which costs and revenue are equal. The further firms' capability utilization rates dropped below the break-even point, the larger their
losses. In the absence of a binding legal-rational structure, pooling agreements
were difficult to enforce because they constituted weak ties among a network of
firms. During economic downturns, pooling agreements typically broke down, resulting in *cutthroat competition:* overproduction and uncontrolled price cutting.
Dominant actors in these federations, such as Andrew Carnegie, frequently cut
prices in order to eliminate competition (Roy 1997).

Their dependence on accumulating capital and the weak ties among a network
of firms constrained capitalists' ability to predict the need for additional production capability. To strengthen their ties, capitalists pursued several strategies. Their
objective was to centralize control over independent firms competing for the same
market.

The transportation industry was among the first to consolidate (Chandler
1977; Dobbin 1994; Roy 1997). After completing the east-west trunk lines in the
early 1850s (e.g., Pennsylvania Railroad Company, Baltimore & Ohio), railroad

companies began to implement various consolidation strategies, including mergers and long-term leases. The New York Central Railroad was formed by merger during this period (Cochran and Miller 1942). Some railroads obtained special rights from state legislatures to form holding companies. In 1853 the Pennsylvania legislature granted the Pennsylvania Railroad Company the right to own stock in other railroad companies equivalent to 15 percent of its own capital (Haney 1920; Thorelli 1955). Stock ownership through the holding company form soon became the preferred consolidation strategy among the largest railroads.[9] The holding-company had two major advantages over previous forms of business consolidation (e.g., mergers): it more tightly coupled independent business enterprises, and it did not require complex reorganization of independent firms under a single administration. As J. P. Morgan maintained, mergers were organizationally and legally complex to unscramble. In contrast, if a holding company did not achieve the desired effect, it could be unscrambled by selling the stock of its unwanted parts.

Although the holding company strengthened ties among previously diverse and independent firms, this form of consolidation was not widely used. Few capitalists wanted to risk public exposure of their consolidation strategies (Chandler 1977). The formation of a holding-company still required a special act of a regional state legislature. Because legislatures, at their discretion, could reject a proposed holding company charter most large capitalists established *trusts:* an organization of owners of competing companies within an industry who gave voting power to a group of trustees. Unlike the holding company, trust agreements did not require a state charter.

Unlike previous forms of business organization, trusts constituted a sharp break between ownership and control. Smaller capitalists within the trust typically gave up control of the business to the larger capitalists and were issued trust certificates entitling them to a share of the profits. The oil industry, for example, established the Standard Oil Trust that gave trustees control of more than 90 percent of the industry (Hogan 1971; Chandler 1977).[10] The cattle, cordage, cottonseed oil, linseed oil, salt, leather, lead, sugar, and whiskey industries also created trusts.

Trusts implemented several strategies, including exclusive distribution systems, control of raw materials and patents, price cutting, and centrally controlled advertising (Ripley 1905; Stevens 1913; Jones 1921; Watkins 1927; Tennant 1950). Trusts were typically adopted in industries where a significant degree of consolidation had already occurred. Pooling agreements continued to be used in industries with many producers because trusts were difficult to organize in industries with ownership widely distributed among many small firms (Hogan 1971).

The emergence of trusts and their potential market power generated concern among other capitalist class segments (i.e., small businesses, farmers) and the working class. Pressured by small capital and the working class over, for example, the creation of the Distiller's and Cattle Feeder's Trust and the Sugar Trust, state

TABLE 2.1 Forms of Business Organization, 1860s-1930s

Business Organization	Characteristics	Period	Form of Control	Legal Status
Agreement	Setting minimum prices, and establishing a fund from profits to be divided among the members.	1865–1875	Informal	None
Pool	Collective agreement on output, setting minimum prices, and establishing a fund from profits to be divided among the members.	1875–1895	Informal	None
Trust	The allocation of authority by members to a group of trustees, collective agreement on output, setting minimum prices, and establishing a fund from profits to be divided among the members.	1879–1890	Informal	None. Illegal after the Sherman Act.
Holding Company I*	Authority allocated to owners through laws of incorporation. Setting output levels and prices. Profits were distributed to the owners.	1800s	Stock Ownership	Legal, but required a state charter and a special legislative act.
Holding Company II	Authority allocated to owners through laws of incorporation. Setting output levels and prices. Profits were distributed to the owners.	1888–1930s	Stock Ownership	Extensive legal rights. Did not require a special legislative act.

* Widely used in transportation, but not in manufacturing.

managers and the courts at both the regional and federal levels began to examine trust activities. Eight states adopted laws prohibiting certain forms of trusts. In response, big capital began to look for an alternate mode of organization. A problem confronting manufacturing enterprises was they lacked legitimacy. In the absence of laws legitimating their activities, manufacturing corporations were subject to critical review by the public and regional state managers. Table 2.1 is a summary of the forms of business enterprise that existed in the late nineteenth and early twentieth centuries.

Restructuring Institutional Arrangements: Twentieth-Century Capitalism

Federalist State Structures and the Emergence of the Modern Corporation

Ironically, throughout most of the nineteenth century laissez-faire ideology limited capitalists' consolidation agendas. Crucial was the way regional state laws of incorporation defined *foreign corporation:* a firm with no legal rights outside its state of incorporation. This dimension of the political-legal structure constrained capital accumulation in two interrelated ways. First, expanding production frequently required access to raw materials and markets located outside the firms' state of incorporation. Consolidation was limited, however, because the firm had to be incorporated in the state where it conducted business and it could not own stock in other firms. Vertical integration could not occur if the raw materials were located outside the state of incorporation. As a result, the corporation had to purchase raw materials from other corporations. Dependence on other firms for raw materials made the corporation vulnerable to price swings. Second, to ensure its survival in periods of rapid economic swings and expanding production capability, the firm wanted to increase its control over regional markets. Although corporations attempted to resolve the problem of market competitiveness with pooling arrangements and trusts, the weak ties of these organizational forms limited their effectiveness. Cooperation among semiautonomous capitalists was difficult to maintain when competition increased (e.g., recessions, depressions).

The capital-dependent relationship between the regional state and capitalists had profound effects on regional state business policy. Throughout the eighteenth and into the nineteenth century, regional states obtained most of their revenues from their own economic activity. By the late nineteenth century, most regional states began to disengage from business activity. Regional states became dependent on private enterprises to provide revenues and create jobs.

New Jersey—which granted firms special concessions to encourage economic development—was particularly dependent on revenues from business. As early as the 1830s, New Jersey granted a monopoly to the Camden and Amboy Railroad Company for the lucrative New York–Philadelphia route and exempted the railroad from regional state taxes (Thorelli 1955; Grandy 1993). In exchange, the company agreed to collect a transit duty tax on passengers and freight. Since the New York–Philadelphia route was used primarily by out-of-state passengers, this agreement shifted much of the state's tax burden to nonresidents. While this business policy provided New Jersey with substantial tax revenues, it provided the Camden and Amboy Railroad Company with a monopoly over a crucial railroad line and guaranteed the firm profits.

Prior to the Civil War, revenues from railroad firms accounted for approximately 90 percent of New Jersey's operating budget, making it possible to eliminate the state's property tax. The costs of war making, however, required additional revenues and necessitated the reinstatement of property taxes. New Jersey's business policy of providing tax-exempt and monopoly status to a railroad company while imposing property taxes on its citizens elicited a political response from residents. They demanded tax reform (Grandy 1993). Momentum for tax reform increased in 1871 when the Pennsylvania Railroad gained control over the Camden and Amboy Railroad. This gave a "foreign corporation" (i.e., one incorporated outside New Jersey) special tax exemptions and a monopoly over this lucrative railroad line.

By the early 1880s, politicians in New Jersey were confronted with several interrelated problems: (1) resistance to state taxes, challenging the legitimacy of government (2) preexisting agreements with business enterprises, limiting capacity to impose property taxes on them, and (3) dependence on insufficient external sources of capital, limiting abilities to meet the state's operating budget. These *political economic* conditions preceded one of the most important events in the creation of the modern corporation.

The Political Solution to Economic Constraints: The Modern Holding Company

In response to its fiscal crisis, New Jersey revised its business policy. The first step toward crisis resolution was the New Jersey Holding Company Act of 1888. Subsequent decisions further revised the state's statutes of incorporation. Between 1888 and 1896 New Jersey passed several statutes that radically transformed the political-legal institutional arrangements within which firms operated. These new laws of incorporation provided big capital with the means to gain control over corporations located throughout the United States, not only by purchasing their assets, but also by purchasing their outstanding stock (Eichner 1969). These changes in the institutional environment also created the legal basis for the enormous merger and consolidation movement that occurred at the turn of the century.[11]

The New Jersey legislation extended corporations' rights in several crucial ways. It permitted one corporation to hold stock in another corporation. Previously, unless a regional state passed a legislative act granting special privileges, it was illegal for one corporation to hold stock in another or to issue stock to purchase another. The 1880s' legislation permitted firms to use temporary financing from external capital markets and to raise capital for the sole purpose of taking over another firm. The most important aspect of this legislation, however, was that in 1889, the New Jersey laws of incorporation granted firms the right to purchase property outside the state of incorporation with stock issued specifically for that purpose (Dewing 1941; Cochran and Miller 1942; Kirkland 1967; Chandler 1977). This constituted a sharp break from the past when the regional states' legal-rational authority restricted business activity to the state of incorporation.[12]

Several additional key components of the New Jersey legislation improved the corporate environment. First, the New Jersey laws created extremely lenient guidelines for incorporation. They placed no restrictions on the amount of stock issued and they limited stockholders' liability to the assets of the corporation. As a result, this institutional arrangement tended to result in *overcapitalization:* issuing more stock than there were actual assets in the company. Second, the New Jersey laws of incorporation did not require firms to reveal their financial status to the public or to their competitors. In contrast to previous law, firms were only required to provide financial information to stockholders. Because stocks were not widely distributed, very few people obtained information on business activities.

Third, the New Jersey legislation had higher limits on *capitalization* than most states: the amount of outstanding shares in a company (Bannock, Baxter, and Rees 1978). This provision was extremely important because it allowed corporations to issue whatever amount of stock necessary to finance large mergers and acquisitions. Fourth, the new statute limited corporate taxes to a small percentage of corporate capitalization. No tax was imposed for incorporating in the state or for creating franchise subsidiaries (Keasbey 1899). Most important, there was no tax on the transfer of capital from the parent holding company to the subsidiary corporation, or from the subsidiary corporation to the parent company.

Changes in the New Jersey political-legal structure occurred in two stages. Pre-1888 New Jersey corporate statutes focused on firms operating within the state. Post-1888 statutes were directed toward corporations conducting business outside the state, providing corporations with added flexibility in merger activity and stockholding authority. Several subsequent changes were crucial. The 1889 New Jersey law restricted the purchase of stock to certain kinds of businesses. This provision was amended in 1893 to eliminate restrictions on the kinds of companies that could be combined through stock ownership, which allowed corporations to purchase property with stock issued for that purpose.[13] Also in 1893, the New Jersey legislature added a provision that allowed horizontal combinations by permitting corporations to merge with other firms engaged in similar business activities. In 1896, the legislature added a provision encouraging vertical integration through mergers by authorizing corporations to purchase mines, factories, or other business properties (Grandy 1993). New Jersey's business policy appealed to business enterprises that were expanding and wanted access to markets and raw materials outside their state of incorporation.

These business policies had important benefits for the state of New Jersey, solving its fiscal crisis and reducing its dependence on the railroad industry for revenues. By 1899, incorporation fees (i.e., one-time fees paid for forming a corporation) and franchise taxes (i.e., taxes paid annually) in New Jersey exceeded tax revenues from railroads. Between the mid-1860s and 1900, the state's debt declined from $3.4 to $.1 million.

Despite the significance of the New Jersey Holding Company Act of 1888, an emerging anti–big business ideology (e.g., the antitrust movement) led many capitalists to believe that the holding company would share the same fate as the trust. In 1887, regional states began filing antitrust suits. In 1890, the federal government passed the Sherman Antitrust Act that made illegal combinations that attempted to restrain trade or create a monopoly.[14] The state passed this law after middle-class reformers (i.e., small businesses, professionals) and farmers succeeded in passing antitrust legislation in several regional states to monitor or control efforts toward monopolization. In 1887, Louisiana instituted an antitrust suit against the Cottonseed Oil Trust, and Nebraska filed an antitrust suit against the Whiskey

Trust. In 1888, New York brought antitrust charges against the Sugar Trust. In 1890, Ohio sued the Standard Oil Company. Leading the Populist antitrust movement, Kansas passed the first antitrust legislation in 1889. By 1893, fifteen other states passed similar legislation (Cochran and Miller 1942; Thorelli 1955; McNall 1988; McDonough 1994). In response to these legal constraints, business enterprises changed their strategies from gaining control over another company through stock acquisition to consolidation through mergers (i.e., combination through the direct purchase of another corporation's assets) (Bonbright and Means 1932). In summary, the New Jersey legislation provided the legal framework for the holding company. Although questions remained about whether the New Jersey legislation allowed capitalists to use the holding company to consolidate several businesses under a single corporation, this regional state business policy established a legal basis for corporate stock ownership. In 1899, New Jersey was the only state where capitalists could create a corporate shell for the sole purpose of owning and controlling other corporations.

The antitrust movement's challenge to the holding company solicited a response from big capital. This response included a new corporate form. Some historians argue that J. B. Dill, the general counsel for the Standard Oil Trust, convinced Governor Abbett to alter the New Jersey statutes.[15] Others suggest that the initial changes in the holding-company legislation occurred before Dill could have influenced Governor Abbett (Kirkland 1967; Eichner 1969; Grandy 1993). Although ambiguity exists on the degree of influence Dill had on the initial legislation, the historical record shows that he actively promoted the law after it was passed and lobbied regional state managers to make subsequent changes. Dill lobbied state managers to combine the holding company statutes into a single legal code, which occurred in 1893. Also, in 1892, Dill founded the Corporation Trust Company of New Jersey, which he used to create hundreds of corporations. Moreover, a clear distinction did not exist between capitalists and state managers. Allan McDermott, the New Jersey clerk of chancery, served as one of the incorporators of Dill's company. Both Governor Abbett and Secretary of State Henry Kelsey served as directors.[16] In short, both regional state managers and capitalists participated in promoting, defining, and setting up the holding company form.

The New Jersey legislation was important not only because it created the holding company and extended a range of legal rights to corporations, but also because it established the legal basis of the modern corporation. By providing business with legal rights, the New Jersey legislation established the foundation for corporate law and the basis of legal battles and state business policy throughout the twentieth century.

The New Jersey business policy was a step toward the institutionalization of corporate rights that are similar to the rights of individuals. The New Jersey legislation extended stock purchasing and ownership rights—previously restricted to individuals—to corporations. This became the basis of corporations' property rights, which treats them similar to individuals under the law. This has had important long-term consequences because corporations are able to accumulate massive resources compared to most individuals. These institutional arrangements create clear advantages for corporations when individuals attempt to obtain restitution (e.g., injury due to faulty products).

Further, the capacity to issue stock created additional means to generate capital internally. This simultaneously reduced business enterprises' dependence on external sources of capital. Now, businesses could simply issue stock to pursue their consolidation strategies. In addition, the political-legal structure allowed individuals to avoid certain taxes by incorporating themselves as corporations, which further blurred the line between corporations and individuals. Thus, depending on which was more advantageous, wealthy individuals could retain their legal status as individuals or incorporate as a business entity.

The behavior of the framers of the New Jersey business policy is best understood within the prevailing ideology. These political actors attempted to incorporate utilitarian principles and laissez-faire ideology into the political-legal structure to provide a framework for capitalists to pursue their self-interests. The new business policy assumed that unconstrained business behavior contributed to social and economic progress. Its proponents employed utilitarian arguments to claim that providing business enterprises with rights previously restricted to individuals allowed them to pursue their self-interest, and that these pursuits would be beneficial to society. The only restrictions placed on corporations (i.e., limited liability) were those that protected people with financial relationships to corporations (i.e., stockholders, creditors). Further, enforcement structures in the state to protect these individual rights were weak or absent. After individual rights were institutionalized as corporate rights, state business policies that limited business activity were viewed as interventionist and criticized for undermining the capacity of the corporation to advance their interests, which they presented as synonymous with society's interests.

There is a flawed logic of equating corporations with individuals. Polices that advance the interests of the corporation do not always advance the public good (Thorelli 1955). Most important, this distortion of laissez-faire ideology has made if difficult for citizens and policymakers to think straight about business policy. Among other things, this distortion of laissez-faire ideology camouflages the use of public resources by regional and federal states to advance the interest of big business (Sklar 1988; Roy 1991).[17]

Political Capitalism: State Antitrust Legislation and Corporate Consolidation

The turn-of-the-century antitrust movement and subsequent legislation had limited effects on state business policy. Despite accounts of trust-busting associated with the Sherman Antitrust Act, the antitrust movement never posed a serious threat to big capital's consolidation strategies. The primary outcome of the act was to mediate the conflict between populist opposition to consolidation and the interests of big capital. Although Congress created the Bureau of Corporations in 1903, the federal government, especially the executive branch, opted for regulating rather than punishing or dismantling giant firms that exercised market control. Despite notoriety as a trustbuster in the popular and business presses, President Theodore Roosevelt did not oppose concentration of capital through corporate consolidation and viewed antitrust legislation as a means to regulate corporations. President Roosevelt stated:

> The line of demarcation we draw must always be on conduct, not on wealth. Our objection to any corporation must be, not that it is big but that it behaves badly. (In Kolko 1963:69)

The Sherman Antitrust act contained a crucial shortcoming: violation was based on whether a corporation's behavior was "reasonable." State managers and the courts exercised their discretion to determine whether corporations engaged in "unreasonable restraint of trade." This ambiguity made regulation open to interpretation, which made it difficult to implement and enforce. Some state managers recognized this problem and regarded the Sherman Antitrust act as "delusion and a sham, . . . an empty menace of the ignorant and unreasonable" (Senator Aldrich in Cochran and Miller 1942:171). Senator Orville Platt (R–Connecticut) described the Sherman act as a compromise that did not address the trust problem.

> The conduct of the Senate . . . has not been in the line of honest preparation of a bill to prohibit and punish trusts. It has been in line with some bill with that title that we might go to the country with. The questions of whether the bill would be operative, of how it would operate, . . . have been whistled down the wind in this Senate as idle talk, and the whole effort has been to get some bill headed: "A Bill to Punish Trusts" with which to go to the country. (Cochran and Miller 1942:172)

These objections to the Sherman Act were well founded. After the turn of the century, corporate lawyers began to assume that the holding-company structure was immune from antitrust laws, and to advise their clients to restructure as holding companies. As Theodore Roosevelt wrote, the New Jersey legislation entailed "the absolute nullification of the anti-trust law" (Roosevelt 1913:427). New Jersey holding-company legislation legalized what had been universally prohibited; it allowed a merger through holding companies because they did not involve contracts or agreements between competitors (Cochran 1957).

Under New Jersey law, a trust could be transformed into a holding company by simply chartering a corporation to take over the assets held by the trustees (Martin 1959). To change a trust into a holding company only required capitalists to (1) substitute the stock of the holding company for the certificates of the trust (2) substitute a board of directors for the board of trustees, and (3) substitute a permanent transfer of stock or ownership for the trust relationship (Haney 1920). For example, when the sugar trust was transformed to the American Sugar Refining Company, Henry Havemeyer, the president of the trust, became the president of the holding company and the trustees became the board of directors (Eichner 1969). Often little change occurred in the way in which the new enterprises conducted business. Owners simply held stock instead of trust certificates. The primary difference between the trust and the holding company was the latter was embedded in political-legal institutional arrangements that provided it with more rights.

In short, the holding-company form created a winning situation for big capital. Its legal status provided the corporation with a means to consolidate markets in a way less vulnerable than previous forms to antitrust legislation. The holding company provided more effective means to control prices and to coordinate an industry's production capability with market demand. The institutional environment was transformed so that big capital obtained a higher degree of legitimacy to pursue its consolidation strategies. In contrast to the informal strategies of pools and trusts, the holding company embedded business enterprises into a single corporation with formal legal-rational authority over other business entities. Once industrial consolidation occurred within the new holding company, capitalists could better ensure a steady rate of return by implementing policies to control the behavior (e.g., setting prices, limiting expansion) of its network of subsidiary corporations. New Jersey's business policy constitutes a transition in the historical trajectory that provides business with a wide range of rights that were eventually approved by the U.S. Supreme Court.

Competition among Regional States: The "Race to the Bottom"

The Federalist structure provided regional states with a great deal of flexibility to develop the legal parameters of economic activity. Regional states' dependence on business enterprises for revenues created competition to obtain incorporation fees. This situation—together with the standard established by the New Jersey holding-company legislation and pressure from capitalists—initiated a *race to the bottom:* an attempt to provide the most lucrative institutional arrangements for business enterprises. The incentives for regional states to enter this race included the direct revenues from business incorporations and the indirect revenues from economic growth. Although variation existed among regional states, including Connecticut, Delaware, Maine, New York, Pennsylvania, and West Virginia, many replicated the New Jersey laws of incorporation (Thorelli 1955; Grandy 1993). Delaware's original statutes were almost identical to New Jersey's, imposing two kinds of taxes: organization fees and an annual franchise tax (Larcom 1937). However, Delaware's rates were significantly lower than those in New Jersey. Later, to attract business enterprises, Delaware and several other regional states provided corporations with rights, powers, and privileges additional to those available in New Jersey. By 1912, only two regional states prohibited holding companies (Haney 1920).

As they did in New Jersey, capitalists influenced Delaware's business policy. Important changes in the provisions granting corporate charters occurred at Delaware's 1899 convention. Members of the DuPont family and their corporate executives were named as delegates to this constitutional convention. And, a DuPont executive Charles Richards held a position on the committee on corporations (McNamee 1983).

A key provision of the Delaware incorporation laws was the power of self-determination. The 1898 Delaware statute states:

> The certificate [of incorporation] may also contain any provision which the incorporators may choose to insert, for the regulation of the business and the conduct of the affairs of the corporation, and any provisions creating, defining, limiting, and regulating the powers of the corporation, the directors and the stockholders or any class or classes of stockholders; provided such provision is not inconsistent with this act. (in Lacom 1937:29)

This radical laissez-faire provision gave capitalists the legal authority to set the limits and rights of their own corporations. This power of self-determination was used by corporations to define their powers inside and outside the firm. The *external* power of self-determination included the right to purchase and hold stocks of other corporations, to promote other companies, to guarantee the performance of undertakings or obligations of business firms in which the corporation might have an interest, and to purchase shares of the corporation's own stock. The *internal* power of self-determination included the authority to create, define, limit, and regulate the powers of the directors and stockholders. This provision provides corporations with the authority to adjust the internal relationship of groups' interests (e.g., common versus preferred stockholders) in the corporation in the manner deemed best suited to efficient management and financial stability of the corporation (Larcom 1937). For example, the internal power of self-determination allowed corporations to stipulate the percent of stockholder approval for the right to sell the entire assets of a franchise of the corporation.

Capitalists' preference to incorporate in Delaware increased after New Jersey governor Woodrow Wilson—pressured by external interests—passed legislation known as the Seven Sisters. This legislation made trusts illegal, strengthened the criminal code for violations of corporations' financial responsibility (e.g., financial fraud, incorporating for fraudulent purposes), and prohibited stock issues for anticipated versus earned profits. Although New Jersey withdrew some of these provisions in 1917, it lost its position as the preferred state of incorporation. New York's contribution to the "race to the bottom" included an amendment (i.e., the Franchise Tax Law in 1918) that exempted "holding corporations whose principle income is derived from holding the stocks and bonds of other corporations" from the franchise tax (New York Laws of 1918, in Bonbright and Means 1932:11). Delaware eventually won the "race to the bottom," replacing New Jersey in the 1920s as the most favorable state for business incorporation.[18]

There are two crucial implications of the holding company. First, it provides a legal basis to consolidate large amounts of capital under a single more tightly coupled business enterprise. Second, it allows corporations to control assets that significantly exceed their own capitalization by permitting the creation of two or more intermediary companies within a pyramided structure. It is possible to control dozens or even hundreds of business enterprises by owning more than 50 percent of an intermediary company's stock. The intermediary companies, in turn, can control the subsidiary by owning a majority of its stock (table 2.2). In this way, the holding company controls a third-level subsidiary corporation by owning just over 12.5 percent of its stock. This form allows a corporation to control assets many times its own capitalization, reducing its dependence on external sources of capital to consolidate a large number of business enterprises. Through this structure the Rock Island Company controlled $370 million of capitalization in its subsidiary corporations with $25 million of its own stock (Haney 1920; Bonbright and Means 1932; Berle and Means 1991).

The holding company embodied three interrelated advantages over previous business enterprises: (1) a pyramid structure (2) a legal means to consolidate and control the market, and (3) a capacity to finance corporate consolidation strategies and capital requirements by issuing stock. In addition to issuing the parent company's stock, a holding company can use its subsidiaries as *internal capital markets:* issuing stock to raise capital. The capital from subsidiaries' stock issues can be used to acquire other subsidiaries. In this way the holding company also becomes a finance company (Bonbright and Means 1932:14).

TABLE 2.2 The Pyramided Holding Company: Percentage of Ownership to Ensure Ownership Control by the Holding Company

The Holding Company	
First-Level Subsidiary Corporation	Ownership by the holding company = more than 50 percent
Second-Level Subsidiary Corporation	Ownership by the holding company = more than 25 percent
Third-Level Subsidiary Corporation	Ownership by the holding company = more than 12.5 percent

Discussion

The late-nineteenth-century decay-exploration phase was affected by contradictions in the logic of capital accumulation and the exercise of power to resolve those contradictions. The historical context for change included big business' concern with "cutthroat competition," populist opposition to corporate consolidation, a Federalist state structure, and the weak ties among networks of business enterprises. Weak ties limited capitalists' capacity to sustain a unified strategy during economic downturns.

Despite continued political opposition to business consolidation (e.g., antitrust movement), the holding-company form that replaced trusts increased capitalists' capacity to consolidate. Regional states' dependence on revenues from business enterprises provided the institutional context that created compatible business and regional state agenda designed to transcend the decaying institutional arrangements. Representatives of big business (e.g., Standard Oil in New Jersey, DuPont in Delaware) were directly involved in creating the new institutional arrangements. Although the new institutional arrangements provided regional states with an additional source of revenue, the benefits to regional states varied. Capitalists were the real winners.

Intense competition and economic boom and bust characterized the late nineteenth century. In response, the capitalists class mobilized politically to reconfigure the institutional arrangements within which capital accumulation occurs. During boom periods firms expanded by purchasing new plants and equipment, increasing their investment in fixed capital as a proportion of total capital. However, this capital accumulation logic contained a contradiction. Capital-intensive production increased fixed costs, which required higher capability utilization rates to reach the break-even point. The higher capital intensity also reduced businesses' flexibility in lowering costs during economic downturns. Capitalists could more easily disinvest from variable capital (i.e., labor) by laying off workers. Capital in plants and equipment, however, could not be liquidated easily. If capital shortages occurred during an economic downturn requiring the liquidation of assets, these assets would be sold for a fraction of their original costs. To maintain or increase capability utilization rates during economic downturns, businesses cut prices. Although this strategy spread costs over a larger volume, the lower prices raised the break-even point and required corporations to further increase utilization rates. The cycle of lowering prices and raising the break-even point created overproduction in relationship to consumption and put further downward pressure on prices. To overcome these constraints, capitalists sought to strengthen the weak ties among business enterprises by replacing agreements and pools. Although trusts provided a solution, trusts came under public scrutiny as capitalists used them to consolidate capital and control markets.

The prevailing ideology and state structure had important effects on resolving capital-accumulation constraints. Nineteenth-century Federalism, which granted regional states authority over economic activity, was an important component of the political institutional context within which the modern industrial corporation emerged. Along with the right of self-governance went the responsibility to generate revenues. However, the capacity of regional states to generate revenues was constrained by laissez-faire ideology, which advocated small government and opposed taxing citizens. Within this institutional context, regional states' fiscal solvency and legitimacy were dependent on their capacity to establish agreements with business. These institutional arrangements produced a compatibility between the interests' big capital and regional states. Regional states were dependent of revenues from business, and business desired stable institutional arrangements within which to pursue economic activity.

Absent a strong centralized state and advocating laissez-faire ideology that opposed centralized political control by the federal government, capitalists pressured regional states to establish laws of incorporation that were favorable to business. Dependent on businesses for revenue, New Jersey set up laws of incorporation that granted the business enterprise rights similar to those of individuals (e.g., limited liability, the right to own stock in other businesses). New Jersey's business policy initiated a "race to the bottom" among regional states, which granted corporations a wide range of legal rights with few restrictions or responsibilities. These institutional arrangements created the legal framework for the modern corporation.

Change in the historical trajectory was affected by capital accumulation constraints, business political behavior, and the Federalist structure of the U.S. state. Capitalists were concerned with maximizing profits during boom periods and surviving during periods of economic bust. The survival of their businesses, not cost efficiency, motivated capitalists to mobilize politically to reconfigure their institutional arrangements. Capitalists' behaviors were based on their desire to reduce the effect of market competition. The holding company was the outcome of their experiments to establish the institutional arrangements that allowed them to pursue their consolidation agenda. This historical transition and corporate transformation occurred during a short time frame.

Although the *new* holding company is important for many reasons, significant are its internal capital markets and right to own the stock in other corporations. As John D. Rockefeller, the president of Standard Oil, asserted, the *new* holding company signaled the triumph of the corporation; now corporations could be created solely to combine with other corporations through stock transactions (in Kirkland 1967). The right to establish ownership control through stock transactions was the basis of subsequent corporate consolidation.

CHAPTER 3

Restructuring the Business Enterprise to Obtain Market Control, 1890–1905

Regional state laws of incorporation provided the institutional arrangements and legitimacy for the modern corporation to pursue its consolidation strategy. Two interrelated processes were crucial: the emergence of the holding-company form, and the growth of finance capital. Among the most important aspects of the new institutional arrangements were the extremely lenient financial guidelines. These guidelines allowed high capitalization limits and placed few limits on debt-to-asset ratio and stock issues (Sklar 1988). For example, owners could issue stock to raise capital, use this capital to purchase assets and other corporations, and issue stock based on the assessed value of new subsidiary corporations. Despite these institutional arrangements, a crucial obstacle impeded corporate consolidation. Industrial capitalists, consisting almost solely of entrepreneurs who reinvested into their own businesses, had neither the experience with capital markets nor the capital to pursue consolidation strategies. As a result, industrial growth occurred through the *concentration* of capital: an increase in the value of each firm (Marx 1977:625). Further, little demand existed for industrial stock, which made industrial capital dependent on financiers.

The Expansion of Finance Capital: Corporate Consolidation and Big Business

Before the creation of the late-nineteenth-century holding company, banking and industrial capital remained separate.[1] The holding company, however, created capital-accumulation opportunities for both the banking and industrial capitalist class segments. These opportunities created an incentive to merge industrial capital with banking capital to create *finance capital* (Zeitlin 1974; Roy 1991).

Throughout most of the nineteenth century, private investment bankers focused on the transportation and communication industries. During the last two decades of the nineteenth century almost one-half of all private investment occurred in the railroad industry (Baran and Sweezy 1966). Savings banks were restricted from dealing in common stocks, lacked the knowledge and organization to market stocks, and typically did not have the capital to underwrite consolidation activities. In short, despite the existence of a state structure that allowed consolidation of business enterprises and the view among industrial capitalists that consolidation was a viable means to avoid "cutthroat competition," industrialists did not have the capital necessary to carry out this strategy.

Private financiers' interest in industrial capital increased in the 1890s, however, as the financial stability of the railroad began to weaken, and a depression from 1893 to 1897 resulted in financial collapse in the railroad industry. Scores of railroads went bankrupt after 1893 (Chernow 1997). By 1894, twenty-five percent of railroad investments were in receivership (Campbell 1938; Roy 1991).[2] This prolonged economic downturn resulted in a steady decline in railroad investment (Baran and Sweezy 1966). As revenues declined, the flaws in this financial structure emerged. As John Moody stated:

> No single financial problem in the previous history of the world equaled in difficulty or magnitude with this reorganization of the railroads of the United States. These crazy financial structures had been patched together by any possible method of cohesion. (In Josephson 1962:410–11)

Instability in the transportation sector created an incentive for private investment bankers, brokers, and investors to look for alternate opportunities. Private investment bankers familiar with the holding company's use in the railroad industry recognized the advantages of this corporate form's stock-issuing privileges. In particular, they recognized that it was possible to make profits using this corporate form by simply marketing and manipulating the value of industrial securities (Larcom 1937; Chandler 1977; DiDonato, Glasberg, Mintz, and Schwartz 1988). Financiers such as J. P. Morgan used the stock exchange to sell securities issued by new and existing corporations.[3] Demand for stocks in the expanding industrial sector raised stocks' market valuation and allowed corporations to issue them at high values. This capital was frequently used to advance corporations' consolidation strategies.

This arrangement also created a capital-dependent relationship between financiers and industrialists. Because industrialists had little access to capital, they depended on financiers to arrange mergers and acquisitions. For their capital, service, and expertise, financiers frequently received payment in the form of stock (Chandler 1977). Although financiers often made millions of dollars on a single merger, they also demanded a seat on the board of directors and the right to appoint board members and top managers of corporations (Josephson 1962).

Through these arrangements, by the turn of the century financiers became influential in the management of nearly all large industrial corporations (Cochran and Miller 1942; Kirkland 1967; Gordon et al. 1982). Finance capitalists (i.e., Morgan, Villard) played a crucial role in forming General Electric (1892) and U.S. Steel (1901) (Kirkland 1967). J. P. Morgan and his partners helped form International Harvester and held a position on its board of directors. The Rockefeller group financed Standard Oil and controlled several other companies. One way financiers exercised control was by influencing decisions concerning the type of stock issued. Thus, they defined the voting rights of shareholders (e.g., common stock does not provide voting rights while preferred stock does), thereby defining their opportunities for input into the management of the corporation.

Four factors are frequently cited as motivating the concentration and centralization of capital. First, capitalists argued that consolidation of product lines would result in greater efficiency. Second, smaller independent companies became concerned about self-protection as the consolidation movement developed. The smaller firms found survival difficult, but felt they could endure—as subsidiary corporations—by joining larger companies. Third, industrial capitalists continued to express concern over "cutthroat competition." Fourth, they also became aware of the shortcomings of trusts. As Andrew Carnegie stated:

> There is no possibility of maintaining a trust. It is bound to go to pieces, sooner or later, and generally to involve in ruin those foolish enough to embark on it. (*New York Times,* 1888)

Together with the late-nineteenth-century regional state laws of incorporation, financial capitalists enabled industrial capitalists to replace the weak ties of pools and trusts with the more tightly coupled holding company. This corporate form established a legal basis to control the behavior of member companies entering these combinations.

The Holding Company: The Fast Track to Monopoly and Oligopoly

The following case study illustrates the strategy pursued by turn-of-the-century industrialists. The steel industry case is typical of late-nineteenth- and early-twentieth-century industrial consolidation practices in several ways: (1) it used the holding company form (2) it represented the merging of banking capital and industrial capital to create finance capital, and (3) it attempted to eliminate "cutthroat competition" by gaining control over regional and national markets. However, the steel industry is also atypical compared to other industries: (1) the consolidation of almost two hundred previously independent steel companies into eleven corporations was more extensive than in some industries (Hogan 1971), and (2) the degree of market control was less than in several other industries. I selected the steel industry because its behavior was typical of turn-of-the-century corporate attempts to control markets. In the following, I show how historically specific institutional arrangements affected consolidation. How well the specific outcomes in the steel industry (e.g., the number of companies consolidated) typified the period is less important than illustrating how the institutional arrangements provided the context for capitalists' strategic decisions.

The First Consolidation Phase: The Carnegie Steel Company

Consolidation in the steel industry occurred in two phases. The first began during the depression in 1873. Andrew Carnegie used external capital markets (i.e., a loan from Judge Thomas Mellon) to purchase several steel related properties (Hogan 1971; Cochran and Miller 1942). For the next several years, Carnegie pursued a strategy of expanding during depressions when he could purchase bankrupt or near bankrupt steel facilities at reduced prices and build new facilities at lower costs (Hessen 1975). By 1888 Carnegie had expanded his steel business through a series of mergers and acquisitions.

Carnegie's success was due to a combination of internal and external controls. Carnegie's internal management strategy stressed the rapid movement of materials through the production process. The cost controls Carnegie set up were significantly more precise than those in other industries (i.e., textiles, petroleum, tobacco) (Chandler 1977). By increasing the rate at which materials moved through the production process and maintaining high capability utilization rates, Carnegie maximized the use of equipment, lowered per-unit energy costs, and reduced semifinished inventory. These managerial practices reduced per-unit costs and ensured rapid capital turnover and high cash flow.

Externally, Carnegie pursued two strategies. He reduced costs through vertical integration by purchasing key resources upon which steel production depends (e.g., raw materials, coke-making facilities). Carnegie also pursued horizontal integration strategies by purchasing companies competing for the same markets. By 1887, The Carnegie Steel Company had established a regional monopoly in its primary product group (i.e., rails).

In 1889, Allegheny Bessemer Steel Company in Duquesne threatened Carnegie's dominance in western Pennsylvania. It developed a more cost efficient method to manufacture steel rails. Allegheny's rail-manufacturing process eliminated the reheating stage by rolling rails directly from the ingot. This innovation improved cost efficiency and made it possible to sell rails cheaper than those produced by conventional methods. This technological innovation exposed a fundamental contradiction in large industrial business enterprises and posed a significant threat to Carnegie's steel company. On the one hand, Carnegie had massive capital investments in conventional technologies. High fixed capital investment limited organizational flexibility. It was not financially feasible for Carnegie to replace his production facilities with the new technology. On the other hand, competition threatened market share and market control. This situation elicited a response.

Carnegie wrote a letter to several railroad companies warning that rails made by the direct rolling process were dangerous (Hogan 1971). By implying that the use of rails manufactured by this new process could result in derailed trains, Carnegie persuaded the railroad companies not to use the Allegheny Bessemer Steel Company products. The Allegheny Bessemer Steel Company had to settle for rail contracts with low profit margins. As a result, Allegheny Steel came under financial pressure. Henry Frisk—a top operating manager and major stockholder at Carnegie Steel—initiated negotiations to purchase the company. In November 1890, the expanding Carnegie Steel empire acquired the Duquesne plant of the Allegheny Besmer Steel Company. Although Carnegie had established innovative cost controls to monitor the efficiency of operations, his market-control strategy blocked a major technological innovation, which significantly improved efficiency, from spreading throughout the industry.

After Carnegie acquired the Allegheny Bessemer Steel Company, he sold the steel it produced by the more efficient direct-rolling method at prices set by his regional monopoly. This strategy proved to be extremely profitable. The cost-efficient Duquesne plant paid for itself in slightly over a year. By 1890, the Carnegie Steel Company also acquired several raw material holdings and established market dominance in the Pittsburgh area. To facilitate continued expansion, the firm reorganized as a holding company in 1892. It incorporated in New Jersey as the Carnegie Steel Company Limited (Hogan 1971).[4]

In 1889, while Andrew Carnegie was building a regional monopoly in Pennsylvania, Ohio, and West Virginia, Judge Elbert Gary was creating the Illinois Steel Company in the Midwest. He produced this large steel corporation by consolidating several raw material holdings and three Chicago companies that owned five steel plants in Chicago and Milwaukee. By the late 1890s, Illinois Steel Company realized it needed better manufacturing facilities and access to raw material reserves to compete with Carnegie Steel (Hogan 1971). Thus, financed by J. P. Morgan & Company, Illinois Steel acquired Minnesota Iron Company, a company almost as large as Illinois Steel itself. Because Illinois business policy did not allow one corporation to own the stock of another, the new $200 million Federal Steel corporation was incorporated in 1898 as a New Jersey holding company (Larcom 1937; Hogan 1971). J. P. Morgan appointed Judge Gary as president of the new holding company that controlled five subsidiaries (Hogan 1971). About one-half of the total authorized capitalization under the incorporation agreement was issued in preferred and common stock.

Carnegie Steel Company and Federal Steel Company shared three important characteristics: (1) both their primary product lines were steel rails, billets, plates, and structural steel (2) both had an excess of raw steel-making capacity, and (3) both sold their raw steel to manufacturers of finished steel products (Hogan 1971). However, unlike Carnegie who concentrated his manufacturing facilities in one region, Federal Steel located its manufacturing facilities in Illinois, Ohio, Pennsylvania, and Wisconsin.

A third large consolidation in the steel industry created National Steel Company, another New Jersey–based holding company. National Steel included eight companies concentrated primarily in Ohio. Unlike Carnegie Steel and Federal Steel, National Steel acquired three companies that consumed raw steel (i.e., American Tin Plate Company, American Steel Hoop Company, American Sheet Steel Company). This strategy created internal markets for National Steel's products. National's consolidation was financed by another private investment banker—W. H. Moore—who placed himself on the board of directors of National Steel and its three steel-consuming subsidiary corporations.

Three crucial conditions affected these consolidations. First, the political-legal structure governing incorporation made it possible for one corporation to gain control of another by owning just over 50 percent of the acquired company. Second, private-investment bankers had access to capital and expertise in the securities market. Industrial capital depended on private-investment banking for financing and financial management. The completion of these consolidation deals further combined private investment banking with industrial capital. Third, the giant holding companies forged resource-dependent relationships with other firms. For example, although many independent steel companies continued to exist, they depended on the "big three" (i.e., Carnegie Steel, Federal Steel, National Steel) for raw steel. Most of the independent steel companies manufactured finished products from raw or semifinished steel.

The Second Consolidation Phase: Creating the United States Steel Corporation

The "big three" steel companies created price-setting monopolies in regional market. However, as they expanded into each other's market areas and attempted to control the national market, competition for market share emerged. Federal Steel Company controlled 15 percent of the production capability of the nation's steel capability. This jeopardized Carnegie's position as the industry's price setter. Unlike National Steel Company, which had steel-consuming subsidiaries to buffer the effects of market downturns, neither Carnegie Steel nor Federal Steel had ownership control over steel-consuming subsidiaries. Ownership control in the holding company entails owning more than 50 percent of another corporation's stock, which allows the parent holding company to determine policy in the subsidiary (e.g., where to purchase raw steel). Also, Carnegie Steel and Federal Steel had more raw steel-making capacity than finishing capacity, which made them dependent on the smaller independent steel makers to purchase their raw steel.

The regional monopolies of the "big three" were further threatened when the smaller independent steel companies, realizing the implications of their dependence on the larger ones (e.g., high purchase prices), began building raw steelmaking facilities of their own. In 1899, National Tube Company constructed a raw steel-making facility to reduce its dependence on Carnegie Steel. It located this facility, organized as a subsidiary, in Benwood, West Virginia. American Steel and Wire Company also constructed steel-making facilities. It acquired raw material properties and ore carriers to transport ore from the Mesabi Range (Hogan 1971).[5] In 1901, Inland Steel Company began producing raw steel.

Although the Carnegie Company expanded into new markets (e.g., wire, tubes), the potential constraints on capital accumulation of this industry structure elicited a response. Andrew Carnegie became concerned about losing outlets for his raw steel and a return to "cutthroat competition." In 1890, Carnegie invited Judge Gary of the Federal Steel Company to a meeting and suggested a pooling arrangement. Judge Gary agreed to the pact. However, it was subject to the same limitations as previous pooling agreements. Market arrangement based on personal agreements were hard to maintain. Also, the effectiveness of the Carnegie-Gary pool declined because independent steel companies continued to construct their own steel-making facilities and reduced their dependence on the "big three" for raw steel. As in the pre-trust period, it was difficult to preserve price controls based on personal agreements in the face of market competition. During the following decade, the "big three" steel corporations continued to be concerned over a return to "cutthroat competition." In 1900 Judge Gary approached J. P. Morgan to arrange a combination of the Carnegie and Federal Steel companies. Although this first effort failed, it prepared the way for the successful consolidation of the "big three" in the following year.

Just as they had in the first phase, private investment bankers played a crucial role in the second phase of consolidation. In fact, the first phase of consolidation created problems that structured investment bankers' interests in initiating a second phase of consolidation in the steel industry. As were many business enterprises created through the holding-company form, two of the "big three" steel companies were overcapitalized (Thorelli 1955).[6]

Overcapitalization occurred, in part, because regional states provided capitalists with the legal authority to set the valuation of their own stock. One method to establish capitalization considered the amount paid for the subsidiary, the working capital for a specified period, the expenses of the incorporation, and the profit anticipated from the subsidiary. Another method estimated the subsidiary's anticipated earning power. The problem of overcapitalization was exacerbated because corporations were allowed to pay dividends on overcapitalized assets. Paying dividends on overcapitalized assets drains capital from the asset and further reduces the actual value of the stock (Haney 1920).

Although overcapitalization was less problematic for the "big three" than for some corporations, none of these steel companies could ignore the potential implications of a drop in stock values. Although National Steel and its steel-consuming subsidiaries were in a strong market position, they were overcapitalized. Overcapitalized corporations are vulnerable to a sharp drop in cash flow and to bankruptcy if a price war emerged. Federal Steel and Carnegie Steel were well financed but in weak market positions. Corporations with few outlets for their raw steel would experience a dramatic drop in demand. All three big steel corporations could suffer severely if a price war occurred. This possibility of "cutthroat competition" created a frightening prospect for both financiers and industrialists. After the first consolidation phase, private investment bankers had substantial investments in steel corporations. Thus, their financial stability depended on stability in the corporations they had financed. A price war meant a severe drop in earnings and created conditions for bankruptcy. Thus there were strong incentives for capitalist class segments to pursue consolidation strategies and establish control over national markets.

Instability in the steel industry signified trouble for finance capitalists in at least three ways. First, as stated above, return on their investment depended on economic stability in the steel industry. Second, growth in other segments of the economy (e.g., railroad)—where investment bankers also had significant holdings—depended on a steady supply of steel. Third, if a bankruptcy occurred, the losses to finance capital increased as they invested larger amounts of capital into the expanding industrial firms. It was one thing for one previously independent small steel company to go bankrupt. It was quite another for one of the "big three" to go bankrupt. It was still another problem for the "big three" to become involved in an uncontrolled price war that might ruin all three holding companies and bankrupt financiers (e.g., Mellon, Moore, Morgan).

In short, the network of resource-dependent relations that emerged from the first phase of consolidation made these capitalists extremely vulnerable to an economic downturn and a return to "cutthroat competition." Finance capitalists argued that it was necessary to eliminate the possibility of "foolhardy competition [that] could [result] in a major panic" (Hogan 1971). If a large number of investors sold their securities in an overcapitalized corporation, the corporation may not have the capital to buy back these stock and the remaining stock may decline in value. A decline in value of corporations' stock means losses for financial capitalists. However, finance capital had the resources (e.g., capital, expertise) to circumvent this potential crisis.

In 1901, J. P. Morgan financed the creation of the United States Steel Corporation, another New Jersey–based holding company. It was by far the largest consolidation in the history of the United States. Morgan produced the first $1 billion company with a capitalization of over $1.3 billion. However, consolidation did not solve the overcapitalization problem. The overcapitalization of many firms was simply rolled into one firm. Like the companies from which it was created, United States Steel was overcapitalized. Although the corporation only reported tangible assets of $682 million, Morgan underwrote and offered for sale $1.321 billion in mortgage bonds, preferred stock, and common stock (Josephson 1962). In other words, almost one-half of the securities issued represented *water:* securities that are not backed by assets. Unaware of U.S. Steel's financial structure, middle-class investors purchased a large portion of these securities.

U.S. Steel was so overcapitalized that Andrew Carnegie refused to accept stock and negotiated to receive his payments in the form of bonds (Chernow 1997). Other major stockholders in Carnegie Steel such as Henry Frick and Henry Phipps sold their holdings in the new corporation (Josephson 1962). Henry Frick sold almost $50 million of his shares at $55 in 1901. Less-knowledgeable investors were not as fortunate. U.S. Steel stock dropped to $9 by 1904 (Kolko 1963).

Not even the Standard Oil Company approached the scale and scope of United States Steel Corporation. By April 1901, the corporation controlled ten first-level subsidiary corporations. In the following months, the new holding company acquired additional steel-manufacturing, raw material, and transportation companies. Like other holding companies, U.S. Steel raised the capital to acquire these subsidiaries by issuing stocks and bonds that exceeded the value of the securities of the acquired firms (Hogan 1971). The new holding company was fully integrated, both horizontally and vertically. It owned and operated raw material, transportation, and manufacturing facilities in nearly all types of steel products. Like the parent holding company, most of the first-level subsidiary corporations were incorporated in New Jersey.

Consolidation in other industries also used a pyramided structure. Within this corporate form, the proportion of the parent company's investment in the subsidiary corporations inversely related to the level of the pyramided structure. The parent company could achieve ownership control with a relatively small proportion of actual ownership of subsidiaries' stock.

By November 1901, the United States Steel Corporation consolidated more than two hundred companies. It acquired or controlled approximately 785 steel plants, including over 60 percent of the steel-production capability in the United States.[7] Most of the subsidiary corporations were single function organizations (i.e., producers of a single product). It liquidated the stock of thirty-nine previously independent companies creating 188 subsidiary corporations (Haney 1920).

U.S. Steel's strategies did not appear to increase efficiency. Although records show that Carnegie Company manufactured steel rails for $12 per ton, similar cost records are not readily available for the new U.S. Steel Corporation. Therefore, it is not clear whether the new company was less cost efficient. However, it is clear that the new company was less efficient from a societal perspective. Soon after this consolidation in the steel industry the price of steel rails increased to $28 per ton. The old Carnegie Steel Company sold the same product for $23.75 per ton. Either the new company was less cost efficient or the corporation engaged in price setting. In either case, consumers paid more for this product after the consolidation.

The political and economic institutional arrangements structured the form of the corporation. The institutional arrangements included: (1) regional states' legalization of the new holding company form (2) extremely liberal regional states' laws of incorporation (3) the Sherman Antitrust Act (1890) that challenged trusts and legitimated the holding company, and (4) a decline in the profit-making opportunities in the railroad industry that created an interest in the industrial sector among financiers.

Justifying Consolidation: Prevailing Ideologies

Centralization by big business did not go unnoticed by the public. An article in the popular press characterized the creation of Federal Steel Company and its struggle with Carnegie as initiating

> one of the greatest contests for supremacy that the world has ever seen. It is a fight between the new concern and the Carnegie interests, both backed by almost unlimited capital. (*New York Commercial*, September 10, 1898, in Hogan 1971:266)

This contest for supremacy was short-lived. Federal Steel and Carnegie Steel consolidated, which created the conditions for market control. As in the past, laissez-faire utilitarian ideology was evoked to legitimate consolidation. The leading iron and steel trade journal countered criticisms by asserting that the consolidation was for the greater good.

> As for the smaller industrial concerns which may be forced out of existence or adapt their business to new conditions, their sacrifice is only a part of the price which must be paid for progress.
>
> Whatever is for the greatest good must prevail in the end, and if a concern capitalized at millions can produce at a lower cost than one with only thousands involved, no amount of sympathy for the "little fellow" will save him from being crowded out. (*Iron Age* 1898, September)

This debate between the rights and interests of corporations and those of the public did not disappear, but continued throughout the first half of the twentieth century. It is questionable whether the centralization of capital resulted in a greater good. It is clear, however, that this period of rapid corporate consolidation benefited big business.

Transformation to the Holding Company

Financing Consolidation

To capitalists skeptical of entering into business combinations, the 1893 depression provided an incentive; prices fell less rapidly and losses were less severe in consolidated industries (Eichner 1969). By the late 1890s, corporate trasnformation and market consolidation were underway. Three crucial institutional arrangements provided incentives to restructure as a holding company. First, unregulated and high capitalization limits provided a source of capital. Corporations could issue stock and use the capital to pursue consolidation strategies. Second, the pyramided financial structure of the holding company provided the legal framework for capitalists to control more assets than they owned. Third, corporate lawyers assumed that the holding-company form legitimated consolidation by placing business combinations beyond the legal restrictions of the Sherman Antitrust Act (Martin 1959). By 1904, the reorganization of assets within the industrial holding-company skyrocketed. The total value of common stock of publicly held manufacturing corporations increased from a little over $.5 billion dollars in 1898 to over half of the total book value of all industrial capital in 1904 ($11.6 billion) (U.S. Bureau of Census 1975; Roy 1991). Between 1898 and 1904, more than $4 billion in new securities were issued solely for industrial consolidation (Cochran and Miller 1942).

Incorporation as a New Jersey holding company was particularly widespread in industries where capital was most centralized. In 1890, 61 of the 83 (i.e., 73.5 percent) companies with capitalizations of over $1 million were incorporated in New Jersey (Larcom 1937). From the year (1888) that New Jersey passed this legislation to 1903 almost 56 percent (i.e., 192 of 345) of the total incorporation in the U.S. occurred in New Jersey. The next highest states for holding-company incorporation were Pennsylvania with 31 and New York with 30. By lowering the cost of ownership control, the holding-company form provided an inexpensive means to pursue market control. The holding-company form was crucial in the historical process of transforming capitalism from many small entrepreneurial firms in competitive markets to a few giant corporations in monopolistic and oligopolistic markets.

Although consolidation in the steel industry created the largest U.S. corporation (i.e., U.S. Steel), its market share (i.e., 60 percent) was far from the highest in the industrial sector. The steel industry operated as an oligopoly: corporate executives met to fix prices and distribute market share. Several industries, however, were effective *monopolies:* market control by a single corporation. Of the sixty-three largest corporations created by consolidation or mergers between 1895 and 1904, forty-three gained control of between 70 and 95 percent of their industry's market share.

TABLE 3.1 Industry, Corporation, and Market Share, 1904

Industry	Corporation	Percentage of Market Share
Gypsum	U.S. Gypsum	80
Explosives	DuPont	85
Farm Equipment	International Harvester	90
Tobacco	American Tobacco	90

U.S. Gypsum, American Tobacco, DuPont, and International Harvester, controlled 80 percent or more respectively of their markets (table 3.1) (Nelson 1959).

Consolidation in the explosives industry followed a historical trajectory similar to that in the steel industry. In 1872, the Gunpowder Trade Associate was formed when overproduction threatened prices. During the 1870s depression that followed, Henry DuPont purchased the majority of the stock in several large powder companies. However, within its current administrative structure the DuPonts were unable to exercise control over these subsidiary corporations. To consolidate control, between 1902 and 1903 the DuPonts purchased the remained stock in these companies and several more companies in the explosives industry for cash or an exchange for stock in the new E. I. du Pont de Nemours Powder Company (Chandler 1962).

Advantages of the Holding-Company Form

The holding company replaced the weak ties among business enterprises organized as pools and trusts by making it possible to establish ownership control of firms by embedding subsidiary corporations into a single corporation. This more tightly coupled structure and the institutional arrangements that defined the rights of corporations established the context for the decision to pursue industrial consolidation. Consolidation strategies were feasible because this social structure established the means to raise the capital (i.e., stock sales) necessary to carry out these strategies, and a corporate form that legitimated ownership control of many corporations by a single parent company.

The holding company had several advantages over other corporate forms. First, establishing ownership control through stock had several advantages over *mergers:* the acquisition of assets. Consolidation through ownership of stock required less capital than consolidation through ownership of assets. By purchasing just over 50 percent of their stock, the parent holding company gained ownership control over many more assets than it owned. Thus consolidation through ownership of stock made control less costly to achieve. Also, in most states, mergers required the support of two-thirds of the stockholders. Stockholder approval in the holding company required a simple majority.[8]

Second, the holding company provided a means to camouflage ownership. Consolidation through stock ownership could go unnoticed by the public. This reduced the probability that renewed opposition to corporate consolidation would emerge. In fact, consolidation could occur without the knowledge of the company being acquired. J. P. Morgan gained control of the American Bridge Company for the United States Steel Corporation before American Bridge's executives or directors were aware of the transaction. No negotiations concerning price occurred and no actual capital changed hands between the companies. The law required only that the holding company exchange its stock with individuals for the stock of the company it intended to take over. To takeover this corporation, J. P. Morgan simply circulated an offer to exchange U.S. Steel stock for American Bridge stock and made the exchanges (Haney 1920; Bonbright and Means 1932).

Third, because ownership changes could occur through stock purchases, consolidation in the holding company did not require a reorganization of the corporation or its management. In contrast, a merger required compatibility among the corporate entities that made up the new merged or amalgamated company.[9] This institutional context also saved corporations restructuring as holding companies millions of dollars in legal and underwriting fees (Bonbright and Means 1932).

Fourth, the holding company allowed firms to control other firms that were geographically dispersed in several regional states. Prior to the industrial holding company, most regional states required firms to incorporate in the state where they conducted business. In contrast, subsidiary corporations' legal status allowed the parent holding company to incorporate a subsidiary in virtually any state. For example, Clariton Steel and Union Steel Co., subsidiaries of U.S. Steel, were incorporated in Pennsylvania. The U.S. Steel corporation itself was incorporated in New Jersey. These institutional arrangements made possible regional consolidation of entire industries.[10]

Fifth, the holding company created a *liability firewall:* losses in subsidiary corporations were contained within that corporate entity. Limited-liability laws together with the legal separation of subsidiaries from parent companies protected the latter and their financiers from breakdowns in subsidiary corporations. Parent companies were not even liable for subsidiaries' debt. The liability firewall was rarely disregarded by the courts.

Sixth, through the holding-company form, corporations engaged in intercompany transactions to give the appearance of financial strength. These intercompany transactions included selling the assets of one subsidiary to others, shifting business from one subsidiary to others, concealing subsidiary losses, and selling inventory from one subsidiary to others (Berle and Means 1991). Intercompany transactions frequently appeared as profits in the parent company while the subsidiaries lost money in the long term. This situation benefited the stockholders of the parent company because records of strong earnings produced high, often over-valued, stock values (Berle and Means 1991). These overvalued parent company and subsidiary stock were frequently sold to naive individual investors.[11]

Seventh, the holding company increased corporations' self-financing capability by establishing *internal capital markets:* transforming fixed "assets into capital" by issuing securities (e.g., stocks, bonds) (Prechel 1997b:158). The new institutional arrangements allowed corporations to purchase property with stock issued for that purpose. Also, few limits were placed on the capitalization of these new subsidiaries. Further, as part of an acquisition agreement, corporations could issue stock in the proposed subsidiary corporation in order to finance the acquisition. This self-financing capability provided the context for decisions to pursue consolidation strategies.

Eighth, the holding company increased organizational flexibility. Parent companies could organize as a *pure holding company* that owned the stock of operating companies and exercised little or no managerial authority over operating managers. They could also organize as an *operating-management holding company*, that held the stock of subsidiary corporations and managed them. Some holding companies engaged in both activities: the *mixed holding company*, for example, could own-and-operate one plant and simply own the stock of others. Standard Oil Company of New Jersey, American Cotton Oil Company, and American Steel & Wire Company organized as mixed holding companies. Still other variations of the holding company concentrated on finance and investment. They created subsidiaries to promote their financial operations. For example, General Electric (GE) owned the stock of the Electric Securities Company and Electric Bond and Share Company. GE organized these subsidiary corporations to promote, under-write, and buy the bonds of other electric companies. Through these financial subsidiaries, GE pursued a forward integration strategy, gaining control over companies that purchased its products (Haney 1920). The holding company benefited corporations in other ways: market embeddedness of subsidiary corporations provided a measurement of their effectiveness (i.e., capacity to realize a profit) (Prechel 1997b:410).

Ninth, the holding company/subsidiary form increased corporations' flexibility. If a subsidiary corporation could not compete in its market niche, the parent holding company could disinvest by selling the subsidiary's stock (Douglas and Shanks 1929; Bonbright and Means 1932; Dewing 1941).

Decisions to restructure and consolidate were made within a specific institutional context created by social actors (e.g., capitalists, state managers) attempting to advance their interests. The new macro-level institutional arrangements provided a context for corporations to organize as holding companies (i.e., meso level), which provided flexibility and granted rights but established few constraints.

Disadvantages of the Holding-Company Form

Despite its advantages, the holding-company form was not without problems. Although the holding company strengthened the weak ties that existed among business entities organized as pools and trusts, aspects of the holding company remained loosely coupled. The holding company had limited management and monitoring capabilities. Holding companies centralized certain financial controls. Operating control, however, was typically decentralized to the subsidiary managers. These middle managers—some of whom were the previous owners of these subsidiaries—frequently conducted business in ways that did not follow the strategies stipulated by top management of the parent holding company. Industrial holding companies did not contain the authority structures to ensure that the managers of the subsidiary corporations complied with the interests or pursued the agendas of its new owners. Loose coupling between top management of the holding company and middle management responsible for operating subsidiary corporations frequently resulted in conflict. The holding company's limited monitoring capability also increased the possibility of fraud within the subsidiary corporations.

Although the holding company's internal capital markets created an important source of capital, they were frequently less financially sound than a merged company. Subsidiary managers typically had the authority to take on debt. High debt in subsidiary corporations weakened the financial structure of the parent holding company. The holding-company form also had high managerial costs and, sometimes, high taxes. In most states, each subsidiary corporation was required to pay annual franchise taxes.[12] Also, each subsidiary within a holding company typically had a separate board of directors, staff of executive officers, and accounting controls. These duplications resulted in high operating costs.

As a partial solution to these problems, holding companies began to buy subsidiary corporations' stock, thereby obtaining total ownership of their subsidiaries. For example, the largest industrial consolidation between 1904 and 1914 created General Motors Company (1908). This automobile company purchased the majority of the assets of several other corporations. Like other corporations (e.g., United States Steel), this holding company attempted to standardize its accounting system to control its subsidiary corporations that operated semiautonomously from the holding company (Chandler 1962). Later, General Motors purchased the remaining assets of its subsidiaries and restructured and reincorporated as an operating company (1916), General Motors Corporation. This strategy increased centralized control by eliminating the possibility of dissenting minority shareholders objecting to the principle owners' strategies and agenda (Bonbright and Means 1932). The Consolidated Tobacco Company restructured in a similar manner. In short, consolidation entailed two steps. The initial step included ownership control of subsidiary corporations to obtain market control. The second step, which required more capital, involved total ownership of these corporate entities. Ownership of subsidiaries, however, did not address cost-efficiency issues. Few controls over the managerial process existed. The efficiency considerations of industrial consolidation were not addressed for several decades (chapter 5).

Discussion: The New Institutional Arrangements and the Modern Corporation

Until the late nineteenth century, industrial business enterprises had few legal rights. Business enterprises (e.g., pools, agreements) could only be loosely coupled, which limited organizational capacity to control members' responses to market fluctuations. The depressions of 1873–1878, 1882–1885, and 1893–1897, and the potential for "cutthroat competition" eroded capitalists' confidence in the institutional arrangements based on laissez-faire ideology. New institutional arrangements were established in response to economic crises. Although restructuring as a corporation via the holding company was initiated by the 1888 New Jersey laws of incorporation and was well underway by 1890, it accelerated after New Jersey provided even more favorable institutional arrangements by revising its incorporation laws in 1893. These laws eliminated most restrictions on purchasing property with stock issued for that purpose. These new institutional arrangements gave corporations the autonomy to engage in a wide range of business activities.

These new institutional arrangements also increased corporations' autonomy from regional and national states. It was much more difficult to prosecute a holding company than a trust even when they engaged in the same restraint of trade activities. It was one thing to sue a trust that organizes several independent businesses to control the market. It is quite another thing to sue a single business enterprise for controlling production levels and setting prices in its own subsidiary corporations. A legal framework for the latter did not exist.

Autonomy from state regulation resulted in strategies that rapidly increased corporate size. As the size of corporations increased so did *fixed costs* (e.g., interest on borrowed capital, the cost of administrative staff, depreciation of assets, raw material inventories). Whereas high fixed costs created incentives to set prices, ownership control of production capacity in regional markets provided capitalists with the power to engage in price fixing and other oligopolistic behaviors. Although some regional states had laws prohibiting these practices, their dependence on big business for revenues and jobs produced a countervailing force that frequently kept them from exercising their authority. Restricting Standard Oil or U.S. Steel from engaging in price fixing created an incentive for these companies to relocate to a different regional state. For politicians, the perceived advantages of allowing price-setting practices outweighed the perceived disadvantages.

Political protests against the centralization of capital intensified. In response, state managers in the U.S. Congress introduced several bills between 1900 and 1914 to control corporations. However, the Federalist state structure and laissez-faire ideology limited the national state from controlling corporations. Although the rate of centralization of capital alarmed small businesses, they were also concerned with an intrusive federal government that might compromise small-business interests. The capacity of the federal government was further impaired by regional states' opposition to national incorporation laws because of potential loss of incorporation-fee revenues (Seager and Gulick 1929; Urofsky 1982; Sklar 1988; Grandy 1993).

Conclusion

The modern corporation did not evolve naturally out of the competitive economy of the late nineteenth century. Rather, social actors exercised power to dismantle the competitive structure of the economy. Capitalists advanced their interests by pressuring regional states to establish new institutional arrangements that granted them rights and imposed few restrictions. By 1935, the business policies of twenty-nine states allowed virtually unlimited authority to corporations in acquisition and holding stock (Larcom 1937). The most highly capitalized consolidations occurred in states where corporation laws set the highest limits on capitalization and allowed the greatest freedom in organizing financial structures (Nelson 1959). These new institutional arrangements legitimated the industrial holding company and paved the way for industrial consolidation.

This analysis provides the basis to unravel the theoretical logic underpinning efficiency theories. These institutional arrangements made it possible for capitalists to use their capital in an extremely efficient manner. Through the holding-company corporations could establish ownership control by owning just over 50 percent of a first-level subsidiary's stock, just over 25 percent of second-level subsidiary's stock, and so forth. However, efficiency for capitalists—individually or as a group—is not equivalent to efficiency for society. As in the late nineteenth century, contemporary efficiency arguments assume a utilitarian logic: the capacity of capitalists to pursue their self-interests contributed to the greater good. Thus, the greater good must be evaluated in terms of the benefits to society. Using this criterion, little support exists for efficiency arguments. After corporations consolidated, prices increased in some industries, and little evidence exists that prices dropped in others. Further, advocates of efficiency arguments frequently equate the survival of the industrial corporation and expansion of the U.S. economy with the efficiency of the corporation. In the absence of another history to compare with the one that occurred, this is an assertion. It is not a valid basis for social-science conclusions. There is no evidence to support the assumption that a different historical trajectory would have produced a less efficient corporation.

Although the holding-company form provided the top management of parent companies with authority to intervene in the management of its subsidiary corporations, top management typically delegated authority to subsidiary managers. Few controls existed to hold these middle managers responsible for the success of subsidiary corporations. Cost efficiency in this corporate form at this time in history required *responsible autonomy:* a strategy to win the loyalty of employees by giving them leeway in their work activities and by encouraging them to adapt to changing situations in a manner beneficial to the firm (Friedman 1977).[13] Because they lacked internal monitoring systems, top management in the parent company had little capacity to determine whether responsible autonomy existed, or whether the decision-making process in subsidiaries entailed efficiency considerations that were superior to those in smaller firms where owners managed at the point of production.

CHAPTER 4

Political Capitalism: The Rise and Demise of the Industrial Holding Company

Changes in the institutional arrangements provided the context for capitalist decisions that contributed to the rise and later to the demise of the industrial holding company. The legitimacy of the holding company was affected by economic conditions, the Federalist state structure, regional and federal state business policy, and the political behavior of class segments and subclass segments. In contrast to class segments that are divided economically and politically because of their structural relationship to the capital-accumulation process as a whole (e.g., industrial capital, financial capital) (Poulantzas 1978), *subclass segments* are divided by their structural relationship to capital accumulation within a segment of the economy (i.e., an industry). Although the automobile and steel industries are part of industrial capital, their interests do not always coincide with the class segment that they are part of. It is important to identify capitalist subclass segments. The failure to conceptualize them as a part of the capitalist class and to view them as competing groups ignores the reality that their political and economic bases of power far exceed that of noncapitalists.

The late-nineteenth-century capital structure in the industrial sector had two similarities with the transportation sector: corporations in both economic sectors were capitalized at much higher rates than the business enterprises from which they were formed, and both required capital beyond that generated by profits (Roy 1991). Railroad entrepreneurs used internal capital markets (e.g., selling stocks and bonds) to raise capital because this form of financing reduced dependence on external capital markets. Although selling stock surrendered partial ownership and control, it was preferred to borrowing. Stock sales eliminated interest costs in an industry already financially strained by high construction and operating costs.

Financiers preferred bond financing because it limited risk to investors. However, there were several disadvantages to bond financing for railroad entrepreneurs. It entailed annual interest payments and mortgaged the enterprise's assets. Because private-investment bankers preferred bond financing, railroad entrepreneurs pursuing consolidation strategies had little choice but to comply. As a result, large proportions of railroad enterprises were capitalized by bonds, frequently at high interest rates. These interest costs together with other fixed costs kept operating costs high throughout the nineteenth century. Railroads used more than 20 percent of their gross earnings to pay interest (Livesay 1975). When a railroad could not pay its bonds, investment bankers would frequently issue new bonds to cover the older bonds. By 1890, many railroads were carrying up to three layers of bonds and other forms of debt (Roy 1991), and interest costs consumed almost half of the gross revenues of some railroads (Campbell 1938). These high fixed costs constrained cash flow throughout the industry.

By the mid-1850s, to limit the risk of managing a business with high debt and operating cost, railroad entrepreneurs attempted to establish market control. They argued that prices must be based on actual costs, not established by market forces (Livesay 1975). Price setting, however, placed heavy burdens on businesses dependent on railroads. The constraints imposed on railroad entrepreneurs by private investment bankers contributed to high operating costs that were passed on to these small capitalists. Estimates suggest that, by the early 1890s, one-half of every dollar paid to railroads by farmers and merchants for shipping fees went to private bankers (Roy 1991). As the railroads began to extract more capital from farmers and merchants, these capitalist class segments mobilized politically to protest the price-setting practices of big capital.[1] These small capitalists were joined in some regions by the working class who also recognized the growing power of big business.

By guaranteeing business enterprises rights similar to individuals, regional and federal state business policies and enforcement structures defined the direction of the U.S. political economy in favor of big business. Before the New Jersey Holding Company Act, the law did not allow business enterprises to acquire the stock of others unless it was approved by a special legislative act. The regional state "race to the bottom" initiated by New Jersey's laws of incorporation resulted in extremely lenient statues of incorporation. Between 1888 and 1905 many of the largest industrial corporations were formed.

Although there were widespread political protests opposing industrial consolidation, until 1914 (i.e., Clayton Act), the state's response to corporate consolidation entailed a series of weak and piecemeal policies. The only significant attempt to limit business combinations was the Sherman Antitrust Act of 1890, which declared illegal restraints on interstate commerce and "combinations in the form of trusts or otherwise in restraint of trade." Although it was used to initiate an inquiry into the behavior of a few giant enterprises and to bring a claim against the Standard Oil Trust (Hogan 1971; Chandler 1977), the act did not clearly define restraint of trade. Enforcement was generally ineffective. Most important, despite the fact that the Sherman Antitrust Act was passed two years after the New Jersey Holding Company Act of 1888, it was not clear whether the antitrust legislation prohibited consolidation through the holding-company form. Indeed, consolidation continued to occur at a rapid rate after the state passed the Sherman Antitrust Act.

After the 1893 depression, three events stimulated business combinations. First, during the depression prices declined at a slower rate in industries that consolidated. This created an incentive for consolidation. Second, diversification (i.e., investment in other economic sectors) became less appealing. For example, the capital structure, debt, and high operating cost in the railroad industry increased risk to investors. Third, after the economy emerged from the 1895 depression, the stock market rebounded. Thus, demand for industrial stock increased (Eichner 1969).

Institutionalizing the Holding Company

The first important test of the Sherman Antitrust Act occurred in 1895 when the federal government filed a case against E. C. Knight. The recently organized American Sugar Refining Company either merged with or acquired all of its competitors in the Philadelphia area, including several that resisted takeovers. The Supreme Court ruled that combinations in manufacturing that took the form of a holding company chartered by a regional state were beyond its jurisdiction. This Federalist logic was extended to relations among regional states. The courts also considered corporations chartered in one state to be immune from the laws of other states (Eichner 1969).

By ruling that regional states had authority over consolidation, the courts eliminated uncertainty concerning the legality of consolidation through the holding-company form. When they could confirm intent to establish monopolistic market control, the courts used the Sherman Act to stop mergers (i.e., consolidation of assets). After the *United States v. E. C. Knight* decision, however, corporate attorneys assumed that consolidation through the holding-company form was immune from federal legislation (Thorelli 1955; Eichner 1969). In short, "the New Jersey Holding Company had passed the scrutiny of the law" (Eichner 1969:17). The E. C. Knight decision established the holding company as the preferred corporate form for the next nine years (Eichner 1969; Grandy 1993).

The Supreme Court's ruling in *U.S. v. Addyston Pipe & Steel Co.* (1898) created an additional incentive to transform trusts into holding companies. The decision declared trusts in the form of cartel market-sharing agreements illegal. The decision, written by William Howard Taft, considered all restraint of trade in the form of trusts illegal, even if the restraint was not unreasonable. In short, the court effectively eliminated cartel agreements and left the holding company the primary alternative for consolidation. By the turn of the century, many large business enterprises began to abandon their trust agreements and reorganize as holding companies. To accomplish this, corporations simply shifted their assets from trusts to holding companies and continued to pursue their consolidation strategies. The Sherman Antitrust Act was important not because it slowed corporate consolidation but because it encouraged corporations to organize as holding companies.

Although the holding-company form is important, regional state laws of incorporation are most important for another reason. Prior to regional state laws of incorporation that granted business enterprises status similar to that of individuals, the only rights that they held were those specified by law. After business enterprises were granted status similar to individuals, the only restrictions on their rights were those prohibited by law. The holding company became the preferred corporate form not only because it was legal under regional state law, but because it granted a new status to the business enterprise. This historical transition effectively turned the table on the relationship between the state and the business enterprise. Instead of requesting rights to be placed in their incorporation charters, corporations could engage in behaviors similar to those granted to individuals. These behaviors were legal unless laws were passed to define them as illegal.

Within these institutional arrangements, the state was incapable of controlling consolidation through litigation. The state had neither the resources nor an adequate enforcement structure to investigate and control the behavior of big business. The Antitrust Division of the Department of Justice remained weak through the Taft and Wilson administrations. The inclusion of "reasonable" as a criterion to determine anticompetitive activity allowed state managers a great deal of flexibility when interpreting the Sherman Act. President Taft (1910–1913) moved away from Theodore Roosevelt's focus on using the Sherman Act to differentiate "good" from "bad" trusts toward using it to stop combinations that were established to restrict competition. The Taft administration was also less prone to accept arguments justifying consolidation to realize economies of scale when those combinations also restricted competition. Taft shifted the emphasis from restraint of trade (i.e., "good" versus "bad" trusts) to intent (Eichner 1969). Although Taft's interpretation of the law appears to be a step toward controlling consolidation, proving intent became a major obstacle to antitrust enforcement.

Thus, throughout the early twentieth century, the state was incapable of litigating antitrust violations. Until Franklin Roosevelt's presidency, the total budget of this part of the state structure remained below $1 million.[2] Even high-priority cases required years of investigation and pretrial testimony before the state was prepared to go to trial (Eichner 1969). The Federalist state structure was crucial. Whereas regional states "raced to the bottom" to attract big capital, the state did not have the laws or structures necessary to slow the consolidation of industrial corporations.

The merger rate increased dramatically after the Supreme Court's E. C. Knight (1895) decision. Between 1895 and 1904, 79.1 percent of the total capital consolidation in the U.S. occurred in New Jersey (Nelson 1959). The second highest proportion of consolidations occurred in New York (9.7 percent), Pennsylvania (7.2 percent), and Delaware (3.8 percent). The number of corporations that disappeared due to mergers increased from 26 in 1896 to 69 in 1897 to 303 in 1898 to 1,207 in 1899. For the next three years (1900–1902), the number of mergers averaged 378 per year (Chandler 1977; Nelson 1959). There were 3,653 mergers between 1898 and 1902, twenty-five times the number in the succeeding five years (Nelson 1959; Gordon et al. 1982; McDonough 1994). Most important, more than 50 percent of the consolidations resulted in a market share of over 40 percent for the new corporation. At least one-third resulted in a market share of 70 percent (Lamoreaux 1985). Between 1895 and 1904, 157 holding companies consolidated more than 1,800 firms and controlled more than 40 percent of the capital invested in the entire industrial sector (Hogan 1971; Keller 1990).

Only after the 1904 Supreme Court ruling on the Northern Securities Company did the rate of corporate consolidation slow. Northern Securities Company was formed as a New Jersey holding company to hold stock in the Northern Pacific Railway Company and the Great Northern Railway Company. To the surprise of most corporate attorneys, the Supreme Court ruled against the Northern Securities combination. The Northern Securities case was considered "unreasonable restraint of trade" primarily because of the holding company's pyramided structure. The decision was not based on consolidation per se. Rather, the ruling was based on the form of consolidation. The pyramided holding company provided a financial structure to gain ownership control with considerably less capital than the asset value of the acquired companies. However, since the Northern Securities case involved railroad companies that were considered natural monopolies, it was not clear whether the decision applied to industrial corporations.

The 1911 Supreme Court ruling against the American Tobacco Company clarified state business policy concerning the use of the holding company (Thorelli 1955; Martin 1959; Chandler 1990). Similar to Northern Securities, American Tobacco Company used the pyramided holding company to control several subsidiary corporations and gain market control. The Court held that the pyramided structure of the American Tobacco Company constituted "unreasonable restraint of trade." The American Tobacco and Northern Securities decisions showed that the state was becoming more concerned about the use of the pyramided corporate structure to gain market control than about market control per se. It was the ability of corporations to control markets by controlling the assets of subsidiaries they did not fully own that state managers found problematic.

These decisions must be understood as a response to the uneasy tension between laissez-faire utilitarian ideology, which allowed corporations to pursue their self interests, and the socially constructed reality (i.e., state business policies) that made it possible to consolidate through the holding-company form. This ideology advocated unhampered private competition to create the greatest social and economic good. Regional state business policy, however, gave corporations the legal right to control markets through partial ownership of subsidiary corporations, which increased corporations' anticompetitive practices. That is, regional government business policies contradicted the laissez-faire ideology by making it easier for big capital to gain control over markets. In the absence of these business policies, corporation consolidation and market control could not have occurred at this pace.

Not only did political-legal institutional arrangements result in monopolistic market control that contradicted the laissez-faire principle of unhampered competition, they also provided advantages to the most powerful members of society. State intervention in the economy did not equitably advance individual interests and, therefore, the public good. In fact, it provided opportunities for big capital and limited the capacity of entrepreneurs (e.g., small businesses, farmers) to compete (Wiebe 1967). Together with the Populist Movement, these contradictions compelled state managers to reconsider the relationship between private interest and the public good. The discrepancy between ideology and reality informed the debate, challenging the legitimacy of the holding company.

Continued opposition to consolidation from political actors both inside (e.g., elected state managers) and outside the state (e.g., farmers, small businesses) generated a response that slowed the rate of consolidation. It is important, however, to place the state's response in historical context. By 1904, giant corporations already controlled a large percentage of their respective markets. The courts applied the "rule of reason" when making restraint-of-trade decisions; in general, corporate behavior that restrained trade was acceptable. Only when corporations stepped over an ambiguously defined line based on "reason" were the restraint-of-trade laws enforced.

In the end, the Sherman Antitrust Act had little effect on consolidation. The Sherman Act was designed to limit consolidation through trusts. By the time the Sherman Act was passed, however, capitalists already viewed the weak ties of the trust as inadequate for long-term organization. The new business policy that gave individuals' rights to corporations through the holding company (e.g., stock ownership) created a mechanism to establish monopolies through partial ownership.

It was the Clayton Act that limited the holding-company form of organization. The Clayton Act is important because it shifted the focus toward how corporate consolidation was financed.

Challenges to the Holding Company and Corporate Consolidation

The Clayton Act

The ineffectiveness of state business policy generated additional political opposition to industrial consolidation, and Congress began to discuss proposals to strengthen the Sherman Antitrust Act (Grandy 1993). The view that the holding company was the source of the problem redefined the parameters of this debate from concerns over "restraint of trade" to limiting the use of the holding company. The change was important because it emphasized the difference between consolidation by acquisition of stock versus assets. The way in which this concern was resolved had long-term consequences.

By the time the Clayton Act was passed, several state managers had accepted consolidation but proposed changes in its form to curtail the misuse of power. For example, in 1907, Herbert Knox Smith, the U.S. commissioner of corporations stated: "It is not the existence of industrial power, but rather the misuse, that is the real problem." (Reports of the Department of Commerce and Labor, Washington D.C., 1907:33, in Martin 1959:21). Similarly, Oscar S. Straus, U.S. secretary of commerce and labor stated:

> It is becoming more and more obvious that the work of the Government in regulating corporations should not be directed at the mere existence of combination itself, as such, but should deal rather with the way in which the combination powers are used, so as to prevent as far as possible the misuse of these industrial forces. (Reports of the Department of Commerce and Labor, Washington D.C., 1908:33, in Martin 1959:21).

The focus on the holding company intensified during the 1912 presidential campaign. The Democratic Party platform directly criticized the holding company as a form of consolidation. It proposed to limit the rights granted by regional state laws of incorporation including constraints on the way in which corporations engaged in "interstate trade, including, among others, the prevention of holding companies, of interlocking directorates, of stock watering, [and] discrimination in prices" (Martin 1959:28). In that same year, elected state managers began to introduce legislation to curtail uses of the holding company. Senator Robert W. La Follette introduced a bill to add several sections to the Sherman Act restricting a corporation from doing business under any name but its own. Any other name might conceal its identity or misrepresent its ownership.

By 1913, officials in President Wilson's new administration articulated the relationship between consolidation and the holding company more directly. U.S. Secretary of Commerce William C. Redfield stated that corporations should "not hold stock in the competing companies, and that neither a person nor a corporation shall at the same time own a controlling interest in two or more competing corporations" (Reports of the Department of Commerce and Labor, Washington, D.C., 1913:71, in Martin 1959:21). Legislation introduced to limit consolidation focused directly on the holding company as the source of unfair business practices. Senator John Sharp Williams introduced a bill prohibiting a corporation from owning stock in other corporations or having its stock owned by another corporation. Senator Albert B. Cummins proposed legislation restricting interstate stock ownership. None of these bills limited consolidation by merging assets (Martin 1959). Rather, they attempted to limit corporations from controlling other corporations through partial stock ownership.

Like the regional state laws of incorporation in the late 1800s, big business was directly involved in defining federal laws regulating their own behavior. Capitalists succeeded at blurring the distinction between their private interest and the general interest of the public (Veblen 1923). In fact, state managers invited proposals from those capitalists whose behavior they were attempting to control. The Senate Committee on Interstate Commerce requested that Judge Elbert H. Gary, president of the United States Steel Corporation, submit a draft of a bill designed to control corporate consolidation. Predictably, in defense of the holding-company form, Judge Gary's proposal maintained that the federal government should determine whether consolidation "unreasonably" restrained trade and injured the public (Hearings on the Control of Corporations, Persons, and Firms Engaged in Interstate Commerce, U.S. 62d Congress, 2d session, 1912:2407–2412, in Martin 1959:25). Political momentum, however, had begun to shift against big capital's use of the pyramided holding company. The U.S. secretary of commerce issued a report arguing that corporations should be required to submit the names of other corporations in which they held stock and President Wilson argued that the federal government should prohibit the use of holding companies (Martin 1959).

The Clayton Act was proposed to limit antitrust behaviors of big business. It contained four main sections designed to make illegal under certain conditions: (1) price discrimination (2) exclusive dealing and tying contracts (3) holding companies, and (4) interlocking directorates. A crucial component of the Clayton Act, Section 7 focused on the use of the holding company. Throughout the legislative process, lawmakers referred to Section 7 as the holding-company section (Martin 1959). However, capitalists' lobby efforts succeeded at limiting the extent to which Section 7 restricted holding companies from purchasing stock of other companies. It did not prohibit all holding companies or make all corporate-stock acquisition illegal. Section 7 restricted these corporate behaviors only when they substantially lessened competition (Martin 1959). To ensure that the bill was not too restrictive, the term "holding company" was deleted from the final version of the bill. A main provision of the bill was worded as follows:

> No corporation engaged in commerce shall acquire, directly or indirectly, the whole
> or any part of the stock or other share capital of another corporation engaged also in
> commerce, where the effect of such acquisition may be to substantially lessen com-
> petition between the corporation whose stock is so acquired and the corporation
> making the acquisition, or to restrain such commerce in any section or community,
> or to tend to create a monopoly in any line of commerce. (Section 7 of The Clayton
> Act, Act of October 14, 1914, 38 Stat. 730; also see Bonbright and Means 1932)

In the end, Section 7 of the Clayton Act placed few restrictions on the use of the holding company for corporate consolidation. It did not prevent corporations from forming subsidiary corporations and establishing ownership control over them when it did not "substantially lessen competition" (Section 7 of The Clayton Act, Act of October 14, 1914, 38 Stat. 730). Section 7 of the Clayton Act only prohibited the acquisition of the stock of a competing firm if the effect of the acquisition unreasonably constrained trade. It allowed the purchase of the physical assets of another corporation with the approval of the Federal Trade Commission (FTC) (Bonbright and Means 1932; Kudla and McInish 1984; Martin 1959). In the end, Congress failed to prohibit consolidation of the assets (versus ownership control through stocks) of two or more companies into a single corporation (Bonbright and Means 1932; Neale and Goyder 1980; Martin 1959). Moreover, Section 7 did not apply to individuals (versus corporations) purchasing stock solely for investment or using their voting rights to lessen competition.

While the logic of disallowing one form of consolidation and allowing another was challenged by some state managers, they had little effect on the bill. Most important, no attempt was made in the legislative process to define "substantially lessen competition" (Martin 1959), leaving restraint of trade open to interpretation.

Despite its weaknesses, Section 7 of the Clayton Act eliminated two key advantages of the holding company: (1) the ability to secretly gain control of another corporation, and (2) the ability to acquire and control another corporation by purchasing a majority of its stock. The most serious flaw in the Clayton Act was articulated by Victor Murdock, the leader of the Progressive Party:

> The Clayton bill . . . attacks the form of monopoly, not its substance, in its attempt to
> eliminate "holding companies." When in time the courts reach with banning decrees
> this provision the offenders will change the form of the monopoly and escape with the
> substance of monopoly as before. (*Congressional Record*, in Martin 1959:51, 205).

Despite its weaknesses, Section 7 of the Clayton Act closed the stock loophole for consolidating different business enterprises if the consolidation could be shown to restrain trade. However, restraint of trade was never specified. Thus, the definition of restraint of trade became politicized and its interpretation was effected by historically specific conditions.

Enforcement of Section 7 of the Clayton Act

The case that established how the courts would interpret Section 7 of the Clayton Act did not occur until 1921 when Aluminum Company of America (ALCOA) attempted to gain control over Aluminum Rolling Mill Company in a stock acquisition. Cleveland Metal Products Company created a subsidiary corporation and sold 73 percent of the mill's stock. Most of the stock was purchased by ALCOA. The FTC investigation revealed that Cleveland Metal Products Company was a competitor of ALCOA's, and that the Aluminum Rolling Mill Company was created to gain control of the market. The FTC ordered ALCOA to sell the stock to businesses unconnected with ALCOA or its subsidiaries. Although ALCOA appealed, the United States Circuit Court of Appeals upheld the FTC's decision (1922).[3]

The case was complicated when Aluminum Rolling Mill Company became insolvent and ALCOA attempted to purchase its assets. The FTC petitioned the circuit court to block ALCOA. Despite FTC objections, the court allowed the acquisition. The court's decision was based on the form of consolidation. Although the court did not allow intercorporate stock ownership between the two firms, it did allow intercorporate asset acquisition. The court's ruling clarified Section 7 of the Clayton Act and closed the stock loophole as a means of consolidation. However, it left the asset loophole open. The degree to which consolidation lessened competition became secondary to the form of consolidation, whether it occurred through asset or stock acquisition. The former required complete ownership of the acquired corporation. The later permitted ownership control through partial stock ownership. Important to this decision was the contradiction between laissez-faire ideology and regional state business policy that made it possible to control other corporations with partial stock ownership. The small business coalition was successful because they pointed out that these institutional arrangements provided advantages to big business who had access to capital markets and could use this capital to takeover small business and gain control over markets.

The FTC, however, recognized the importance of the asset loophole. In 1921, the FTC petitioned Congress to include asset acquisition in Section 7 of the Clayton Act. The FTC, joined by other state agencies and commissions, continued to press Congress to strengthen the Clayton Act (U.S. Federal Trade Commission. Annual Report, 1921, in Martin 1959). However, these appointed state managers failed to persuade elected state managers to close the asset loophole.

The Arrow-Hart and Hegeman Case finally resolved the federal government's position on the form versus the effect on competition of consolidation. In October 1927, the Arrow-Hart and Hegeman Company, Inc. organized as a holding company for the purpose of acquiring all the voting stock of the Arrow Electric Company and the Hart and Hegeman Manufacturing Company. The FTC filed suit against the new holding company. The regulator argued that this acquisition would eliminate competition between the two operating companies and violate Section 7 of the Clayton Act. Before the FTC had time to take action, however, Arrow-Hart and Hegeman Company created two new holding companies, distributed the stock of the two operating companies between the new holding companies and dissolved the original holding company. In December 1928, the two operating companies and the two holding companies merged under the laws of incorporation of Connecticut. These maneuvers changed the form of consolidation from acquiring stock to merging assets into a single parent company.

Based on its new legal status, the company petitioned the Second Circuit Court of Appeals. However, the court affirmed the FTC's order to disinvest. The company appealed this decision to the Supreme Court. Although the initial FTC complaint was issued prior to the incorporation of assets into the parent company, five of the nine members of the Supreme Court voted to block the FTC from ordering the parent company to disinvest. The 1934 Supreme Court ruling stated that the FTC did not have the power under the Clayton Act to order the divestment of physical property (i.e., assets). In short, the parent holding company avoided disinvestment of its acquisitions by transforming the form of control from stock ownership to asset ownership.

The courts specified policy in more detail during the following ten years. Under certain conditions the courts gave the FTC authority to stop acquisitions that reduced competition and did not involve the transfer of stock (Martin 1959). Under most conditions, however, the asset loophole allowed corporations to acquire corporations. To summarize, there were two phases of the Supreme Court's rulings on Section 7 of the Clayton Act. The first phase (1914–1927) addressed the issue of reducing competition in regional markets. Even when market dominance existed and the FTC obtained proof of restraint of trade, however, the Court appeared to interpret "substantial lessening of competition" solely within the legal definition of *monopoly*: a single firm selling a particular product line. If corporations did not sell almost identical products in the same regional market, their cases were dismissed. The Court ruled that preexisting substantial competition was lacking.

The Court based decisions in the second phase (1927–1934) on competitiveness in national markets. The Arrow-Hart and Hegeman and the Monsanto Chemical Company and Atlantic Chemical Company cases set the precedent during the second phase of Section 7 enforcement. The Supreme Court's 1934 decision on the Monsanto-Atlantic case was a crucial event because it placed the burden of proof on the FTC, which further curtailed its authority and capacity to block consolidation. The Court required the FTC to provide evidence that the acquiring and acquired companies had been selling, rather than could sell, the same product(s) in the same market(s). Although the FTC demonstrated that competition existed between Monsanto Chemical Company and the Atlantic Chemical Company, the

Court concluded that "acquisition will not tend toward monopoly, because . . . there are a large number of concerns in the United States engaged in the manufacture and sale of heavy chemicals" (Federal Trade Commission, in Martin 1959:170, 195). By defining restraint of trade in national markets in this way, the state's business policy allowed further consolidation. Only after consolidation occurred could the FTC take action. With its small budget and staff, this dimension of the state structure did not have the capacity to contain corporate consolidation.[4]

In the end, the primary effect of Section 7 of the Clayton Act was to slow the rate of consolidation. By limiting consolidation through stock acquisition (i.e., using the holding company), Section 7 made consolidation more expensive (Bonbright and Means 1932). To gain control over another firm, the parent corporation had to purchase all of the firm's assets, not just a controlling share of its stocks. By focusing on the form through which consolidation could occur, the state did little to prohibit consolidations that involved purchasing the assets of another company (Mueller 1970). The importance of Section 7 of the Clayton Act exists in the restrictions it placed on the use of the holding company as a means of consolidation. It prohibited corporations from controlling other corporations through partial stock ownership. Whereas the 1921 ALCOA case was important because the FTC filed complaints against corporations using the stock loophole to consolidate, the 1934 Arrow-Hart and Hegeman case ended speculation on how the courts would interpret Section 7 of the Clayton Act. Thus Section 7 made consolidation more expensive. Now, the parent company had to acquire 100 percent of another corporation (i.e., asset acquisition), which typically entailed debt financing and more dependence on external capital markets. These policies set up important, but not sufficient, conditions to deinstitutionalize the holding-company form.

Conflict within the Capitalist Class: Protectionism and Price-Setting

Monopolistic practices in tariff-protected industries generated an additional source of opposition to the holding company. Resolution of the subsequent conflicts entailed mediating class and class segment conflicts with the state's agendas.

By the turn of the century, state managers and capitalists began to argue that free trade with low-wage European countries would undermine domestic economic stability and national security. Members of the Republican Party (e.g., William McKinley) argued that free trade polices were incompatible with high wages and living standards (Eckes 1995). By the 1890s, Congressman William Kelly of Philadelphia maintained that free trade would weaken the steel industry, make the United States dependent on foreign steel, and reduce the nation's defense capabilities. Other state managers, typically members of the Democratic Party, opposed these arguments. They held that tariffs reduced domestic competition and encouraged the creation of monopolies that benefited big business and undermined consumers' buying power.

In the decade following the 1893 depression, the debate over tariffs and free trade changed several times, typically relative to the strength and stability of the economy and the export-import ratio.[5] Small businesses, consumers, and some state managers opposed big businesses' agendas to set up protectionism and market monopoly. During his presidential campaign, Woodrow Wilson argued that tariffs create a system of special privilege and monopolistic advantage, and are "at the heart of every other economic question" (in Eckes 1995:48).

This conflict was mediated by the state. As early as 1898, through a trade association (i.e., Structural Steel Association), the steel industry established a pricing system. The most elaborate and extensive pricing systems in the steel industry emerged during the trade association's meetings at the Gary dinners in Gary, Indiana and the Waldorf Astoria in New York. These price-setting behaviors were formalized in 1907 when a trade association committee was established by corporate leaders for the sole purpose of establishing steel prices. Capitalist subclass segments that consumed steel began to challenge monopolistic practices that restricted profit making in their economic sectors and, in 1911, the House of Representatives appointed a committee to investigate the conduct of Judge Gary and the United States Steel Corporation (USS). After this congressional investigation, the Department of Justice charged USS with violation of the Sherman Antitrust Act and took legal action to dissolve the corporation for attempting to establish a monopoly in the steel industry. Legal maneuvers and state managers' concern that such action would disrupt the steel supply necessary for the state's warmaking agenda during World War I, however, allowed USS to delay this litigation until 1920 when the courts ruled against the Department of Justice.

The Federal Trade Commission (FTC) developed a separate case against U.S. Steel for price-setting practices by the industry's trade association, Pittsburgh Plus. These practices originated in the Pittsburgh area and later extended to other parts of the United States (Hogan 1971). In 1919, the Western Association of Rolled Steel (WARS), a trade associate of steel consumers, filed a complaint with FTC against USS. Although the FTC denied its first complaint, WARS succeeded in filing a grievance for price setting against U.S. Steel and eleven of its subsidiaries. The FTC charged USS with exercising "general control, supervision, direction and guidance over the policies of and business conducted by its said respondent subsidiaries" (in Hogan 1971:1103–1104). USS's top management claimed that its only relationship to its subsidiaries was as a stockholder and that it did not exercise managerial control over these business enterprises. In July 1924, after three years of investigation, hearings, and testimony, the FTC issued a cease and desist order. In 1925, the FTC ordered USS to end the Pittsburgh price-setting system (Hogan 1971).

In summary, conflict between capitalist subclass segments (i.e., steel producers, steel consumers) emerged within the state. State managers mediated this conflict by prohibiting parent holding companies from setting prices through their subsidiaries. The new business policy placed additional limits on the use of the holding-company form by challenging its viability as a mechanism to exercise market control. Although there was nothing to stop capitalists from setting prices for products produced within a single corporation, to do this required corporations to restructure so that the assets of the corporate entities were 100 percent owned by the parent company.

Price setting and other oligopolistic practices made some state managers and members of the public increasingly critical of the growing holding-company form. By 1928, most of the largest industrial corporations were holding companies. Among the 573 corporations listing their securities on the New York Stock Exchange, 556 were holding companies. Of these corporations, 395 were holding company-operating company hybrids, 92 were pure holding companies, and 69 of the pure holding companies were industrial corporations (Berle and Means 1991). Of the 92 pure holding companies, only 15 existed in 1910, and 23 and 54 were added respectively between 1913 and 1920, and 1921 and 1928 (Berle and Means 1991).

Corporate restructuring as holding companies, however, came to an end in the 1930s as the public became more aware of the practices of big business. Federalism and laissez-faire ideology had produced regional and federal state business policies that placed few constraints on big capital. Big business, however, failed to uphold its part of the social contract and the working and middle classes began to challenge its legitimacy when the Great Depression resulted in massive unemployment. As bankruptcies in overcapitalized firms became widespread, additional political opposition to the holding company emerged. Section 7 of the Clayton Act had placed limits on using the holding company to pursue consolidation strategies. The 1924 FTC ruling had prohibited the use of subsidiaries to set prices. Next, the New Deal revised state business policy to further deinstitutionalize the holding company. In contrast to previous regulations that focused on the holding company as a vehicle for consolidation and price setting, New Deal policies affected all corporations organized as holding companies.

As the domestic and global economies moved into depression, rather than adjust state business policy to these new conditions, the federal government continued to support foreign trade policies that protected big business. The state extended its previous protectionism policy by passing the Republican Party-backed Hawley-Smoot Tariff Act (1930). This bill was important not because it changed tariffs, but because it retained existing tariffs as commodity prices dropped. The import duty remained constant although the price of the item declined. Maintaining high tariffs while prices declined raised the average import duty to 59 percent by 1932. A twenty-cent tariff on a one dollar commodity equals 20 percent of its price. A twenty-cent tariff on the same commodity when its price drops to fifty cents is a 40 percent tariff. In 1932, as a response to United States protectionism, many countries refused to buy U.S. goods. Such retaliation slowed world trade and spread the depression throughout global markets (Eckes 1995). To mediate the conflict with its trading partners, the federal government passed the Trade Agreement Act of 1934 that established the "most favored nation" status. This act required participating countries to give all "most favored nation" trading partners trade concessions. The public debate over tariffs was important because it brought additional attention to big business, which became increasingly associated with the holding company.

The New Deal and Deinstitutionalization of the Holding Company

Throughout the early twentieth century the banking system and money reserves continued to grow. Cooperation among the Federal Reserve System and banks in Britain, France, Germany, and the United States appeared to assure domestic and economic stability (Friedman 1963). However, the economic contraction in 1929 and the failure of several large banks in 1930 drained much of the money reserves from the banking system. Between 1929 and 1933 bank failures ranged from 1,350 to 4,000 per year (Greider 1989). By 1933, a series of bank runs reduced money reserves in the United States by one-third and produced bankruptcy or merger in one-third of its banks (Friedman 1963).

Although several factors contributed to the Great Depression, the crash of 1929 exposed the weaknesses in the holding company's financial structure. John Kenneth Galbraith defined the problem as *reverse leverage* where corporations used stock dividends to pay the interest on bonds of the upstream holding companies. As long as the demand for goods and services ensured high-capability utilization rates within the subsidiaries, the subsidiaries realized profits and could pay stock dividends to the parent companies. However, the 1920s economic downturn lowered capability utilization rates and profits, which created a liquidity problem and reduced subsidiaries' capacity to pay dividends. With the interruption of dividend payments from their subsidiaries, the parent holding companies defaulted on bonds, producing bankruptcy. Corporate bankruptcy drained the money reserves in banks and bank affiliates that held bankrupt corporations' securities.

Several years passed before the federal government realigned the institutional arrangements governing the holding company's financial structure. After failed attempts to end the depression, President Herbert Hoover felt that a small but powerful group of bankers on Wall Street were part of the problem. Hoover believed that these investors were undermining his efforts by artificially depressing stock prices. Hoover and other state managers also objected to other investment bankers' practices (e.g., selling short) (Carosso 1970).[6] The president threatened a congressional investigation if they did not stop. The investment community did not respond to Hoover and in 1931 the president initiated an investigation. In 1932, a congressional subcommittee appointed Ferdinand Pecora to examine the practices of investment banking. Pecora's first investigation examined the practices of the failed complex holding company created by Samuel Insull who created a holding-company pyramid that allowed him to control up to two thousand dollars of assets in a subsidiary by investing a dollar in the parent holding company, Corporate Securities Company of Chicago (Cochran 1957). Many investors lost large amounts of capital from their investments in this holding company.

Pecora discovered several unethical practices of investment bankers including floating new issues of corporate stocks and bonds that were of questionable value, and financing them from deposit customers and trust accounts (Greider 1989). Also, as did the Pujo Committee twenty years earlier, Pecora challenged the practice of investment bankers holding positions on the board of directors of corporations whose securities they sold (Carosso 1970).[7] These institutional arrangements allowed investment bankers to promote stock sales in corporations where they held substantial financial interests without informing potential buyers of their financial interests.

Pecora's investigation of National City Co., the security affiliate of the National City Bank of New York, revealed that investors in extremely high-risk securities were given little or no information on the risk of their investment. National City Bank (later renamed Citicorp) also shifted approximately $25 million in bad loans to its affiliate banks at the expense of the affiliate's stockholders who had no knowledge of the transaction. Other practices of the executives of National City Bank included voting themselves large salaries and substantial bonuses and avoiding taxes by transferring securities to their relatives.

Some of the most disturbing practices that were uncovered, however, occurred in the large private investment bank of J. P. Morgan Company (Carosso 1970). In addition to promoting the speculation on new corporate-stock issues, J. P. Morgan Company developed a preferred list. List members were allowed to purchase riskier common stock at the same lower prices as J. P. Morgan Company. Moreover, although most stockholders had little or no information on the risk of their investment, list members were provided risk information on stock. This list included the names of numerous politicians (Carosso 1970). These discoveries fueled the public's suspicions of investment bankers and contributed to a political and ideological climate for bank reform.

The subsequent Banking Act of 1933 (i.e., sections of which are known as the Glass-Steagall Act), the Securities and Exchange Act of 1934, and the Banking Act of 1935 weakened finance capital by severing some of the links between commercial banking and private investment banking (Carosso 1970; Burk 1988). Although these laws placed controls on the flow of capital into corporate securities through private investment bankers, the Glass-Steagall Act had the most profound effect on the holding-company form. It reduced the available capital for investment in manufacturing by placing tighter restrictions on commercial banks.

The National Bank Act was passed by Congress during the Civil War to separate national banks from stock ownership companies. Banks, however, circumvented the National Bank Act by dealing in corporate securities indirectly through affiliates. By 1930, near one-half of all new corporate securities were issued by bank affiliates (Roe 1994:95). Concerned that the collapse in the value of stock held by bank affiliates caused bank failures, Congress passed the Glass-Steagall Act, prohibiting banks from underwriting corporate securities through their affiliates.

In addition to limiting the risk to personal savings, the Glass-Steagall Act restricted commercial banks from lending more than 10 percent of its capital to corporations, subsidiaries, or affiliates. Because investment bankers were dependent on deposits in commercial banks to underwrite stock issues, the Glass-Steagall Act limited their access to this source of capital. Thus, after 1933, private investment bankers had limited capacity to issue industrial stock and underwrite corporate consolidation (Seligman 1982; De Long 1991; Wolfson 1994). Moreover, the Securities and Exchange Act of 1934 required that corporations disclose financial information. It prohibited and regulated various practices (e.g., selling short) and required companies to report on earnings and operations (e.g., annual reports) (Carosso 1970). Whereas the disclosures required by the Securities and Exchange Act of 1934 made potential investors more informed about the risk of investment, the Glass-Steagall Act curtailed the flow of capital from commercial banks to investment bankers. The state also allocated to the Securities and Exchange Commission (SEC) the authority to supervise stock exchanges.

These state business policies further deinstitutionalized the holding-company form. New institutional arrangements reduced the capital available to issue stock in holding companies and subsidiary corporations. Estimates show that in 1929 the security affiliates of National City Bank and Chase Bank had a capital surplus of $221 million. In contrast, the capital available to the eight largest private investment banks between 1934 and 1939 was less than $75 million (Carosso 1970). As a result, security issues dramatically declined in the 1930s (table 4.1).

Also, New Deal corporate tax policies created financial disincentives to use the holding-company form. With the support of President Franklin D. Roosevelt, in 1932, Budget Director Lewis Douglas proposed taxing corporate dividends (Leff 1984). After much debate, the Senate Finance Committee passed a 5 percent tax on dividends paid to individuals, and taxed capital stock and excess profits. This provision of the NIRA (National Industrial Recovery Act) taxed income that individuals received from stock ownership (Leff 1984). However, it did not tax income that parent holding companies received as dividends from subsidiary corporations. Also, wealthy individuals avoided the individual dividend tax by using a tax loophole that allowed them to incorporate themselves as holding companies.

Additional business-policy changes that deinstitutionalized the holding company were the 1934 and 1935 revenue bills. During the policy debates, President Roosevelt outlined a tax policy for economic recovery that contained provisions

TABLE 4.1 Corporate Security Issues, 1929–1939 (In millions of dollars)

Year	Preferred	Common	Total
1929	1,695	5,062	6,757
1930	421	1,105	1,526
1931	148	195	343
1932	10	13	23
1933	15	137	152
1934	3	31	34
1935	86	22	108
1936	271	272	543
1937	406	285	691
1938	86	25	111
1939	98	87	185

Source: U.S. Bureau of Census, 1972.

to tax the rich. Roosevelt and his new secretary of the treasury, Henry Morgenthau Jr., were joined by the Progressive Party in an attempt to change corporate taxes. The group tried to eliminate provisions governing corporate reorganization that allowed tax-free intercorporate dividends.[8] These state managers also attempted to stop the practice of allowing corporations organized as holding companies to pool their revenues to offset taxable profits in one subsidiary with losses in another. Despite capitalist efforts to retain this practice, the 1934 Revenue Act prohibited pooling of revenues to avoid taxes. Senate Finance Committee Chairman Harrison also successfully argued to keep the capital-stock/excess-profits tax (Leff 1984). The oil industry lobbied particularly aggressively and convinced state managers to retain the deduction for subsidies for discovery and depletion costs. Although Senate Progressives lost several battles to increase taxes on corporations and wealthy individuals, they were able to add amendments to the final 1934 revenue bill. These additions made it possible to more closely monitor corporations' tax payments by abolishing consolidated tax returns and examining corporate salary payments (Leff 1984). When the bill shifted to the House, big business pursued an aggressive lobby effort to eliminate the tax on dividends, the temporary capital-stock/excess-profits tax, and the restrictions on depreciation allowances. The political efforts of big business were successful. Although the 1934 Revenue Act changed corporate tax laws, it contained several tax loopholes and generated little revenue.

In 1935, President Roosevelt again attempted to plug tax loopholes for the wealthy. He proposed an individual inheritance, gift, and income tax, a corporate income tax, and an intercorporate dividend tax (Leff 1984). Roosevelt viewed the intercorporate dividend tax as a fight against monopolies, big corporations, big incomes, and big fortunes (*Addresses of FDR*, in Leff 1984). Corporations in the chemical industry (e.g., DuPont, Union Carbide, Allied Chemical & Dye, Monsanto, Dow, American Cyanamid) lobbied heavily against the dividend tax. Many of these taxes were excluded from the final version of the 1935 Revenue Act. However, the bill contained two important provisions. First, it closed the loophole in the 1934 Tax Act that allowed individuals to incorporate as corporations to avoid the tax on dividends. Second, it contained an intercorporate dividend tax (Leff 1984; Gordon 1994). Although the tax was scaled down from Roosevelt's proposal to a maximum of 1.5 percent, it did tax the transfer of capital via dividend payments from subsidiary corporations to their parent holding companies. This intercorporate dividend tax increased the cost of operating businesses within the holding-company form by taxing transfers of capital between holding companies and their subsidiaries. This state business policy was important because it eliminated a crucial benefit of holding-company form: tax-free capital transfers across corporate entities.

Taken together, the court's interpretations of Section 7 of the Clayton Act, the FTC ruling against using subsidiaries to fix prices, and the New Deal policies eliminating tax-free capital transfers among holding companies and their subsidiaries, deinstitutionalized the holding company. Almost immediately after the passages of the New Deal policies, the number of newly created subsidiaries began to decline. To avoid the intercorporate dividend tax, parent companies that were organized as holding companies began to transform their subsidiaries to divisions, which consolidated their operations into single corporations. Capital transfers within a single corporation were not taxable.

The analysis here suggests that the holding company emerged because it was a legal means to pursue industrial consolidation strategies. Through the holding-company form, parent companies obtained market control and the capacity to set prices by controlling a large proportion of the production capabilities in an industry. Big business began changing to a divisional form after state business policy (1) limited the use of the holding company for industrial consolidation and price setting (2) limited the use of consolidated tax statements that covered up the practice of using losses in one subsidiary corporation to offset taxable gains in another, and (3) taxed capital transfers from subsidiaries to parent companies.

This historical sequence shows that the holding company decline was not caused by its functional inefficiency: inability to coordinate day-to-day operating activities (Chandler 1962; Williamson 1985). Instead, the holding company was deinstitutionalized over two decades of political struggle beginning with Section 7 of the Clayton Act and concluding with the New Deal.

Institutional Arrangements and Change to the Multidivisional Form

Capital Dependence and State Business Policy during World War II

Although the flow of capital from the banking industry slowed, industrial capital found a new source. A significant proportion of the expansion within the emerging divisional form was financed by the state. As World War II intensified and the demand for military-industrial products from Europe escalated, the federal government became more dependent on industry to achieve its goals and agendas. To meet the state's political-military obligations to the Allies, President Roosevelt appealed to the private sector to redirect production toward the war economy and expand production capability. Many industrial capitalists, however, refused to cooperate. Industrial capitalists maintained that low profit during the depressed 1930s, and wartime price controls, left the industry without sufficient capital to finance the construction of additional capability. Representatives from the steel industry argued that wartime expansion would undermine long-term profits by leading to higher fixed costs and production capacity in product-lines that were not compatible with peacetime demand (Tower 1941; Broude 1963). As the war progressed, the steel industry admitted its forecasts underestimated demand. Dependent on external capital and reluctant to borrow it, this subclass segment refused to expand until the federal government accelerated tax amortization rates to allow corporations to deduct their investments at a faster rate (Broude 1963).

In response, the government passed the Revenue Act of 1940 that allowed industry to depreciate 100 percent of its investments in new facilities over a five-year period. Normally, corporations depreciate their capital investments over twenty years. After this business policy was passed, profits in the steel industry, for example, soared from $147.5 million in 1939 to $281.2 million in 1940. These rates compared "favorably with earnings in the boom year, 1929" (*Iron Age* 1941; American Iron and Steel Institute 1943). Moreover, these returns were sustained, averaging $275.2 million between 1940 and 1942. Despite the massive increase in liquidity (e.g., cash), the steel industry still refused to invest at the level the state considered adequate to ensure a strong national defense and to meet its political-military obligations to the Allies. In 1943, the War Production Board became directly involved in industrial production to ensure its national defense agenda. This business policy entailed a massive underwriting of the construction and operation of steel-making facilities. The state used tax dollars to construct twenty-nine open hearth furnaces and seventeen electric furnaces and engaged in twenty joint ventures with private corporations (Hogan 1971; Tiffany 1988). In short, to meet its national defense agenda, the state created a publicly owned steel industry because this subclass segment refused to expand. The total cost of the expansion, almost

$2.7 billion, was divided between the steel corporations and the government. When the war concluded, the War Assets Administration sold these properties to private enterprise at prices considerably below construction costs.

Industrial capitalists benefited substantially from this state business policy. Between 1940 and 1944, more than $25 billion was invested in new plants and equipment and the federal government contributed over two-thirds of the capital. Corporate profits increased from 6.3 percent in 1939 to 10.3 percent in 1944. Most important, industrial corporations were able to expand their capability while retaining a large proportion of their profits, dramatically strengthening their financial position. All investments in enemy territory were written off or paid by the federal government, and all investment in war production was either financed by the federal government or charged as an operating cost under the five-year amortization provision (War Production Board 1945). Corporations' investment in non-war plants and equipment was lower than depreciation charges. As a result, industrial corporations' working capital doubled and their net worth increased by approximately one-third during World War II. The Industrial sector's long-term financial position was further strengthened by approximately $25 billion in unused tax credits (War Production Board 1945).

These state business policies had an important effect on institutionalization of the multidivisional form. In contrast to the turn-of-the-century expansion when most industrial capitalists were dependent on external capital markets, much of the post-1930 expansion was financed by the state or internally generated capital. Their strong liquidity position in the 1940s allowed industrial corporations to obtain complete ownership of their corporate entities, which reduced their need to organize as holding companies. Also, complete ownership of their operating entities and organizing them as divisions reduced parent-company problems of controlling their corporate entities. Subsidiary top managers, frequently the former owners who retained partial ownership, often attempted to manage autonomously from the parent company, which produced power struggles within the corporation.

The Celler-Kefauver Amendment

By the 1950s, the political, financial and ideological bases of the holding-company form were delegitimized. However, some big businesses continued to use the holding company to consolidate market power. In response, in 1950, Congress passed the Celler-Kefauver Amendment. This legislation was important because it reversed the previous policy initiative, which obligated the FTC to establish intent. Under the Celler-Kefauver Amendment if mergers resulted in firms' having a large share of the market, the courts could block or dissolve the merger even if no restraint of trade could be demonstrated. The Celler-Kefauver Act was important because it acknowledged the shortcomings of business policy designed to reverse consolidation after it occurred. In this respect it was a proactive policy to stop mergers before monopoly was established (Mueller 1970). It changed the focus of state business policy from the means to consolidate (i.e., via stock ownership) to the effects of corporate consolidation on market control.

As with previous legal cases, enforcement was not simply a matter of law but of interpretation of the law. Interpretations were affected by corporate profits and economic conditions. For example, by 1950, competition in the flour-milling industry intensified and profits declined. In 1951, Pillsbury acquired the assets of Ballard and Ballard Company (1951) and the Drug's Baking Mix division (1952) of American Home Foods Corporation. In June 1952, the FTC issued a complaint charging Pillsbury Mills, Inc. with violating Section 7 of the Clayton Act. The FTC alleged that these acquisitions constituted excessive concentration of ownership and market control. The initial investigation showed that, prior to the acquisition, all three firms were engaged in the sale of the same or similar products. Seven companies had made 70 percent of the prepared flour-base mixes (Martin 1959; Sobel 1984). Despite the implications for market control, the FTC allowed these mergers. The FTC justified its decision by stating:

> [C]ompetition is a constantly changing phenomenon. It has never been sharply defined. Injury to competition, as distinguished from injury to the competitor, is seldom capable of proof by direct testimony and may therefore be inferred from all the surrounding circumstances. . . . [C]ompetition between the big companies continues to protect the consumer interests. (Federal Trade Commission 1953, in Martin 1959:290)

Although it is unclear how these state managers were defining consumer interests, it is evident that a concern for corporate profits affected the FTC's (1953) interpretation of the Celler-Kefauver Amendment. This FTC decision shifted the criterion for allowing mergers away from market control to profit levels. It allowed the merger in a highly concentrated industry because profits were low. This decision produced a significantly weaker business policy than the amendment's framers intended. The problem with using historically specific conditions to establish general business policy is that competition varies historically. When capital accumulation conditions improve, state managers rarely reverse decisions based on a different set of historical conditions.

By the 1950s, corporations were organizing their assets as divisions in the multidivisional form (MDF) (Fligstein 1990) or in *conglomerates:* widely diversified MDFs. Conglomerates were underway in firms whose original business was tied to defense procurement. Dependence on defense procurement could result in financial disaster when wars ended and the Defense Department canceled its contracts (Boies 1994). Several other historical conditions affected capitalists' motives and behaviors that resulted in conglomerates. First, most major industries were consolidated by the 1950s, profits were high, and corporations were looking for outlets for their excess capital. Second, the flexibility of interpreting state business policy made corporations vulnerable. Further consolidation could result in restraint of trade allegations. Third, a price drop could have serious adverse effects on corporations with all (or most) of their investments in a single product line. Fourth, if firms spread their investments over several industries, it was more difficult for the state to prosecute mergers because antitrust laws focused on limiting market control. Thus, a conglomerate philosophy of management emerged in the 1950s that stressed a diversified portfolio of product lines. This strategy was driven, in part, by the assumption that temporary failures in one product line could be offset by investments into others.

The Spread of Oligopolies

The new institutional context for corporate strategic decision making shifted the historical trajectory of corporate strategic consolidation from monopoly (table 3.1) to oligopoly (i.e., the domination of an industry by a few sellers). In 1947, the largest four firms in the gypsum, primary aluminum, metal cans, industrial trucks and tractors, motors and generators, sewing machine, and aircraft engines and parts industries controlled between 57 and 100 percent of their respective market (table 4.2).[9] Capital also became highly centralized in the industrial sector as a whole. In 1958, the largest fifty industrial firms held approximately 50 percent of the assets of the largest five hundred industrial corporations in the United States (Prechel and Boies 1998a:322–23).

A crucial feature of oligopolies is the high degree of cooperation among top-level decision makers of the largest firms. Members of the oligopoly generally abide by group decisions even when they do not participate in making them (Bannock, Baxter and Rees 1978). Members of oligopolies collude on two types of decisions to exercise power over the market. First, oligopolistic firms, to guarantee

TABLE 4.2 Market Concentration of the Four Largest Firms in an Industry, 1947

Industry	Percentage of Market Share
Industrial Trucks and Tractors	57
Motors and Generators	59
Aircraft Engines and Parts	72
Sewing Machines	78
Metal Cans	80
Gypsum	85
Primary Aluminum	100

Source: Census of Manufacturers, 1963.

profits, engage in price setting, a markup over costs agreed to and acknowledged by all members. Second, oligopolistic firms, to avoid declining prices due to over-production and underconsumption, limit rivalry for market share by coordinating market demand with production capability.

Since oligopolies curtail competition few incentives exist to cut costs. Instead, strategic decisions within these institutional arrangements are based on maintaining market share and high utilization rates. Although smaller companies entered these industries, their decisions were structured by the institutional context. Oligopolistic price-setting structures meant high prices and high profits for large and small companies. Also, small companies rarely challenged the prices set by the big corporations who could cut prices and force them into bankruptcy.

Summary

Decades of political protests by small capitalists, farmers, and the working class pressured state managers to reduce the rights granted to corporations by regional states. The outcome of political struggles in the first fifty years of the twentieth century restructured the institutional arrangements so that the holding-company form was deinstitutionalized.

Initially, it was not clear how the federal courts were going to treat the holding company. As a result, most of the consolidations during the first phase (1889–1897) were achieved through the merger of assets. Of the large monopoly-seeking consolidations formed at the turn of the century, only the American Cotton Oil Company used the holding company and purchased stock of acquired firms. The 1895 Supreme Court decision in *United States v. E. C. Knight Co.* eliminated threats to the holding company under the Sherman Antitrust Act, and financiers and corporate attorneys considered the holding company immune from antitrust laws. Immediately following this decision, unprecedented activity occurred in the industrial securities market representing a second phase of consolidation through the purchase of other corporations' stocks. Sixteen of the twenty-nine consolidations between 1900 and 1903 occurred within holding companies (Haney 1920). Even more industrial consolidations occurred through the holding company between 1913 and 1928 (see above). The holding company became the vehicle to simultaneously consolidate markets and *centralize capital:* the fusion of different capitals under a single ownership. Centralization allows a few people to control large amounts of capital that are spatially distributed throughout a regional, national, or global economy.

The state mediated class conflict by allowing anticompetitive practices by big business but limiting the form of those practices by disallowing corporations from using the holding company to establish market control. State managers' interpretations of the law (i.e., "unreasonable restraint of trade") were also affected by the state's own agenda to ensure economic stability. If economic growth was threatened by low corporate profits, state managers tended to allow corporate consolidations. The problem with using historically specific economic conditions to establish general business policy is competition and profits vary historically. When economic conditions improve, state managers do not reverse decisions that were justified by previous historical conditions. Further, once policies allowing corporate consolidation are established, few incentives exist for capitalists to introduce more efficient means of organization. Capitalists did not set up consolidation strategies so that they could control costs. The agenda of big capital was to gain market control in order to set prices.

Although the Celler-Kefauver Amendment (1950) affected the form of consolidation, it had little effect on the holding company or the centralization of capital. Most large corporations stopped using the holding company to consolidate their control over markets prior to passage of the Celler-Kefauver Amendment. After the Celler-Kefauver Amendment, centralization of capital simply took a different form. Rather than centralizing capital within an industry, centralization of capital occurred across industries.

It was the New Deal that had the most significant effect on deinstitutionalization of the holding company. New Deal business policy represents a historical transition that produced a transformation to a corporate form where complete ownership over corporate entities exist. Most corporations listed with the New York Stock Exchange prior to the New Deal were holding companies or holding-company/operating company hybrids. In contrast, by 1948, only five of the largest firms were holding companies (Berle and Means 1991) and that number remained relatively stable through 1979. New Deal bank regulations had important effects on this corporate-form change by cutting off the flow of capital to private investment bankers. Dependent on capital from commercial banks, private investment bankers were unable to underwrite corporate stocks and bonds at the same rate as in previous decades. Capital dependence on financiers, however, was a short-term constraint on industrial consolidation. Demand for industrial goods in the 1940s stimulated economic growth and improved cash flows. State business policy (e.g., tax policy, direct government investment) also increased cash flows in the industrial sector, which further reduced corporations' dependence on external capital markets.

By the 1930s, industrial capitalists had already experimented with three organizational forms to control markets. First, *pools, arrangements, cartels, and trusts* allocated decision-making authority over prices and production capability to a central body. These organizational forms were designed to avoid cutthroat competition. The weak ties among business enterprises, however, made compliance with decisions made by the centralized administrative body difficult to enforce. Individual entrepreneurs frequently cut their prices to gain market share, especially during recessions and depression when demand declined. Although trusts created stronger ties than pools and cartels, trusts had few legal rights and their informal ties were also vulnerable to economic downturns. Even Andrew Carnegie stated that trusts are "bound to go to pieces, sooner or later" (*New York Times* 1888). By the late nineteenth century, capitalists began to pressure regional states to create the institutional context to establish stronger ties among business enterprises competing in the same markets.

The second organizational form, *holding companies*, formalized control through stock ownership (i.e., more than 50 percent) of a subsidiary corporation. A crucial advantage of the holding company was its formal political-legal status that provided corporations with a range of rights including the right to own other corporations. Incentives to use the holding-company form declined after three decades of political protests that resulted in revisions to state business policy. Policy changes included Section 7 of the Clayton Act (1914), the FTC's 1925 decision to restrict U.S. Steel from setting prices through its subsidiaries, and the FTC's 1934 decision to force Arrow-Hart and Hegeman to divest. New Deal policies restructuring financial arrangements had the most profound effect, however, by taxing intercorporate capital transfers and by cutting off the flow of the public's capital to corporations; private investment bankers no longer had access to individuals' savings deposited in commercial banks. It was access to the public's capital, versus the personal wealth of financiers, that provided them with the power to consolidate industry. Financiers such as J. P. Morgan underwrote industrial consolidation with capital that they obtained from National City Bank, later renamed Citicorp, and other commercial banks.

The third category of organizational form entailed organizing all assets under a single legal entity. Two widely used corporate forms fit the category where owners controlled 100 percent of corporations' assets. The *functional departmentalized form* had few product lines, divided the organization along discrete tasks (e.g., manufacturing, sales, finance), and centralized decision-making authority. Many corporations set up this form in the late nineteenth and early twentieth centuries (e.g., DuPont). In 1920, after it implemented a diversification strategy, DuPont set up the *multidivisional form* (MDF), organizing geographically dispersed operations and corporate entities with multiple product lines as divisions (Chandler 1962).

Corporate restructuring at DuPont and General Motors occurred because of an incompatibility between strategy and structure and the subsequent lack of managerial control. Diversification at DuPont made its centralized functional-departmentalized form inadequate. Consolidating many small automobile companies under a holding company at General Motors resulted in a lack of control and high operating costs. The incompatibility between their respective strategies and structures resulted in profitability crises in these corporations during the

1920's depression. Their family fortune threatened, the DuPont family, who had substantial investments in General Motors, financed both corporate restructures to the MDF (see chapter 5 for more detail).

Corporate restructuring at DuPont and General Motors, financed by one family, are important historical events. These two events, however, do not represent a transformation of the corporate form. A shift in the historical trajectory of the corporate form occurred in response to New Deal policies when a large number of corporations changed to the MDF. The events at DuPont and General Motors, however, are important because they represented the spread of finance capital. The line between industrial and financial capital became increasingly blurred; by the 1920s, industrial corporations were financing other industrial corporations. DuPont's ownership of General Motors stock also constituted a diversification strategy whereby one industrial corporation diversifies its capital investments by owning stock in another large corporation that manufactures a different product line.

Conclusion

The theoretical logic employed here shows that institutionalization and deinstitutionalization of the holding company was a complex process that was affected by the capacity of competing classes and class segments to advance their interests. The Federalist state structure, a weak national state, laissez-faire ideology, and the power of financiers had important effects on the policy formation process that created the institutional context for industrial consolidation using the holding-company form. The institutional arrangements in the late nineteenth century (1) provided corporations with the legal rights to incorporate (2) limited parent companies' liability for their subsidiaries' actions (3) made financing easier by creating internal capital markets (4) avoided the need for complex management structures, and (5) granted to corporations rights previously reserved for individuals. These institutional arrangements allowed consolidation with a low *investment-asset ratio:* proportion of investment capital to the assets controlled. Corporations exercised their new rights (e.g., stock ownership) to establish ownership control over other corporations.

Regional state business policy that granted corporations rights previously reserved for individuals had important long-term effects. Regional state laws of incorporation provided the institutional context for business decisions and further politicized capitalism. It was one thing for the state to grant corporations specific rights to engage in business activities. It was quite another thing for corporations to have the right to engage in any business activity that was not illegal. In the latter case, it required a legislative act to prohibit corporate behaviors. These institutional arrangements restructured the relationship between the state and business so that the state had to stop an already existing corporate behavior. Further, the fact that corporations were engaged in an activity meant that they had invested in social structures to carry out that activity. Passing laws that prohibited an existing activity were costly to the corporation, which created additional incentives for capitalists to engage in politics.

Despite the political pressure from small capitalist class segments and the working class to eliminate advantages granted to big business, the federal government's response to industrial consolidation was, at best, piecemeal. The state's first policy to contain consolidation (i.e., the Sherman Act), which was designed to control trusts, was outdated by the time it was passed. Subsequent business policy to control industrial consolidation was effected by the state's own agenda to ensure economic stability. When profits declined "reasonable" became a core consideration by state managers interpreting antitrust laws. In many cases, decisions to consolidate were not made to take advantage of new technological developments and economies of scale as asserted by functional efficiency arguments (Chandler 1962; Williamson 1985). Most subsidiaries used the technology that they had prior to being controlled by a parent company. In some cases, consolidation occurred to eliminate competition from companies with more advanced technologies (e.g., Carnegie's takeover of Allegheny Bessemer Steel Company).

Historicizing the corporation, which includes giving attention to crucial events, shows that corporate change is a dynamic process. Change was driven, in part, by inconsistencies and incompatibilities within corporations' institutional arrangements. A central dimension of these institutional arrangements was laissez-faire ideology. Capitalists' capacity to modify laissez-faire ideology was decisive to legitimating the holding company. Although mid-nineteenth-century capitalists publically endorsed laissez-faire ideology, they viewed the absence of state intervention in the economy as an impediment to expansion. Absent laws allocating rights to business enterprises, capitalists had few legitimate means to pursue their agenda. After capitalists convinced regional state managers to create a business policy granting more rights to corporations, big business reemployed laissez-faire ideologies: the right to pursue their interests unencumbered by government business policy. Capital dependence was the issue around which capitalists' political strategies pivoted. When capital dependence increased, big business lobbied for state intervention. When capital dependence did not constrain their capacity for goal realization, big business opposed state intervention in the economy.

The success of small capitalists and the working class was due to their capacity to expose a contradiction: the institutional arrangements create inequality of opportunity. State business policy created state structures that benefited big business. After decades of political protest, state managers passed legislation that deinstitutionalized the holding company because the state's legitimacy was challenged by (1) classes and class segments who exposed the contradiction between laissez-faire capitalism and the institutional arrangements that unfairly benefited big business, and (2) the corporate practices (e.g., overcapitalization) allowed by these institutional arrangements . To restore its legitimacy, the state set up policies that deinstitutionalized the holding-company form.

Part II
Transformation of the
Managerial Process

Transformation of the Managerial Process

Few sociological examinations of the managerial process exist. This is surprising given the centrality of organizational studies in sociology and the degree to which change in the managerial process affect the organization of the corporation and labor process. The managerial process includes incentives to induce decision-making behavior, an evaluation procedure, and an apparatus of discipline and reward to elicit cooperation and compliance of managers. Managers are social actors who are embedded in a complex of structural arrangements that are designed to achieve corporations' agenda. The account-control system is a crucial aspect of the managerial process. It is the historically specific mode of rational calculation designed to achieve organizational standards, targets, and goals.

Several researchers argue that the dispersion of stock in the modern corporation had the effect of replacing entrepreneurial with managerial capitalism where managers, not capitalists, controlled the corporation (Chandler 1977; Williamson 1985). This argument was challenged by other researchers who argued that once stock is dispersed capitalists can exercise control over the corporation with a small proportion of stock ownership (Zeitlin 1989; Mintz and Schwartz 1985). The analysis here moves beyond this argument and examines the institutionalization of control inside the corporation. It shows that controls over managers' behavior were the outcome of conflicts and political struggles among capitalist class segments. These controls were established in the early twentieth century and few changes in the assumptions upon which these controls were based occurred until the economic crises in the 1970s and 1980s. The analysis also shows that controls that are established over managers are only rational from the perspective of those who win the power struggles. It cannot be assumed that managerial controls are rational from some universalistic conception of efficiency because different capitalist class segments have different conceptions of efficiency.

In chapter 5, I examine the development of account controls in the late nineteenth century, how profitability crises and power struggles among capitalist class segments transformed cost controls into financial controls by the 1920s, and the gradual incremental changes that institutionalized financial controls in the following decades. Using a historical case-oriented study, chapter 6 shows how financial controls produced contradictory behaviors (e.g., decisions) when evaluated in relationship to corporate substantive goals (e.g., profits). Resolution of this contradiction in the 1980s entailed a restructuring of the managerial process.

CHAPTER 5

From Product Cost Controls to Financial Controls

While industrial consolidation mitigated the meso-macro contradiction and created the institutional arrangement for steady profit making, it exacerbated the micro-meso contradiction between the corporate form and the managerial process. Unlike the holding-company form that embedded its subsidiaries in the market, combining assets into a single corporation (e.g., functional-unitary, MDF) made top management more dependent on internal controls to monitor performance in corporate entities. Big business was confronted with a new obstacle: how to maintain control over the giant corporation.

Social structures that define managerial control and autonomy are core features of the managerial process. Berle and Means [1932] (1991) point out that by the 1930s a power shift occurred that facilitated the agendas of finance capitalists and their managers. (Authors who describe Berle and Means often fail to point out the context of their analysis. They were commenting on the pyramided holding company, which created a capital structure that shifted control from industrialists to a few large stockholders [i.e., financial capitalists such as J. P. Morgan] and their managers.) Berle and Means concluded that the dispersion and diffusion of stock in the pyramided holding company entailed a revolution in property rights where individuals and families no longer exercised control in most corporations. Industrialists' dependence on external capital markets to pursue consolidation strategies allowed a small group of financiers and their managers to exercise control over the corporation.

Other researchers maintained that the increased size and diversity of the corporation separated ownership from control. This managerial thesis suggests that unless capitalists became career managers they did not have the time, information, or experience to make top-level decisions (Chandler 1977). Therefore, authority was allocated to managers who set long-term policy and managed operating activities. Managerialists argue that this transformation from family to managerial capitalism entailed a power shift (Gordon 1945; Galbraith 1967; Rumelt 1974; Chandler 1977; Williamson 1985).

There is no doubt that the role of management increased significantly by 1930. Also, managerial hierarchies expanded throughout the middle decades of the twentieth century. It has not been demonstrated, however, that the emergence of managerial hierarchies entailed a power shift from capitalists to managers. Advocates of the managerial revolution thesis do not provide an account of the historical sequences to document this transformation. In particular, they fail to examine the effects of family and financial capitalists on the managerial process. It is one thing to suggest that managerial hierarchies emerged and that managers' motives and behaviors did not advance the interests of capitalists. It is quite another thing to show that managers gained control over the corporation and that their behavior deviated from the directives they received from capitalists. Managerialist arguments assume that managers had adequate autonomy from capitalists to construct governance structures that deviated from those set up by capitalists, allowing managers to pursue their own agenda. The analysis here shows *why* managers' interests deviated from capitalists' interests. This requires an analysis of the *managerial process:* the collective behavior of managers and the incentive structures to motivate them and control their behavior.

An examination of historical sequences shows that financial capitalists exercised their power to set up the system of control. The dependence of industrial capital on family and banking capitalists allowed the latter to coerce industrial capitalists to conform. *Coercive pressure* exists when actors controlling essential resources require organizations dependent on those resources to conform (Pfeffer and Salancik 1978). In this chapter, I show that the system of control was designed to provide decision makers with information that linked their decisions to the interests of financiers.

Prevailing Theory

Prevailing conceptions of the managerial process rely on marginal utility and agency theories to explain managers' behavior. Agency theory assumes that inefficiencies in the firm are a consequence of conflict between the interests of managers (i.e., agents) and capitalists (i.e., principles). The theory assumes that managers act in a self-interested manner. Managers act independent of the managerial process or define it in such a way that it advances their own interests (e.g., growth versus profit maximization). Rather than examining the effects of managerial process and its incentive structure on managers' behavior, like managerialism, agency theory assumes that power is transferred from capitalists to managers who advance their own interests, which may be inconsistent with capitalists' interests.

One version of principle-agency theories is transaction cost analysis (TCA). Like other managerial theories, this perspective assumes that the MDF emerged because it economized on bounded rationality by creating a managerial division of labor between operating and strategic decisions. Williamson (1985) argues that inefficiencies followed from the opportunistic behavior of managers. The lack of information (i.e., asset specificity) creates opportunities for "self-interest seeking with guile" and increases the need for internal governance to attenuate opportunism (Williamson 1985:211). A problem with TCA is that it attributes managerial behaviors that undermine efficiency to opportunism without examining the alternate hypothesis: *managers' behaviors are responses to the incentive system—in which they are embedded—that were created by capitalists.* TCA fails to examine whether inefficiencies emerge from the system of control itself.

Two key areas of inquiry are conspicuously absent from current analysis. Researchers have not shown (1) whether corporate incentive structures are created by managers, or capitalists, and (2) whether inefficiencies emerge because managers' behaviors are consistent with the incentive structure within which they are embedded. In short, existing conceptual frameworks undertheorize the power of principles to create the structures designed to control managers, and then fail to investigate it. This problem exists, in part, because researchers' focus is on the immediate decisional and behavioral aspects of management, which fails to consider the social structural determinants of behavior.

The key to understanding the managerial process entails identifying the incentive structure and how it affects managers' actions. My analysis challenges two interrelated assumption of agency theory: (1) attributing rationality to the formal system of control, and (2) attributing the causes of inefficiencies to opportunistic managers (i.e., agents). *Efficiency* is defined as the ratio of inputs like labor and raw materials to outputs (Chandler 1962: 37). Efficiency improvements entail doing what the organization does better (Pfeffer and Salancik 1978). In manufacturing corporations, improving efficiency entails converting inputs into outputs at a lower cost.

To examine these issues, I study the historical sequences between the midnineteenth and mid-twentieth centuries that produced two historical transitions that affected the decision-making process: (1) market controls to product cost controls, and (2) product cost controls to financial controls. Internal corporate-account controls are divided into two main categories. *Managerial accounting* is designed to enhance the ability of operating management to plan, make decisions to control and reduce costs, improve quality, and increase productivity (Maher, Stickney, Weil, and Davidson 1991). *Financial accounting* is the valuation and verification of opportunities for profit making and a comparison of this valuation at the beginning of a period to the end of a period (Weber 1978; Maher et al. 1991). Financial accounting is designed to report the financial position of an entity (i.e., corporation, corporate unit) at predetermined time intervals (e.g., monthly, quarterly). It accounts for assets, equities, revenues, and expenses of a business. The analysis shows how financial accounting—rather than managerial accounting—became the primary means to ensure control in the largest U.S. corporations. I also show how financial accounting did not provide the kind of information necessary to evaluate or monitor the efficient use of resources.

Nineteenth Century Cost Controls

In the early 1800s most firms engaged in relatively simple manufacturing processes and produced few products using few raw materials. Entrepreneurs sold these products in competitive markets. If the firm was profitable, entrepreneurs could assume that the production process was efficient because the market provided a measure of the relationship between the cost to manufacture the product and its selling price. Because entrepreneurs engaged in the day-to-day production decisions they knew the input costs on the few products they produced. If a firm became unprofitable, entrepreneurs had the knowledge to scrutinize cost inputs. As long as these firms pursued *scale* strategies (i.e., increased output) to reduce unit costs, entrepreneurs did not need elaborate cost-accounting systems. The few products manufactured consumed resources at a relatively uniform rate and the market identified when the costs to manufacture a product exceeded competitors' costs (Johnson and Kaplan 1991). If firms owned more than one facility, comparing costs and profits from the different facilities provided a second measure of firms' cost efficiency.[1]

From Market Controls to Product-Cost Management, 1800–1870

As corporations began to vertically integrate, markets could not monitor product costs. Integration occurred in two stages: integrating separate processes into a single firm, and integrating separate products into a single firm. Textile firms were among the first to integrate separate processes (e.g., sheep shearing, spinning, weaving) (Johnson and Kaplan 1991). Integration generated a problem. After separate processes were integrated, the market no longer differentiated among the costs of the various interim products. Therefore, integrating several processes into a single firm required an internal costing system to detect product costs. Further, *scope* strategies, which increased the number of different products manufactured in one facility, required more cost-accounting detail to identify the additional cost inputs. Vertical integration required more formally rational calculation so that entrepreneurs could identify the many costs of producing several products and interim products in a single firm.

By the early 1800s, entrepreneurs in the United States and Britain began to place more emphasis on product cost accounting. They designed cost-accounting techniques to identify the three basic components of manufacturing cost (i.e., material, labor, overhead). As early as 1815, some firms had developed a system to identify and monitor *conversion costs* (i.e., overhead and labor costs to convert raw materials into final products) in each of its separable processes (Johnson and Kaplan 1991). The system charged mills with their respective share of raw material, labor, and factory overhead. Overhead, which included the cost of repairs, fuel, freight, and insurance, was distributed among the mills based on floor space, number of looms, and the rated horsepower of water turbines.

Two interrelated features of this account-control system are crucial: (1) it compared total product costs to market prices for each product, and (2) it directed managers' attention toward shop-floor activities to identify and reduce production costs (Kaplan and Johnson 1991). These account controls provided mill managers with cost data on the various phases of the manufacturing process, which they used to compare the productivity of one or more processes over time. In short, this account-control system provided decision makers with information to: (1) identify labor and nonlabor costs, including raw material, inventory, and factory overhead, and (2) monitor, evaluate, and control the production process. This enabled entrepreneurs to identify cost variations over time, examine the cause of the variation, and make changes in the production process to reduce costs (e.g., improvements in machinery, plant design). By the 1880s, the textile industry had developed an accurate system of allocating costs to products (Chandler 1977; Johnson and Kaplan 1991).

Expansion, Economic Crisis, and the Intensification of Account Controls, 1870–1900

By the late nineteenth century, the increased size and complexity of manufacturing facilities altered the spatial characteristics of manufacturing. Whereas previously, close proximity existed between inputs and the final product, the new system organized a sequence of operations over an extended area. In some early-twentieth-century corporations, raw materials delivered at one location came out as finished products two miles away (Nelson 1975). These spatial changes and the increased organizational complexity undermined the capacity for entrepreneurs to supervise operations at the point of production. Moreover, organizational expansion increased owners' administrative activities (e.g., purchasing raw materials, distribution), which diverted their attention away from production.

In response, entrepreneurs began to decentralize control over the production process. As late as the 1840s, however, there were few middle managers in the United States (Chandler 1977). Thus, owners allocated control over the manufacturing process to *foremen* whose responsibilities spanned three basic areas of decision making and control: (1) determining the manner and timing of production (2) ascertaining the cost and quality of work, and (3) supervising employees (Nelson 1975; Edwards 1979). Entrepreneurs also hired *inside contractors*, which delegated even more authority at the point of production to nonowners. Inside contractors typically emerged from the ranks of foremen. They used the entrepreneurs' machinery and equipment, maintained complete control of manufacturing, and hired, fired, and paid workers. Inside contractors were responsible to the owners for the economic performance of their contracted organizational units (e.g., blast furnace, weaving mill) (Nelson, 1975). While inside contracting reduced the problem of monitoring, supervising, and controlling diverse and frequently highly skilled workers, owners soon became detached from the point of production. Therefore, efficiency improvements usually benefited the inside contractors. Some inside contractors earned incomes comparable to the major stockholders of the company (Clawson 1980).

This system of decentralized controls remained stable until the recessions, depressions, and economic crises between 1873 and 1896. By the early 1890s, growth in gross national product (GNP) declined to .19 percent from 5.58 percent in the 1870s. These historical sequences produced a profitability crisis, labor unrest, production bottlenecks, and the increased frequency of stock-market panics.

Because of these events, capitalists became concerned with the risks of ownership. By the 1880s, capitalists were uneasy with a system where they assumed the major financial risk, but had limited control over costs and profits. Together these events resulted in a shift in the formally rational system of control. To increase their control over the firm, owners of many large corporations initiated strategies to eliminate inside contractors and centralize control over foremen. Two strategies were at the heart of this change.

First, large corporations set up programs to enhance harmony and morale to offset labor unrest (e.g., strikes, radical labor politics). This strategy was known as *welfare capitalism:* programs based on the belief that voluntary efforts by employers to improve the life and work conditions of employees contributed to a value orientation that encouraged self-betterment, loyalty, and cooperation. Programs to improve life conditions included educational and recreational programs, housing, plans for saving and lending money, and provisions for insurance pensions. Initiatives that focused on improving work conditions included safety programs, incentive wage plans, and apprenticeship training. Welfare capitalism was a paternalistic program based on the belief that these initiatives would encourage worker loyalty and cooperation. Capitalists assumed that these programs would simultaneously create a better person and worker (Nelson 1975).

The second effort to regain control over the manufacturing process entailed the creation of *managerial hierarchies:* where superordinate managers have authority to provide guidelines for the subordinate managers and workers. Initially, product-cost accounting was a key component of the managerial process. By the late 1800s, entrepreneurs in the iron and steel, foodstuffs, petroleum, chemicals, and machinery industries began to set up product-cost controls similar to those used in single-activity firms (Johnson and Kaplan 1991). The Carnegie Steel Company was among the first multi-activity corporations to develop a detailed product-cost accounting system. Between 1872 and 1902 Andrew Carnegie developed an accounting system that collected cost data on each product as it moved through the manufacturing process. These included raw material costs (e.g., iron ore, limestone, coal), interim products costs (e.g., coke, pig iron), costs accumulated in the blast furnace and rolling mill stages, and labor costs at each manufacturing stage. Carnegie designed the system to establish *responsibility accounting*, identifying the manager responsible for costs. For Carnegie, success was dependent on "the introduction and strict maintenance of a perfect system of accounting so that responsibility for money or materials can be brought home to every man" (in Livesay 1975:85). Carnegie's major innovation was to collect cost information on each of the firm's separable manufacturing processes. During this period, capitalists paid little attention to *financial accounting*, which assesses the performance of capital (e.g., return on investment). Using this system, Carnegie kept his costs lower than other integrated steel corporations. The fundamental premise of Carnegie's account-control system was: "Watch the costs and the profits will take care of themselves" (Carnegie in Livesay 1975:101).

Capitalists set up a more detailed cost system for two reasons. First, the increased complexity of the manufacturing process undermined their capacity to understand their costs or predict profits. Lacking an account-control system that identified product costs, capitalists had little capacity to assess the relationship between product cost and market prices or estimate cash flows. Second, after the economic crisis of the late nineteenth century, capitalists became concerned with the risks of ownership. Their solution was to obtain more precise cost information to better understand the relationship between the cost to manufacture individual products, and market prices.

The Dual Focus of Scientific Management, 1900–1920

The desire for more precise cost data increased as corporations continued to expand. Much of this expansion was the outcome of vertical integration from the merger wave between 1897 and 1903. Also, by the turn of the century, companies began to mass produce machine-made metal goods (e.g., sewing machines, rifles, reapers, locks, scales, pumps) that contained many input costs. The owners of these corporations were confronted with the same problem as those in industries (e.g., steel, textile) that had already begun to manufacture many different products. When several products are manufactured from the same raw materials in a single facility, the market cannot differentiate among the costs to produce each product. Increased organizational complexity made it difficult to locate costs, and capitalists could no longer assume that if the corporation was profitable that each product was profitable. Capitalists began to set up scientific management to resolve the disparity between the increasingly complex manufacturing process and the availability of decision-making information.

Capitalists in mass-production industries began to employ engineer-managers to design and develop information-gathering systems to track the flow of material and labor costs. In fact, several capitalists began to attend the annual meetings of the American Society of Mechanical Engineers where they solicited mechanical engineers to develop a more advanced cost system. These engineer-managers developed methods of scientific management to control costs and gain control of the labor process. Two distinct types of control emerged.

Frederick Taylor developed a system to monitor labor and material costs. Taylor collected cost data on the manufacturing process and used it to establish standards for planning the flow of work (e.g., elaborating work rules) to identify and standardize the "one best way" to use labor and material. Beginning in the 1880s, Frederick Taylor began to develop his method, and in 1903 and 1905, he presented papers at the American Society of Mechanical Engineers (ASME) that contained core ideas in his conception of scientific management (Noble 1977).

At the same ASME conference where Taylor presented his work, engineer-managers such as Alexander Hamilton Church discussed an account-control system that established "standard rates at which material and labor should be consumed in manufacturing tasks" (Johnson and Kaplan 1991:49). Standard rates were used to compare projected with actual costs to identify cost variances, and to assess the performance of products in relationship to profits. Church attempted to convince owners to develop a product-costing system capable of (1) identifying specific costs (wages, materials, indirect shop charges, selling expenses) of each product, and (2) connecting those product costs with the overall profitability of the corporation (Church 1914). Church advocated using product-cost information to identify the relationship between the profits earned on each product and the firm's overall profitability. Church even began to devise a way to calculate the cost associated with each machine's idle time (Nelson 1975; Chandler 1977; Johnson and Kaplan 1991). Others (e.g., Arnold Emerson) argued for developing a product cost system capable of centralizing control, delegating responsibility, and holding lower-level managers and workers accountable for costs.

By applying their technical expertise to cost accounting, these engineer-managers quickly developed sophisticated information-gathering systems. By 1918, engineer-managers began to show how information on standard costs allowed managers to differentiate between costs that can be controlled and costs that are beyond operating managers' control (Johnson and Kaplan 1991). Despite the capacity of a standard cost system to assess the relationship between managerial decisions and firm profits, the large vertically integrated corporations formed during the great merger wave did not set up these account controls. By the 1920s, Taylor's version of scientific management became the primary means to control the manufacturing process. This shifted managers' attention away from controlling cost in general to controlling labor.

Capital Dependence: Cost Management to Financial Management

As discussed above, few industrial capitalists had sufficient capital to finance late-nineteenth- and early-twentieth-century corporate consolidation. Therefore, they were dependent on external capital markets. This capital dependence resulted in two important changes: (1) the formation of *finance capital*: the merging of private investment banking and manufacturing capital, and (2) the restructuring of the form of control. Intracapitalist class politics effected this transformation. Pressured by financiers—upon whom they depended to pursue their consolidation strategies—industrial capitalists set up controls to evaluate the efficient use of capital.

External Capital Markets: Finance Capital and Financial Management

Private investment bankers were not satisfied with allowing manufacturing capitalists to simply use their money. Financiers required documentation of corporations' financial stability. They were also concerned that corporations would anticipate income and authorize dividend payments out of operating capital, rather than profits. In the long term, this practice could drain capital from the corporation and weaken its financial position. Existing accounting techniques, however, could not detect this behavior.

J. P. Morgan and Company was among the first investment banks to assert its power and become involved in the management of industrial corporations. In exchange for financing the McCormicks and Deerings consolidation, J. P. Morgan and Company demanded input into restructuring the new International Harvester Corporation (1902). By 1906, George W. Perkins, a J. P. Morgan partner, replaced members of the McCormick and Deering family with professional managers. Similarly, private investment bankers influenced the expansion and restructuring of AT&T in the early 1900s. Dependent on external capital markets, AT&T was forced to accept J. P. Morgan's demand to appoint Theodore N. Vail, previously a banker, as the president of the restructured corporation. These decisions were made to ensure that corporations implemented a financial conception of control.

Capitalists employed accountants to develop account controls that would provide them with information to make capital decisions. Among the most widely used methods was the inventory-averaging system. Although rarely used before 1900, after 1910 most large corporations adopted *inventory-costing procedures:* an aggregating bookkeeping procedure that separates "the production expense of an accounting period from the cost of manufactured product inventories at the end of a period" (Johnson and Kaplan 1991:130). Inventory costing places a numerical value on: (1) units of in-process and unsold products the end of a period, and (2) units of products sold during the period. Separating sold from unsold products during a specific time provided inventory costs that were presented on the balance sheet. Inventory accounting also provided information to compare aggregated production costs to revenues, which were reported on the income statement (Johnson and Kaplan 1991). The balance sheet and income statement became the primary financial reporting documents in most corporations.

Inventory accounting is in sharp contrast to product costing. Whereas product-cost accounting provided managers with information on how to cut costs by attaching input costs to specific products, inventory accounting used product-cost information to identify the impact of costs on aggregate profits. This aspect of financial accounting integrated cost accounts into the double-entry bookkeeping system by assigning costs as the product moved through the factory. It aggregated input costs and combined cost and financial accounts into a single account.

After several stages of aggregation, it became impossible to identify the part of the total product cost in the income statement that represented the product cost of a particular stage of the manufacturing process. Moreover, in facilities that manufactured many different products, there was no way to trace costs to products. Without information to identify the costs (e.g., labor, material, overhead) to manufacture a particular product, management could not generate reasonable estimates of variable or fixed costs (Johnson and Kaplan 1991).[2] Variations in energy consumption, for example, to manufacture specific products were lost. Therefore, indirect costs were frequently allocated based on a common cost basis, typically labor hours.

Most important, combining the costs at one stage of the manufacturing process with costs at the next stage reduces decision-making information. Aggregating these data lost the detail necessary to identify the products a corporation produced at a lower or higher cost than its competitors. Capitalists became less concerned with evaluating the efficiency of manufacturing individual products for two reasons. First, by 1910, oligopolies existed in several industrial sectors allowing capitalists to coordinate production capacity with market demand and set prices. Second, firms began to produce more products. Capitalists assumed that producing a wide range of products would buffer the firm from short-term downturns in the price of specific products.

As long as corporations retained the holding-company form and subsidiaries retained a narrow product line, the market embeddedness of subsidiaries provided information measuring the capacity of subsidiary corporations to profitably manufacture their products. Also, production managers retained better understanding of the cost structure when there were few input costs. As corporations pursued vertical integration and began producing many products and interim products, however, it became difficult for production managers to understand product costs. The situation worsened when corporations restructured their assets as divisions. Within the divisional form, capitalists and top managers lost more information on the relationship between product cost and price.

Ironically, at the historical juncture when corporations began manufacturing more products, operating managers had less product-cost information upon which to base their decisions. The dimension of the account-control system that made it possible to evaluate the efficient use of manufacturing facilities and the relationship between product profits and total profits disappeared. Product cost-accounting, which traced cost to particular products, was replaced with account controls that traced costs to a particular time (e.g., monthly, quarterly, annual reports). The aggregate inventory averaging system directed managers' attention toward inventory valuation and away from product cost. As a result, little information existed to evaluate firms' capacity to efficiently produce its expanding product line. These changes virtually eliminated capitalists' (i.e., principles) capacity to evaluate whether managers (i.e., agents) made cost-efficient decisions. While the account-control system became less relevant for production management, it satisfied external capital markets.

Family Capitalists and Financial Controls

Among the most influential family capitalists to effect the transition to the financial conception of control were the DuPonts. By 1903, the DuPont family bought several independent firms and consolidated them into one functional, departmentalized corporation. As a result, DuPont Company became a centrally managed multi-activity corporation that coordinated manufacturing, distribution, and purchasing activities.

To assess the corporation's financial strength in order to make capital allocation decisions, the DuPonts assigned to their financial staff the task of developing more precise profit measurements and establishing criteria to evaluate financial performance (Chandler 1962, 1977). Pierre DuPont (president) and Irénée DuPont (chair of the Executive Committee) supervised this project and expanded the financial staff from twelve in 1903 to more than two hundred in the following year. Donaldson Brown, one of Pierre DuPont's subordinates, developed the profitability measurement that later became the industrial standard. Brown attempted to capture the flow (i.e., speed, volume) of materials through the manufacturing process. Alfred Chandler (1977:446) describes Brown's concept as resting on the assumption

> that if prices remained the same, the rate of return on invested capital increased as volume rose and decreased as it fell. The higher the throughput and stock-turn, the greater the rate of return. Brown termed this rate of flow "turnover." He defined it as value of sales divided by total investment. Brown then related turnover to earnings as a percentage of sales (still the standard definition of profit in American industry). He did this by multiplying turnover by profit, which provided a rate of return that reflected the intensity with which the enterprise used resources.

By 1910, these accounting methods became the standard tool to evaluate the productivity of capital in corporations and their functional departments.

This dimension of the account-control system gave immense importance to *return on investment* (ROI), which measured performance and evaluated return in corporate entities by their contribution to corporate agendas and goals. ROI became the sole basis of capital decisions concerning (1) the allocation of new investments among competing corporate entities, and (2) the financing of new capital requirements (Chandler and Salsbury 1971; Johnson and Kaplan 1991). By 1918, corporations extended ROI to plan, control, and motivate managers in the sales and purchasing departments. ROI remained the primary means to evaluate corporate entities through the 1970s.

The DuPonts also developed *budget controls* to identify costs within the corporations' operating units. Although budget controls were used to evaluate production managers' capacity to control costs, they were based on the same principles as other financial controls. They used aggregated cost data, which did not identify the relationship between specific product costs and profits. The chemical, railroad, metal-working, electrical, and steel industries were among the first to adopt budgetary controls. Budgetary controls summarized manufacturing information in two monthly reports. The *works cost report* (i.e., budget) contained information concerning the mill superintendents' area of responsibility. It compared the operating efficiency of mills in the same departments. Although budget controls identified whether one mill was more efficient than another, they did not identify costs. Thus, the works cost report could not determine mills' capacity to produce particular products cost efficiently.

The *profit and loss sheet* contained information on all manufacturing costs, operating income, and return on investment. Top management used this information to assess the earnings and ROI by mill and product line. When ROI was initially introduced, only top managers used it to assess the efficient use of capital. Also, mill managers were not compelled to achieve ROI targets. Top management used data from the profit and loss statement (ROI) to make decisions concerning alternative uses of capital, and evaluate mill managers' capacity to remain within assigned budgets (Johnson and Kaplan 1991).

These financial controls created an incentive structure within which middle-level managers made operating decisions. Owners and top managers used budget controls, which emphasized the efficiency of the manufacturing process, to evaluate operating managements' cost efficiency by measuring the cost consumed in each operating unit. As a result, mill superintendents focused on managing the organizational unit (e.g., mill) as efficiently as possible based on inventory-movement criteria. These budget controls created an incentive structure encouraging mill superintendents to act as if they managed single-activity factories, which encouraged managers in the same firm to compete with one another. These financial controls assumed that an incentive structure encouraging managers to cut costs in their organizational units reduced total cost to manufacture a product. In the long term, this assumption proved to be seriously flawed. ROI and budgetary controls directed operating managers' attention away from product costs (i.e., the shop floor) and toward the performance of capital (Kaplan and Johnson 1991).

In summary financiers are responsible for two key changes that shifted product-cost accounting to financial accounting. First, to satisfy investment bankers, inventory-costing procedures were introduced to develop a means to assess the efficient use of capital. Second, financiers introduced financial controls to more precisely measure ROI. Industrial capitalists set up account controls (1) to replace inside contractors with managers (2) to reduce the authority of foremen, and (3) to satisfy external capital markets' demands for information on the productivity of capital.

Critics identified flaws in these financial controls by 1923. J. Maurice Clark criticized the trend toward financial accounting (e.g., the use of income statements and balance sheets) because of the arbitrariness of the distinction between relative and fixed costs. Clark (1923) pointed out that many costs that appear to be fixed over a short time are variable with respect to long-term decisions. He also argued that the standard cost system did not accurately capture costs that vary with different business situations. To overcome these weaknesses, Clark developed concepts such as *differential costs*, which are costs that vary with respect to a given decision. These different uses of cost accounting include detecting the profitability of individual products, and the efficiency of different processes and departments (Johnson and Kaplan 1991). As described above, engineer-managers developed these measures by the years 1910–19, but they were not implemented.

Financial Controls in the Multidivisional Form

The extension of financial control is closely tied to the emergence of the multidivisional form (MDF). These changes were, in part, attempts to resolve crises and problems of bounded rationality that emerged at DuPont in the 1920s. The demand for explosives during World War I was extremely profitable for DuPont and contributed to its strong liquidity position. However, declining demand for explosives in the postwar era left DuPont with unused production capacity. To increase capability utilization rates, DuPont diversified its product line and manufactured artificial leather, rayon, dyes, varnish, paint, and celluloid products. Initially, DuPont tried to manage this diversified product line through its functional form. The cognitive limits of top management were strained, however, by the need to establish resource allocation policies in several product lines, appraise corporate unit performance, coordinate departments, and maintain adequate, but not excessive, inventories.

The economic depression that resulted in a profitability crisis at DuPont in 1920 exposed the weaknesses of its existing organizational form. While diversification increased organizational complexity, DuPont had limited capacity to assess their ability to manufacture products cost efficiently. Thus, the DuPonts attempted to restructure the managerial process to obtain more precise financial measurements. The first step entailed creating *divisions*: corporate entities organized as product lines (Chandler 1962). After they created divisions, the DuPonts and their top managers obtained ROI measurements on divisions' performance. This is in contrast to the use of ROI in the functional departmentalized form where it was used to allocate capital among the firm's functional activities. Within the MDF, ROI measurements entailed even more aggregation: a single measurement included several functional activities of an entire product line. Owners and their top management also started to use ROI to assess middle managers' performance to determine who deserved promotions, salary increases, and investment capital. These financial controls created an even stronger incentive structure that stressed the efficient use of capital, but less emphasis on assessing the corporations' capacity to manufacture individual products cost efficiently.

General Motors also adopted the MDF. The founder of General Motors, William C. Durant, consolidated previously independent marketing, manufacturing, and purchasing activities. Incorporated in 1908, General Motors was a giant holding company for ten automobile, three truck, and ten parts subsidiaries. Like the DuPonts, Durant assumed that the consolidated enterprise would exceed the combined profits of the individual units operating as separate companies. General Motors, however, was poorly managed. Further, availability was the primary criterion for acquisition and little emphasis was placed on the compatibility of the acquired firms. As a result, many of GM's subsidiaries were unprofitable. GM's survival depended mainly on the profits from Buick and Cadillac (Rae 1984). By 1910, GM was close to bankruptcy. However, private investment bankers, Lee, Higginson and Company of Boston, saved the corporation.

Although Durant restructured the holding company as an operating firm and transformed the subsidiaries to divisions, these corporate entities continued to operate independently. Unlike the DuPonts, Durant did not set up a managerial process capable of directing and coordinating the activities of a diversified corporation. Durant became immersed in the detailed activities of the production units, and gave limited attention to general policy and coordinating activities. Like most large corporations, General Motors remained profitable during World War I. During this period, the DuPont family invested heavily in General Motors. A crisis occurred at GM, however, during the 1920–1921 economic depression. With the family investment threatened, Pierre DuPont took steps to resolve the crisis. To restore stockholder confidence in General Motors, the DuPonts improved the company's cash flow and purchased Durant's 2.5 million shares of GM, contingent on his withdrawal from the corporation. When this transaction was complete, the DuPonts held 23 percent interest in the corporation (Rae 1984).

Pierre DuPont took over as president of General Motors and hired Donaldson Brown to set up the account-control system that he developed at DuPont Company. DuPont also hired Alfred P. Sloan Jr., and together DuPont, Brown, and Sloan constructed a financial conception of control that Brown described as centralized control with decentralized responsibility (Chandler 1962). The president held centralized authority over the divisions and delegated responsibility to execute control over the managerial process to the executive and financial committee (Rae 1984). DuPont and his top managers also created centralized research, advertising, and product-planning units that advised the divisional managers.

Like financial controls at DuPont, the system at General Motors was designed to do three tasks. First, it compared division goals with the company-wide financial goals. Second, ROI was used to allocate resources and reward managers. Third, financial controls provided sales reports and flexible budgets that showed whether actual sales or costs deviated from projections. *Flexible budgets* include projected receipts and expenditures of corporate entities. They provide three controls over the managerial process. First, flexible budgets distinguish between variable and fixed costs, making it possible to forecast costs and profits at different utilization rates. Second, they calculate the projected net ROI at estimated utilization rates and selling prices to assess the contribution of divisional activities to corporate profitability goals. Third, flexible budgets detect if variations from expected performance levels occurred, which monitors each division's actual performance (Rae 1984; Chandler 1977; Johnson and Kaplan 1991).

General Motors also developed a transfer pricing system to ensure that the transfer of products from one division to another did not result in overcharges. *Transfer prices* are costs one corporate entity charges another for a product or service. Transfer prices are designed to keep one division from advancing its ROI at the expense of ROI in other divisions and, thereby, undermine company-wide profitability goals. This financial control, however, did not monitor transfer pricing of interim products among operating units within divisions. After Pierre DuPont restructured the managerial process at GM (1923), he appointed Sloan as president to coordinate the divisions and to monitor their performance.

The efficiency of financial controls in the MDF depended on their capacity to do three tasks better than the market: (1) create an internal auditing system to link managers' decisions to performance (2) create incentives and motives for middle managers that direct their decisions toward corporate profitability goals, and (3) develop a monitoring system to identify the high-yield units within the corporation, ensuring that capital is allocated to those units. Efficiency depended upon the capacity of financial controls to create an internal quasi-capital market that ensured managerial decisions were consistent with the profitability goals of the corporation. Most important, financial accounting assumed that profits would take care of themselves if corporations maximized ROI within divisions. This is in sharp contrast with *managerial accounting*, which assumed that if corporations controlled product costs, profits would take care of themselves.

In response to their capital-dependent relationship with external capital markets, industrialists set up financial controls. Financial accounting replaced managerial accounting and became the means to provide decision-making information, evaluate the performance of corporate entities, and centralize control over diverse corporate units. By 1950, managerial accounting (i.e., tracing the costs to manufacture each product) virtually disappeared, and corporations relied on financial accounting (i.e., return on investment) to make operating decisions. The shift from cost management to financial management created an incentive structure that encouraged divisional managers to maximize the use of capital and operating managers to remain within assigned budgets. Capitalists and their top managers assumed that embedding operating managers in this incentive structure—oriented toward advancing the financial goals of operating units—would simultaneously advance the profit-making agenda of the corporation.

Means-Ends Contradictions: Using Financial Accounting to Control Product Costs

By the end of World War II, critics identified two crucial problems with using information derived from financial accounting to make operating decisions. Financial controls fail to (1) adequately separate fixed from variable costs, and (2) provide current cost data. Later critics pointed out that inventory costs do not provide an accurate assessment of product costs (Johnson and Kaplan 1991). Although production cost changed on a daily basis and many production decisions are made each day, financial data was available on a monthly or quarterly basis.

By the 1950s, most corporations developed cost centers and allocated pooled overhead costs to those centers. A *cost center* is frequently a production unit. *Pooled overhead costs* are incurred to complete productive activities not directly associated with identifiable cost centers (e.g., clerical, research, janitorial). Corporations developed the "second stop method" to assign these costs. This account control has two important features: (1) it allocates a portion of total pooled overhead cost to each cost center, and (2) it divides these costs by the estimated labor hours in specific areas of the cost center. This system established the rate of assigning overhead costs to each labor hour (Johnson and Kaplan 1991). Using this method, labor rates were used to estimate future overhead costs in each period (e.g., month, year).

This system had several flaws that originate in the aggregation of cost data to create financial controls. First, like the financial controls described above, labor rates did not disaggregate product-cost data from the financial accounting system. This made it impossible to locate the cost inputs of a particular product and identify the cost to manufacture that product.

Second, pooled overhead costs overestimated labor costs. As manufacturing processes became more automated and less labor intensive, pooled overhead cost became more misleading. These rates were sometimes several times higher than the actual labor rate (e.g., wages paid to workers) (Johnson and Kaplan 1991; Drucker 1990). Meanwhile, the increasing proportion of nonlabor costs (e.g., utilities, property taxes, depreciation, insurance, rent) on total product costs went undetected. These distortions created large errors in estimating product costs.

Third, using inflated labor rates to assign overhead costs directed operating managers' attention almost solely toward reducing labor costs (Johnson and Kaplan 1991). Exaggerated labor rates gave the false impression that even small reductions in labor had major effects on reducing costs. As a result, these account controls created an incentive structure that encouraged managers to spend a great deal of time and effort reducing labor time, which had trivial effects on lowering costs.

Fourth, financial accounting overestimates product costs of low labor-intensive products and underestimates product cost of high labor-intensive products (Johnson and Kaplan 1991). Moreover, these account controls do not capture product costs that vary with indirect labor costs (e.g., materials handling, energy, inspection). As a result, pooled overhead costs cross-subsidize product costs by overestimating the cost of manufacturing high-volume products, and underestimating the cost to produce low-volume products. This problem did not surface when corporations were manufacturing a wide range of products in oligopolistic markets. However, when competitive markets returned in the 1970s and 1980s, managers could not determine whether they could compete with foreign corporations' product costs.

Fifth, these aggregated data do not provide production managers with cost variations that occur with changes in product mix. Although the accounting system was sensitive to changes in total cost, it did not provide the data to detect the source of this variation. Also, cross-subsidization of cost contributed to product proliferation because the higher costs of developing and setting up facilities to manufacture new products was absorbed in the aggregated costs to produce an entire product line.

Throughout the middle decades of the twentieth century, manager attention was directed almost solely on reducing labor costs. As the production process became increasingly capital intensive, changes in labor rates had only minor effects on total costs. This managerial behavior, however, had important effects. Strategies to cut labor costs by extracting more labor from the labor power purchased, contributed to conflict between workers and managers. By the 1960s and 1970s, corporate leadership acknowledged some of the weakness of the financial conception of control, and accountants attempted to make financial accounting data more useful to production managers. This resulted in incremental changes in the area of capital budgeting and ROI. These procedures, however, were not implemented in time to circumvent the cost-control crisis that emerged in the early 1980s.

Financial Accounting and Lost Relevance

This examination of historical sequences from the late nineteenth through the mid-twentieth centuries shows that two transformations occurred in the mode of control. After the prolonged crisis between 1873 and 1896, industrial capitalists began to endorse scientific management and the standardization of manufacturing by identifying the "one best way" to use labor and material. By 1910, most corporations established a managerial hierarchy to control the labor process, and set up controls over its expanding managerial hierarchy. These early account controls assessed the impact of product costs on profits. Some engineer-managers even developed systems to identify the managers responsible for product costs. Industrial capitalists set up these account controls to gain control over the manufacturing process because inside contractors were making high profits, not because inside contracting was a cost-inefficient method of production (Clawson 1980). After these controls were set up, capitalists reduced the authority of foremen and replaced inside contractors with professional managers.

Industrial capitalists' dependence on external capital markets produced a second shift in the mode of control. Financiers demanded that corporations develop methods to evaluate firms' financial strength and the efficient use of their capital. Dependent on these external capital markets, industrialists transformed cost management to financial management. Corporations set up centralized financial controls to assess corporate entities' ROI, evaluate the cost efficiency of corporations' product lines, and monitor middle managers' capacity to realize ROI and budget goals. However, there was an irrational dimension to these controls. Because corporations used the same technologies to make many products, financial controls did not measure variations in the costs to manufacture individual products.

Financial controls did not provide accurate information to monitor operating activities, assess the contribution of particular products to corporate profits, or evaluate the efficiency of managers' decisions. The information derived from these financial controls was misleading or irrelevant for product assessment and development decisions (Elnicki 1971; Johnson and Kaplan 1991). A crucial flaw was the assumption that the variable portion of the budget varies with direct labor activity. As labor intensity declined and corporations produced a wider range of products, pooled overhead costs and time-dependent financial data (e.g., monthly, quarterly) distorted the actual causes of product costs. Although capitalists lost sight of product costs, they did not lose sight of the benefits of the increased concentration and centralization of capital. The absorption of smaller firms by larger firms through mergers and acquisitions extended oligopolistic market power. This situation lowered the standard for cost efficiency satisficing. As corporations gained market power and the capacity to set prices, cost efficiency became less necessary to ensure profits.

Summary

This analysis shows that industrial capitalists' dependence on external capital markets created the context that allowed financial capitalists to set up a financial conception of control. Financial management was a crucial aspect of managing the modern corporation. Beginning in the early 1900s, financiers placed managers with finance backgrounds in the top managerial positions and on the board of directors of the largest industrial corporations. By the 1920s, financial and family capitalists set up financial controls over the managerial process.

My analysis is consistent with dimensions of previous sociological formations of the financial conception of control, but it also differs in important ways. Previous formulations of the financial conception of control emphasize short-term profits and the manipulation of assets to ensure growth through mergers and diversification (Fligstein 1990:2). My formulation of the financial conception of control, however, also stresses the emergence of finance capital and the effects of this capitalist class segment on (1) merger and acquisition strategies and (2) the development of internal managerial controls that stressed short-term return on investment. My analysis also contrasts with Fligstein's (1987, 1990) argument that the shift toward the financial conception of control occurred after the passage of the Celler-Kefauver Act (1950), the spread of the MDF, and the hiring of firm presidents with a background in finance. He suggests that the financial conception was only well established by 1979 when 33 of the largest 120 firms had presidents with a background in finance (Fligstein 1987:47, table 2). In contrast, my analysis shows that corporations have been pursuing merges and acquisitions to increase profits and appointing top managers with financial backgrounds since the turn of the twentieth century. Further, the emphasis on short-term profits began in the 1920s when financial and family capitalists began to set up time-based financial controls over the managerial process that emphasized return on investment.

My study suggests that efficiency arguments are misleading. There is no doubt that professional management grew throughout the twentieth century as managerial theory suggests. However, capitalists, not managers, restructured the system of control. Managers were embedded in an incentive system handed to them by capitalists to realize capitalists' agenda. Therefore, it is misleading to suggest that a managerial revolution occurred in the early twentieth century. It is more accurate to say that a revolution of finance capital occurred. This capitalist class segment exercised power and set up financial accounting to control professional managers. The financial concept on control was spread throughout the industrial sector when it became risky for these capitalists to invest all of their capital in one corporation or industry. After financiers invested in other corporations, they exercised their power and set up financial controls to assess and monitor the efficient use of their capital.

The study does not support marginal utility arguments, which assume that cost efficiency is the overriding incentive that explains capitalists' behavior. Similar to the managerial thesis, marginal utility perspectives assume that organizational change occurs when the marginal cost of discovering opportunities for gain within the firm exceeds the marginal costs of discovering opportunities for gain in the market (Williamson 1975). These arguments assume that capitalist behaviors are governed by a collective and unified conception of rationality. As shown here, capitalist class segments have competing interests based on their respective relationship to the capital accumulation process, and they exercise their power to achieve those interests. Thus, they have different conceptions of rationality. Their respective conceptions of rationality affected the kinds of account controls capitalist class segments set up and passed on to managers. Industrial capitalists set up product cost controls to ensure that they could manufacture products profitably. Later, financial capitalists set up financial controls to evaluate return on investment. Because industrial capitalists were dependent on these external capital markets they had little choice but to comply.

Because prevailing perspectives ignore conflict and power they cannot account for crucial empirical events. For example, this theoretical blind spot leads transaction cost analysis (TCA) to make several errors. Oligopolistic practices protected corporations from market competition. Case studies of General Motors, DuPont, Standard Oil of New Jersey (now Exxon), and Sears Roebuck are typically used to support these efficiency arguments. Each of these corporations exercised a significant degree of market power, making them inappropriate cases to test the TCA thesis. Further, because TCA undertheorizes power it never examines who set up financial controls and for what purpose. Because these researchers do not investigate these phenomena, they fail to acknowledge that the financial controls used in most corporations throughout the twentieth century were poorly equipped to assess costs. Controls over managers were based on ROI criteria, not cost efficiencies. They may have been rational from the perspective of financial capitalists, but not rational from the perspective of controlling costs. TCA fails to acknowledge that financial control did not provide managers with the kind of information to accurately evaluate the cost efficiency of their decisions. Further, in the absence of a managerial accounting system directing operating managers' attention toward product costs, TCA cannot evaluate whether managers made efficient or inefficient decisions.

Variations on marginal utility theory from Frederick Taylor to contemporary advocates of TCA assume that social actions are motivated by economic self-interest. Although self-interest affects behavior, it is not the only variable that effects social action. A central problem with TCA is it does not adequately acknowledge that social actors are embedded in social structures that create incentives and produce behaviors. A close examination of TCA's claims exposes a contradictory aspect of its argument. On the one hand, TCA suggests that the MDF is efficient because the reporting system put enormous pressure on divisional managers to comply with top-level goals. In this instance, they assert that social structures control behavior. On the other, TCA attributes inefficiencies in the MDF to self-interested behaviors (i.e., opportunism with guile), which suggests that social structures do not control behavior. TCA does not reconcile these contradictory arguments. If the reporting system in the MDF put enormous pressure on managers to comply, how is it possible for these same managers to pursue opportunism with guile?

TCA advocates represent a long tradition in managerial theory (e.g. Chester Barnard), which assumes that social structures are rational and create the appropriate incentives to achieve desired ends and that individuals are irrational. That is, only self-interested behaviors produce inefficiencies, not behaviors that occur in response to incentives established to achieve certain ends (e.g., financial control).

Others have pointed out that marginal utility explanations do not conform to realistic empirical situations. Agency theory uses simple decision-making situations in firms that represent one stage of the manufacturing process and produce few products (Johnson and Kaplan 1991; Kaplan 1982). This is in sharp contrast to the reality of the modern corporation where managers are confronted with decisions concerning the production of hundreds and frequently thousands of products.

By failing to account for historical sequences, efficiency arguments incorrectly assume that financial controls created an incentive system that structured managers' motives and actions so that these controls could produce behaviors that advanced corporations' agenda. Efficiency arguments falsely assume that the means were adequate to realize the ends. These arguments fail to acknowledge that capitalists constructed financial controls intended to monitor and assess the efficient use of their capital. They also fail to examine the effects of the financial conception of control and the concomitant incentive structure on managers' behavior.

CHAPTER 6

The Management of Managers at American Steel, 1920–1970s

Managerial and economic perspectives champion the efficiency of the modern corporation. Alfred Chandler (1990) argues that although oligopolies emerged in many industries, competition within industries pressured managers to increase their strategic and operating skills. Oliver Williamson considers the MDF more efficient than the departmentalized functional and holding-company forms because it establishes strategic planning, resource allocation, and monitoring and control systems (Williamson 1985). These researchers assume that large corporations are efficient because of the way in which they have internalized market functions. They narrowly conceptualize efficiency as an organizational attribute and assume that inefficiencies are recognizable and managers and owners set up rational and efficient methods to solve organizational dilemmas. They assume that basis of corporate change is the dynamic interplay between managers and the organizational structure whereby managers transform the organization to make it more functionally efficient, and that the mode of control within which managers are embedded creates an incentive structure that produces rational managerial actions (i.e., decisions) when evaluated in terms of corporate goals (Prechel 1991:425).[1]

In contrast to these theories, capital-dependence theory does not attribute rationality or efficiency to the corporation. Rather, the theory suggests that efficiency considerations are historically contingent and the mode of control is, in part, the outcome of power struggles within the capitalist class. During historical periods when profits are at acceptable levels, little emphasis on efficiency exists. In contrast, efficiency considerations become pivotal under other historical conditions. Moreover, many variables external to the firm affect efficiency and result in increased emphasis on efficiency. External variables may result in higher operating costs, which lowers cash flow and the capacity to generate the capital necessary to finance operations from internal sources (Prechel 1991:437).[2]

The theoretical logic explicit within capital-dependence theory suggests that corporations' embeddedness in institutional arrangements affect their efficiency. State business policy including corporate income-tax rates, depreciation schedules, and tax credits affect cash flow and corporations' capacity to finance operations. Also, changes in the economic environment (e.g., energy costs, inflation rates, interest rates, slow economic growth) can undermine efficiency by increasing costs-per-unit output. Further, the entrance of a more cost-efficient producer into a market niche can depress prices, reducing the existing producers' efficiency whose costs remain stable. Even if prices remain stable (e.g., in an oligopolistic market structure), a new producer that employs more advanced technologies will have lower costs. Although the second scenario is a less serious threat to short-term effectiveness (i.e., profit rates) when oligopolistic markets exist, corporations' relative efficiency is important because financiers are less attracted to corporations whose per-unit costs exceed their competitors' cost structures. Corporations with high cost structures receive lower bond rating and must pay higher interest rates. This constrains cash flow and their capacity to attract capital from external capital markets. This situation reduces corporations' capacity to reinvest into more efficient manufacturing facilities, reducing effective pursuit of organizational goals (Raff and Temin 1991).

Changes in market demand also affect efficiency. Rapid economic growth and high demand increase *capability utilization rate*: the ratio between production capability and output. Organizational contradictions and irrationalities that contribute to higher costs, therefore, do not always lower formal efficiency measurements because high utilization rates reduce per-unit costs (Child 1972:17). In contrast, economic downturns lower utilization rates, which lowers efficiency measurements by increasing per-unit costs. Macro economic changes that undermine efficiency may block goal realization because higher costs relative to revenues undermine profits. That is, declining efficiency can but does not always undermine effectiveness (Prechel 1991:428). Disequilibrium within the corporate form manifested as declining efficiency, therefore, is typically only acknowledged by management when the corporate form moves into disequilibrium with its environment followed by effectiveness *crisis*, the failure of the corporation to realize goals.

Unraveling Efficiency and Effectiveness

Despite the emphasis placed on efficiency by organizational researchers, little progress has been made toward resolution of efficiency debates. The failure to resolve these debates is due to methodological and theoretical shortcomings.

Few attempts are made to measure efficiency. Thus, researchers fail to provide a criterion to ascertain when an organization is efficient or inefficient. Instead of examining the efficiency of the managerial process, managerialist and TCA proponents assume that if a corporate form survived it is efficient (i.e., economizes on costs). Many factors contribute to organizational survival. Inefficient corporations may survive and even prosper under some conditions. Economic and managerial theories fail to acknowledge that an inefficient corporate form may prosper if principles have the power to influence the state so that business policies protect corporations from competition, provide access to external capital markets, or improve internal cash flows.

Important conceptual shortcomings restrict an understanding of efficiency. For example, key concepts are too often presented as empirical absolutes, rather than as theoretical constructs that aid in the understanding of the empirical (Prechel 1990:650). Characterizing the functional departmentalized form as centralized and the MDF as decentralized may be useful for broad comparisons of corporate forms. The failure to treat centralization and decentralization as theoretical constructs that aid in the understanding of phenomena, however, results in a distorted and flawed understanding of empirical reality. Beginning with Chandler (1962) many researchers from different theoretical perspectives associate extreme decentralization with holding companies, centralization with departmentalized functional form, and decentralization with the MDF (Williamson 1985; Fligstein 1990). Centralization and decentralization *within* corporate forms, however, is historically contingent; General Motors' MDF was centralized in the mid-1930s, decentralized in the 1940s, and centralized in the 1960s (Freeland 1996). A problem with prevailing organizational theories is they narrowly defined the parameters of the empirical inquiry and then ignore important variables. As a result, theories frequently encourage insufficient depth of analysis. This becomes particularly problematic when alternate theories do not emerge that challenge the conclusions of prevailing theories, identify alternate variables, and formulate alternate hypotheses that direct researchers' attention toward different phenomena.

One important shortcoming in current organizational theory is the failure to examine the ways in which the combination of controls—whether centralized or decentralized—affects incentive structures that direct managers' behavior. In this chapter and in chapter 8, I examine historical processes in an attempt to unravel the issues of centralization and decentralization and their effects on managers' motives and behaviors. To do so, I move beyond current theory that tends to conceptualize decision making and authority as the same variable (Prechel 1994b:726). That is, decision-making authority is frequently presented as centralized or decentralized. As a result, control and decision making are frequently incorrectly understood as located in the same place in the corporation.

Rather than making assumptions of organizational rationality and efficiency, the analysis here acknowledges the potential for irrationality and conflict among dimensions of the social structure, and the temporality of equilibria. This theoretical framework suggests that formal rational control may be irrational in relationship to substantively rational goals of the corporation. It cannot be assumed that formal rationality produces substantively rational outcomes. The objective is to understand better the internal dynamics of the managerial process. Explicit within this analysis is that efficiency is only one of many variables that affects whether a corporate form or a managerial process survives. Efficiency must be understood in context of a range of other variables including the historically specific conditions that affect corporations' capacity to accumulate capital. For these reasons, I employ a case-oriented method because it provides sufficient depth of analysis to examine the many variables—including the incentive structure—that affect managers' behavior.

The following focuses on micro-level dynamics to examine how meso-level phenomena (i.e., corporate governance, incentive structures) affect behavior. Particular attention is given to how financial control affects the incentive structure over time, its effects on both the interests and actions of managers, and social relations among managers at the point of production. Analyses of the point of production are crucial. This is the organizational level where the controls are ultimately oriented toward and, historically, where operating decisions are made. If irrationalities or contradictions in the managerial process exist, they should be manifested at this level.

Historical Case-Oriented Study: American Steel

The following is a historical case study of the managerial process in a large integrated steel plant (i.e., a plant that produces steel from raw materials). This corporation was created in the depression during the late nineteenth century and became one of the largest U.S. steel corporations by the late 1970s. While other corporations are larger than American Steel (a pseudonym),[3] it has one of the largest steel plants in the United States, covering approximately nineteen hundred acres. By the late 1970s, the average employment in this plant was 24,000, which included 6,000 managers. This corporation was selected because it is typical of many other industrial corporations: (1) it operated in oligopolistic markets throughout much of the twentieth century (2) it operated a large manufacturing facility where decision-making authority was delegate to middle managers, and (3) it controlled operating managers through an account-control system based on financial controls.

American Steel is an appropriate case to study. Throughout the middle decades of the twentieth century it was more efficient and effective than other steel corporations. American Steel was considered by steel industry analysts to have the most progressive management of the large integrated steel corporations. Therefore, it was not less efficient than other corporations. Yet I will show glaring inefficiencies in its managerial process. If a shortcoming in selecting American Steel for this case study exists, that flaw is because this corporation may underestimate inefficiencies in the managerial process in other U.S. corporations.

The Capital Accumulation Strategy in the Oligopolistic Era

A distinctive characteristic of the U.S. steel industry between the early 1900s and the 1960s was its oligopolistic structure, comprising two important dimensions. Prices were based on a markup over costs, and market demand was closely coordinated with industry production capability. This oligopolistic behavior ensured high utilization rates and a stable rate of return for the major integrated producers. Although these oligopolistic practices eliminated "cutthroat competition," the large integrated producers continued to compete for market share to maximize utilization rates.

To capture a large market share, like other expanding corporations, American Steel manufactured a wide range of products and maintained a high degree of flexibility in its manufacturing process. This flexibility allowed the corporation to adjust to market shifts, ensuring high utilization rates. The flexible manufacturing strategy, however, was not cost efficient per unit because production changes increased labor costs and increased the probability of managerial error. As a result, initial runs often produced low-quality steel. Despite its inefficiencies, as long as the steel oligopoly coordinated prices with costs, this strategy remained superior to manufacturing a narrow product line, liable to low utilization rates upon market shifts.

Controlling the Production Process

In addition to articulating corporate strategy, like other large corporations (Chandler 1962; Johnson 1991), American Steel's top management remained engaged in day-to-day manufacturing decisions through the first four decades of the twentieth century. Two features contributed to top managements' knowledge of the manufacturing process. First, like most corporations in this period (Chandler 1990), American Steel had a policy of promotion from within. Top managers' tenure with the corporation typically began in production, which frequently included training through apprenticeship programs and other formal technical training in areas such as engineering and metallurgy. The acquisition of technical and craft knowledge familiarized top management with the company's technologies and manufacturing processes.

Second, once promoted to the top jobs, top managers remained involved in day-to-day operating decisions. For example, at American Steel, top management met every morning to review incoming orders, schedule the production units, and coordinate the manufacturing process. Moreover, American Steel's CEOs made regular site visits to the manufacturing facilities. (This practice continued through the 1960s.) Regular contact with the point of production continually updated top managements' understanding of the manufacturing process. Knowledge obtained from these nonaccounting sources allowed top management to directly oversee and monitor a wide range of operating and coordinating decisions. Moreover, because of their knowledge of steel-making and regular contact with operating management, top managers could monitor the cost-cutting efforts of these managers. Top management's participation in manufacturing decisions provided them with an understanding of both the process and the cost associated with the various phases of manufacturing.

Changes in American Steel's economic environment, however, resulted in strategic decisions that changed the corporate structure so that top managerial control at the point of production became less feasible. The Great Depression (1929–1933), a second economic contraction (1937–1938), and slow economic growth throughout the 1930s lowered American Steel's utilization rate below the *break even* point, the utilization rate required for profit (figure 6.1).

American Steel's strategy to overcome this capital-accumulation crisis and to reduce the threat to profit making during future economic contractions included forward integration into the market, resulting in horizontal differentiation of the corporation. Many of these acquisitions were incorporated as subsidiaries. This strategy guaranteed steel markets, increasing American Steel's capability utilization rate. As a middle manager told me: "These acquisitions were all an extension of our steel making strategy. In other words, the biggest reason for acquiring them was to sell more of our own steel, to market our own steel." In the late 1930s, American Steel implemented a strategy to exploit the profit-making opportunities that occurred because of the economic recovery and wartime demand for steel, further expanding its production capability, size, and degree of horizontal differentiation. Growth and more complexification, however, resulted in bounded rationality, undermining top management's ability to coordinate day-to-day operations. This delayed manufacturing schedules, which lowered utilization rates and the efficient use of resources (e.g., labor, machinery).

Although American Steel's top management maintained control over several organizational activities during the first decades of its history, expansion and the manufacture of many different products restricted top managerial control. Like top management of other expanding corporations, American Steel applied scientific management (e.g., Taylorism, Fordism) techniques to the production process to increase productivity and control the labor process. The primary means to ensure control included centralizing quantitative data into planning offices where engineers established behavioral controls, which included work rules, reducing jobs to

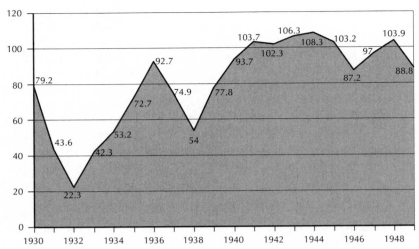

FIGURE 6.1 Capability utilization rate at American Steel, 1930–1949. Utilization rates are higher than 100 percent when production facilities exceed their technical rating, which is based on a specified number of operating hours in a given time period. *Source:* Corporate documents.

their elemental components, and identifying and discarding perceived inefficient movements.

However, several obstacles limited the application of scientific management in industries such as metalworking and steel making. Manufacturing in these kinds of industries includes numerous variables and many permutations of these variables for each product. In addition, many products have unique specifications. Taylorism undermined flexibility strategies in two important ways. First, establishing and setting up rules restricted the manufacturing flexibility necessary to meet the unique product specifications of customers. Second, and most important, corporations' wide product line limited the degree to which bureaucratic controls could be set up. Establishing and setting up rules governing the manufacture of thousands of products is not only complex, but it restricts the flexibility to adjust the manufacturing process when problems emerge at the point of production. Hence, in these kinds of industries it is often easier to provide guidelines than definitive rules for every variable, and the modifications of these variables for each product (e.g., melting time, temperature, rolling pressure, etc.) (Shaiken 1984; Thomas 1994).

These developments created a contradictory situation between top management's desire to maintain centralized control—which entailed embedding production managers in an elaborate set of bureaucratic controls—and the need to retain flexibility at the point of production. The complexity of the manufacturing process restricts the degree to which Taylorism and Fordism could separate conception from execution and establish the "one best way" to manufacture a product. To overcome this incompatibility between centralized control and organizational complexity, top managers allocated decision-making authority over the steel manufacturing process to middle managers. As a manager at corporate headquarters put it:

> Around the 1940s, top management was convinced by outsiders or consultants that [retaining control over the manufacturing process] was no way to run a business. You get the orders to the factory to make sure the production process is not delayed.

Unable to overcome the contradiction between centralization and flexibility, the loci of discretion over many decisions were allocated to the point of production where managers exercised decision-making discretion based on their knowledge and understanding of the manufacturing process. The technical limitations of scientific management resulted in decentralized control over production (also see Burawoy 1979, 1985; Silver 1982).

Decentralization of decision-making authority continued during the late 1940s when post–World War II economic expansion resulted in rapid growth throughout the steel industry. To take advantage of the market opportunities between 1945 and 1959, American Steel expanded its iron making capability, almost doubled its steel making capability, and purchased a large Canadian iron-ore reserve to ensure a steady supply of low-cost raw materials.

In summary, the capital accumulation constraints throughout the first half of the century resulted in four organizational changes. First, expansion into the market furthered *horizontal differentiation,* the diversification of organizational units (Hall 1987). Second, organizational complexity and bounded rationality required top management to decentralize control over the managerial process. Third, like most large corporations (e.g., DuPont, General Motors), top management established bureaucratic controls and financial account controls to monitor lower- and middle-level management. Fourth, the limitations of bureaucratic controls required that top management allocate decision-making authority to operating managers. Financial control became the primary source of top managerial control. As a corporate middle manager told me: "From that point on financial controls were determined at the general office, but that was about the extent of the coordination." Whereas American Steel used ROI to evaluate the different product lines of its divisions and subsidiaries (e.g., real estate, steel, containers), it used budgets to evaluate organizational units within the divisions and subsidiaries. Budget control calculates the receipts and expenditures of each unit at the end of an accounting period (Weber 1978; Johnson and Kaplan 1991).

Further Delegation of Decision-Making Authority, 1950s–1960s

By 1960, the size and complexity of the manufacturing facility had increased significantly, and supervision of the functional units exceeded the cognitive limits of the managers and assistant general managers. To overcome these constraints, American Steel delegated decision-making authority from general managers to managers, superintendents, and assistant superintendents. This relocation of the loci of discretion shifted authority further down the managerial hierarchy to managers who based their decisions on their knowledge of the manufacturing process. These middle managers were responsible for the individual production units and retained authority over their respective units. Once top management relinquished direct control, it specified more detailed bureaucratic controls (e.g., span of control, area of responsibility) over these middle managers. Top management devoted most of its time to assessing the problems and prospects of the corporation, formulating strategy, and making capital-investment decisions.

Similar to previous efforts to establish bureaucratic control to routinize decisions, the complexity of steel-making placed limits on the degree to which rules could effectively routinize decisions. On the one hand, bureaucratic controls could not govern decisions regarding coordination because it is difficult to establish rules governing processes that require the linking of several production units. As in other expanding corporations, personal cooperation among middle managers became the means of coordinating the production units and aligning the flow of materials through the manufacturing process (Chandler 1977). On the other hand, the numerous variables in the steel-making process, together with the extensiveness of American Steel's product line, made it difficult to establish rules and regulations to govern production decisions.

The complexity of steel manufacturing restricted the degree to which the corporation could set up centralized control in two functional areas of the corporation. On the one hand, informal control remained the primary means of governing many production decisions and coordinating linkages among the production units. On the other, middle managers retained decision-making authority at the point of production where they based decisions on their understanding of the manufacturing process. Taylorist and Fordist efforts were limited because it is difficult to establish work rules over manufacturing processes that require flexibility and frequent changes.

Like top management, middle managers obtained knowledge of the manufacturing process by working their way up the managerial hierarchy, which typically included apprenticeship programs whereby they learned the craft tradition. After they were assigned to a manufacturing facility, production managers obtained much of their decision-making information informally, and based their decisions on their general knowledge of the manufacturing process. The manager of a mill that had more than five hundred employees stated: "[I would obtain information] from the morning reports, what the assistants would tell me, from walking around, watching the production sheets, and a general feel of what was happening." Middle-level production managers had access to the information, processed that information, determined what was to be done, authorized what was to be done, and executed the decision (Mintzberg 1979). In short, these managers retained control over the four conception steps and the final execution step of the decision-making process. After the loci of decision-making discretion were decentralized, the operating units functioned semiautonomously of one another.

Throughout this period, American Steel had a hybrid corporate form. Its large steel business was organized like a division and the relationship between the central office and this large corporate entity resembled the MDF. Decision-making authority was delegated to middle managers and top management used account controls (e.g., ROI, budget) to monitor them. American Steel also had several product lines organized as subsidiaries that operated independently of the central office.

Incremental Changes in the Account-Control System

Expansion and diversification resulted in trends toward decentralized decision making. Like other corporations, American Steel's top management relinquished control over the operating units. Very little information was available, however, to evaluate whether operating managers efficiently used the resources allocated to them. To overcome this impediment to top managerial control, American Steel collected more detailed data to monitor and control managerial behaviors.

Changes in the account-control system were driven, in part, by product merger and acquisition strategies. Different corporations frequently used different methods of accounting and financial reporting. After some corporations acquired others, incompatibilities between accounting methods and financial reports made it difficult to compare their contribution to the parent company's capital-accumulation goal. This lack of standardization created problems for the accounting staff responsible for establishing a system of cost control, assessing the financial strength of the corporation, and providing a basis for top management to make capital-allocation decisions.

To overcome this problem the *standard cost system* was established to standardize and centralize cost information, and improve the accuracy and comparability of cost data from various organizational units. The standard cost system collects cost data over a period of time to determine average costs, and establishes a standard cost that is comparable to actual costs. By the 1950s, most firms incorporated the standard-cost system (Johnson and Kaplan 1991). During this period, American Steel also moved the comptroller position (i.e., the chief accountant) to a higher level in the managerial hierarchy, just below the vice president of finance.

Centralizing the comptroller function was part of the shift toward placing more importance on accounting activities and allocating more authority over corporate governance to this activity.

In addition, the standardized cost data provided top management and its administrative staff with information to establish operating budgets for the various departments within the steel-making segment of the business. This change placed more emphasis on budget controls, which became the primary means to determine the technical efficiency of each department. These gradual, incremental changes embedded lower- and middle-level production managers more deeply into this formally rational system of control.

A second sphere of rational calculation entailed the development of more precise forecasting models. By the early 1960s, American Steel began to collect more detailed product-cost data and used cost and market data to develop increasingly sophisticated financial-modeling systems to specify its forecasts. *Financial modeling* derives a set of equations that describe the input and output flow of materials and services, the costs incurred, and the revenues generated to evaluate alternative financial strategies. Management considered these developments a major breakthrough in profit forecasting and cost management. As one of American Steel's middle managers stated:

> Modeling provided the means to open up a whole new spectrum of profit planning and economic evaluation. Financial modeling was a major breakthrough in financial and strategic planning comparable to the development of computers and rockets.

Historically, corporate forecasting served two separate purposes. Forecast provided a means to evaluate operations by comparing the rate of return on investment (i.e., ROI) of operating units to its product-pricing strategies, and to identify the conditions under which to allocate capital for expansion.

Forecasting was also used to manage cost. Forecasts are intended to serve the dual purpose of comparing production cost with prices, and controlling internal operations. This dimension of the account-control system provided a mechanism to evaluate internal operations in terms of market considerations (Weber 1978; Chandler 1962). Financial modeling uses two types of data to control costs, coordinate production with consumption, and monitor the managerial process. On the one hand, financial modeling treats *cost data* (e.g., standard manufacturing and processing costs, yields, labor productivity) as if it were time independent. On the other, *market data* are treated as time dependent because they are subject to changes in the market (e.g., prices). The financial model used these data to test alternative planning assumptions and strategies for the annual budget and profit plan. American Steel's specific objectives included the development and continual improvement of a five-year profit plan, the analysis of facility investment alternatives, and the improvement of cash-flow forecasts.

Global Competition and Intensification of Rational Calculation

By the early 1960s, capital accumulation conditions in the U.S. economy began to change. While the U.S. economy was built, in part, on consumption demands in World War II and in the postwar era, by the late 1950s and early 1960s many European countries had reconstructed their industries and were shipping products to foreign markets. Because of its extensive markets, the United States was a prime target for the expanding industries abroad. These changes became apparent first in the steel industry. By the late 1950s, imports exceeded exports. Whereas the mean steel imports were 1.8 percent between 1955 and 1958, imports captured 5.8 percent of the market between 1960 and 1964.

Its market threatened, American Steel implemented two strategies. On the one hand, American Steel mobilized politically with other steel corporations and industrial capitalists to lobby for legislation to protect U.S. markets and improve its cash flow (see chapter 7). On the other, it intensified rational calculation to better control operating cost in its increasingly competitive economic environment. The corporation placed more emphasis on accounting activities. Corporate accountants identified and collected more cost points to better predict and control corporate entities' cost.

By the late 1960s, American Steel began to redesign its account-control system to evaluate the relationship between product cost and profitability. This system—derived from the standard cost and forecasting systems—added a crucial component to American Steel's account-control system. *Profitability accounting* uses cost data to identify specific product costs in more detail, thereby moving away from average product costs. These more precise calculations made it possible to generate the average cost and profit estimates for eighteen of American Steel's most important product-groups, versus its product lines. This development is important because is represented a major step toward more precise calculation of product costs from product lines to product groups (e.g., flat rolled steel, bar steel). However, it is important to note that each product group may include dozens of products. Once American Steel set up financial modeling and profitability accounting, the accounting activity focused on increasing the accuracy of the cost and profit estimates of these product groups. These estimates had two effects. First, they provided information to calculate more precisely the income-yielding power of the various departments. Second, these changes embedded production managers into a more precisely defined set of controls, creating incentive to ensure certain behavior and allowing top management to more closely evaluate the cost efficiency of their behavior (e.g., decisions).

These changes occurred in response to historical contingencies. When economic conditions constrained capital accumulation, American Steel intensified its account controls. American Steel attempted to develop a system that allowed them to capture cost changes within an accounting period (e.g., month, quarter) to increase control. As a corporate accountant stated:

> It was very much historical in nature, the feeling developed that it would be very advantageous if we could develop some systematic profit forecasting while the [accounting] period was alive so that remedial action could be taken. And that led to a formal consolidated profit estimate every Monday morning. There was an ongoing emphasis, throughout that period, on the value of this weekly forecasting as an immediate *control tool.*

These developments are important because they reflect how American Steel attempted to overcome a crucial flaw in financial accounting: the inability to provide production managers with current information. The conceptualization of what was necessary to ensure control costs, however, remained unchanged. Like previous controls, these account-controls aggregated product cost to evaluate organizational units. These changes simply provided a more precise means to compare actual costs to standard costs, and to monitor and evaluate operating managers' capacity to control organizational unit costs.

Concomitant with these changes, American Steel intensified *Systems:* the organizational entity that develops and integrates computer applications into the managerial and production processes. Throughout this period, Systems was financed from the budgets allocated to organization entities, and provided support services to those entities. Hence, Systems remained decentralized and responded to the specialized needs of the various organizational entities. Systems was initially divided into two units: (1) *Business Systems* which was located at the corporate offices and performed accounting functions for the sales department, and (2) *Accounting Systems* which performed services for the steel-manufacturing units.

As competitive pressures in the steel industry increased in the mid-1960s, however, American Steel began to centralize Systems and its disparate databases. In 1967, Systems was centralized under the comptroller of steel manufacturing. This change provided the organizational structure to centralize two critical dimensions of its information gathering activities. First, American Steel merged sales and manufacturing data into one location.[4] This centralization allowed the corporation to provide more precise information to its customers, which gave it a competitive edge over other integrated steel corporations. American Steel became the first integrated steel corporation to provide customers with expected completion dates on their orders. Second, in 1966 American Steel began to integrate its accounting system with the financial modeling process, and in 1969 it completed a computerized financial model for the steel-manufacturing operations. To better understand the cost associated with capital investments in plant, equipment, and personnel, American Steel began to use computerized forecasting techniques to anticipate future economic conditions and steel demand. By the 1970s, extreme fluctuations in

the steel market, due partially to imports of selected products, made it more difficult to predict profit-making opportunities. Top management became more reliant
on financial modeling to forecast market demand and plan operating activities.

In summary, throughout the 1960s, American Steel collected more precise data,
developed more precise forecasting models, introduced more powerful computing
technologies, and integrated accounting and market data into a centralized database. Despite these advances, because American Steel's account-control system was
based on a financial conception of control (i.e., return on investment), it continued
to base its cost projections on entire product groups, and cost controls focused on
organizational units. Middle management continued to use these data to improve
the production-control functions. That is, the intensification of rational calculation made more information available, but its use varied little from the 1950s. Like
other corporations, financial accounting at American Steel examined the flow of
inventory through corporate entities in its large steel-manufacturing unit.

Declining Efficiency and Further Diversification

Despite changes in American Steel's account-control system, its costs steadily increased. American Steel's escalating costs are illustrated by examining the relationship between capability utilization rates and *operating profit margin*: the percentage of gross revenues remaining after all costs and expenses other than
non-operating expenses such as interest and income taxes are deducted (Moody's
1987). Trends in the operating profit margin indicate corporations' degree of con-

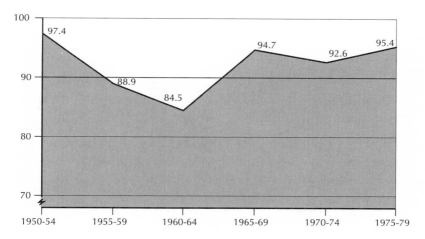

FIGURE 6.2 Capability utilization rate at American Steel, 1950–1979. The utilization
rate in 1958 and 1959 declined in part because of the 1958 recession, and the 116 day
strike in 1959. *Source:* Corporate documents.

trol over operating expenses (e.g., labor, raw material, energy) (Moody's 1987; Hage and Aiken 1970; Prechel 1991:429). Generally, as capability utilization rates increase, operating profit margins increase because per-unit costs decline. However, despite increasing utilization rates—from 88.9 percent in the second half of the 1950s to 94.7 percent in that of the 1960s (figure 6.2)—operating profit margin declined by 3 percent (figure 6.3). While American Steel's costs increased, the more cost-efficient domestic minimills and foreign steel makers began to expand their market share. As a result, the oligopolistic market structure of the steel industry began to erode.

However, in 1966 economic forecasters projected a 2 percent increase in demand per year over the next five years. Although this is a relatively low growth rate, the future looked bright for the U.S. steel industry because these growth rates were in addition to the high production levels of the 1965–66 boom years when steel shipments jumped from 76.6 million tons in 1963 to 92.7 million tons in 1965. To increase efficiency and to take advantage of these capital accumulation opportunities, most steel corporations initiated a strategy to invest into more productive and cost-cutting technologies.

American Steel's top management assumed that it would have little trouble raising the capital to finance its strategy. Two political economic conditions limited its dependence on external capital markets. On the one hand, despite rising costs, economic growth and high utilization rates generated high cash flow throughout the 1960s.[5] On the other, two state business policies strengthened American Steel's

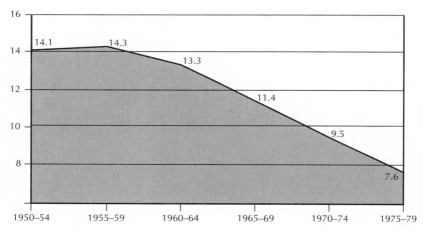

FIGURE 6.3 Operating profit margin at American Steel, 1950–1979. *Source:* Moody's *Handbook of Common Stocks,* various years.

cash flow. First, the construction of the interstate highway system increased demand for steel throughout the 1960s. Second, the *Revenue Tax Act of 1962* provided tax credits to manufacturing corporations and shortened depreciation periods. The shorter depreciation periods were particularly advantageous to capital-intensive industries such as steel.

Diversification Strategies and Higher Costs

Economic forecasts for the steel industry were based on faulty assumptions; analysts failed to account for the decline in the *steel intensity* of the economy (i.e., steel's percentage of the gross national product) (Barnett and Schorsch 1983). By the late 1960s, analysts predicted that long-term growth in demand was unlikely. Together with declining profits this situation resulted in a drop in steel stocks from 169 percent to less than 50 percent of their book value between 1958 and 1971 (Acs 1984). This combination of high cash flow and low stock-market prices created cash cows of most steel companies, making them attractive takeover candidates. The acquisition of such companies improves the acquiring corporations' cash flow.

Five of the top twenty steel corporations were the targets of takeovers in 1968, and nine steel corporations were acquired by conglomerates (Hogan 1972; Scheuerman 1975). In addition to the incentives for taking over corporations with high cash flow, interest on debt securities issued to acquire these corporations are defined as business expenses and therefore, tax deductions. The largest takeover in U.S. history ($425 million), to that date, was the acquisition of Jones and Laughlin Steel (J&L), the seventh largest steel company in the U.S. The takeover of J&L Steel by Ling-Temco Vought (LTV) caused steel corporations to pressure the federal government to test the applicability of the antitrust laws to conglomerate mergers.[6] On May 24, 1969, the Justice Department filed a suit to stop the acquisition. On May 27, 1969, however, the Justice Department made an agreement with LTV to allow it to retain ownership of J&L if LTV allowed J&L to operate as an independent company (i.e., as a subsidiary).[7]

Although the LTV-J&L case reflected a more critical approach by the Justice Department to conglomerate acquisitions, this event was most important because of the way in which it affected corporate consolidation strategies. First, this antitrust decision reversed the institutional arrangement discouraging corporations from incorporating mergers and acquisitions as subsidiaries. Now, incorporating a merger or acquisition as a subsidiary appeared to reduce the probability of an antitrust challenge. Several subsequent consolidations in the steel industry occurred through subsidiaries. Granite City Steel Company was taken over by National Steel and incorporated as a wholly owned subsidiary corporation. Crucible Steel became a subsidiary of Colt Industries (Hogan 1972).

Second, this takeover resulted in two defensive strategies by steel corporations: (1) increasing their dividend payments and (2) diversifying into nonsteel industries.

Both decisions were based on the prevailing conception of the legitimate corporate strategy. Steel corporations increased dividends to raise stockholders' and stock analysts' confidence, assuming that higher stock values would follow, increasing the cost of takeover, and reducing this threat. They diversified into more profitable industries to simultaneously raise profits and stock values. Higher stock values impede takeovers because they increase the cost of acquisition. Also, diversification increases organizational complexity, which requires a wider range of skills to manage, also making the corporations less desirable takeover targets. Although takeover threats catalyzed diversification in the steel industry, this strategy was also pursued because the prevailing managerial ideology assumed that a diversified company was best able to survive fluctuations in economic sectors.

Like the industry as a whole, American Steel's failure to control its costs and its eroding profit levels steadily lowered the value of its stock throughout the 1960s. American Steel was threatened with a takeover in the late 1960s. In response to the takeover threat and the increasingly competitive economic conditions, American Steel implemented a diversification strategy into more profitable industries. As a corporate manager put it:

> The acquisitions were done to protect against a takeover, and exploit opportunities for profitable growth in areas outside the traditional spheres of activity that had a better profit outlook.

Between 1969 and 1970, American Steel entered into two joint ventures and formed a subsidiary that included four additional companies. By the mid-1970s, it controlled eight properties in unrelated markets, including the plastic, real estate, computer, and machine industries. Diversification further decentralized decision making. By the 1970s, American Steel had a combination of divisions and subsidiaries.

These decisions at this historical juncture (i.e., mid-1960s–early 1970s) were crucial because they diverted funds away from cost-containing modernization projects in the steel industry at a time when the industry had a high cash flow. Capital expenditures on diversification increased from $131 million in 1956 to $1.14 billion in 1975; the steel industry spent 30 cents of every investment dollar on nonsteel business activities between 1969 and 1971 (Acs 1984). In short, efficiency considerations were secondary to defending against a takeover and pursuing profitability opportunities in other industries.

Profit-Making Opportunities, Expansion, and More Organizational Complexity, 1970s

In the early 1970s, both global and domestic steel consumption increased—the latter from 97.1 (1970) to 122.5 (1973) million tons—raising certain product-line prices. For example, the market prices of steel plates rose from $119 a ton in January 1972 to $560 in August 1974 (Hogan 1983:16). In 1973, imports declined to 12.4

from 16.6 percent (1972), and economic forecasters predicted a 3 percent annual increase in domestic steel consumption throughout the decade (American Iron and Steel Institute 1974; Hogan 1972:1–3). Higher demand increased utilization rates, mitigating profitability problems. In 1974, American Steel realized the highest rate of return since 1950, and its rate of return in the second half of the 1970s was its highest since 1955–59 (figure 6.4).

Moreover, American Steel's rate of return on equity was 10 percent for the 1970s, a slight increase from the 1960s. Although American Steel's capability utilization rate remained approximately the same (figure 6.2), its operating profit margin (i.e., efficiency) dropped from 12.4 in the 1960s to 8.6 in the 1970s (figure 6.3). In short, although its efficiency declined, because of price increases American Steel's effectiveness remained stable (figure 6.4).

To exploit these profit-making opportunities, American Steel implemented a strategy to expand its steel operations. The corporation increased its raw material holdings, expanded its coke-producing facilities, and constructed one of the largest basic oxygen furnaces in North America. These changes significantly increased its steel-making capability, and increased its size and degree of horizontal differentiation. Expansion during this historical juncture resulted in profit levels throughout the 1970s similar to those in the 1960s.

Although American Steel centralized certain activities (e.g., coordination of sales and manufacturing), expansion and diversification increased complexity and decentralization of other activities. The corporation realigned top management,

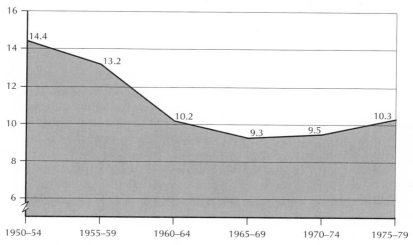

FIGURE 6.4 Rate of return on equity after taxes at American Steel, 1950–1979.
Source: Moody's *Handbook of Common Stocks,* various years.

created more levels in the managerial hierarchy, and allocated decision-making authority to operating managers. By the mid-1960s, American Steel had eight layers of management within its steel-manufacturing operations.

To maintain control over the various organizational units, top management continued to rely on financial accounting, using budgets and ROI to evaluate the efficiency of the organizational entities. As the managerial hierarchy increased and operating units expanded, these accounting controls became the primary criterion to evaluate middle managers' skills and to "ascertain if they merited a salary increase" (American Steel manager). These policies were a continuation of past policies where organizational entities operated *semiautonomously:* they retained control over internal operations but were financially responsible to the general office. These organizational controls embedded operating management in an account-control system that evaluated their performance by budgetary controls, ROI, and the flow of inventory, creating an incentive structure that encouraged operating managers to rapidly move material through the production process.

In summary, change in American Steel's strategy and structure throughout the 1960s and 1970s was affected by changing macro-level conditions of capital accumulation and state business policy. The *Revenue Tax Act of 1962* increased cash flow, providing corporations with additional capital to modernize their manufacturing facilities. Although the desired effect of this state policy was to improve cash flow, these tax breaks were so lucrative that they made steel corporations potential takeover targets. To avoid a takeover and take advantage of capital-accumulation opportunities in other economic sectors, American Steel used much of the capital from this state business policy to diversify and pay high dividends. And, in the mid-1970s, American Steel implemented an expansion strategy to take advantage of the booming steel economy. By the late 1970s, American Steel had one of North America's largest and most complex integrated steel plants, employed six thousand managers, and manufactured more than five thousand different steel products. These changes all contribute to expansion and complexification of the corporate structure and gradual, incremental decentralization of decision-making authority. American Steel controlled its operating managers' behavior by embedding them in systems based in a financial conception of control.

There were two long-term contradictory dimensions to American Steel's strategy. First, the dividend-payout ratio siphoned away capital from debt reduction and modernization programs that would improve American Steel's capacity to efficiently manufacture steel.[8] Second, the expansion and diversification strategies significantly increased its debt. As one top manager at corporate headquarters told me: "Our financial problems were accentuated by the fact that we added another layer of fixed costs to our operations by these investments."

Financial Control, Social Embeddedness, and Inefficiencies

Despite American Steel's changes to increase control over the managerial process, the utilization rate to operating profit margin relationship worsened as the corporation increased its scale and scope. While American Steel's average utilization rates were almost 7 percent higher in the second half of the 1970s than in that of the 1950s (figure 6.2), its operating profit margin was approximately one-half its rate in the 1950s (figure 6.3). That is, as utilization rates increased—which normally improves efficiency because it reduces per-unit costs—operating profit margins declined. The crucial question is: Why did American Steel's cost efficiency decline at such a rapid rate?

In the following, I analyze micro-level behaviors and show how the mode of control—based on financial accounting—generated inefficiencies. My analysis focuses on three critical flaws in the financial conception of control. First, embedding operating management in an account-control system based on budgetary and ROI controls creates incentives that encourage managers to be concerned with the cost within their area of responsibility.

Second, centralized account controls, together with bureaucratic controls, entailed hierarchical reporting, which discourages lateral communication and creates barriers among the various organizational entities, resulting in cumbersome decision-making processes that slow managers' responses. These controls over managers contain a fundamental contradiction: centralized controls undermine the lateral communication necessary to coordinate the manufacturing process. This contradiction is a core source of managerial inefficiencies.

Third, the account controls used by large corporations did not provide an adequate understanding of their costs. As corporations implemented scope strategies in the 1960s and 1970s, it became more difficult to make a reasonable assessment of the relationship between product costs and market prices. Aggregated product-cost data may make it possible to evaluate a product line or product group, but it does not evaluate the cost efficiency of manufacturing specific products (see chapter 5). The aggregation of costs necessary to create financial controls—to satisfy external capital markets—consolidates the information necessary to identify specific product costs. These financial controls made it virtually impossible to target specific cost reductions, coordinate prices with a product's costs, and establish manufacturing policy based on the profitability of individual products.

Mid-Twentieth-Century Financial Controls and Incentive Structure

Top management and its administrative staff established an authority system based on financial account controls to monitor costs and capital expenditures. This authority system embedded operating managers in an incentive structure that encouraged them to make decisions that keep budgets low, ROI high, and inventories moving through the manufacturing process. This incentive structure generated motives and behaviors at several levels within the managerial hierarchy. Control over the managerial process also entailed bureaucratic controls, which conveyed authority rights throughout the managerial hierarchy. *Authority* is a social structural attribute; it is the capacity of superordinate members of the hierarchy to control subordinates because of their position in a social structure. This is in contrast to power, which is an individual attribute. Power is often affected by individuals' position in the authority structure. Authority structures in corporations are designed to ensure rapid and clear decisions, and stringent discipline among their members (Weber 1978). Together, financial and bureaucratic controls embedded managers in a control structure that resulted in decisions that contradicted corporate profitability goals.

In the following, I show how control over the managerial process entailed creating responsible autonomy (Friedman 1977; also see chapter 3 herein). In contrast to previous conceptions of responsible autonomy that focus on management's strategies to control workers, I examine how responsible autonomy is set up to control the managerial process. I show that responsible autonomy within the formally-rational set of incentives based on financial controls produced the unintended effect of encouraging micro-level behaviors (i.e., decisions) that were inefficient in terms of the corporation's substantive profit-making goals.

While the flexibility necessary to manufacture a wide product line requires responsible autonomy, an account-control system based on budgets and ROI created incentives and motives that resulted in social action that over time opposed corporate substantive goal rationality. The concern here is with how formally rational controls shaped the managers' interests so that their decisions opposed the corporation's substantive goals (e.g., low costs, profits, product quality). The specific form of this contradiction is important because its resolution shaped the mode of control in the 1980s and beyond.

As size and complexity increased, and with the introduction of more technical manufacturing processes, *bounded rationality*—the cognitive limits of individual decision makers (Simon 1957)—limited top managements' capacity to evaluate operating management. Centralized controls relied on account controls derived from financial accounting and the rule-based Taylorist version of scientific management. However, limitations restricted the introduction of centralized rule-based control in manufacturing corporations that produce many different products. Manufacturing steel includes numerous variables and several modifications of these variables for each product. Establishing and setting up a separate set of rules for thousands of products that have unique production specifications restricts the manufacturing flexibility necessary to ensure product specification. These technical limitations required that the loci of discretion over many decisions be at the point of production where managers exercised decision-making discretion based on their knowledge and understanding of the manufacturing process.

Once the loci of decision-making discretion were decentralized, American Steel's production units operated semiautonomously of one another. This created a vacuum in the managerial process. After top management relinquished control over the operating units little useful information was available to evaluate whether resources within these units were being used efficiently. Top managers and owners falsely believed that financial controls provided useful and adequate information on the efficient use of resources.

Inefficiencies within Subsidiaries

As in many corporations, each subsidiary and division at American Steel operated as an independent business unit. After corporations created a range of diverse corporate entities, top management no longer used its firm-specific knowledge of the manufacturing process, but depended on aggregate financial data to monitor corporate-entity performance (Johnson and Kaplan 1991). Because they could not identify product costs, these account controls did not distinguish between low ROI caused by costs associated with product development and low ROI caused by poor managerial performance. ROI does not provide information on the costs associated with, for example, operating decisions.

Despite this flaw, after early-twentieth-century capitalists made the decision to focus primarily on controlling the labor process, owners and top managers used ROI as the *primary basis* for strategic decision making and allocation of capital funds. Most important, low ROI began to be interpreted as low performance by the managers responsible for the various organizational entities. This evaluation criterion and the emergent incentive structure—where aggregate accounting data became the basis to evaluate whether the middle managers deserved a salary increase or promotion—encouraged these managers to make decisions that maximized subsidiaries' ROI. Over time, together with the increased size of corporate entities, these controls created an incentive structure that stressed short-term profitability goals among operating managers (also see Lazonick 1991; Johnson and Kaplan 1991).

On one occasion, a middle manager responsible for one of American Steel's coal-producing subsidiaries made a decision not to purchase a $.5 million coal dryer because the investment would increase costs and erode the subsidiary's ROI. However, the higher-quality coal produced with the coal dryer would have saved the steel-manufacturing business unit $4 million dollars per year in manufacturing costs.

Although the decision enhanced subsidiary ROI, it undermined the capacity of the steel manufacturing division to produce low-cost steel. This decision appeared to be efficient based on ROI criterion, but it opposed the corporation's substantive goals to produce high-quality steel at the lowest possible cost. These controls over the managerial process and the subsequent incentive structure generated a substantive goal rationality within the subsidiaries that opposed the corporation's ultimate substantive goal.

Inefficiency between the Sales and Steel-Manufacturing Departments

More serious flaws in the financial conception of control were the obstacles to efficiently coordinate American Steel's product mix with the market. Once cost data were aggregated for financial accounting purposes, it was virtually impossible to locate individual product-cost data. In the absence of product-cost data for individual products, pricing decisions were based on cost data from product groups.

As a result, the sales department, which made pricing decisions, would often unknowingly sell products with high manufacturing costs. This undermined corporations' substantive profitability goal because costs vary within product groups; the specific configuration and composition of each corporations' manufacturing facilities creates significant variation in product cost among corporations manufacturing the same product. Companies will have higher or lower cost, for example, if a manufacturing process in one company requires more time, energy, or labor than in another company. Although significant cost variations exist within the production process, the managerial process was unable to detect these variations. In short, managerial hierarchies replaced the market function of determining price. However, the financial conception of control did not provide information to decision makers to determine product costs. In some cases, American Steel's sales managers would sell products that were below the cost to manufacture those products.

This problem was exacerbated because sales personnel were evaluated on the volume of their sales. This incentive structure encouraged sales personnel to sell products even if they knew that the profits were low on those products. Higher sales volume resulted in better evaluations, increasing the chances of a bonus, salary increase, or promotion. Neither the efficiency of the policy nor the selling strategy were evaluated because the data to carry out such an evaluation was inaccessible. The flaws in financial controls emerged when foreign steel corporations began to gain market share in specific products. American Steel could not identify its product costs on specific products to determine whether it was making or losing money on them. (This was a common problem in U.S. manufacturing corporations [Johnson and Kaplan 1991]). Managers were embedded in a formally rational system of control that was irrational from the perspective of the corporation's substantive goals (e.g., controlling total costs).

Inefficiency between the Steel-Manufacturing and Raw Material Departments

The incentive structures created by formal rational budgetary controls generated inefficient decision making by creating contradictory substantive goal rationalities in the steel-manufacturing and raw materials departments. This problem is illustrated by the following.

A responsibility of the raw materials department was to transport iron ore from the raw material subsidiaries to the manufacturing site. When the shipment of raw materials arrives at the manufacturing site, the steel-manufacturing department becomes responsible for unloading the ship. The cranes used to unload the iron ore are assigned to the manufacturing department because they are normally used to load the iron ore and other raw materials into the blast furnaces.

On one occasion a shipment of iron ore arrived on a weekend when one of the cranes needed repairs, and operators were using the other crane to load raw materials into a blast furnace. Rather than calling the mechanics in on the weekend, the superintendent made the decision to wait until Monday to have the inoperable crane repaired. The manager made this decision because the additional labor cost to bring in a repair crew on the weekend would have created a budget overrun in his area of responsibility, reflecting poorly on his managerial skills. This decision saved the blast furnace department between $200 and $500 in overtime costs. Meanwhile the ship and its 30–35 crew members remained idle for twenty additional hours, which cost the raw materials subsidiary approximately $20,000 in labor and capital-investment costs. As one American Steel manager stated, the superintendent made this decision because

> the guys who ran the blast furnace were only interested in their blast-furnace productivity. They didn't give a damn about how long the ship sat there. They were a different department and there was no charge to them.

The incentives created by the account-control system generated a substantive goal rationality (i.e., to stay within assigned budgets) in the blast-furnace unit that opposed corporate substantive goals. Although failing to repair the crane on the weekend was efficient within the narrowly defined budgetary criterion, this decision opposed the corporate substantive goal to minimize total costs. The incentive structure undermined cooperation among the middle managers and increased total operating costs. This contradiction emerged because formally rational controls gradually became reified into substantive subunit goal rationality.

There are two crucial aspects of the managerial process that produced this decision. First, as the corporation increased in size and complexity, department managers were granted responsible autonomy because it was difficult to establish rules governing every decision at the department level. Second, budgetary controls within which managers were embedded created an incentive structure that encouraged the manager to keep costs low within his area of responsibility. The alternate decision to call in the repair crew on the weekend would have generated a cost overrun and a potential negative evaluation of the manager.

Inefficiency between Operating Units within the Steel-Manufacturing Department

Although the contradictory aspects of the managerial process undermined efficiency in various spheres of the corporation, it was most extreme in the steel-manufacturing department. These managers were embedded in an incentive system that encouraged them to make decisions that kept budgets low and inventories moving through the manufacturing process, creating motives and behaviors that contradicted the corporation's intended goal of keeping corporate-entity costs low. This contradiction manifested itself in two ways that undermined the corporate substantive profitability goal: (1) it encouraged managers to maximize output to reduce per-unit costs, and (2) it encouraged managers to make decisions that kept flawed steel in the manufacturing process.

If mill superintendents stopped the manufacturing process to reroll defective steel, their operating costs increased. High operating costs typically result in budget overruns, which reflected poorly on managers' abilities. As one manager put it, this incentive structure resulted in decisions where

> one mill would pass on steel that really didn't meet specifications, hoping that it would slip through. Nobody wanted to take the hit on poor quality. They regularly tried to pass on the defective material to the next mill and let them take the hit.

Decisions to keep defective products in the manufacturing process, however, increased costs (e.g., labor, energy, raw materials) of products that were typically sold at a lower price, scrapped, or rerolled because they did not meet market standards. Although these decisions ensured that managers remained within their budgets, the production of low-quality steel increased manufacturing costs and decreased revenues, undermining the corporation's substantive product quality and profitability goals. This behavior was not detected because the account-control system did not monitor transfer pricing of interim products among operating units, and because oligopolistic price-setting behavior ensured profits (see chapter 5).

Moreover, these decisions created conflict among managers, which undermined cooperation and further undermined cost efficiency. The formal budgetary controls encouraged these managers to disregard the consequences of their decisions for downstream production units or the substantive corporate goals. As one manager stated:

> There was a tendency for people to optimize in their area. If you are in steel production you may do things to make your balance sheets look good, but it may hurt the ironmakers, hot-rolling, or cold-rolling area. There was a tendency for each [manager] to do their own thing, make it look good for them.

Together with an incentive structure encouraging managers to make decisions to pass defective material to the next mill, the increased size and complexity of the production process undermined informal cooperation. Over time each middle manager began to view his or her operating unit as autonomous. This condition was a consequence of the contradiction between the lateral nature of production processes and hierarchical controls. While lateral communication is necessary to ensure efficient linkages and coordination of the production process, account controls encourage hierarchical communication. Hierarchical controls produced lateral conflict among managers because it provided an incentive to pass flawed products on to downstream managers who became responsible for those products. In retrospect, managers described the problem in the following way:

> You had superintendents of mills, little kings; that was their fief. All they were concerned about was their mill. And they passed their products on to the next guy, who was only concerned with his mill. This turf business . . . is a problem. It does not provide the greatest effectiveness. It certainly does not give you cost efficiency.

Over time this situation, of passing cost on to the next production unit, created lateral conflict and deep-seated "divisions" among these middle managers and, in several cases, "rivalry and open hostility." These conflictual social relations undermined the personal cooperation among department managers necessary to ensure the efficient linking and coordinating of the manufacturing process. Besides keeping American Steel's manufacturing costs high, conflict contributed to lower product quality, creating important obstacles to capital accumulation in the long term.

Like between the raw materials subsidiary and the steel-manufacturing unit, formal controls within the steel-production units became reified into substantive production-unit goals, which encouraged decision making that contradicted corporate substantive goals. This contradiction was not detected because managers' actions were not judged against the profitability goals of the corporation. The financial conception of control that emphasized budgets and ROI by itself did not guarantee efficiency because formal rationality is indifferent to whether accounting is carried out according to substantively rational principles (Weber 1978).

Using financial accounting to control costs is also flawed because it associates cost transactions with the *location* in the corporation where the cost was incurred, not with the *decision* that caused them. Although identifying costs with the location in the corporation where transactions occurred made sense for external reporting purposes, it made little sense from a cost-efficiency perspective. Financial account controls "did not reflect the underlying categories of work, or activities, that cause costs" (Johnson 1991:52; Johnson and Kaplan 1991; Raff and Temin 1991). This shaped motives and actions (i.e., decisions) that negatively affected corporate performance (Armitage and Atkinson 1990; Johnson and Kaplan 1991).

For example, to keep their costs low and remain within their budgets, the purchasing department would sometimes buy low-quality raw materials. The inefficiencies for the corporation of such decisions were not detected by the account-control system because the effects of using low-quality materials are not associated with the decision in the purchasing department. Instead, the higher energy costs to transform low-quality raw materials into high quality steel are assigned to the steel-making operations where the cost is incurred. That is, higher cost may occur because of a decision made in a corporate entity over which the unit where the cost is incurred has no control.

In several crucial ways, formal budgetary controls became increasingly inadequate to attain the corporation's substantive goals. First, as the size and complexity of each organizational unit increased (some units contained more than five hundred employees), the managers of the various manufacturing units rarely saw one another. This eliminated the opportunity to develop or maintain lateral informal lines of communication. Over time responsible autonomy led to a situation where middle managers became increasingly concerned with the activities within their formal span of control. Second, just as increased complexity of the manufacturing process resulted in bounded rationality and the removal of top management from operating decisions in the 1940s, by the early 1960s upper-level middle managers (i.e., general managers, assistant general managers) became removed from the day-to-day production operations. As a result, they became less capable of evaluating whether cost increases were justified. Third, because budget controls evaluated production managers by their ability to remain within predetermined budgets, they created an incentive structure that encouraged these managers to make decisions based on how those decisions would affect their particular production unit. Fourth, although the managerial process was unable to identify the manager responsible for passing on low-quality interim products, the downstream production managers knew when a substandard product was passed on to them and who made that decision. This situation generated lateral conflict among these managers.

The situations described above expose important irrationalities that emerge when centralized hierarchical financial controls are set up in large complex manufacturing processes. The fundamental problem is the disjuncture between the hierarchical control system and the laterally connected production system. The production process is most efficient when it flows along a continuum from one stage to the next. To minimize input costs, it is important to maintain a smooth flowing continuous production process because even minor disruptions increase energy and labor costs. Centralized control, however, entailed a hierarchical reporting system, which discouraged lateral interaction and communication. Lateral conflict among managers hindered the informal cooperation within the managerial process upon which the coordination of the manufacturing process depended.

How Did American Steel Continue to Realize a Profit?

American Steel continued to realize a profit because it was effective enough to generate an acceptable rate of return in its oligopolistic environment. Despite these seemingly glaring inefficiencies, American Steel was more effective (i.e., profitable) than other steel corporations. American Steel's after-tax rate of return on equity was significantly higher than the industrial average; whereas American Steel's rate of return averaged 9.8 between 1960 and 1979 (figure 6.4), it was 7.9 percent for the steel industry.

During this historical period of adequate cash flows and profits, inefficiencies at American Steel were not detected. As long as managers remained within their budgets, they met the internal formally rational criteria of success. As long as the corporation continued to realize a profit, management did not reexamine the cost efficiency of the managerial process. Financial controls were inadequate in two ways. First, since budgetary and ROI controls focus on entire organizational units, they provided little information on the cost efficiency of operating decisions or the relationship between product cost and market price. Second, budgetary controls cannot identify the managers responsible for coordinating decisions or the costs associated with linking technologies that require the joint effort of several managers and generate a single outcome. Although efficiency of the managerial process depended on the cooperation of middle managers responsible for coordinating activities and decisions, account controls designed to evaluate the financial position (e.g., ROI) of the corporate entity were incapable of evaluating these costs. At best, aggregated financial data provided a diagnostic tool to determine whether there was a failure in an operating unit that needed to be discovered and corrected (Johnson and Kaplan 1991). Financial control provided neither the basis for identifying the failure nor an understanding of what needed to be changed.

These findings demonstrate that something is not in itself irrational, but rather becomes so when examined from a specific rational standpoint (Weber 1958:53, footnote 9). In this case, middle managements' decision-making motives and behaviors were rational when examined in relationship to the incentive structure created by the formally rational controls (Prechel 1991, 1994b). These decisions were, however, irrational from the substantive profitability goals of the corporation as a whole. These irrationalities continued to persist because financial controls were incapable of identifying the costs associated with product-cost decisions, precluding the possibility of identifying when decisions undermined corporate substantive capital-accumulation goals.

Discussion: Financial Controls and the Managerial Process

The formally rational financial conception of control contradicted the corporation's substantively rational agenda and goals. Whereas bureaucratic controls defined managerial responsibility and the span of control, financial controls became top management's primary means of monitoring operating managers. Initially implemented to monitor the efficient use of capital, ROI became the means to evaluate the cost efficiency of divisions and subsidiary corporations. And, budgets became the means to monitor and control costs within the smaller corporate entities (e.g., departments). Information from the standard cost system was used to estimate the operating cost of each production unit, establish budgets for these units, and determine whether middle managers remained within their budgets. Middle managers, in turn, pressured subordinate managers to keep their costs low.

Together with bureaucratic controls, financial controls created an incentive system that encouraged operating management to focus on its area of responsibility and disregard the implications of its decisions on downstream units, producing lateral conflict and undermining cooperation. Operating managers based their decisions on the peculiar priorities and problems of their specific subunits, such that formally rational budgetary controls were reified into substantive goal rationality for these decision makers.

These findings point toward an important question: Why did American Steel continue to use a financial conception of control to evaluate corporate entities? There are four interrelated explanations. First, American Steel was required to provide finance capital with information on the efficient use of capital (e.g., ROI). Second, the emphasis on a financial conception of control was furthered by legislation, which required corporations to make financial information available to the public. Third, the contradiction between corporate and subunit substantive goals went undetected, in part, because financial accounting was incapable of detecting cost inefficiencies. The contradiction became increasingly difficult to detect as the corporation expanded and the managerial process became more complex. Fourth, the inability of the account-control system to evaluate the profitability of specific products did not present a significant problem in the oligopolistic era when markets expanded and prices were set in relationship to costs. As long as the corporation remained profitable, product costs and the profitability of specific products attracted little attention.

Conclusion

American Steel's strategy conforms to that of other larger manufacturing enterprises as presented by the managerialist perspective. It increased its scale and scope in response to expanded market opportunities. American Steel also decentralized decision-making authority and used ROI and budgets to control its corporate entities. Financial controls were created to provide both the division heads and corporate executives with an understanding of present performance and anticipated conditions. Managerialists argue that these data "made possible the administration of the operating divisions without inhibiting or interfering with the authority and responsibility of the general managers" (Chandler 1962:307). Although it is technically correct to say that these controls did not interfere with managerial prerogatives, managerial theory fails to consider how responsible autonomy—the leeway and authority provided to managers—within this incentive structure affected operating managers' behavior.[9]

This case-oriented analysis shows how many variables, internal and external to the corporation, affected the system of control and the incentive structure that undermined efficiency. The theoretical framework here posits questions that are in sharp contrast to those raised by prevailing theories. Chandler (1990) argues that corporations in oligopolistic industries remain efficient by sharpening and enlarging the skills of management. Managerial skills may have increased in the twentieth century, but this is not the question. More skills do not automatically increase efficiency. Rather, the question is: How did the incentive structure within which managers were embedded affect decision making and efficiency? It is the application of skills that is important, not simply the existence of skills.

Similar to the managerialist perspective, TCA assumes a simplistic functional argument: if corporations survive, it is because they economize on costs (Williamson and Ouchi 1981; Williamson 1985). TCA suggests that bureaucratic and financial controls constitute mechanisms to ensure efficient decision making among middle and lower-level management. In contrast to these claims, the analysis here shows that financial controls are not complete bundles of information and do not provide an accurate comparison of cost to price. Also, because financial controls do not contain accurate and timely product cost or price data they do not ensure that operating units are governed in a quasi-market fashion. Financial controls neither capture the wide range of costs in complex manufacturing corporations nor necessarily serve the needs of the organization as a whole. Because of their insufficient depth of analysis, TCA theorists fail to acknowledge that financial controls are aggregated cost data and do not provide information on specific product costs to accurately evaluate the relationship between product costs and market prices.

The analysis here shows that corporations can remain profitable and even increase their profits when efficiency declines. Although one objective of financial control was to harmonize motives and behaviors and direct managers' attention toward corporate goals, it created incentives for operating managers to make decisions that contradicted the substantive profit-making goal of the corporation. The response to declining efficiency is historically contingent. In contrast to the era of global competition, the adverse effects of the financial conception of control on decision making had little effect on corporate behavior in the oligopolistic era when profits remained high.

PART III
Historical Transitions in Corporations' Institutional Arrangements, 1940s–1990s

Historical Transitions in Corporations' Institutional Arrangements, 1940s–1990s

This part of the book examines the institutional arrangements that contributed to corporate stability in the middle decades of the twentieth century (1940s–1970s), the change in institutional arrangements in the 1980s, and big businesses' political and organizational response. Chapter 7 shows how corporate political behavior contributed to corporations' capacity to make a profit in light of the deep-seated irrationalities and inefficiencies in the managerial process between 1940 and 1970. By 1980, changes in corporations' environment further integrated the U.S. economy into the global economy. These new institutional arrangements increased corporations' capital dependence. In chapters 8 and 9, I examine the corporate response to these changing institutional arrangements. The case-oriented method in chapter 8 illustrates how American Steel restructured its account-control system and managerial process to control the behavior of operating managers in such a way as to better ensure that their decisions advanced the corporation's goals and agenda. Chapter 9 examines the social forces that produced changes at American Steel to the *multilayered subsidiary form* (MLSF): "a corporation with a hierarchy of two or more levels of subsidiary corporations and a parent company at the top, operating as a management company" (Prechel 1991, 1997a:407). After providing an in-depth case study, I switch to a variable-oriented analysis in chapter 10 to examine change to the MLSF in the largest industrial corporations in the United States. Chapter 11 examines the implications of these changes.

CHAPTER 7

More Political Capitalism: Changing Economic Conditions and Corporate Political Behavior, 1940–1985

In order to provide sufficient depth of analysis to explain the complexities of big business political behavior, this chapter focuses on a single industry. The focus on one industry does not preclude an analysis of big business in general because the success of this subclass segment was dependent, in part, on its capacity to align itself with the general interests of the industrial capitalist-class segment. I examine corporate political behavior during the middle and late stages of the oligopolistic era (1940–mid-1970s) and during the transition to global competition (mid-1970s–1980s).

The historical case-oriented method used here identifies transitions in the social construction of corporations' institutional arrangements. I show that the content of business policy is affected by the historically contingent capital-dependent relations between corporations and the state, and the capacity of capitalists to exercise power. I examine the conditions when corporations have adequate social power to define the political environment within which they are embedded. The contingent theory of business unity elaborated here is distinct from state-centered conceptions, which argue that states are autonomous (Skocpol 1980, 1985). Theoretical perspectives that assume state autonomy define away the effects of powerful political actors outside the state, and then ignore them empirically. As a result, these theories fail to explain how political-legal arrangements between corporations and the state become institutionalized and deinstitutionalized.

I selected the steel industry to illustrate historical shifts in capital-state relations for three reasons. First, it represented a subclass segment that controlled resources upon which economic growth and stability depended throughout most of the twentieth century. The steel industry generated the largest proportion of the Gross National Product (GNP) in the manufacturing sector between 1929 and 1958 and only two industries had a higher share of the GNP in 1974 (U.S. Department of Commerce 1960–1979). Second, because steel was used in many industrial products during much of the twentieth century, the behavior of the steel industry affected industrial output, employment, defense preparedness, and profits and wages in other economic sectors. That is, the political and economic behavior of this subclass segment did not occur in isolation from the broader capital accumulation process or the state's agendas. Third, like many industrial sectors, economic concentration is high in the steel industry. Although several industries were more concentrated than steel, in 1950, the eight largest steel corporations accounted for more than 75 percent of all domestic steel production (U.S. Census of Manufacturers 1972; U.S. Federal Trade Commission 1977). The high degree of economic concentration in the steel industry makes it an appropriate object of analysis to determine whether subclass segments have the capacity to develop political coalitions and influence state business policy.

Theoretical Debates

There is considerable disagreement among researchers who examine the policy formation process. Several studies that emphasized social forces external to the state argue that agreement exists within the capitalist class, interclass conflicts are resolved outside the state, and elites representing the capitalist class influence policy. Others have argued that the state is relatively autonomous in its relationship with capitalist groups, and that the content of policy is the outcome of the state's efforts to mediate class and interclass conflict. In rebuttal to these arguments, the state-centered perspective emphasizes the autonomous political action of the state. A key issue in this debate is how each perspective conceptualizes class and its relationship to the state.

The *class-unity* argument maintains that consensus exists within business (Miliband 1969). Some adherents of this approach argue that a unified capitalist-class perspective emerges from the policy-formation process that originates outside the state (Domhoff 1979). Others have argued that a dominant coalition of banks exercises hegemony over corporations and takes into account the long-run interest of the economy (Mintz and Schwartz 1985). Still others have argued that classwide rationality is articulated by representatives of the capitalist class who sit on multiple corporate boards and act on the basis of what is best for business as a whole. This inner circle "has the informal organizational ties, the formal organizational capacity, and the general vision of business needs to serve as a vehicle for classwide political mobilization" (Useem 1983:119–20).

In contrast, *state autonomy* arguments suggest that the political action of the state is autonomous from these external forces and the state's organizational structure and agenda are important forces in shaping policy. States are conceived as organizations that formulate and pursue goals that are not simply a response to the demands or interests of social groups, classes, or society (Skocpol 1980, 1985). State autonomy theory assumes that the state is a complex of organizations with a life and structure of its own that is independent of the dynamics of capital accumulation, and its responses to the economy are traceable to administrative arrangements, government institutions, and political parties (Skocpol 1980).[1]

The *class segment* perspective suggests that divisions emerge among major business sectors because of the differential rates of accumulation within the various segments of capital (Offe 1975; Poulantzas 1978; Aglietta 1979). Class segments conform to the relationship each branch of capital has with the economy, and are strongest in industries where economic concentration is high (Baron and Sweezy 1966). As a consequence of their distinct location in the social process of production, class segments have specific political economic requirements and concrete interests that may be contradictory to those of other class segments and, therefore, the potential to develop a specific variant of interclass consciousness and common action in relation to other class segments (Zeitlin, Neuman, and Ratcliff 1976; Zeitlin 1980). As a result, whereas market constraints that are shared by economic sectors result in similar political behavior, conflicting economic interests generate opposing political interests (Berg and Zald 1978; Mizruchi 1989). Moreover, the policy-formation process itself generates political divisions among class segments because business policies do not affect all capitalist class segments equally (Prechel 1990). Business policy designed to overcome obstacles to growth in the economy as a whole or in one segment of capital often impedes growth in other economic sectors. The class-segment argument suggests that just as the economic realm is not dominated by a unified logic of capital accumulation, the political realm is not occupied by a single class or class segment, but by a capitalist "power bloc" whose composition can vary historically (Poulantzas 1978). This perspective suggests that states can only be *relatively autonomous* from the capitalist class because both are part of the mode of production (Poulantzas 1978; Levine 1988). The capitalist class and the capitalist state are dependent on one another to ensure economic stability.

There are two theoretical shortcomings creating obstacles to resolution of this theoretical difference. First, the central concepts (i.e., class unity, state autonomy) are articulated in such a way that they cannot account for historical variation (Prechel 1990). Second, the empirical studies that document each perspective lack sufficient historical depth. That is, they do not operate within a sufficiently long time frame to determine the variations in these relationships in different historical contexts. What is needed, therefore, are modifications in the conceptualization of these variables, and historical studies with sufficient depth to investigate the conditions under which class unity and state autonomy exist. The disagreement between society-centered and state-centered arguments is due, in part, to insufficient theoretical detail. State autonomy and class unity are too often interpreted as empirical absolutes, rather than understood as theoretical constructs. The central concepts in this debate—class unity and state autonomy—should be conceptualized as *ideal types* that exist only rarely at the empirical level, but that serve as abstractions that provide a means to aid in the description of the empirical level (Weber 1949).[2] Class unity can be seen as existing at one end of a continuum, with intraclass divisions at the other. Likewise, in a separate continuum, state autonomy can be considered at the opposite end of the continuum from the concept of the state as an instrument of the capitalist class. The key issue to understanding capital-state relations is not whether class segments are united or divided, but rather the historical conditions under which the capitalist class is more or less unified or divided. Similarly, the key issue is not whether states are autonomous from the capitalist class or class segments but rather the historical conditions under which the state is more or less autonomous.

Drawing from perspectives common in organizational theory, I conceptualize the policy-formation process as affected by (1) internal organizational arrangements, and (2) the institutional arrangements in corporations' environment. This formulation makes it possible to identify the conditions when classes are more or less divided and when states are more or less autonomous. My objectives are to (1) elaborate a contingency model of business unity that accounts for the relationship between capitalist class unity and historical conditions, and (2) examine the effects of the capitalist class and class and subclass segments on the state's structure and agenda. My theoretcial framework suggests that variation in capital dependence effects business unity among capitalist class and subclass segments, and alliances and conflicts between capitalists and the state.

Historical Contingent Model of Business Unity and Corporate Political Behavior

Although there is a single capitalist class, it includes competing class segments and subclass segments. These class and subclass segments sometimes agree on policy and form alliances to ensure that those policies are passed and implemented. Their unique relationship to the economy, however, divides them on certain issues. The presence or absence of political alliances and the respective power of class and subclass segments have profound effects on state business policy. Therefore, state theory must be formulated in such a way that it takes into account historical variations in political unity within the capitalist class, and the historical conditions under which these outside political actors attempt to influence the policy-formation process. I argue here that a useful view of the relationship between the capitalist class and the state is one that begins by explaining how capitalist class and subclass segments might come to have different interests, and allowing for the possibility of conceptualizing class power and state power as *independent variables* whose relationship must be ascertained in specific historical circumstances.

Class Power

Research that is sensitive to historical variation in the relationship between the state and outside interests demonstrates variation in the power of external political actors (Zeitlin 1984 Prechel 1990). An explanation of how economic interests are expressed must also account for how economic groups mobilize politically.

Throughout the twentieth century, organizations increasingly became the basis of collective action, and the vehicle through which powerful political coalitions expressed their power (Offe and Wiesenthal 1980; March and Olsen 1984). Organizations are the vehicle through which political agendas are pursued by capitalists (e.g., Business Roundtable), workers (e.g., unions), and international coalitions such as the Organization of Petroleum Exporting Countries (OPEC) and the European Economic Community (hereafter EEC) (Laumann and Knoke 1987; Prechel 1990). Organizations that represent political coalitions affect policy by pressuring the state to amend legislation when existing policies conflict with their economic interest, and provide the basis to forge alliances with other political coalitions when their interests coincide.

An important basis of political alliances and conflicts within the capitalist class and between the capitalist class and the state is capital dependence. These capital-dependent relations are historically contingent, and the historical form of this dependence has important effects on state business policy. Although capital dependence always exists between the state and corporations, this dependence is most pronounced during periods of economic downturn. During recessions and depressions the capitalist class unifies behind a business policy favorable to capital accumulation in the dominant economic sectors. Capitalist class and subclass segments unify because the state, historically, is the only organization with the authority and power to implement the society-wide policies necessary to overcome economic constraints. Moreover, because the state is dependent on corporate revenues to maintain its increasingly large bureaucracy and carry out its agenda (e.g., social welfare, war making), it attempts to alter the institutional arrangements to facilitate economic growth (Offe and Ronge 1975; O'Connor 1973). Their mutual capital dependence increases cooperation among big business and the state to create institutional arrangements that improve their cash flows or access to capital.

During periods of steady economic growth, however, when corporations have adequate cash flows and access to capital, class and subclass segments pursue their independent economic agendas. Moreover, political unity within the capitalist class declines because there is less need to mobilize and pursue their economic agendas politically. Despite the lack of unity within the capitalist class, the state is least autonomous during periods of rapid economic growth. Under these conditions, the capitalist class is less dependent on the state and the state has less power over them. Powerful segments of the capitalist class pursue economic strategies that may conflict with the state's goals. When this occurs that state can only react to big business.

State Power and the Organizational State

This emphasis on political actors in the state's environment is compatible with the thesis in organizational theory that internal structures and environments affect goals and decisions. The state's *agendas* are defined by its claim to being the guardian of universal interests and its attempt to preserve the state's unity (Rueschemeyer and Evans 1985). These state agendas include economic stability, international relations, and national defense. Although the state's agendas are often generated outside the state and are endorsed by the capitalist class as a whole, they may not be shared at all times by all capitalists because general policies may undermine class segment's specific economic agenda. For example, the state's agenda to maintain free-trade policies may not be shared by capitalists whose market shares are eroded by imports. Similarly, the capacity of capitalists to affect policy does not preclude state structures from affecting policy. Just as changes in the environment affect organizational decisions and structures, existing structures affect future action.[3]

The theoretical formulation here suggests that the state is a complex organization whose structure includes separate large supra-units (i.e., executive, judicial, legislative) and disparate subunits (e.g., treasury, commerce). The U.S. state is a single organization because the Constitution defines functions of these supra-units as interrelated. No single part of the state has the authority to set up policy. Both the executive and legislative branches engage in the policy-formation process and the final policy must meet judicial requirements. Thus, the state does not constitute a set of detachable parts, but exhibits an *apparatus unity* (Poulantzas (1978).[4]

The state as a complex organization does not preclude the possibility of the bureaucratic sphere (e.g., Federal Trade Commission) becoming more autonomous from the representative sphere (e.g., Congress) over time, or of parts of the state acting autonomously under certain historical conditions. In fact, increased complexity creates conditions where state bureaucratic structures can become more independent and act autonomously (Weber 1978). Just as corporate subsidiaries may act autonomously from their parent holding company under certain conditions, the U.S. Department of Defense may act autonomously from the executive branch. However, the capacity of the various parts of an organization to act autonomously does not make them independent organizations. In both cases, the political-legal structure (i.e., business law, the Constitution) establishes authority relations among these organizational entities. The political-legal structure embeds these entities into a single organization.

State structures are important, first, because they define the limits of the state's formal authority and parameters for future policy. Second, existing structures affect policy through the alignment they provide for competing interests both inside and outside the state, which has consequences for implementation. Policies that can only be implemented with great difficulty have less chance of acceptance than those whose implementation is more straightforward. Thus, the *state* is an organization that is affected by its own structure and agenda and by political coalitions in its environment. Whereas the organizational arrangements within the state become the accumulated product of a history of past policies, these arrangements develop into an organizational structure and a network of interests both inside and outside the state that constrain present choices (Beetham 1987; Prechel 1990).

Capital-dependent conditions and state structures are linked in two analytically distinct ways. First, when economic crises emerge, capitalists are dependent on the state to create new institutional arrangements to overcome those constraints. Resolution of crisis produces new policies and state structures to implement them. Over time the state develops an elaborate structure oriented toward resolving economic crisis and mediating capitalist-class conflict. Second, historical variation in the dependence between the state and the capitalist class is crucial to the policy-formation process. The nature of their dependence affects the capacity of capitalists to align their interests and exercise power over the state. These historical processes have important implications. Through its expansion, the state does not necessarily become more powerful or autonomous. The state's legitimacy, however, does become more dependent on economic stability because state activity is increasingly oriented toward maintaining steady economic growth. Also, over the long term, this process shifts authority from representative state structures to bureaucratic state structures (Weber 1978). Once formal enforcement structures exist they provide a legal basis for capitalists to pressure the state to enforce policy, which reduces the state's autonomy from the economy and the interest of the capitalist class.

That is, counterintuitive power relationships emerge when the state's authority is extended over more areas of economic activity and more complex enforcement structures are established. The extension of the state's authority may reduce its autonomy because new organizational structures provide class and subclass segments with legitimate mechanisms within which to exercise political power. As demonstrated in previous chapters, U.S. business enterprises had few legal rights until the late nineteenth century, which constrained their economic activity. When regional states began to establish laws governing business behavior, however, those laws provided corporations with a legitimate means to pursue their agendas. Once established, it is different to dismantle state structures because they become the means to advance a particular agenda, and the focus for a network of political actors both inside and outside the state. Despite the concerted political pressure from small capitalists, farmers, workers, professionals, and state managers, nearly four decades passed before the state was able to establish policies (i.e., New Deal) that prohibited the use of the pyramided holding company as a means of industrial consolidation. Moreover, the concomitant expansion of the state and shift of authority from representative state structures to the bureaucratic state structures provided more outlets for capitalists to channel their lobby and legal efforts to influence policy. The following analysis shows that over the long term, this process produces a state that is more prominent, but less autonomous from the economy and the capitalist class.

Subclass Segment Political Power

The capacity of the steel industry to act as a subclass segment was established by the early 1900s when it set up an oligopolistic market structure and used its trade associations (e.g., American Iron and Steel Institute [hereafter AISI]) to develop its political and economic strategy. This strategy included price setting, and coordination between production capability and market demand, which ensured a high capability utilization rate. Since profits are closely tied to utilization rates, the steel industry resisted expansion during periods of economic growth because unused capability undermined profit making on the downside of the business cycle. That is, because of its specific location in the social process of production, the steel industry had its own political economic requirements and concrete interests. As a result, under certain historical conditions the interests of the steel industry were contradictory to those of other capitalists. For example, the strategy of the steel industry to control production capability had important effects on other capitalists because steel was necessary to build the nation's infrastructure (e.g., roads, bridges, factories), ensure growth in the economy as a whole, and to manufacture consumer commodities in other economic sectors (e.g., automobile, appliance).

The steel industry is a subclass segment because it is a group within a class that shares interests with the class as a whole but, by virtue of its common and specific relations to the means of production, also has interests that conflict with those of other subclass (e.g., automobile) and class segments (e.g., industrial capital) of the capitalist class.[5] That is, it has many of the attributes of class segments (Poulantzas 1978). The high degree of internal economic concentration and the number of interlocking networks (Fusfield 1958; Scheuerman 1986) allowed for extensive planning and coordination, which provided the steel industry with the capacity to unify its economic and political power. The way in which the steel industry pursued its political and economic interests resulted in particular relations to the capital-accumulation process as a whole and to other capitalist groups.

An analysis follows of how the steel industry affected the content of business policy through its specific location in the social process of production, its capital-accumulation strategy, and its particular relations with other political economic actors (including the state).

Capital-State Dependence and Business Political Behavior

The Political Economy of Expansion

As World War II intensified, the demand for military-industrial products from Europe escalated, creating economic opportunities. To meet the state's political-military obligations to the Allies, President Roosevelt appealed to the private sector to redirect production toward the war economy and expand production capability. The steel industry, however, was reluctant to cooperate voluntarily. It maintained that low profits during the depressed 1930s and wartime price controls left the industry without sufficient capital to finance the construction of additional capability. This subclass segment claimed that expansion would undermine long-term profits by leading to excess capability, higher costs, and a product line that was not compatible with peacetime demand (Broude 1963; Tower 1941). As the war progressed, the steel industry admitted that its forecasts underestimated demand, but refused to expand until the federal government accelerated capital-generating tax amortization rates (Broude 1963).

Resource Dependence and Capitalist Class Conflict with the State

Dependent on a crucial war-making resource, the government passed the Revenue Act of 1940, allowing industrial capitalists to depreciate 100 percent of its investments in new facilities over a five-year period. After this state business policy was passed, profits in the steel industry soared. Although this state business policy increased cash flow, the steel industry did not invest at the level the state considered adequate to ensure a strong national defense; the steel industry expanded capability from 81.8 million tons in 1939 to 88.9 million tons by 1942. In 1943, the state began construction of a "public" steel industry to ensure its national defense agenda. Under the direction of the War Production Board, the federal government invested more than $471 million between 1940 and 1944 in a steel plant in Geneva, Utah and sold these properties to the U.S. Steel Corporation for 440 million after the war (U.S. Congress 1946) (for more detail see Chapter 4).

The steel industry was not the only big business that benefited from this policy. The industrial capitalist class segment as a whole benefited. The federal government contributed over two-thirds of the capital that industry invested between 1940 and 1944, dramatically strengthening industrial corporations' financial position. Investment in war production was either financed by the federal government or charged as an operating cost under the five-year amortization provision of the Revenue Act of 1940. This provision was so lucrative that corporations' investment in nonwar plants and equipment was lower than depreciation charges. At the end of World War II, industrial corporations had dramatically improved their financial position and expanded their capital investments while taking on little debt or issuing few stocks. The strong capital structure of the steel industry produced a high degree of autonomy from the state in the following decade.

When the domestic economy returned to peacetime activity, demand increased in virtually every steel-consuming industry. Although demand exceeded the production capability of the industry, there was little threat that new steel companies would be formed in this capital-intensive industry; collusion among steel producers made it possible to cut prices and force new competitors out of the market. Despite the increased demand and pressure from the federal government to increase steel-making capability, the steel industry did not expand. Citing the rapid decline in capability utilization rates to 35 percent following World War I, the AISI maintained that capability estimates should include economic downturns, and expansion would not be profitable when the postwar economic boom subsided. The trade association also argued that expansion would undermine long-term profits because an economic downturn would occur once the immediate consumer needs were filled.

Conflict among capitalist groups emerged in Congress when representatives from other capitalist subclass segments (e.g., oil, agricultural machinery) and class segments (e.g., small businesses), argued that an inadequate supply of steel undermined growth in their industries (U.S. Congress 1948). In late 1949, the executive branch entered the debate and publicly criticized the steel industry for failing to expand. President Truman, the Department of Agriculture, and the Small Business Administration argued that a steel shortage would limit business activity throughout the economy and suggested that Congress authorize the construction of steel capability if the steel industry did not reinvest (U.S. Congress 1950a). In addition, while several members of Congress maintained that the steel shortage was undermining economic growth and would raise prices, fuel inflation, and threaten national security, the steel industry argued that adequate capacity existed (U.S. Congress 1950a). The executive branch and Congress viewed the steel industry's failure to comply with its agenda as the outcome of interdependent decision making and oligopolistic resistance to ensure higher prices. Meanwhile, the "net income of 50 steel companies increased from $264.5 million in 1946 to $542.1 million in 1949 and the rate of return on steel investment was higher in 1948 than in any year since 1917" (U.S. Congress 1950b).

Conflicts within the industrial capitalist class segment and between the steel industry and the government intensified when the United States entered the Korean War. President Truman threatened to return to World War II strategy and authorize the construction of steel-making facilities if private industry failed to expand. Despite these demands, "the steel industry was very definite in asserting that it would not expand capability without being able to take advantage of accelerated amortization" (Edward Welsh, Reconstruction Finance Corporation, in Broude 1963:293). To resolve this conflict between the profit-making goals of this subclass segment and the government's national defense and economic agendas, the federal government passed the Defense Production Act of 1950. This legislation redefined the depreciation period from twenty years to depreciate 100 percent of investments to five years to depreciate 85 percent of investments, substantially increasing the cash flow and providing reinvestment capital for the entire industrial class segment. Following this concession by the state, annual expenditures on new plants and equipment in the steel industry almost doubled—from $608 million in 1949 to $1.2 billion in 1951—and reached $1.5 billion in 1952, increasing capability from 95.5 million tons in 1949 to 108.6 million tons in 1952 (Broude 1963; American Iron and Steel Institute 1949, 1960).

The federal government, however, considered this level of investment inadequate to meet its national security agenda, and in 1952 the president nationalized the steel industry under executive authority of the Defense Production Act of 1950. In response, the steel industry argued that nationalization of private enterprise was illegal and used the state structure and its legal apparatus to challenge the legality of Truman's decision. The steel industry prevailed and the Supreme Court ruled this nationalization unconstitutional. This decision—which clarified the state's dependence on the steel industry to ensure its agendas of economic growth and a strong national defense—had an important effect on the subsequent political behavior of this subclass segment. As during previous historical junctures when the state's agendas were dependent on the steel industry, the business policies that followed generated capital for the steel industry. In 1957 and 1960, respectively, these capital-generating policies financed 45 and 60 percent of investments in the steel industry (*Fortune* 1966).[6]

In summary, dependent on the steel industry to realize its national defense and economic growth agendas, the state subsidized expansion in the steel industry. This subsidization occurred despite record profits and government studies concluding that the steel industry could expand without public assistance. As in the 1940s, expansion occurred only after the state accelerated amortization rates (Broude 1963; Hogan 1971).

Two types of conflict contributed to the redefinition of institutional arrangements. First, economic conflict emerged between the steel industry and the steel-consuming industries because their logics of capital accumulation did not coincide at this historical juncture. This conflict reemerged at the political level when political coalitions representing capitalist groups in the steel-consuming industries convinced members of Congress and the executive branch that the steel shortage undermined growth within their respective industries (U.S. Congress 1948). Second, conflict emerged between the state and the steel industry because the capital-accumulation strategy of the steel industry impeded the state's agendas to ensure economic stability and national security. The state resolved these conflicts by implementing new legislation that provided financial incentives for the steel industry to expand production capacity. Business policy was redefined because this subclass segment pursued a unified political strategy during a period when the state depended on a resource that it controlled.

Although this business policy ensured the state's national security and economic agendas, it had detrimental consequences for the steel industry because the market did not justify the expansion. While the growth in steel capability averaged 3.9 percent between 1950 and 1960, growth in steel consumption was .4 percent (Barnett and Schorsch 1983). Moreover, capital investments at this historical juncture, in conjunction with three critical events in the next decade, undermined the long-term profitability of the U.S. steel industry. First, by the end of the 1950s the much more efficient basic oxygen furnace (BOF) was available for commercial use, which made the open-hearth steel-making facilities outdated by the time construction was completed. Second, the domestic steel industry invested in Canadian ore deposits. In the 1960s, however, higher quality iron ore was discovered in Brazil, Venezuela, and Australia. Japanese and European steel makers purchased these raw materials, which reduced their production costs and increased the quality of their steel. Third, the construction of large ocean vessels lowered the cost of transporting raw materials. These events significantly lowered production costs for foreign steel makers, which eliminated the cost advantages U.S. steel producers enjoyed in the immediate post–World War II era.[7]

The Intensification of Global Competition

The high manufacturing cost and oligopolistic pricing structure in the steel industry made domestic markets lucrative to foreign steel producers and industries that were able to replace steel products (i.e., aluminum, plastic). By 1959, steel imports exceeded exports for the first time. Most important, whereas consumption increased by 1.8 percent per year in the 1960s and 1970s, domestic steel shipments grew at an annual rate of one percent (Barnett and Schorsch 1983). That is, foreign steel makers captured almost one-half of the expansion in steel demand, and the domestic steel industry found itself in a crisis of overproduction and underconsumption, expanded capability and insufficient demand. As global competition intensified, profits in the steel industry dropped from 11.4 percent (1957) to 6.2 percent (1961). Although profitability problems were more pronounced in the steel industry, profits declined throughout the industrial sector of the economy (U.S. Federal Trade Commission, 1950–1982).

In short, by the late 1950s, indicators suggested that the steel industry was unable to compete with its foreign rivals. However, little attention was given to the efficiency of the managerial processes. Instead, the steel industry continued to pursue an aggressive political strategy.

The declining rate of return in the steel industry during the second half of the 1950s coincided with the eroding balance of trade and profits in the manufacturing sector as a whole. By early 1961, as profits steadily declined and corporations' dependence on external sources of capital increased, the executive branch became increasingly convinced that state intervention was necessary to end the 1960–61 recession, and proposed a tax credit to stimulate reinvestment and modernization of industry to ensure U.S. competitiveness in global markets (U.S. Congress 1961, 1962). Industrial capitalists opposed this policy and lobbied for accelerated depreciation allowances (*Congressional Quarterly Almanac* 1961). The unified political behavior of this class segment prevailed and the subsequent *Revenue Act of 1962* included both the accelerated depreciation allowances and a 7 percent tax credit (U.S. Federal Trade Commission 1977). As with the Defense Production Act of 1950, industrial capitalists supported this policy because it facilitated capital accumulation in the industrial sector of the economy.

This capital-generating business policy increased cash flow in the steel industry from $900 million (1961) to $1.7 billion (1965) (*Fortune* 1966). With the capital made available by this state business policy, by the mid-1960s, the steel industry had replaced many of its open-hearth furnaces with the BOF and was producing lighter, stronger, higher-quality steel. However, there was a contradictory dimension to this strategy. Although the BOF was more efficient, the additional steel-making capability lowered utilization rates, which increased per-unit costs. Moreover, the competitive market conditions, in conjunction with pressure from the executive branch, restricted price increases.[8] As the marketplace established quality standards and prices, steel profits declined to 7.7 percent in the 1960s compared to 11.2 percent for all manufacturing industries.

The Politics of the Decay-Exploration Period: State Agendas and Class Unity

As competition intensified, profit making in the steel industry became increasingly associated with its capacity to organize as a political coalition and exercise political power. In contrast to its antagonistic relations with both the state and other capitalist subclass segments in the oligopolistic era, the steel industry's strategy during the decay-exploration period was to align its interests with other capitalists and the agendas of the state. On the one hand, the steel industry's political strategy incorporated the state's argument that a strong steel industry was necessary to ensure national security and long-term economic growth. On the other hand, it attempted to establish a political coalition with other industrial subclass segments and with segments of the working class (i.e., United Steel Workers of America [USW]). The primary objective of the steel industry was to establish import quotas.

AISI maintained that import quotas were necessary because low wages abroad and government subsidies represented unfair competition, which eroded the balance of payments, created unemployment, and increased dependence on foreign steel (U.S. Congress 1968). In the late 1950s, the USW rejected the steel industry's argument that imports were responsible for declining profits and employment opportunities. In 1963, however, when foreign competition began to pose a serious threat to wages and job opportunities, USW leadership supported the industry's argument that protectionist legislation was the best means to ensure employment (Bernstein 1975; Scheuerman 1986). By 1967, a political coalition including USW and the textile, oil, and steel industries obtained enough support in Congress to introduce import-quota legislation. President Johnson, however, threatened to veto this protectionist legislation because it conflicted with a state agenda. State managers feared that import quotas would jeopardize the credibility of the U.S. commitment to international trade agreements and could result in trade retaliation by foreign nation-states (*Congressional Quarterly Weekly Report* 1968).

Despite this opposition from the executive branch, Senator Hartke of Indiana and thirty-six cosponsors introduced a steel import quota bill. To forestall the imposition of mandatory import quotas, Japanese and German steel makers approached the House Ways and Means and Senate Finance Committees to establish guidelines to voluntarily restrict exports. In 1968, the State Department negotiated a three-year (1969–1971) *Voluntary Restraint Agreement* (VRA) with European and Japanese corporations to provide the steel industry with the opportunity to modernize and reestablish its competitive position in the global economy.

Although imports dropped in the short term, many foreign producers shifted to different and often higher-value products not covered by VRAs, which maintained or increased the value of their imports (U.S. Federal Trade Commission 1977). VRAs did not solve either the balance of trade or steel-import problem, and in 1971 steel imports increased to 17.9 percent of the market share and profits in the steel industry dropped to less than one-half of the average for all manufacturers. AISI renewed its lobbying efforts and sought more stringent enforcement measures and more specific product coverage. In May 1972, the Nixon administration established a second set of VRAs (1972–1974) that included more stringent and comprehensive controls. The 1972–74 VRAs, however, were not tested in the marketplace because demand for steel in the global economy temporarily increased from 640 (1971) to 783 (1974) million tons. As a result, prices significantly increased, imports declined to 12.4 percent (1973) of the market share, and profits in the U.S. steel industry reached record levels. Although the VRAs did not establish import quotas, they signified a shift from revenue-generating legislation to protectionism.

Despite record profits in the steel industry and the accelerated depreciation allowances under the *Revenue Act of 1971*, AISI continued to lobby for import quotas because VRAs did not establish a solid legal basis to block imports.[9] A political solution became more complicated, however, as the steel industry became less central to economic growth and capitalists in the service sector (e.g., computer, electronics) began to benefit from free trade. In addition, the executive branch continued to be concerned that protectionist policies would initiate a trade war with the EEC, where the United States had a substantial trade surplus.

Redefining State Structures, 1970s

Increased imports of steel and other industrial products (e.g., autos) in the early 1970s were coupled with serious domestic economic problems. Neo-Keynesian policy reached its limit, stagflation became a serious problem, and a major recession in 1974–1975 jolted the economy. The conflicting interest of capitalist subclass and class segments, especially energy-dependent industrial capital, were redirected toward a concern with the economy as a whole when OPEC quadrupled its oil prices in 1973. These economic conditions became the basis of mobilizing a coalition of academics, politicians, labor leaders, and business executives (Vogel 1989; Akard 1996). The interest of this coalition coincided with the concern in Congress and the executive branch that shifts in the global economy would undermine domestic economic stability.

To take advantage of this new political climate, as in the late 1960s, the steel industry articulated its interest in such a way that it was consistent with the interests of other powerful political actors and the state's agendas. Supported by a coalition of other capitalist subclass segments with protectionist interests (i.e., textile, footwear, glass) and the USW, AISI argued that assistance was necessary to finance the expansion programs necessary to meet future demand, and that without a viable steel industry the domestic economy would become dependent on imports and vacillations in the global economy. They also used an argument previously employed by the state itself: that a weak manufacturing sector would threaten national security and economic stability (U.S. Congress 1973). The political clout of this coalition led to the formation of the *Congressional Steel Caucus*, which represented the interest of the domestic steel industry in Congress.

To avoid mandatory import quotas, the Nixon administration introduced legislation (1973) that provided the steel industry with protectionist possibilities while minimizing the threat of foreign retaliation that quotas would have created. A crucial component of the subsequent business policy was the *Trade Act of 1974*, which redefined dumping. Whereas the 1921 antidumping (AD) law defined *dumping* as the sale of foreign products below prices in their domestic market, the trade act required foreign firms to demonstrate that their prices include the full cost of production, a 10 percent mark-up for fixed costs, and an eight percent rate of return (U.S. Congress 1978; Scheuerman 1986). Most important, the trade act redefined two dimensions of the state structure that established the legal basis to enforce protectionism. First, it increased the authority of the executive branch by formalizing presidential power to impose import quotas. Second, although the

trade act gave the executive branch a significant degree of autonomy over enforcement of the dumping laws, it established the organizational structure and legal
mechanism to file complaints against foreign steel corporations that did not comply with the AD laws (*Congressional Quarterly Weekly Report* 1974). This legislation
designated the shift from voluntary trade agreements to establishing the legal
mechanism within the state to restrict imports. This dimension of the state structure became the cornerstone of AISI's political strategy.

In 1976, AISI pressured the executive branch to enforce the trade act when the
demand for steel on the global market declined and imports increased from 12.4
(1973) to 14.1 (1976) percent. The Ford administration, however, was concerned
over trade retaliation and favored reestablishing VRA's. Although Japanese producers agreed to reduce imports, EEC refused. To avoid plant closing and retaliation from EEC, President Ford imposed a three-year import quota on European
specialty steel (*Iron Age* 1976). The failure to protect the large carbon steel markets
meant that the quotas had little effect on imports.

As imports escalated, beginning in March 1977 the steel industry filed dozens
of AD suits against European and Japanese steel producers under the Trade Act of
1974. This political action is important because it denotes a strategic shift within
this subclass segment from exerting political or economic pressure on the state to
using the state's legal structure to achieve its economic goals. However, President
Ford did not litigate the AD suits because he was concerned that such action
would initiate a trade war with foreign nation-states. Moreover, because the agendas of other capitalist subclass and class segments conflicted with those of the steel
industry they began to lobby the state. Finance capital, for example, pressured the
Executive Branch to avoid protectionist policies. This capitalist class segment was
concerned that trade restrictions would undermine the ability of less developed
countries to repay their loans (*Forbes* 1984).[10]

After the steel industry failed to obtain protectionism from the executive
branch, it developed a media campaign to sway public opinion. The ideological
strategy focused on a media campaign to solicit support from industrial communities affected by imports. As unemployment increased, political coalitions within
these communities (i.e., local governments, USW locals) exerted pressure on their
representatives in Congress to obtain a political solution. Meanwhile, AISI intensified its political and ideological efforts in Congress and argued that unfair
foreign competition was responsible for the continued decline in profits. These
lobbying efforts resulted in an expansion of the Congressional Steel Caucus to 180
members by 1977, which made it one of the largest political coalitions on Capitol
Hill. The capital-accumulation constraints of the steel industry reemerged as political conflict within the state when the chairman of the House Ways and Means
Committee criticized the executive branch for failing to resolve the steel crisis
(U.S. Congress 1977). This conflict reached a high point when members of the

Congressional Steel Caucus introduced five protectionist bills in October 1977 (*Congressional Quarterly Weekly Report* 1977).

As was the case with previous administrations, President Carter did not enforce AD laws because they conflicted with the state's agendas. Specifically, the executive branch was concerned that protectionism would initiate a trade war with foreign nation-states, interfere with the Tokyo Multilateral Trade Negotiations, reduce the supply of steel, increase prices, and stimulate the already rapid rate of inflation (Levine 1985; Jones 1986). Despite the perceived effects of AD laws on these agendas, the executive branch could not ignore the domestic political implications of plant closing, the unemployment of thousands of steel workers, and the erosion of the economic base of entire communities.

To mediate this political crisis in such a way that the outcome did not undermine the state's agendas, President Carter established the White House Conference on Steel to complete a detailed analysis of the industry. The subsequent *Solomon Plan* liberalized depreciation schedules and issued $365 million in loans to steel companies and depressed steel communities (U.S. Congress 1978). The most important dimension of this legislation was the *Trigger Price Mechanism* (TPM) under which the Treasury Department monitored eighty-four categories of steel products, representing 90 percent of all steel imports (U.S. Office of Technological Assessment 1981). Based on the cost of producing and transporting Japanese steel to the United Stayes, beginning in May 1978 the TPM established a minimum pricing formula for imported steel. While this legislation induced U.S. steel companies to withdraw their AD complaints, it also increased protectionism beyond the 1974 antidumping legislation. Although TPM did not substantially alter the flow of imports until 1979, it provided a pricing system that allowed producers to raise prices, which increased their profits.

However, TPMs only protected U.S. markets from Japanese imports, and the steel industry argued that subsidized steel from Europe continued to penetrate domestic markets. However, to limit international political resistance, this subclass segment did not act until the foreign nation-states settled the Tokyo Round of the General Agreement on Tariffs and Trade (GATT). When the Tokyo Multilateral Trade Negotiations were completed, the AISI intensified its efforts to restrict imports of European steel and with the support of the Steel Caucus, Congress passed the *Trade Agreements Act of 1979*. This legislation required the federal government to prosecute AD and *countervailing duty* (CVD) (i.e., laws regarding subsidies foreign steel makers received from their governments) allegations within 150 days (Congressional Quarterly Almanac 1979).[11] Most important, it subjected the actions of the International Trade Commission (ITC) to judicial review, which provided the steel industry with a more effective legal basis to force the executive branch to act on AD and CVD litigation and thereby reduced its autonomy over enforcement of protectionist legislation.

In March 1980, when EEC imports began to surge, is politically unified sub-class segment filed AD petitions against 75 percent of all imported steel, which included steel from seven European countries (Walter 1983). To avoid taking legal action that would threaten international relations, the executive branch suspended the TPM. To resolve this international political crisis, President Carter established the Steel Tripartite Advisory Committee (STAC). With the support of the EEC, which recognized the added strength of the new AD and CVD laws, the executive branch negotiated a new set of TPMs that were 12 percent higher than the 1978 TPMs. The STAC also recommended liberalization of depreciation rules, tax investment credits, and relaxation of pollution controls to improve cash flows in the steel industry. In return for these concessions by the state, the steel industry dropped its AD suits.

In summary, the lack of an enforcement mechanism in the *Trade Act of 1974* ensured state autonomy over implementation of protectionism. However, the redefinition of the state structure and dumping provided the steel industry with the legal mechanism to file AD complaints and established a legal basis to argue that foreign steel makers violated U.S. trade laws. The trade act became a critical dimension of the steel industry's political strategy; it legitimated protectionist arguments in Congress and to the public. Public opinion was crucial because it allowed the steel industry to solicit support to establish stronger forms of protectionism in the future. This political strategy resulted in *The Trade Agreements Act of 1979*, which required the state to act on AD and CVD complaints. The 1979 trade agreements act was the outcome of the capacity of the steel industry to legitimate its protectionist arguments and establish political alliances with other capitalists. Whereas the 1974 trade act was important because it created a legal basis and an organizational structure to file AD complaints and legitimated the protectionist arguments, the 1979 trade act was important because it designated a shift from political struggles over the principle of protectionism to creating the institutional arrangements so that this subclass segment could force the state to administer existing forms of protectionism. These changes in state business policy were important because they established a legal structure to initiate litigation against steel producers in foreign nation-states. The political behavior of this subclass segment redefined business policy in such a way that it increased protectionism and reduced state autonomy over enforcement of protectionism.

Capitalist Class Unity, 1980s

While the steel industry was attempting to advance its economic interests by aligning itself with other capitalist class and subclass segments, business unified to reverse a series of political defeats in the early 1970s (Vogel 1989). The business community's agenda included improving corporations' cash flow by reforming tax policy.[12] Initially, they attacked capital gains legislation. In 1978, the American

Council for Capital Formation and other business groups argued that capital gains taxes reduced the availability of investment capital. Despite President Carter's plan to increase the capital gains tax, the business lobby prevailed and the final version of the 1978 Revenue Act reduced the capital gains tax. In addition, the legislation lowered the corporate tax rate and provided business with a 10 percent investment tax credit (Vogel 1989). These policies increased corporations' cash flow.

These tax breaks and protectionist legislation, however, did not solve the capital shortage in the steel industry. Moreover, by 1981, TPMs no longer provided an effective means to protect domestic steel markets. Foreign steel producers avoided TPM regulations by including hidden rebates, manipulating price statements on customs declarations, and setting up firms in the United States to sell steel. As profits declined and imports increased, the steel industry intensified its efforts to establish import quotas. Import quotas, however, were not compatible with the increased emphasis on free trade in the Reagan administration, and the executive branch continued to be concerned that protectionism would undermine international political relations and initiate a trade war with EEC. However, the political position of the steel industry was strengthened in the early 1980s. The back-to-back recessions (i.e., 1980, 1981–82) and internationalization of the U.S. economy unified industrial capital. In 1980, foreign producers had captured a significant proportion of the market in several industries, and by 1983 imports exceeded exports in the economy as a whole and the trade gap had increased from $28.5 billion in 1978 to $60 billion.[13] In response, the capitalist class established a political coalition that pressured the federal government to stimulate economic growth.

In response to the first recession, the Reagan administration proposed the *Economic Recovery Tax Act of 1981* (*RA81*). The *RA81* was designed to increase capital formation, in part, by creating incentives for personal savings (Bowles et al. 1983). The objective was to increase capital flows into the industrial sector for modernization of plants and facilities (Prechel 1990).

Though skeptical of the policy, a coalition of business organizations agreed to support it in return for the inclusion of accelerated depreciation schedules, which industrial capitalists had been lobbying for since 1978 (*Congressional Quarterly Weekly Report* 1981a; 1981b). The most active business coalition was organized in 1975 by the American Business Conference and The Carlton Group, which provided a political vehicle to advance the interests of industrial capital and other capitalist groups. This political coalition included representatives from the Business Roundtable, the National Association of Manufacturers, the American Council for Capital Formation, the Committee for Effective Capital Recovery, and the Retail Tax Committee. The business segment of the *RA81*, the *Accelerated Cost Recovery System* (ACRS), liberalized depreciation schedules and tax credits. It has been estimated that ACRS write-offs were so generous that profits from new investments were higher after, rather than before taxes (McIntyre and Tipps 1983).

This legislation generated so much capital that low-profit industries such as steel could not take full advantage of these tax breaks. It provided the steel industry with an estimated $400 million in 1982 and 1983 (Scheuerman 1986). In order to take advantage of this policy, capitalists lobbied for a special tax-leasing provision that allowed low-profit corporations to sell their unused tax credits to more profitable corporations. The government also passed the *Steel Industry Compliance Act* in 1981, which amended the *Clean Air Act* and allowed steel corporations to postpone compliance with air pollution standards if they reinvested.

Although the ACRS facilitated accumulation and temporarily halted the steel industry's efforts to enforce protectionism under AD and CVD laws, it did not resolve permanently the political crisis. The tax breaks did not restore profits and several European producers continued to sell steel in U.S. markets considerably below their production costs. During the 1981–82 recession imports increased to 18.9 (1981) and 21.8 (1982) percent, capability utilization rates dropped to 48.4 percent (1982), and the steel industry did not realize a profit for the first time since the Great Depression in the 1930s. In January 1982, as in the past, the steel industry used the organizational structure of the state to achieve its economic objectives. The seven largest U.S. steel corporations filed 110 AD charges against forty-one foreign producers, which included every major foreign steel producing country except Japan (Walter 1983). As the investigation proceeded through the ITC and the commerce department, EEC attempted to obtain a political solution and in May 1982 the commerce secretary and the under secretary for international trade opened negotiations with EEC.

International political conflict escalated again in June when the Commerce Department issued a preliminary ruling on $1.4 billion of imported steel against corporations in West Germany, Italy, Britain, Belgium, the Netherlands, Luxembourg, France, Brazil, and South Africa (Walter 1983). These trade violations were subject to an immediate bond of 20 to 25 percent of the import values to be forfeited if the final decision supported the preliminary ruling. In response, EEC developed a list of products exported by the United States that benefited from U.S. government subsidies. EEC maintained that the action of the U.S. government violated the Versailles Summit commitment to continued trade liberalization, which challenged the legality of U.S. trade policy under the GATT.

In addition, domestic political conflict emerged between the steel industry and USW. Although USW and the steel industry fought bitterly over labor issues, they had agreed on tax policy since the 1940s, and beginning in 1974 the USW supported the steel industry's protectionist strategy. The political alliance between the USW and the steel industry dissolved when employment in the steel industry dropped from 449,000 (1978) to 289,000 (1982) (American Iron and Steel Institute 1983), and many steel corporations disinvested from steel. USW argued that the steel industry used the capital from the existing business policy for diversification and refused to support legislation that did not mandate modernization.

To resolve the domestic and international political crises, the executive branch intensified negotiations with EEC and reached an agreement to limit exports of ten categories of steel if AD complaints were withdrawn. The steel industry would not agree to this proposal because it did not include the legal means to block imports. In response, Congress passed a narrowly defined trade law that amended the *Tariff Act of 1930* by requiring a valid export license for steel products (*Congressional Record* 1982). This agreement went into effect in November 1982 with an official ending date of December 1985 when EEC agreed to stop subsidizing its steel industries. The amendment, however, proved inadequately protectionist because, as in the past, the EEC diverted exports toward other product lines. In addition, EEC limited steel imports from newly industrialized countries (NICs) such as Brazil and Korea, which diverted their exports to U.S. markets. By 1983, foreign steel makers captured over 20 percent of the U.S. market share.

To increase protectionism, the steel industry pursued three interrelated political strategies. First, it continued to use the organizational structure of the state to achieve its capital-accumulation goals, and in January 1984 the steel industry filed dozens of AD complaints against EEC producers under the Trade Act of 1979. Second, Bethlehem Steel Corporation with the support of USW petitioned for import restrictions under section 201 of Article 19 of GATT, which allows a government to impose temporary trade protection for an industry that has suffered serious injury due to a surge in imports (*Congressional Quarterly Weekly Report* 1989). Third, the steel industry broadened its political base. By 1983, it had obtained the support of the congressional *Trade Reform Action Coalition*, which represented numerous industrial capitalist subclass segments threatened by imports including the textile, chemical, footwear, nonferrous metal, metalworking, and television industries. In response to the unified lobby efforts of these capitalist groups the House passed the *Fair Trade in Steel Act of 1983*. This legislation limited imports in forty-seven product lines to 15 percent of the domestic market, and mandated modernization.[14] The 1983 steel act simultaneously increased protectionism and resolved the conflict between the USW and the steel industry. This legislation, however, allowed the secretary of commerce to "amend or lift the quota in cases of short supply" (U.S. Congress 1984), and this subclass segment continued to argue that the Executive Branch had too much discretion over enforcement of trade laws.

The steel industry's efforts to use the state structure to realize its agenda succeeded when, in June 1984, the ITC voted to place import quotas on most steel products (International Trade Commission 1984). The decision by the ITC forced President Reagan, who was campaigning for reelection, to revise his free-trade agenda. On the one hand, enforcement of the ITC recommendations could have initiated a trade war or international legal battles. On the other, failure to support the steel industry and the USW ran the risk of losing electoral votes to Senator Mondale in key steel-manufacturing states including Illinois, Indiana, Maryland, Ohio, Pennsylvania, and Texas. To avoid implementing the protectionist recommendations of the ITC, while maintaining political support during an election year, President Reagan replaced the ITC recommendation with a new set of VRAs (1984–1989) that set imports at 18.5 percent of the market share. These agreements, however, were no longer voluntary. This legislation included a licensing system that prevented foreign steel makers from switching their product mix (Reagan 1984), which made it possible to enforce the quotas on a product-by-product basis. This more precise legislation significantly reduced the autonomy of the executive branch in the enforcement of the quotas.

The import quotas were the outcome of a capitalist subclass segment's long-term political strategy (1967–1984) and its capacity (1) to articulate its interests in such a way that it was able to establish alliances with other capitalist subclass and class segments and USW during crucial historical junctures (2) to pressure Congress to implement a protectionist judicial system of trade dispute settlement, and (3) to use the state structure in such a way that enforcement of existing legislation would have conflicted with the state's agenda to maintain stable relations with foreign nation-states.[15]

Findings

There are several important findings. First, organizations that represent political coalitions of capitalist class and subclass segments were a basis of collective action and constituted a means to exercise political power. The AISI was the organizational vehicle that solidified the power of steel producing corporations, forged alliances with other capitalists, and articulated a strategy to realize this subclass segment's political economic interests within a wide range of historical conditions.

Second, the specific form of dependence between the state and the steel industry affected this subclass segment's political and economic strategies. It established a strategy to limit expansion of production capability in the oligopolistic era when the state was dependent on resources that it controlled. Also, through the AISI, the steel industry articulated a political strategy to revise state business policy during the decay-exploration period when the economic strength of the steel industry declined and it was dependent on capital controlled by the state (e.g., tax concessions). Capital dependence of this subclass segment resulted in political mobilization during several historical junctures that resulted in new state business policies, which financed a significant proportion of each major expansion and modernization project within the steel industry since the 1940s.

Third, the rate of economic growth affected business unity. Business unity among the domestic capitalist class was highest when OPEC oil prices (i.e., 1973) and foreign competition (i.e., 1979–82) undermined capital accumulation in the economy as a whole. Threats that weakened corporations' cash flows and increased their dependence of the state for capital (e.g. tax concessions) resulted in political alliances among capitalists who lobbied state managers in representative state structures (i.e., Congress, the executive branch), and bureaucratic state structures (e.g., FTC) to implement policies to overcome constraints to profit making. In contrast, business was less unified during periods of rapid economic growth when corporations had adequate capital to pursue their economic agendas. This finding suggests that when corporations' capital dependence increases, the capitalist class mobilizes politically and moves toward the unified end of the class unity/division continuum to change state business policy. Capitalists' unified political behavior succeeded in obtaining substantial government subsidies to the industrial capitalist class segment throughout the middle decades of the twentieth century.

Fourth, although the steel industry had the resources and political power to successfully advance its specific interests during several historical junctures, this subclass segment developed coalitions with other industrial capitalists when it became less central to growth in the economy as a whole.

Fifth, the state was least autonomous in relation to the steel industry during periods of rapid economic growth, and when the state's national defense and economic stability agendas were dependent on a steady supply of steel. Under these historical conditions the state implemented capital-generating business policies before the steel industry expanded production capability. When economic stability became less dependent on domestic steel and the rate of accumulation in the steel industry declined, this subclass segment was able to exercise less control over the state. This suggests that the state moves toward the less autonomous end of the continuum during periods of rapid economic growth, and toward the autonomous end of the continuum when the rate of capital accumulation declines.

Sixth, when the political strategy of the steel industry undermined profit making in other capitalist subclass segments (i.e., post–World War II), these constraints emerged as political conflicts that were mediated within the state by revising business policy. Moreover, the state's structure and agenda and the way in which the agenda conflicted or coincided with the interests of the steel industry affected the content of the subsequent business policy. State intervention in the oligopolistic era occurred in the form of capital-generating business policy (e.g., tax credits) because the steel industry's strategy to limit production capability undermined the state's agenda to ensure steady economic growth, a strong national defense, and to meet its political-military obligation to foreign nation-states. Similarly, capital-generating business policies (e.g., 1962, 1971, 1981) were implemented during the decay-exploration period to ensure the state's agenda to maintain steady economic growth.

Seventh, after 1974, when protectionist policies were incorporated into the state structure, the steel industry used the state's organizational structure of trade dispute settlement to force the state to enforce litigation against foreign steel producers. A key component of this capitalist subclass segment's political strategy was the coordinated filing of AD complaints (i.e., 1977, 1980, 1982, 1984), which, if enforced, would have conflicted with the state's foreign policy agenda. The executive branch, therefore, resisted enforcement of the AD laws. The state structure established under the *Trade Agreements Act of 1979* provided this subclass segment with the political-legal mechanism to force the state into conflicts with other states that required solutions. Through this historical process the resolution of each conflict resulted in a revised business policy that redefined the state structure and specified the parameters of its formal authority. The capacity of this subclass segment to establish a long-term unified political strategy and to manipulate the state structure explains how the steel industry obtained the highest form of protectionism in the history of the United States during the Reagan administration, one of the most adamant free-trade administrations in the post-World War II era.

The historical sequences examined here show that the state's autonomy declined over time. This decline in state autonomy occurs as it becomes more involved in economic activity. Despite the steel industry's weakened economic position in the 1970s and 1980s, the cumulative effects of its political strategy produced a state structure that reduced state autonomy. Once a political-legal system of trade dispute settlement was established within the state, rather than attempting to influence legislation through its lobbying efforts where success was dependent on support in Congress, the steel industry pursued a legal strategy to achieve its economic agenda. Despite consistent opposition, especially from the executive branch, the steel industry's use of the laws governing trade dispute settlement significantly increased its capacity to exercise power over the state. For example, in 1982 the steel industry rejected the state's proposed business policy, and refused to withdraw AD complaints until the state implemented a licensing agreement to govern steel trade.

While these state business policies facilitated capital accumulation, they are best characterized as a series of short-term policies that have frequently contradicted one another and placed significant financial burdens on society. Estimates suggest that the higher steel prices that followed the 1984 import quotas alone cost consumers 7 billion dollars annually (*New York Times* 1989). Also, policies designed to generate capital in steel corporations (e.g., tax credits, shortened depreciation allowances) reduced government revenues by billions of dollars.

Conclusion: The More Prominent, Less Autonomous State

This examination of historical sequences demonstrates that historical variation in economic growth and stability structured the motives and actions of capitalists. Their motives and actions were affected by the particular form of resource dependence. During the oligopolistic era, when this subclass segment had control over resources upon which the state depended, it unified politically and did not expand until the state supplied much of the capital. During the decay-exploration period, capital accumulation in the steel industry had become increasingly dependent on capital under the state's control (e.g., depreciation allowances, tax credits). In the 1960s, the steel industry organized and launched long-term lobbying and coalition-building strategies to obtain tax concessions. During this period of capital dependence, this subclass segment's capacity to align its interests with the state's economic agenda and establish coalitions with other subclass and class segments redefined business policy to subsidize corporations' modernization and expansion strategies.[16] Through these alliances this subclass segment succeeded in establishing protectionist structures within the state despite resistance from state managers and other capitalist class segments.

During the decay-exploration period, the steel industry's success entailed the exercise of power to restructure crucial state agencies. The organizational structure of the state was redefined in such a way that it required the federal government to litigate complaints filed by steel corporations. Once these state structures were established, this subclass segment expanded its lobbying efforts from the representative parts of the state structure (i.e., executive, legislative) to the bureaucratic structure. The presence of these state structures reduced the capacity of state managers to deny this class segments' demands. The steel industry's success at subordinating the state structure to its profit-making agenda forced the executive branch to accept a system of import protection that it would otherwise have refused (Levine 1985). These institutional arrangements made it possible for this subclass segment to exercise control over the state even when the steel industry was dependent on capital (e.g., tax breaks) under the state's control.

This capital-dependence model of business behavior illustrates the historical conditions that resulted in corporate political behaviors that shaped and transformed state business policy. I identified two themes that affected the content of business policy: conflict between the capital-accumulation agenda of a powerful subclass segment and the agendas of the state, and conflict among capitalists. Both conflicts occurred at the economic level and were mediated at the political level. State business policy was affected by the historically specific conditions of capital accumulation that defined class alliances, the state's agendas, and the historically specific legal and organizational structure of the state. Once the protectionist mechanisms were incorporated into the state structure, each change in business policy redefined the state structure and the parameters of its formal authority. The policy formation process and the degree to which the state acts autonomously in policy making is contingent on historical variation in corporations' capital dependence, the state's structure, economic conditions and the resulting network of capitalist interests and political alignments.

While the state played an increasingly prominent role in these corporations' capital accumulation strategy during the decay-exploration period, it became less autonomous. The state's more prominent role was an outcome of its efforts to resolve the reemerging contradictions between the state's agenda and the capital-accumulation agenda of a powerful subclass segment. The resolution of these contradictions, at each historical juncture, progressively expanded the state structure in such a way that the state became increasingly subordinated to the capital-accumulation demands of this capitalist subclass segment. The historical shift in state power from representative to bureaucratic structures reduces state autonomy. Once established, bureaucratic state structures provide a legal basis for capitalists to pressure the state to enforce existing laws even when enforcement does not coincide with the state's agendas.

CHAPTER 8

Transformation of the Managerial Process, 1980s

Challenged by foreign competition and constrained by rising costs, by the late 1970s, U.S. corporations were unable to compete in the global economy. Decades of protectionism and state subsidies did not produce a competitive industrial sector. Corporations' capital dependence increased, and customers demanded higher quality products at lower costs. Industrial corporations were unable to generate the capital necessary to modernize and restructure. Further, capital shortages in the economy as a whole undermined external capital markets; (i.e., finance capital) capacity to ensure an adequate flow of capital to the industrial sector. This capital shortage was a symptom of the larger problem; the economy was reaching the limits of its capacity to carry debt, threatening long-term stagnation (Bowles, Gordon, and Weisskopf 1983; Greider 1989). Further, historic high interest rates raised the cost to borrow capital.

The recessions in the early 1980s (i.e., 1980, 1981–82) resulted in a profitability crisis in many corporations. This crisis was a consequence of several long-term strategies and trends in U.S. industry, and its further integration into the global economy. These strategies included big businesses' efforts to eliminate or reduce market competition. Many of the largest corporations operated in oligopolistic markets where competition was limited by setting prices and by closely coordinating production capability with market demand (Edwards 1979; Gordon et al. 1982; Chandler 1990; Prechel 1990).

Meanwhile the economies of Japan and several European countries recovered from World War II and expanded their production capabilities beyond the consumptive capacity of their domestic markets. As the newly industrialized countries (NICs) matured (e.g., Brazil, South Korea, Singapore, Thailand), they began to manufacture a wide range of commodities previously produced primarily in

North America and Europe. These developments contributed to the rapid expansion of productive capability in the global economy while markets expanded at a much slower pace. These events changed the structure of the global economy and increased competition.

Although corporate political strategies succeeded in obtaining protectionist legislation that limited competition from imports, investment tax credits, and extremely generous depreciation allowances (chapter 7), these changes in their institutional arrangements did not result in an adequate rate of return. Moreover, protectionist policies did nothing to reduce the domestic competition associated with the new flexible technologies and methods of organizing manufacturing that made it possible to assemble and manufacture many commodities in smaller companies (Piore and Sabel 1984; Thomas 1994). Thus, corporate political strategies did not resolve the emerging meso-macro contradiction. Unable to create a better structure-environment fit by redefining their institutional arrangements politically, corporations began to focus on internal matters.

A second contradiction exacerbated the first one. A fundamental problem confronting large corporations was the disjuncture between their increasingly complex organizational structures and their information-gathering system. As shown in chapters 5 and 6, the system of control within which operating managers were embedded (i.e., financial account controls) generated motives and behaviors that were irrational when evaluated in terms of corporate goals and agendas (i.e., micro-meso contradiction). Several long-term trends and historical conditions contributed to this disjuncture. First, corporations began to manufacture more products from the same technologies. This trend occurred in three phases: (1) the emergence of multi-activity firms that manufactured numerous products from the same raw materials in the first decades of the twentieth century (2) diversification into more product lines in the 1950s and 1960s, and (3) the 1970s and 1980s production of more specialized products within each product line. Together, these changes increased the complexity and number of manufacturing decisions, increasing the need for more precise product-cost information. However, the account-control system that aggregated product-cost information did not provide these data to decision makers.

Second, because the high capability utilization rate kept profits at acceptable levels from 1950 through the 1970s, few incentives to control costs existed.

Third, top management used rates of return on investment (ROI) to assess the performance of entire product lines organized as divisions, and budgets to assess the performance of smaller corporate entities (e.g., departments). These financial controls did not evaluate corporations' capacity to efficiently manufacture specific products. Because product-cost accounting did not evolve at the same rate as organizational complexity, U.S. corporations could neither identify the costs associated with their diverse and complex activities, nor make detailed cost information available to decision makers.

By the 1980s, critics began to raise numerous questions about the industrial sector. Finance capitalists pressured industrial capitalists to restructure their internal organizational arrangements during this decay-exploration period. Institutional stockholders (e.g., Teachers Insurance and Annuity Association-College Retirement and Equities Fund [TIAA-CREF]), California Public Employees' Retirement System (CALPERS) and organizations representing small stockholders (e.g., United Shareholders Association [USA]) mobilized to make the industrial capitalist-class segment improve profits and return on investment (Lazonick 1992; Useem 1993). TIAA-CREF, the largest institutional investor, began to assess the performance of boards of directors and management, and develop strategies to address corporate government governance issues. Industrial corporations responded to their increased capital dependence, to the contradictions in their organizational arrangements, and to pressure from one another capitalist class-segment in three ways: (1) transforming the managerial process (2) merging with and acquiring other corporations in the same or related product lines, and (3) restructuring the corporate form. This chapter examines transformation in the managerial process.

The Theoretical Framework

I suggest that—like the labor process during a previous historical period (Braverman 1974; Noble 1977; Edwards 1979; Clawson 1980; Gordon, Edwards, and Reich 1982)—control over the managerial process in the contemporary era is being centralized. Researchers who address changes in the managerial process have diametrically opposed views. Some suggest that corporations are establishing decentralized cooperative work teams, extending managerial freedom, weakening the boundaries between managers and the managed, emphasizing informal networks, and increasing autonomy and participation (Piore and Sabel 1984; Kanter 1989). Others have argued that the managerial process is becoming more centralized: Managers are further removed from decision-making centers, autonomy is declining, and middle-managerial work is being degraded (Shaiken 1984; Carter 1985; Heydebrand 1985; Burris 1993). Some argue that the ideology of managerial decentralization obscures this degradation (Carter 1985; Smith 1990).

Little progress has been made toward resolution of this debate because current theories fail to address the following question: *How does a corporation maintain control over complex manufacturing processes that involve hundreds of managers while improving product quality and increasing the corporation's capacity to respond to the changing conditions of capital accumulation* (e.g., markets) (Prechel 1994: 724)? I suggest that the failure to address this question is due to the failure of organizational researchers to examine the *spatial* dimensions of the managerial process. There are two interrelated obstacles to answering this question. First, empirical studies of corporate restructuring lack sufficient depth to show *where* decision-making information is located and who has access to it, and *what* is being central-ized and decentralized. Second, the *conception* and *execution* of managerial deci-sions are presented as located in the same place in the corporation. "Modifications in the theoretical formulation of these variables together with an investigation of the location of decision-making information are necessary to determine whether centralization or decentralization is occurring" (Prechel 1994b: 724).

The focus in this chapter is on *how* restructuring the system of control affects the loci of decision-making discretion, the managerial process, managerial auton-omy, and the distribution of decision-making responsibility and authority in the organizational hierarchy. My objectives are (1) to identify the most salient charac-teristics of the emerging system of control, and (2) to show how changing the loci of decision-making information and discretion results in a different set of controls over operating managers.

Although decision making is a central dimension of organization theory and current formulations implicitly or explicitly acknowledge the role of information in the decision-making process, each conceptualizes information in highly ab-stract terms. These conceptual formulations give little attention to the kind of in-formation used, its location in the organization, who has access to it, or how it is used in decision making. I suggest that to determine whether decision making is tightly controlled or subject to wide discretion, researchers must analyze the *design* of information systems and the *spatial* dimensions of the managerial process: *the organizational distance between the conception and execution of decisions.* Moreover, centralization and decentralization must be treated as theoretical constructs that illuminate empirical processes, rather than as empirical absolutes.

Neo-Fordist Decision Making[1]

In the following, I suggest that *new* methods of formal control over the managerial process are emerging in order to ensure standardization of decisions, manufactur-ing processes, and products. Drawing from Max Weber, contemporary decision-making theory, and neo-Marxist conceptions of control, I develop a theoretical framework to explain this dimension of corporate restructuring. These methods of control represent both continuity and change from previous controls. On the one hand, like previous forms of control, neo-Fordist controls are based on rational cal-culation. On the other, these controls entail a sharp break from the past when de-cision making and authority tended to be located in the same place in the corpora-tion. In the following, I will illustrate that the introduction of technically advanced accounting and information processing systems makes it possible to centralize au-thority, while decentralizing the responsibility to *execute* activities *conceptualized* at higher levels in the managerial hierarchy. Unlike contemporary conceptions of de-cision making, which assume that decision making and authority covary (Child 1984), my theoretical framework suggests that authority and decision making can be located in different places in the corporation. Therefore, I treat decision making and authority as separate variables, so that the location of authority apart from the location of decision making can be considered.

Decentralization of authority exists, for example, when the organization's controls of one level over a lower level are so abstract as to leave decision-making discretion with the lower-level manager (Stinchcombe 1990). Therefore, the defining feature of decentralized authority is the *abstractness of information flows and the specificity of how to use that information.* To address this issue, the subterranean processes of collecting, analyzing, and using information must be analyzed.

As Max Weber (1978) argued, rational calculation creates the possibility of establishing a single decision-making criterion, and a unified system of formal control over distinct spheres of the corporation. These efforts to increase economic performance cannot be dissociated from authority because profitability "is a concept which is applicable to every discrete act which can be individually evaluated in terms of business accounting techniques" (Weber 1978:96). Authority is most centralized in manufacturing because the organization of the production process coordinates many complementary processes under continuous common supervision (Weber 1978). This coordination creates the possibility of subjecting social actors to stringent discipline and attaining standardization of effort and of product quality by establishing incentives and shared interests for each actor in the social structure (Weber 1978; Waters 1990).

Rational calculation has a dual role in the corporation. First, it evaluates operating costs in relation to market opportunities to determine "the expected advantages of every projected course of economic action," including the success of profit-making activities and the income-yielding power of the corporation (Weber 1978:81–92; Kalberg 1983). Second, rational calculation is implemented to ensure control and cooperation through "the rational conditioning and training of work performances" (Weber 1946:261).[2] The application of *formal rationality* extends quantitative calculation to as far as it is technically possible to translate actions into numerically calculable terms (Weber 1978).

Three types of control in the modern corporation are based on rational calculation. All three types of control existed throughout the twentieth century. The emphasis on each, however, is historically contingent. First, *budget control* calculates the receipts and expenditures of each budgetary unit at the end of an accounting period. Corporations use budgetary controls to determine capital allocations and to establish expected profit levels (Weber 1978). Budget controls provide information (1) to determine the operating costs of each organizational unit (2) to evaluate the degree to which managers remain within their budgets, and (3) to measure the optimum profitability of the individual worker (Weber 1946). Second, *bureaucratic control* establishes the possibility of carrying out organizational activities based on objective considerations to ensure calculability of results. Weber, for example, argued that the entire system of management emphasizes calculable rules because the success of the enterprise depends on "increasing precision, steadiness, and, above all, speed of operations" (Weber 1978:974). Third, *technical control* is a bundle of rationally calculated rules embedded in the physical technology of the enterprise, and dictates activity at the point of production (Weber 1978; Braverman 1974; Edwards 1979). The selection of technology involves "the consideration of costs" and the degree to which "these expenditures will pay off in terms of money obtained through the sale of the goods" (Weber 1978:66).

The emergence and development of these types of control are based on historically specific conditions. Like other forms of corporate change, capital dependence increases the rate at which rational calculation occurs. Rational calculation occurs at a slower rate "in the absence of the objective need for it" (Weber 1978:106). Researchers sensitive to historical variation have shown, for example, that unanticipated contingencies and crises between 1870 and 1910 resulted in a shift toward a distinctively more purposive system of control, which required new modes of calculation to deliver more precise information to decision makers (Chandler 1962; Noble 1977).[3] Other researchers argue that new organizing techniques and revolutionary changes emerge from crises, and crises result in formalization and tightening of organizational controls (Stinchcombe 1965; Pfeffer and Leblebici 1973; Hamilton and Biggart 1988; Prechel 1991).

My formulation of neo-Fordist decision making suggests that top managers are restructuring the managerial process in response to historically specific capital-accumulation constraints. Rational calculation is intensified to determine where costs can be cut and to increase control over the manufacturing and managerial processes. These data are centralized, and experts (e.g., accountants, engineers) analyze it and establish more precise control by defining the premise of decision making, and distributing information to operating managers on a "need to know basis."[4]

Based on this theoretical reasoning, I suggest four propositions. First, rational calculation is intensified to restructure the account-control system in order to overcome two historically specific constraints on capital accumulation: high manufacturing costs and low-quality products. Second, to ensure standardization of output, decision-making information is centralized and then distributed on a "need to know basis" to limit the decision-making discretion of managers at the point of production. Third, technologies that deliver information are implemented to increase the rate at which information can be transferred throughout the corporation, thereby increasing organizational flexibility and responsiveness to a changing environment. Fourth, neo-Fordist decision-making controls reduce the information-processing activities of production managers, making it possible to reduce the number of managers and levels of the managerial hierarchy.

Transformation of the Managerial Process at American Steel

The Problem: Good Money and Poor Money

This case-oriented analysis of a contemporary corporation shows that in response to severe capital dependence it developed an account-control system based on the same principles as the one advocated and developed by early twentieth century scientific managers (e.g., A. H. Church) who stressed control over managerial decisions affecting product costs (see chapter 5). This chapter illustrates how changes in American Steel's account-control system became the basis of transformations in the decision-making process and the managerial hierarchy. By 1960, this corporation had ten layers of management and retained this managerial hierarchy until the early 1980s (table 8.1).

There are two main forces driving the increased emphasis on organizational control in the late twentieth century: (1) the demand for higher product quality, and (2) increased competition requiring lower operating costs to ensure a profit. As a corporate accountant at American Steel told me, the successful solution to these problems depended on obtaining more precise information on the manufacturing process.

> The desire to know which of our products we make *good money* [profits] [on] and which of our products we make *poor money* [losses] on, and which of our responsibility areas are functioning cost-effectively and which are not is fundamental to the whole concept of accounting and business management. (My emphasis)

Corporations had to standardize decisions to improve product quality and identify cost points before they could determine which cost could be cut. The solution to these problems required more precise information, and organizational control over the use of that information. The new mode of calculation and control defines the premise of decision making at the lower and middle levels by distributing information on a "need to know" basis. Whereas Taylorism and Fordism operate under the principle of distributing information to *workers* on a "need to know" basis, neo-Fordism operates under the principle of distributing information to *managers* on a "need to know" basis. Among the most salient features of neo-Fordist decision making is the simultaneous extension of control over the managerial and manufacturing processes.

Although American Steel steadily expanded its accounting activities and computer applications to improve customer service and profit projections throughout the 1960s and 1970s (chapter 6), its mode of calculation and control did not adequately improve efficiency or effectiveness.[5] In the 1960s and 1970s, American's mean capability utilization rates were 89 and 94 percent and its mean rates of return were 9.6 and 9.7 percent respectively. By 1980, however, global steel-making capability exceeded demand, and higher-quality imported steel was available in

TABLE 8.1 American Steel's Managerial and Organizational Hierarchy, 1960–1980

Managerial Hierarchy	Organizational Hierarchy
Top Management	
1. President	Corporate
2. Vice-president	
Middle Management	
3. General Manager	Product line*: (e.g., Steel Manufacturing)
4. Assistant General Manager	Product group**: (e.g., Flat products, Shape products)
5. Manager	
6. Superintendent	Production units: (e.g., Cold Rolling Mills,
7. Assistant Superintendent	Blooming Mills, Hot Rolling Mills)
Lower Management	
8. General Foreman	Operating responsibilities within production units
9. Assistant General Foreman	
10. Foreman	

* Product line denotes products in an industrial sector (e.g., steel, automobile, chemical).
** Product group refers to a category within the product line (e.g., Buick, Chevrolet).

U.S. markets. As a result, the oligopolistic price-setting structure of the U.S. steel industry collapsed. Between 1975 and 1981 capability utilization rates declined and manufacturing costs increased by 3.3 percent per year more than prices, a cumulative difference of 23.1 percent.

American Steel's inability to control costs became most visible in 1980 (figure 8.1). Although its utilization rate was approximately 81 percent in both 1958 and 1980, American Steel's rate of return on equity was 11 percent and 2.3 percent respectively. Steel demand improved in the second half of 1980 through early 1981, which resulted in a minor upswing in profits. Profitability problems, however, resurfaced during the 1981–1982 recession (i.e., June 1981–December 1982) when domestic steel consumption declined from 105.4 (1981) to 79.6 (1982) million tons and imports rose from 16.3 percent (1980) to 21.8 percent (1982) of the domestic market (AISI 1983). These events resulted in an intensification of rational calculation. As a middle manager in accounting told me:

> The recession has created intense pressures for cost data. The more knowledge you have of your cost, the better chance you're not going to price below your costs and make a bad decision.

In addition to higher internal costs, several external events increased steel-manufacturing costs. For example, oil and natural-gas prices raised the energy cost to manufacture a ton of steel from $15 in 1973 to $220 in 1981 (Hogan 1983), high interest rates and inflation raised inventory and debt costs, and the rising value of the dollar exchange rate increased domestic steel-production costs compared to

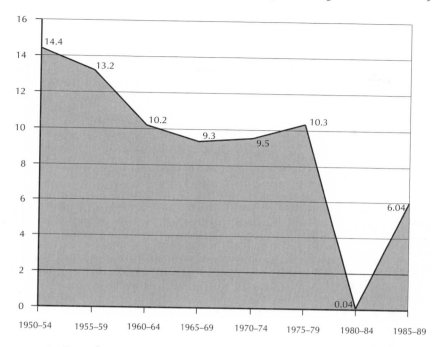

FIGURE 8.1 Rate of return on equity after taxes at American Steel, 1950–1989. *Source:* Moody's *Handbook of Common Stocks*, various years.

foreign producers. In addition, American Steel invested more than 18 percent of its total capital expenditures (1975–1981) to meet environmental protection standards,[6] which reduced efficiency because pollution controls typically increase energy, labor, and maintenance costs. Moreover, market-share competition intensified as imports rose, the steel intensity of the U.S. economy declined,[7] and minimills[8] increased their market share from 2.5 percent (1964) to 20 percent (mid-1980s).

In response to these constraints, American Steel implemented a cost-cutting strategy. Its initial cost reductions, however, did not restore profits to previous levels. By 1982 American Steel's efficiency level declined to where its *break-even point* (i.e., the point at which costs equal revenues) exceeded 80 percent capability utilization. During that same year its capability utilization rate declined to 55.6 percent and averaged only 66.6 percent between 1982 and 1986 (corporate documents). The internal sources of inefficiency, lack of fit with a changing economic environment, and the gap between its break-even point and capability utilization rate created a crisis. The corporation failed to realize a profit for the first time since the Great Depression.

Based on the corporations' calculation of price and cost trends (e.g., raw material, manufacturing, interest), its management projected that American Steel's break-even point would increase from 77 percent of capability utilization rate in 1982 to 86 percent in 1983. Together with the decline of the oligopolistic power of the steel industry, American Steel's efforts to restructure its economic environment through political behavior were not sufficient to ensure a steady and acceptable rate of return. As a top manager in accounting told me these conditions required that American Steel focus on internal restructuring.

> When we realized we couldn't rely on price increases we knew we had to make some internal changes. Without price increases our break-even point also went up, so we had to address the issue.

Restructuring its steel operations was an attempt to create a better fit with the economic environment by reducing internal costs, and creating a structure that was more responsive to shifting market conditions. As a middle manager in sales stated:

> When we went into the reorganization we took the view that the marketplace had changed, our customers had changed, their needs had changed, the demands are changing and as a result of that we have to identify those things better.

In short, the reason the corporation began to restructure the managerial process was to create a better fit with its environment. Restructuring aimed to eliminate subunit goals created by the centralized budgetary controls, delimit middle managerial decision-making authority, monitor managerial decision making, and hold managers responsible for their decisions.

Gradual, Incremental Changes in the Mode of Calculation and Control, 1950–1970s

Prior to the rapid changes that occurred in response to the crisis at American Steel, several incremental changes in its control systems were made that represent a trend toward centralization. While American Steel's accounting department began to define costs in greater detail in the 1950s, the Systems Department implemented more sophisticated computers (i.e., technical controls) to assist in information processing. Historically, Systems is the organizational unit that develops and integrates computer applications into the managerial and manufacturing processes. American Steel began to introduce computers in the 1950s, constructed the first computer-controlled steel-finishing mill in the United States in 1965, and steadily expanded system applications throughout the 1960s and 1970s. A qualitative shift in the use of accounting data to evaluate the manufacturing and managerial processes occurred in the 1970s when the corporation began to emphasize the use of cost-accounting information to make decisions. By 1972 American Steel had identified approximately twelve hundred cost points.[9] To encourage management to focus on costs when making decisions, American Steel established a financial concepts seminar to educate management in the use of financial accounting and cost-accounting information to make better decisions. Although management steadily increased rational calculation, in the absence of market pressures, accounting evolved only slowly throughout the oligopolistic era.

In contrast, when American Steel's internal cash flow eroded and access to inexpensive external capital markets declined in the early 1980s, it accelerated rational calculation. Before the corporation could restructure in such a way so as to improve efficiency, it had to identify its manufacturing costs on each product more precisely and compare these costs to market price. Only after the corporation identified the profitability of each product could it determine which products represented "good money" (i.e., profits) and which products represented "poor money" (i.e., losses).

Restructuring in the Mode of Calculation and Control, Phase One

By 1982 the corporation began to identify and collect cost data in more detail and by 1985 American Steel had identified more than fifty thousand cost points. Moreover, by 1981, systems activities were centralized and moved to the engineering and corporate-planning department. Once American Steel specified the cost to manufacture each product, it analyzed production cost and price data to maximize profits through selective marketing of individual products. Management used this information to identify its least profitable products and product groups, and to shut down or sell the facilities used to make those products. By 1987, American Steel retired its highest cost and least profitable manufacturing units. This downsizing lowered production capability by approximately 30 percent. A top manager with a background in manufacturing initiated these changes, simplifying the corporation structure and reducing horizontal differentiation.

The corporation also used the costing system to identify fixed costs to evaluate alternative production strategies. This process entailed the intensification of *managerial accounting*, the dimension of accounting that transforms standardized cost data into decision-making information.[10] Managerial accounting uses data to, for example, compare the cost of operating a facility at a specific capability utilization rate to the cost of shutting it down and bringing it back up to production. Identifying these costs provides the information to make a decision on whether it is more cost efficient to continue to operate a mill at a specific utilization rate, or to shut the mill down and bring it back up to production. Historically, steel mills were not shut down because of the time necessary to bring them back up to operating temperature. Operating managers typically kept the production facility operating and stockpiled inventories. However, two changes in the economic environment in the 1970s undermined the assumptions that these decisions were based upon. First, energy cost dramatically increased after the oil shocks of 1973 and 1979. Second, double-digit rates increased the cost of capital invested in inventories; in the early 1980s American Steel's semifinished inventories ranged from $750 to $900 million.[11] Moreover, capital invested in inventories could not be used for other purposes. Reducing investment in inventories became increasingly important as corporations became more dependent on expensive external capital. As one manager told me:

> There has been more emphasis on financial data in recent years and a lot of it is tied to the difficult times the steel industry has gone through. I would say that fifteen years ago the primary emphasis was on the income statement, what is the company's profit for the year. As the steel industry and American Steel has gone through some difficult times there has been much more emphasis on the balance sheet and cash-flow analysis. But, I think that is true of industry in general. The emphasis on cash flow increased dramatically in the early 1980s when we went through a period of rapidly escalating interest rates. And that is a macroeconomic event. When the prime rate was 5 percent industry did not pay as much attention to what the cost of carrying inventory was as they did when the prime rate went up to 18 percent.

American Steel placed more emphasis on managerial accounting because it allowed management to determine the most effective operating strategy for each mill, and to evaluate the cost effectiveness of specific managerial decisions. With access to these more precise data management can identify, for example, the total consumption of supplies and raw materials in any given period at a specific utilization rate. More precise calculation of raw material consumption reduces front-end inventory costs, while eliminating bottlenecks in the manufacturing process that occur due to an inadequate supply of raw materials.

American Steel also used these accounting data to develop a strategy to close the competitive gap with steel producers in Japan. Using manufacturing and transportation cost data, American Steel calculated the gap between its costs and the cost of Japanese products delivered in its market area. Based on these calculations American Steel projected a 20 percent gap by 1985 between the cost structure of its primary product groups, and the cost structure of its Japanese competitors for the same products. To improve its competitive position top management introduced a cost-cutting program designed to reduce its manufacturing costs by $82 million in 1982 and $200 million in 1983.

Manufacturing Consent: Corporate Culture and Corporate Values, Phase Two

Like many corporations created around the turn of the century, American Steel employed numerous methods to ensure compliance of its managers.[12] *Responsible autonomy* was one of the key strategies to win the loyalty of corporate managers: giving employees leeway in their work activities and encouraging them to adapt to changing situations in a manner beneficial to the firm (Friedman 1977). Instilling responsible autonomy among managers entailed providing managers with authority over decision making, leeway in making those decisions, and promoting managers from within. As discussed in chapter 6, however, the account-control system provided no realistic means to determine if corporations' quasi-market transactions were cost efficient. Moreover, as the corporation expanded, the effectiveness of these indirect controls declined. The corporate culture did not maintain the degree of unity, communication, and cooperation necessary to ensure the smooth operation of the complex manufacturing process. Over time—encouraged by the existing formally rational controls—employees identified with organizational subunits and subunit goals.

Although the Industrial Relations Department at American Steel was aware of the lack of cooperation among operating managers, the corporation did not confront this problem until the profitability crisis occurred in the early 1980s. Like in many corporations, American Steel's top management was initally influenced by the proposed solution of the corporate culture gurus. Its top management attempted to *manufacture consent* among its managers to overcome the conflicts and contradictions in the managerial process by placing more emphasis on corporate culture. Burawoy (1979) illustrates managements' attempts to manufacture consent among workers to accept workplace discipline. Describing a similar process, Child uses the term *cultural control:* the attempt to maintain "control by ensuring that members of an organization accept as legitimate, and willingly comply with, managerial requirements"(Child 1984:163). The corporate culture chapter of American Steel's restructuring was not as effective as the gurus claimed and its top management had hoped.

In 1983, American Steel hired an outside consulting firm to rearticulate and communicate its corporate culture to its employees in such a way that it addressed its cost-control problems, profitability crisis, and the need for cooperation among all employees. The key component of the cultural dimension of corporate restructuring was an elaborate education program designed (1) to make managers aware of the relationship between their decisions and the profitability crisis, and (2) to encourage management to contribute to cost reductions at every level of the corporation.

Once top management redefined American Steel's corporate culture, it set up a team leadership program (TLP) to better unify the managerial process. Specifically, it attempted to establish a unified set of values to promote cooperation among decision makers (i.e., team management), encourage lateral communication, participatory decision making and problem solving, and shift the delegation of decision making from middle managers to line managers. As a human relations manager stated:

> The team process was an attempt to get all of these people singing the same song—coordinating, thinking the same, communicating *the same values downward*, having the same priorities.

A central component of the revised corporation culture was the attempt to instill how each manager's actions (e.g., decisions) contributed to costs and profits.

The mechanism to transmit these values included an elaborate set of seminars to communicate integrated steel's goals to managers and educate them in how their activities contributed to these goals. This initiative was designed to create a homogeneous value orientation beyond the technical requirements of managerial tasks to improve its "long-term effectiveness by eliminating the barriers among production units" (corporate document).

Initially, middle-level operating management was hostile to these proposed changes, perceiving the sharing of decision-making authority as a threat to their previously uncontested authority. In response to this resistance, top management announced that employees who could not adapt to the new structure were of little value to the corporation. The threat of unemployment or a career change for middle managers in this high-paying industry had mixed consequences. Although some of American Steel's best managers pursued employment elsewhere, few managers left the corporation voluntarily during this period of nationwide middle-managerial retrenchment.

Macro-economic conditions—brought on by global competition and recession—were manifested in the corporation as declining profits and restructuring of the managerial process, eliminating jobs throughout the U.S. economy. This decreased middle-managerial job opportunity and security. This labor market created conditions where middle managers accepted terms of employment that they may have rejected during the labor market conditions of the 1950s, 1960s, and 1970s when a high degree of middle-managerial security, opportunity, and mobility existed.

In summary, concomitant with establishing more formal control, American Steel attempted to elaborate the system of informal control by developing a unified value orientation intended to promote a sense of togetherness and responsibility among managers. While the previous corporate culture stressed the corporation as a community of employees, the new corporate culture stressed the corporation as a community of employees responsible for making a profit.

This strategy constitutes an important shift in the relationship between top management and the other employees. Historically, workers and lower and middle managers were considered members of a corporate community and assigned specific tasks to perform. Profits were considered the responsibility of top management. In contrast, the new corporate culture stressed the individual as a member of the corporate community whose activities are directly associated with the corporation's capacity to achieve its profitability goals. These efforts at instilling a new sense of responsible autonomy, however, did not capture control over the managerial process. The steel industry remained highly competitive, and for the third consecutive year American Steel did not realize a profit.[13]

Quality Control and the Information-Gathering System, Phase Three

American Steel's embeddedness in the manufacturing sector as a whole also constrained profit making. The capacity of U.S. corporations to compete globally required that product quality improve throughout the manufacturing sector because the quality of the output of primary product industries (e.g., steel, glass, rubber, plastic) becomes the input into secondary product industries (e.g., automobile, office furniture), affecting their ability to improve product quality. Low quality in one link of the *commodity chain*—interim products—affects the quality and cost in other links. For example, low-quality iron ore requires higher energy cost to eliminate chemical impurities, or results in low-quality steel. If the manufacturing process does not eliminate the impurities, the lower quality steel does not bend uniformly when it is being shaped into automobile doors, hoods, and fenders. Flawed parts must be discarded as scrap, which increases automobile manufacturing costs. Customers demanded higher-quality steel so they could lower their cost, improve their product quality, and compete in their markets. Dependent on these markets, American Steel had little choice but to comply. However, these demands increased American Steel's manufacturing costs and constrained their capacity to make a profit. As one top manager told me:

> Every year, without exception, the quality parameters became more exact. One reason why this happened, and will continue, is that steel customers realized they could lower their manufacturing costs by insisting on higher quality steel.

By the mid-1980s higher quality became the key to high profits and American Steel further intensified rational calculation to achieve this goal.

Before American Steel could improve product quality to the level necessary to compete globally, however, it had to restructure the way in which it used accounting data. American Steel's accounting system neither provided the costs associated with specific decisions within an operating unit, nor identified how those decisions affected product quality. Operating units continued to be the primary unit of control. In short, this mode of calculation and control provided a diagnostic of whether there had been a failure in an entire operating unit that needed to be discovered and corrected. It provided neither the basis for identifying the failure nor an understanding of what needed to be changed.

To improve product quality while lowering per-unit costs, American Steel redesigned the account-control system to emphasize integrated steel as a single business, not a collection of independent operations. This entailed a shift from the use of return on investment and budgetary controls that evaluated the performance of organization units, to controls that evaluated the contribution of each decision to the overall performance of the corporation. As a top-level accounting manager stated:

> Many people viewed that [profit data in organizational units] as important informa-
> tion. I never did because I knew the numbers were completely unrealistic, but still
> there were people who looked at that and they were made to feel better if they could
> open up a book and see that . . . coal mine earned two million dollars this month
> and . . . ore mine earned $7 million, things like that. Not realizing that the numbers
> weren't worth the powder to blow them to hell.
>
> Things like profits in raw materials, which were really fictitious anyway, were the
> wrong thrust. The raw materials department objective should be to produce the
> highest quality product at the lowest possible cost, which then becomes a cost in the
> steel product.

This point is crucial. Managerialists' arguments that profitability measurements
(i.e., ROI) in corporate units (e.g., divisions, departments) contribute to efficiency (Chandler 1977; Williamson 1985) fail to recognize important flaws in the
financial conception of control that was used through the 1970s (also see Johnson
and Kaplan 1991).

To reduce per-unit costs and increase quality, American Steel redesigned the accounting system to establish a managerial system capable of diagnosing the efficiency of specific manufacturing decisions. As a top accounting manager stated:

> In our manufacturing processes there are a couple of thousand steel specifications or
> recipes. In the past, we had some groups that didn't have specific specifications.
> There are vast differences in the cost alloys, tellurium versus some steel that has rare
> earth additives in it. The cooking time, heating practices, manufacturing process,
> and the raw steel making end of it also create variances in the cost.

American Steel's previous account controls generated budgetary controls for each
production unit and collected general cost data as the product moved through the
manufacturing process. In contrast, internal restructuring entailed the collection
of data on each cost input, and the more precise calculation of the actual cost that
products accumulate. As an accounting manager stated:

> Unless you have considerable detailing of costs, you don't know which of your prod-
> ucts is making money for you. So [the corporation did] extensive correlation of sales
> information by products with the cost center.

A crucial dimension of cost specification included disaggregating data on organizational units previously used for financial reporting. This was accomplished by
separating "out costs that were grouped, that were never identified. Some cost, for
certain variables, you didn't know because you just had cost on the whole unit"
(top accounting manager).

Centralization of Decision-Making Information, Stage Four

After American Steel identified, collected, and relocated these costs into a central
database, it used these data to define cost centers at the point of production, to

establish cost controls for these centers, and to calculate when manufacturing costs exceeded the rationally calculated estimated costs. These activities were centralized into a new organizational unit that combined the previously separate quality control and technology units. This new unit—*the manufacturing decision center*—was elevated to the top of the managerial hierarchy in the steel-manufacturing business segment, equivalent to the plant manager.

The creation of this organizational unit signifies a shift to a different form of control. In contrast to past controls over management that evaluated entire product groups and organizational units, technical experts in the manufacturing decision center used these data to calculate and establish more precise premise controls over the manufacturing of each product. On the one hand, this change shifted the emphasis from product groups to individual products. On the other, it established the premise for making a decision. *Premise controls* restrict behavior by limiting the "content and flow" of information, thereby limiting "the search for alternatives"; premise controls are effective because "the subordinate voluntarily restricts the range of stimuli" used in decision making (Perrow 1986:128–29). Together the specification of information sources and premise controls ensure predictable and consistent decision making. Historically, premise controls were limited to nonroutine decisions, professionals, and operated at high levels of the organizational hierarchy (Simon 1957; Perrow 1986). These centralized data, however, are analyzed in the restructured corporation by a set of highly skilled experts (e.g., technicians, engineers, metallurgists) in the decision center. These changes resulted in centralized control over the manufacturing process by programming production control computers, and defining the premise of decision making at the lower and middle level.

The centralized computer system made it possible for technical experts to aggregate or disaggregate data, depending on managerial needs, and distribute that information on a "need to know" basis. American Steel used these data to establish a *standardized decision-making criterion*, to introduce more precise cost controls, to improve product quality, and to hold managers accountable for their decisions. As one manager stated:

> The processes of defining and organizing objectives are built on the need for *standardization* and conformance to customer specifications. The basic concept behind this process is that once we establish a base, the operating departments are *accountable* for managing to that base.

By 1987 American Steel had placed computer monitors at each decision site to transmit the most recent data from the decision center to the point of production. At the end of 1989, American Steel's engineer-managers had established a standardization index (i.e., production characteristic standards) for 73 percent of its products. The standardization index simultaneously provided premise controls to base decisions on to ensure standardization of product quality, and predict the product cost to manufacture the product at those specifications. Most important, these account controls created a monitoring system capable of holding managers accountable to manage to that cost base. As a senior accounting manager stated:

> The cost center is really a control function. The more cellular the cost-centering structure, the more a cell can be examined [to determine] if it is functioning reasonably. It directs management's attention to where problems are so that they can take some kind of remedial action. . . . Unless you have considerable detailing of costs, you don't know which of your products is making money for you.

The identification of costs also made it possible to intensify *responsibility accounting:* cost accounting by area of responsibility. "One section [of the accounting activity] is called product cost and their basic job is to take the cost information from the standard cost system to identify area of responsibility" (senior accounting manager). The identification of a cost simultaneously locates where that cost occurs in the manufacturing process, which makes it possible to identify the decision maker responsible for that specific cost. In contrast to previous controls that provided a diagnostic of whether a cost overrun occurred in an operating unit, these new controls have the capacity to diagnose if a cost associated with a specific decision exceeds a rationally calculated base cost.

In addition, American Steel intensified *bureaucratic control:* rules defining spans of control, lines of authority, and areas of responsibility, specified in greater detail. This process entailed further centralization of control: "The limits of power or decision making were escalated up the ladder to be more clearly delineated, reviewed, and approved" (senior corporate manager). These rules, together with responsibility accounting, aided in identifying the middle managers responsible for the costs of coordinating the manufacturing process, and the lower level line managers responsible for the specific production costs. Whereas the standard cost system identified the point at which specific cost inputs exceeded predetermined costs, bureaucratic controls identified the manager responsible for those costs. Together these centralized formal controls made it possible to identify even the lowest-level managers and hold them accountable for their decisions.

These controls created the organizational capacity to simultaneously: "increase accountability at each level and enlarge decision-making responsibility throughout the organization" (corporate document). Identifying product cost, the manager responsible for those costs, and more precise monitoring of operating management further centralized authority. As one middle manager stated, operating managers that did not comply were replaced.

> Accountability means we can go back to an individual and say your costs for this product are off by $15. Why is it off that $15? How do you get back up to plus $15? The supervisor can say if you can't do the job . . . maybe you have the wrong people doing it. Ultimately, you may have to make some changes.

Unlike previous controls when operating managers relied on their experience and knowledge of the manufacturing process and remained partially autonomous from centralized controls, restructuring to evaluate the cost-efficiency of specific decisions reduced the autonomy of operating management.

Production problems that could not be resolved readily by premise controls were allocated to management teams. These teams, established by the team leadership program, consisted of the group of managers whose areas of responsibility were affected by that particular decision. Like decisions made by individual managers, the emphasis on formal control redefined the basis of decision making within these teams. Whereas the corporate-culture program emphasized a unified value orientation to make managers aware of the relationship between their decisions and corporate profits, managerial accounting specified the basis of team decisions. Within this structure, when a difference between standard and actual costs was identified, management teams investigated the source and collectively made a decision based on these cost data.

Similar to premise controls over individual decision making, the emphasis on team decision making—together with this predetermined rationally calculated criterion—operated as an *unobtrusive control:* "the control of the cognitive premise underlying action" (Perrow 1986:129). This change shifted responsible autonomy from individual managers to a team of managers. Team management established a mechanism whereby managers supervised each another to ensure that they followed top managerial directives and employed formally rational data in the decision-making process. Team management entails an important strategic shift in controlling managers. Rather than relying on management's acceptance of a unified value orientation to ensure the functioning of the decision-making process, team management places coercive pressures on members of the team to ensure that individual managers use these rationally calculated data in the decision-making process. These coercive pressures function to maintain a unified value orientation that legitimizes the centralized formally rational controls governing the decision-making process.

Team management was part of top management's strategy to transform the basis of decision making from an understanding of the manufacturing process to an understanding of cost data. Rational calculation occurred at a slower rate "in the absence of the objective need for it" (Weber 1978:106), but was intensified in response to capital accumulation constraints in the 1980s. As a senior corporate accountant stated:

> Accounting has become a much more sophisticated area than it was thirty years ago. Operating management has changed. It's no longer a rough and tough John Wayne-type superintendent who can fix anything with an acetylene torch and a sledgehammer. Operating management's sophistication level has risen and the complexity and

sophistication of accounting have greatly increased. When college graduates get to work in industry they find that every time they turn around somebody is rubbing their nose in a computer printout and is holding them responsible for favorable and unfavorable numbers.

Although decisions continued to be executed at lower levels in the managerial hierarchy, in contrast to the previous budgetary control system, many conception functions were concentrated in the decision center. By centralizing the loci of decision-making discretion, American Steel created the organizational capacity to move execution down to the level where inputs occur while centralizing dimensions of the conceptualization process and the monitoring of those decisions.

After specifying cost and bureaucratic controls, American Steel set up *technical controls* under the guidance of engineers from a Japanese steel corporation. The corporation also sent more than one hundred blue-collar and managerial employees to observe the formal controls used in a Japanese steel corporation. American Steel implemented these technical controls to maximize capability utilization rates, to better control the manufacturing process, and to reduce the cost of carrying inventories.

This phase of corporate restructuring centralized coordinating functions of the entire plant in the new *operations control center*. The center programmed computers to schedule orders with similar production specifications to reduce the amount of downtime needed to adjust the manufacturing process to meet different product specifications. This new organizational unit transformed steel making from batch production to *continuous processing*, the organization of steel making that links operations leading to a more continuous flow of steel processing from initial steel making to delivery at the customer's plant.[14] Continuous processing, however, is not merely a different way to organize production; it entails centralization of control. It aids in achieving market-oriented goals by tight coupling and centralizing (corporate document).

The second technical control to improve product quality incorporated *statistical quality control* (SQC) directly into the manufacturing process. Statistical quality control is the application of statistical techniques to help experts (e.g., engineers, managers) solve problems and plan more effective systems, which entails the application of statistical principles and techniques to direct the manufacturing process (Deming 1969).

American Steel's embeddedness in the commodity chain produced coercive pressures that accelerated the application of this formally rational control.[15] By the early 1980s, General Motors began to implement SQC into its manufacturing processes, and in 1984 informed American Steel that it would stop purchasing its steel if it did not use SQC. General Motors knew that it could lower its manufacturing costs if it had higher quality steel, and it assumed that this technical control would improve quality. Although American Steel had begun to implement SQC in 1983, its dependence on this customer in its largest market resulted in a rapid acceleration of SQC applications. SQC is being used on two levels within industry.

On the one hand, customers use *statistical quality improvement* (SQI) programs to measure the parameters of a product to ensure that it meets their manufacturing process. These coercive pressures are described by a middle manager in the computer department.

> Each of our customers is using their statistical quality programs to come up with specific measurements of what they feel the quality ought to be from their steel suppliers. And they are continuing to narrow that window on what the net requirements are. And that net drives our process. We used to inspect quality. But we never had a statistical program in place that we could make sure that we were meeting the quality standard that the customer wanted. [That] dramatically changed our manufacturing process.

On the other, corporations use internal applications of SQC to improve quality and meet the statistical parameters established by their customers in two ways. First, American Steel used SQC to evaluate the tolerance capabilities of a particular technology to determine whether that technology could manufacture a product to meet customers' specifications. Second, once management identified the tolerance capabilities of the manufacturing technology it used *statistical process control* (SPC) to "monitor every production process to make sure that the right material goes in and the right material comes out, and it is measured against consistent standards" (sales middle manager).

By 1986 technical experts in the manufacturing decision center had calculated the standards for all significant product characteristics. When American Steel received an order, sales personnel transferred the product specifications to the manufacturing decision center, where technicians programmed the production-control computers to those predetermined standards. In short, experts in the decision center use these technical controls to incorporate production decisions directly into the manufacturing process. Statistical process control and the production-control computer together established a reiterative control system that repeatedly measures and monitors the product while it is manufactured to ensure conformance to standards. If the product exceeds the tolerance limits calculated for a particular product, the production-control computer automatically adjusts the technology during the manufacturing process to conform to the standards necessary to meet the customer's requirements. "Production units are computer-monitored for conformance to the new standards to assure maximum *control* of manufacturing and the identification and more timely correction of quality problems during manufacturing" (corporate document). One top manager in manufacturing described this process in a similar way as Frederick Taylor described his early-twentieth-century version of scientific management. Technical control

> is a tool for monitoring the output of a process, and *standardization*, which is an approach to guarantee customers their specified product. The idea is to find the *best way* of doing something, then make sure it is done that way every time. (My emphasis)

Like cost and bureaucratic control, American Steel based technical control on rationally calculated quantitative data to ensure standardization. "It is a means to an end. It defines quality as conformance to [preestablished] standards. That is our end" (corporate document). Although SQC represents a more precise form of technical control, like product cost accounting, SQC did not represent a recent conceptual breakthrough. A. H. Church stressed the advantages of cost accounting by product in the early 1900s, engineers in the United States emphasized the advantages of statistical quality control in the late 1930s (Shewhart 1931, 1939), and many Japanese corporations introduced it into their manufacturing process in the 1960s.[16] Neither technique was widely used in the United States until the crisis in the early 1980s.[17]

Formally Rational and Flexible Managerial Hierarchies

The Centralization and Redistribution of Information: The Hierarchical Computer System

Implementation of these controls entailed restructuring the Systems Department. By the late 1980s, Systems' responsibilities shifted from computer applications to database (i.e., information) management. A middle manager in Systems describes this rapid change:

> Since I came to the company [1970s], Systems has moved from a developer of [computer] applications to being responsible for corporate databases. We have to be the people who . . . can make that data available to the people who need it to make decisions. You see that with the growth of our information center. I think that is the same kind of focus that all systems organizations across the country are going to head toward. We have a group at the plant called our systems technology group. Their primary responsibility is automating information, making information easy to access, obtain, manage, print, display, and manipulate. They're looking at all types of ways to get information in and making it easier to access.

Once American Steel located the product cost and market-price data into a centralized database, it developed a computer model to identify the most cost-efficient blend of raw material and process variables (e.g., heat, rolling pressure) required to meet specific product-quality goals. The information-processing capacity of the computer could calculate these data in "less than two minutes"; in the past, "it would have taken a couple of people three or four weeks to make those calculations" (research and development middle manager).

To transmit data to the appropriate location in the corporation, the systems department established a hierarchical three-level computer system. The business computer, at the *highest level*, provided access to information used to coordinate raw material inventory with sales and production schedules, trace each product (i.e., semifinished inventory) from the time it entered the manufacturing process as raw materials to its delivery date, and store information on billing and projected delivery dates.

At the *lowest level*, this system increased *automated management*: the application of computer information processing systems to aid in decision making and in controlling the manufacturing process. American Steel set up programmable individual computers (i.e., computer-aided manufacturing (CAM)) that identify and immediately correct problems within individual manufacturing technologies. CAM "automatically measured the shape and adjusted the rollers to increase the pressure on the stress point," thereby correcting defects during the manufacturing of the product (Systems middle manager). This technical control represented a key component of the rationalization process. A top manager in manufacturing described the change as taking

> the humanistic element out of the decision-making process. The operators used to have to eyeball the strip as it fed through the mill and manually adjust it to ensure flatness. The new [computer controlled] system automatically measures the shape and adjusts the rollers, correcting any shape defects as the steel is being rolled in order for us to make a good, consistent product.

Humans, however, are not completely eliminated from the point of production. As one manager stated: "now and then it [the computer] will holler tilt and you [have] to get a human being in there to find out what is tilting." This dimension of corporate restructuring represented a central scientific management principle. It separated conception from execution in its most extreme form: computers executed decisions conceptualized in the manufacturing decision center. When production problems emerged that were beyond the capabilities of the technology, production managers or managerial teams consulted with the decision center or used managerial accounting techniques to formulate decisions to be used in correcting the problem.

At the *middle level*, the computer-integrated manufacturing (CIM) system connected the individual (CAM) computers to coordinate manufacturing activities into a continuous process. These synchronized controls replaced informal coordination of the manufacturing process that previously had escaped calculation. Together the CAM and the CIM systems coordinated the various stages of the manufacturing process and transmitted product specifications to the appropriate point of production.

This computer hierarchy links order processing, planning, scheduling, manufacturing, and customer-service functions. American Steel implemented this multilevel computer system to standardize decision making, the manufacturing process, and ultimately the final product to meet the increasingly precise and changing quality specifications demanded by its customers. This formally rational technical control is central to contemporary management. By 1992 American Steel had fully set up these controls, which made it possible to continuously cast 100 percent of the steel it manufactured. Continuous casting is designed to increase product quality, to ensure the continuous use of production units, to improve customer service, and to reduce raw material, semifinished, and finished inventories.

This rationalization of the managerial and manufacturing processes mitigated American Steel's capital dependence problem by increasing capital turnover. In contrast to the early 1980s when the amount of capital invested in semifinished inventory levels ranged from $750 to $900 million, in 1992 American Steel's investment in these inventories dropped to $67 million. This reduced American Steel's capital dependence by improving cash flow and allowing it to use this capital for other investments.

Corporate Downsizing: Creating a Tightly Coupled, Flexible, and Flatter Managerial Hierarchy

These changes also increased horizontal and vertical tight coupling of the managerial process. A new *plant planning and scheduling system* tightly coupled each production unit horizontally by centralizing and formalizing the coordinating functions. This dimension of the control system was designed to cut cost by reducing (1) the downtime necessary to realign the manufacturing facilities, (2) the amount of capital invested in semifinished inventories, and (3) the energy required to reheat products manufactured in discrete stages. The corporation implemented this centralized, more tightly coupled manufacturing process to achieve:

> market-oriented goals and maintain a continuous processing strategy. The concept of continuous processing cannot succeed unless functions are *centralized* and performed by an organization whose perspective is the entire production process. (Manufacturing top manager)

Vertical tight coupling occurred in three areas of the corporation. First, management linked the CAM system at the point of production directly to the manufacturing decision center. Second, through this vertical linkage the corporation transmit premise controls to the computer terminals at each decision site to enhance standardization of decision making. Third, the computer system provided the capacity to locate customers' orders. If a customer requests a change in an order, the regional salesperson transmits this information to the sales decision center, where operators can locate and change these specifications minutes before the order enters the manufacturing process. These controls tightly coupled the corporate entities and the corporation to its economic environment. The restructured corporation had the capacity to transmit standardized decision-making information throughout the managerial hierarchy from "operations, or sales, or general management so they can make the *proper decision*, which could vary under different economic situations" (accounting top manager).

In contrast to the previous corporate structure in which production managers had control over both conception and execution, restructuring centralized many conception functions in the decision centers, decentralized execution, and held managers responsible for proper execution. The parameters of conception functions that remained at the point of production were narrowly defined by formally rational controls created at higher levels in the corporation. In contrast to the semiautonomous organizational units where operating managers obtained much of their decision-making information through informal means, this restructured corporation redefined the role of middle managers, reducing their importance to the functioning of the corporation. As a Systems middle manager put it:

> Middle managers used to be the people that provided the information. They acted as an information source. With the increase in information technology, middle management throughout America is threatened because they are no longer the information sources.

TABLE 8.2 Transformation of the Managerial Hierarchy at American Steel, 1980–1985

Manazerial Hierarchy in 1980	*Managerial Hierarchy in 1985*
Top Management	
1. President	1. President
2. Vice-president	2. Vice-president
Middle Management	
3. General manager	3. General manager
4. Assistant general manager	4. Assistant general manager
5. Manager	
6. Superintendent	
7. Assistant superintendent	
Lower Management	
8. General foreman	5. Section manager
9. Assistant general foreman	6. Supervisor
10. Foreman	

Corporate restructuring included a shift in managerial skills from understanding the manufacturing process to understanding this new from of calculation.[18]

Together these controls made it possible to reduce the number of decisions, decision makers, and layers of the managerial hierarchy. American Steel replaced many of the information-processing activities of operating management. Although the managerial hierarchy remained stable throughout much of the oligopolistic era (table 8.2), between 1980 and 1985, it reduced the number of middle levels of management from five to two, and lower levels of management from three to two, reducing the lower and middle levels of managerial hierarchy from eight to four (table 8.2). These changes accounted for corporate downsizing at American Steel eliminating 28 percent of its managers.

The Commodity Chain and the Formal Rationalization of Manufacturing

This case-oriented study leaves us with an important question: Was hyperquantification to centralize control over the managerial process at American Steel an exception? Although the extreme capital accumulation crisis at American Steel may have resulted in an accelerated rate of change, the basis of corporate restructuring at American Steel is typical of other corporations.

Restructuring the managerial process at American Steel was a response to pressure from other corporations with which it had resource-dependent relations defined by its position in the commodity chain. Although American Steel's capital-dependent condition affected these changes, its customers pressured it to introduce these formally rational controls. In an effort to close the quality gap between its foreign competitors and improve their profit-making opportunities, U.S. automakers introduced SPC in the late 1970s. By the early 1980s, this core industry concluded that SPC was an effective way of improving quality. The quality of inputs (e.g., steel, glass, rubber, plastic) obtained from its suppliers, however, restricted the automobile industry's ability to improve quality.

By 1983 this steel consumer began to pressure steel manufacturers to establish techniques to improve delivery schedules and the quality of steel. Automakers (e.g., General Motors, Ford) demanded that steel producers use SPC, and threatened to stop purchasing from those who failed to use SPC in their manufacturing processes. In 1983 Oldsmobile announced that it would not purchase steel for one of its 1985 models that was not manufactured with SPC. Since the automotive industry consumes approximately 30 percent of the integrated steel industry's output, corporations in this industry had little choice but to comply. Additionally, to control its front-end inventory costs, the automobile industry pressured the steel industry to establish more precise delivery schedules. In response, American Steel set up its plant planning and scheduling system (PPSS) to coordinate steel shipments with delivery schedules to achieve just-in-time goals set by customers.

American Steel placed similar constraints on its suppliers. In the late 1980s,

American Steel introduced a policy to only purchase products from suppliers that used SPC. American Steel established a product evaluation program to detect the variability of the most critical input materials in the steel-making process, and provided SPC consultation to suppliers making those products. To enforce compliance, it established inspection teams that used statistical techniques to evaluate suppliers' capacity to meet American Steel's product specifications. American Steel also pursued a strategy of single sourcing (i.e., reduced the number of suppliers) based on suppliers' use of these controls. Like the automakers, if one of its suppliers failed to establish these formal rational controls, American Steel refused to purchase their product.

American Steel became more tightly coupled to fewer suppliers because it assumed that standardization of input materials improved their capacity to more accurately predict how these products react during the manufacturing process and meet quality control parameters. This suggests that tighter resource-dependent corporate networks are emerging, placing pressure on corporations to establish more precise control over the managerial process. These controls reduce output variance by reducing the variance in input materials. Manufacturing corporations have little choice. In a period of heightened competition, corporations must comply with demands set by core corporations that consume their products.

The relationship between large corporations and their suppliers constitutes a variation on late-nineteenth-century subcontracting. However, one important difference exists: contemporary corporations have the information to select those aspects of the commodity chain where the highest profits exist. After corporations identified product cost in detail, they began to subcontract the least cost-efficient aspects of their production process. Also, in the nineteenth century, principals (i.e., capitalists) assumed the financial risk but had limited control over the return on their capital investment. In contrast, within contemporary institutional arrangements large corporations can require agents (i.e., subcontractors) to set up their manufacturing process to meet their (i.e., the principal's) product quality requirements. That is, principals can define the conditions of the contract, but they do not have the financial risk. When demand declines, the principals can stop their orders. Further, these new relations within the commodity chain place downward pressure on profits and wages in noncore industries.

The trend toward subcontracting is rapidly accelerating. Although the automobile industry has subcontracted many of its manufacturing processes for decades, corporations in other industries are setting up this strategy. In the farm equipment industry, Deere & Co. subcontracts most of the parts for some of its tractors and Agco Corporation subcontracts almost one-half of the parts assembled into its tractors. More extensive subcontracting relations recently emerged in the processed-food industry, an industry that historically had not used this strategy. Sara Lee set up an extreme form of outsourcing by selling most of its factories, subcontracting its brand names, and concentrating its efforts on sales. Nike and Coca-Cola have set up similar strategies. Subcontracting is an attempt to extract more profits with less investment in assets. This trend is partially driven by the strategic emphasis on financial management, a strategy that became more prominent in corporations with the multilayered subsidiary form (chapters 8 and 9).

Discussion

American Steel's managerial process ensured an adequate rate of return throughout the oligopolistic era. By the early 1980s, however, the institutional arrangements had changed, and the contradictions and inefficiencies in its managerial process constrained capacity to make a profit. While its high costs constrained cash flow and increased its dependence on external capital markets, the availability of higher-quality, lower-priced steel in U.S. markets forced American Steel to improve quality. The pressure to incorporate formal controls over the managerial and manufacturing processes was heightened by American Steel's position in the commodity chain; steel consumers were under market pressure to increase their product quality and lower their costs.

Transformation of the managerial process at American Steel between 1980 and 1992 produced several important changes. First, the intensification of rational calculation was the basis of American Steel's managerial process restructuring. Together environmental pressures and the impediments to capital accumulation in its previous account-control system caused a renewal of emphasis on breaking down the manufacturing process into discrete activities, identifying the costs of those activities, and centralizing data to more precisely coordinate and control them. American Steel intensified rational calculation to increase formal control over production decisions, to coordinate linkages among the production units, to standardize decision making and product quality, and to guarantee that the operative goals of the production units advanced the substantive goals of the corporation (i.e., lower costs, higher quality, profits). In contrast to the previous organizational structure where several semiautonomous hierarchies existed, American Steel designed its new mode of calculation and control to centralize authority and unify the entire managerial system into one hierarchical system.

Second, control over many decisions was centralized into the manufacturing decision center where experts used more precise rationally calculated data to specify the premise of decisions. Whereas more precise bureaucratic controls identified the managers responsible for decisions, the cost controls detected when managers did not follow premise controls. In combination, cost controls and bureaucratic controls made it possible to monitor and increase surveillance over these managers to ascertain whether they followed the standardized decision-making criterion, thereby extending control over lower- and middle-level operating managers.

Third, American Steel redefined its corporate culture and values to encourage managers to understand the relationship between their responsibilities and the corporation's substantive goals (e.g., profits, product quality, etc.). The emphasis on this corporate culture operated as an unobtrusive control, ensuring that managers used the formally rational criterion in this sphere of decision making. Managerial teams had autonomy in making some decisions, but this team autonomy was premised on the formally rational and standardized data available to them.

Fourth, this intensification of rational calculation created controls to tightly couple production units, and the corporation to its environment. On the one hand, internal tight coupling provided the organization with the capacity to transform more parts of the manufacturing process from batch to continuous processing, and increased its capacity to transmit product specifications to the point of production. On the other, access to the centralized database within this tightly coupled corporation increased its capacity to respond to a range of environmental contingencies. This mode of control reduced the time necessary to transfer information, for example, concerning product specification and input costs throughout the corporation, thereby increasing its flexibility and responsiveness to the environment.

Fifth, the new mode of control—which entailed attempts to redefine the "one best way" to manufacture each product—separated conception from execution by placing production managers farther away from the loci of discretion. Whereas execution occurs at the point of production, American Steel relocated many conception activities (i.e., processing information, determining and authorizing what was to be done) to the decision center where a group of experts stipulate the parameters of a set of more or less coherent and preferred goals for corporate subunits, and determine the activities of production managers. Whereas the previous form of control relied heavily on relatively static budgetary and bureaucratic controls, the contemporary form of control rapidly processes, changes, and transmits decision-making information to various locations in the corporate hierarchy. This spatial separation of managerial activities separates conception from execution.

Sixth, these changes in the managerial process replaced many of the information-processing activities of management. American Steel's control system embedded many decisions directly into the manufacturing process, thus making it possible to reduce the number of managers and levels of the organizational hierarchy. By eliminating many decisions, it was possible to eliminate four of the eight layers of lower- and middle-level management.

Conclusion

Rational calculation evolved only slowly in the absence of capital dependence and competitive market conditions. However, it was intensified in response to crisis. Also, the fact that budgetary controls, for example, were used throughout the middle decades of the twentieth century suggests that the institutionalization of rationalized myths (Meyer and Rowan 1977) rather than their efficiency explains why American Steel and other U.S. corporations continued to use these controls. Once institutionalized it required a crisis to delegitimize and transform this aspect of the managerial process.

The more precise account controls made it possible to program production-control computers from centralized offices, establish premise controls over manufacturing decisions, and identify the manager responsible for executing a decision. Neo-Fordist decision making exercises control over operating managers by evaluating if a difference exists between the cost that resulted from the action of that manager and the predetermined cost established in the decision center. Neo-Fordism entails centralizing control over production decisions while decentralizing decision-making responsibility, and reduces uncertainty by limiting information processing by mid-level operating managers. In short, neo-Fordism limits the search for alternatives at the point of production, which enhanced the probability of predictable outcomes.

These changes in the managerial process simultaneously separate conception from execution functions in a similar way to the separation and centralization of knowledge from workers to managers in the early twentieth century. That is, whereas early twentieth century capitalists used Taylorism to centralize conception functions from the labor process to the managerial process, corporations are now using Neo-Fordism to centralize conception functions from operating managers to manager-engineers. As Harry Braverman observed, once management centralized information on the labor process that information was "distributed on a strict need to know basis" (1974:82). Similarly, once the experts in the decision center set in motion the organizational capacity to centralize, process, and transmit information on the managerial process, general knowledge of the manufacturing process by production managers became less necessary to the functioning of the system. This transformation in the managerial process entails the distribution of information from the centralized decision center to operating managers on a "strict need to know basis."

Although these middle managers initially resisted top managements' efforts to redefine the decision-making process, they had little affect on this transformation of the managerial process. The centralized engineering and designing level of the managerial process distributes information in such a way that it defines the premise of decisions, which reduces the decision-making discretion and autonomy of lower- and middle-level production managers.

Formally rational controls provided the organization with the capacity to extend the basic principles of scientific management (i.e., measurement, quantification, the separation of conception from execution) to previous unrationalized dimensions of the corporation. Neo-Fordist controls extend scientific management beyond the tall and rigid, rule-based managerial system that characterized Taylorism and Fordism in three fundamental ways. First, the new system of control can rapidly process, change, and transmit decision-making information. Second, this stage of scientific management has flatter hierarchies because it replaced many of the information-processing activities of management. Third, this new account-control system is the basis of organizational flexibility. Decision-making information can be transmitted throughout the corporation, thereby coupling the organization tightly while increasing flexibility. These controls make it possible to overcome the dilemma of simultaneous formalization and tightening of the organization in response to environmental pressures, which previously undermined flexibility (Weick 1976).

There are two historical processes that contributed to transformation of the managerial process. On the one hand, coercive pressures have existed since the turn of the century to standardize the manufacturing process because variation in input products (e.g., steel, parts) increase costs and reduce product quality in downstream segments of commodity chains. Thus, the transformation described here was not independent of the long-term trends. Throughout the middle decades of the twentieth century coercive pressure to make fabricated shapes and forms (e.g., electrical apparatus, power machinery, construction equipment) to exact customer specification resulted in centralization to more closely coordinate marketing, manufacturing, and engineering (Chandler 1962). However, corporations' capital dependence was the catalyst for rapid change. The analysis here supports one of Max Weber's important insights. Capital accounting is historically contingent and "dependent on certain quite specific substantive conditions" (Weber 1978:107). When an objective need for capital accounting emerged (e.g., increasing cash flow versus filing for bankruptcy) rational calculation was extended as far as technically possible to embed social actors in a system of control capable of ensuring that managers' actions were based on numerically calculable criteria.

The analysis here is an effort to fill a gap in the organizational research: the managerial process. Capitalists and their managers assumed the efficiency of the managerial process and, for the most part, researchers have failed to challenge this assumption. Although other researchers (Williamson 1985; Chandler 1977) examine efficiency issues, their assumptions preclude the kind of analysis necessary to address efficiency claims. These perspectives also fail to examine the relationships among efficiency, power, and survival. Among the most important implications is the failure of prevailing theories to understand financial controls misrepresented labor costs and directed managers' cost reduction efforts almost solely toward reducing labor costs (chapter 5). The outcome has been workplace antagonism and conflict. This explains, in part, why the United States lags behind in the industrial relations innovations that have been institutionalized in many European countries (e.g., codetermination, worker councils).

Although this analysis suggests that the managerial process was restructured to increase cost efficiency, it does not suggest that this rationalization is an adequate or permanent solution to managerial contradictions and irrationalities. It also does not suggest that the centralization of authority is absolute. Rather, just as the centralization of authority over the labor process was not absolute (Burawoy 1979; Clawson 1980), operating managers retain some discretion. Moreover, contradictions and irrationalities are historically contingent and just as Taylorism and Fordism became inadequate forms of control when macro conditions changed during previous historical periods, new historical contingencies are likely to create new contradictions, irrationalities and conflicts that will be catalysts for future rationalization.

CHAPTER 9

Changing Institutional Arrangements and Transformation to the Multilayered Subsidiary Form

In the 1920s, large industrial corporations began changing to the *multidivisional form* (MDF) (Chandler 1962). Crises at DuPont and General Motors resulted in transforming these firms to the MDF. Little additional corporate-form change occured until after New Deal business policies in the 1930s eliminated financial incentives to organize corporate entities as subsidiaries (chapter 4). After this policy change, more corporations began to change to a divisional form. Fligstein (1985) suggests that by 1959, 49.6 percent of the largest firms were MDFs and by 1979 84.2 percent of the largest 120 firms were MDFs. Beginning in 1969, however, corporations began to make more use of subsidiaries after a Justice Department ruling allowed conglomerate mergers if the acquired company was allowed to operate as a subsidiary corporation (see page 129). This decision encouraged corporations to incorporate mergers and acquisitions as subsidiaries because it reduced the probability of an antitrust challenge. Also, by the late 1970s, the big business lobby succeeded in lowering the capital gains tax (chapter 7). This business policy change reduced the tax on capital transfers—via dividend payments—from subsidiary corporations to parent companies. Changes in corporations' institutional arrangements in the 1980s created additional incentives to organize corporate entities as subsidiaries.

In this chapter, I examine transformation from the MDF to the *multilayered subsidiary form* (MLSF) (figure 9.1). A key component of change to the MLSF entails restructuring divisions as *subsidiary corporations:* separate legal entities whose controlling interest (i.e., more than 50 percent) is held by a legally separate parent company (Dun & Bradstreet 1985; Allison, Prentice, and Howell 1991; Prechel 1997a:409).

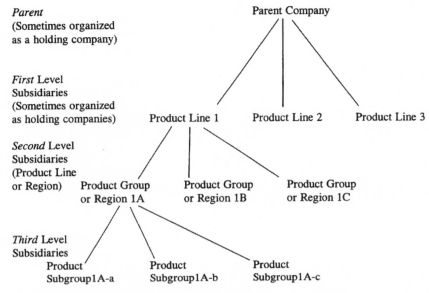

Parent
(Sometimes organized
as a holding company)

First Level
Subsidiaries
(Sometimes organized
as holding companies)

Second Level
Subsidiaries
(Product Line
or Region)

Third Level
Subsidiaries

Parent Company

Product Line 1   Product Line 2   Product Line 3

Product Group   Product Group   Product Group
or Region 1A   or Region 1B   or Region 1C

Product   Product   Product
Subgroup1A-a   Subgroup1A-b   Subgroup1A-c

FIGURE 9.1   The multilayered subsidiary form. From Prechel 1997a.

I employ historical methods and a case study to show that changing economic
conditions in the 1970s and 1980s produced corporate political behavior that succeeded in transforming crucial dimensions of state business policy. These new institutional arrangements created the condition to reorganize corporations as
MLSFs. My research differs from previous studies of corporate-form change in
important ways. I examine change in the 1980s and early 1990s characterized by
changing state business policy, shrinking markets, and falling profits in a competitive and globalized economy. Most corporations changed to the MDF between
the 1940s and 1970s (Chandler 1962, 1990; Fligstein 1990; Roy 1997) when the
economy was relatively stable and markets were expanding. Thus, my research is
unique in a theoretically important way; it examines the corporate response to different historical conditions.

Like in previous chapters, I use the social structure of accumulation (SSA) temporal framework. I focus on the decay-exploration transition, when political capitalism becomes most pronounced. This transition is characterized by state managers and capitalists experimenting to establish institutional arrangements conducive
to steady profit making (Gordon et al. 1982; Bowles at al. 1983; Kotz, McDonough,
and Reich 1994).

Restructuring the Institutional Arrangements

Political Capitalism in the 1980s

Confronted with economic constraints, by the late 1970s the industrial sector mobilized politically to transform their political-legal environment (Vogel 1989; Prechel 1990; Akard 1992; Useem 1993). Capitalists' political strategy resulted in massive tax breaks for capital-intensive corporations (chapter 7). Despite these changes in corporations' institutional arrangements and changes in the managerial process (chapter 8), low profits and high debt continued to constrain profit making and industrial corporations remained dependent on external capital markets. Corporate political behavior intensified in the early 1980s when debt skyrocketed and profits further declined.

One political strategy was motivated by the financial risk of tort lawsuits. Through political organizations such as the American Tort Reform Association and the Chemical Manufacturers Association, large corporations (e.g., Dow Chemical, DuPont, Johnson and Johnson) mobilized politically to reform tort liability laws (Bacas 1986; Moskowitz and Laurie 1986). After this political effort failed, corporations began to restructure their liability-prone porduct lines as subsidiary corporations (Engineering News Record 1986; Prechel 1997b:155).

Also, the massive tax breaks provided to industrial corporations in the *Revenue Act of 1981* did not solve the economic crisis manifested as low profits and high bankruptcy rates. In 1982, approximately sixty-six thousand firms filed for bankruptcy protection, and Dun & Bradstreet reported 24,900 bankruptcy cases, resulting in $15.6 billion in uncollectible debts (Greider 1989). In response, capitalist groups such as the American Business Conference and The Carlton Group developed a second and more comprehensive political strategy. This strategy focuses on redefining corporate tax law (chapter 7). Although the *Economic Recovery Act of 1981* (i.e., *RA81*) improved industrial corporations' cash flow, the *Tax Reform Act of 1986* (*TRA86*) and subsequent legislation (e.g., *Revenue Act of 1987* [*RA87*]) had the most profound effect on the corporate form.

Moreover, current institutional arrangements created new constraints on the state's agendas to ensure economic stability. A contradiction emerged from the *RA81* that exacerbated existing problems, contributing to the fiscal crisis of the state and creating new motives and incentives for state managers to explore alternate business policy. The *RA81* reduced government revenues, increasing the federal debt and dependence on foreign capital (Greider 1989:577). A study of 250 corporations revealed that 42 paid no federal income taxes in 1985, and 130 paid no taxes in at least one year between 1981 and 1985 (e.g., AT&T, Boeing, DuPont, General Dynamics) (*Congressional Quarterly Weekly Report* 1986). Further, business groups representing less capital-intensive industries (e.g., computer, biotechnology) opposed extending existing tax breaks. As a result, the *RA81* became politically infeasible (Prechel 1997b:156). Moreover, the *RA81* failed to generate personal savings that advocates of the bill argued would aid in capital formation. In fact, personal saving rates declined to a new low in the early 1980s. By 1986, family debt had dramatically increased and a large portion of family income was being used to pay it off (Harrison and Bluestone 1988).

By the mid-1980s, the executive branch of the government and the Federal Reserve Board became concerned over the rising debt. The total outstanding public and private debt almost doubled between 1977 and 1984 and increased by 25 percent in 1983 and 1984 alone (Greider 1989). Rising debt undermined the financial sector's capacity to fulfill one of its most important functions: *capital formation*, which entails the flow of capital from financial institutions (e.g., credit unions, saving and loans, commercial banks, insurance companies) into new productive facilities. As a result of capital shortages, industrial corporations did not have access to capital at affordable rates (Prechel and Boies 1998a:336). The prime interest rate reached a historic high point in the early 1980s at over 18 percent (figure 9.2), and corporate and state managers sought a political solution (Stockman 1986).

At this same time, financial analysts began to argue that stock markets undervalued the assets of whole corporations (Useem 1993; Prechel and Boies 1998a:337). They argued that the sum of the parts was more valuable than the whole (Jensen 1984; LeBaron and Speidel 1987; Porter 1987). Indeed, their predictions appeared correct. Wealthy investors (e.g., T. Boone Pickens, Carl Icahn) made fortunes taking over corporations and selling their parts. The task for industrial corporations was to set up a political-legal mechanism and an organizational form that allowed them to "unlock" capital without accruing high tax bills. Thus, a coalition of capitalists set up a political strategy to accomplish this agenda. The business policies of the mid-1980s redefined the institutional arrangements to accomplish industrial corporations' agenda to set up a tax-free mechanism to "unlock" capital in their corporate entities.

In response to political pressure from financial and industrial capital, as during previous crises, state managers experimented with state business policy. Since the 1970s, a coalition of capitalist class segments argued that high interest rates were one of the major causes of slow economic growth. Industrial capital lobbied for lower interest rates so that they would have access to affordable capital necessary to modernize their manufacturing facilities and regain a competitive position in the global economy. Taking on additional debt at high interest rates would add another layer to their already high operating costs. Because finance capital was dependent on industrial capital for revenues and financial stability—they owned a large portion of industrial stocks and bonds—they did not oppose this policy initiative. That is, although the industrial sector was dependent on the financial sector's external capital markets, the long-term viability of finance capital was dependent on profitability in

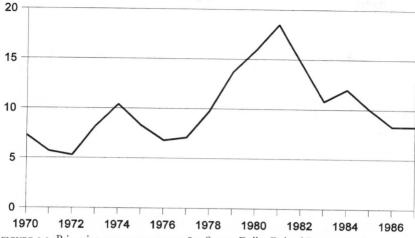

FIGURE 9.2 Prime interest rates, 1970–1987. *Source:* Dallas Federal Reserve Bank.

the industrial sector. These capitalist class segments had similar interests. Declining stock values, lower dividend payments, and bankruptcies in the industrial sector created a serious threat to stability in the financial sector. Finance capital supported this policy because of their location in a capital dependent network with industrial capital. If the decline continued, finance capital would be excluded from valued resources.

By 1983, the Federal Reserve Bank introduced a policy to lower interest rates. This policy was followed by changes in corporate tax law. Restructuring of these institutional arrangements created substantial profitmaking opportunities for the financial sector, which provided the financial underwriting and legal expertise for subsequent corporate restructuring (see chapter 11).

Opposition from various capitalist class segments and consumer groups succeeded in pressuring Congress to discontinue the lucrative investment tax credits. The *TRA86*, however, left the accelerated depreciation write-offs intact.[1] Although this part of the *TRA86* is important, other segments had much more profound effects. With virtually no public discussion or dissemination of information to the public about the implications, the *TRA86* and subsequent legislation dismantled New Deal policies designed to curtail corporations' capacity to use the holding company subsidiary form (chapter 4). New Deal policies taxed capital transfers between subsidiary corporations and their parent companies. The mid-1980s business policy eliminated this tax, which allowed corporations to restructure their assets and debt tax-free. The capital transfers, however, could only occur via stock transactions, which required that corporations restructure their divisions as subsidiary corporations (Prentice-Hall 1987; Wood 1987; Prechel 1997b:157).

The *TRA86* and *RA87* repealed the General Utilities doctrine, which normally meant that the distribution of assets is taxable (Prechel 1997b:156–58). However, important exceptions exist. The distribution of an asset through a tax-free reorganization is allowed under the Internal Revenue Code if the transfer occurs through a subsidiary. These complex regulations that were not finalized until more than two years after the *TRA86* ensured that "if appreciated assets are transferred to a subsidiary, and the stock of the subsidiary is spun off, the distributing corporation will not have a recognized [taxable] gain" (Prentice-Hall 1987:653-54 Cavitch and Cavitch 1995:9–23; Willens 1988). To qualify as tax-free spin-off, the subsidiary must meet other requirements. The reorganized subsidiary must engage in "a valid business purpose" such as continuation of an existing business (versus solely for tax purposes) and it must be engaged in that business for five years (Prentice-Hall 1997:653–54; Cavitch and Cavitch 1995). These provisions are important because they encourage parent companies to expand their existing product lines.

The laws governing tax-free restructuring also allow parent companies to place the debt from their "old" divisions into their new subsidiaries, making the "new" subsidiaries responsible for the debt (Cavitch and Cavitch 1995). Although the restructured parent company can own all of the stock of the "new" subsidiaries, rarely do the courts hold parent companies responsible for subsidiaries debt (Allison et al. 1991; Prechel 1997b:159). This new business policy contributed to a shift in corporate strategy. In the early 1980s, approximately $72 billion in corporate stocks was converted to debt (Greider 1989), which increased corporations' dependence on external capital markets.[2] The new institutional arrangements set up in the mid-1980s, however, allowed corporations to reduce their high interest debt by issuing subsidiary corporations' stock. This method of capital formation (i.e., using subsidiaries as internal capital markets) provided corporations with the capital to implement a range of strategies including paying off debt. Once the high-interest debt was repaid, if necessary, corporations could borrow additional capital from external capital markets at less than one-half of the early 1980s interest rates (see figure 9.2).

There are other important implications of these new institutional arrangements. Corporations could pursue the same strategies as they did in the late nineteenth and early twentieth centuries: obtain ownership control through subsidiaries. Moreover, now, Section 7 of the Clayton Act was the only significant obstacle to corporations' use of variations on the holding-company form to implement strategies to gain control over markets (but see chapter 11). Further, because late-nineteenth-century laws of incorporation provide corporations with similar rights as individuals, parent companies that have ownership control over subsidiaries are treated similarly as individual stockholders. In most cases, limited-liability laws do not hold parent companies responsible for financial breakdowns in their subsidiary corporations.

Also, in 1987 the Federal Reserve Bank abrogated a central part of the New Deal business policy (i.e., Glass-Steagall Act) that prohibited bank affiliates from underwriting asset-backed securities. By 1997, the federal government no longer enforced most of the Glass-Steagall restrictions on bank affiliates, allowing banks to invest larger amounts of capital in corporate securities. This institutional arrangement change is crucial. It aided capital formation by increasing capital flows from banks and other financial institutions to investment bankers (i.e., Goldman Sachs) who underwrite corporate securities.

In summary, by the early 1980s, it was not in finance capital's interest to maintain the kind of capital-dependent relationship with industrial capital that it had for much of the twentieth century. While this capital-dependent relationship benefited finance capital during much of the twentieth century, the capital shortage of the early 1980s together with increasingly high interest rates undermined stability in both the industrial and financial sectors. Two interrelated policies were crucial to the new institutional arrangements. On the one hand, the new tax policies allowed corporations to restructure their divisions as subsidiaries tax-free and issue stock in those subsidiaries. On the other, the Federal Reserve's policy to lower interest rates functioned to shift capital from interest-bearing investments into the stock market. Industrial corporations used the capital from initial public stock offerings to finance its modernization and merger and acquisition strategies. These new institutional arrangements had significant benefits to finance capital who underwrite industrial corporations' recapitalization and stock issuances (see chapters 10 and 11).

Distinctions among Corporate Forms

There are several important differences between the MLSF and previous corporate forms. These differences are best understood in terms of how the corporate entity affects *relational complexity:* "the integration, interconnection, and coordination of organizational entities" (Warriner 1984; Prechel 1997a:409).

Several distinctions exist between the MLSF and the *holding company*, a company that controls one or more other corporations by owning their securities (Bonbright and Means 1932). First, whereas a "pure" holding company does not manage its subsidiaries (Bonbright and Means 1932; Chandler 1962), MLSF parent companies have the organizational capacity to engage in financial management of their subsidiaries and to monitor their subsidiary corporations' operating activities (Prechel 1997a:410–11). Second, most conceptions of the holding company do not capture the intraorganizational relations of the MLSF. "Parent companies can embed several holding companies in a single MLSF"(Prechel 1997a:411). For example, at the third level of its hierarchy, Amoco created a holding company (i.e., Amoco Chemical Holdings) that manages five subsidiary corporations organized by product group (Prechel and Boies 1998a:325–26). Some holding companies manage up to seven levels of subsidiaries (Dun & Bradstreet 1994). MAFCO Holdings, a parent company, owns and controls MacAndrews & Forbes Holdings, a first-level subsidiary holding company. Through this first-level holding company, the parent company owns and controls $5 billion in assets located in several holding-company subsidiaries and operating-subsidiary corporations, including Revlon (cosmetics), Coleman Holdings (outdoor equipment), C&F Holdings (cigars, aerospace), First National Holdings (banking) and Andrews (entertainment and publishing).

Several *distinctions also exist between the MLSF and the MDF* (table 9.1). First, "whereas top management in the MDF is located in the central office, the MLSF locates top management in a legally separate parent company" (Prechel 1997a:410). This legal separation of the parent company creates a more explicit organizational separation of financial and operating management. The MLSF is also distinct from the *conglomerate MDF:* "divisional firms that . . . are diversified in sufficient degree to warrant assignment to the conglomerate category" (Williamson 1975:157; Chandler 1977:480). "Most corporations that transformed to conglomerates in the 1960s and 1970s organized their assets as divisions" (Lazonick 1991; Prechel 1997a:411).

Second, the MLSF reduces the parent company's financial risk by creating separate legal entities. The MLSF reduces financial damage to parent companies from liability cases caused by, for example, dangerous work environments (e.g., mining) and product liabilities (i.e., silicone breast implants, asbestos, pesticides, tobacco) that occur in subsidiary corporations. This *corporate veil* protects the parent company's assets by containing economic losses, bankruptcy, and tort liability lawsuits to the subsidiary corporation (Prechel 1997a:415). The litigation on silicone breast implants illustrates how the MLSF isolates liability to subsidiary corporations, reducing the financial risk to parent companies. Dow Corning Inc., a large producer of silicone breast implants, is a joint venture of the parent companies Dow Chemical and Corning Inc. The courts ruled that both parent companies were exempt from tort lawsuits because they were not engaged in the development or manufacture of the product. Exempting Dow Chemical was challenged, however, because it was alleged that this parent company completed tests on breast implant components (Prechel and Boies 1998a:339). In short, if the parent company does not engage in product development or manufacture, the liability firewall protects the parent from financial responsibility from the activities that occur in its operating subsidiaries. This protection exists even when the parent company receives substantial profits from the subsidiary where product development and manufacture occur, as was the case in the Dow Corning, Dow Chemical, and Corning arrangement.

Third, the MLSF reduces parent companies' dependence on external capital markets and increases corporations' self-financing capability. Organizing corporate entities as subsidiary corporations creates an *internal capital market:* transforming fixed "assets into capital" by issuing securities (e.g., stocks, bonds) (Prechel

TABLE 9.1 Salient Characteristics of the MDF and MLSF

Multidivisional Form	Multilayered Subsidiary Form
The central office is legally part of the same corporation as other organization entities.	The parent company and each subsidiary are separate legal entities.
No liability firewalls.	Liability firewalls between the parent company and its subsidiary corporations and among all subsidiary corporations.
No internal capital markets.	Each subsidiary corporation constitutes a potential internal capital market.
The entire corporation is embedded in the market.	Each subsidiary corporation is embedded in the market.

1997b:158).[3] After corporations restructure, parent companies can sell stock of a subsidiary. The MLSF improves parent companies' flexibility in self financing (Prechel 1991:439) by (1) raising capital through subsidiary stock and bond sales (i.e., initial public offerings, partial spinoffs) (2) transferring subsidiary corporations' profits to the parent company as stock dividends, and (3) repurchasing subsidiary stocks when the parent company's cash flow increases. During the 1980s, initial public offerings (IPOs) of subsidiaries' stock were an increasingly common source of financing. Because subsidiary corporations are a source of capital through stock sales, the MLSF creates an incentive to restructure, especially in a period of increasing dependence on expensive external capital markets, as in the 1980s (figure 9.2).

Fourth, embedding subsidiary corporations in the market creates a means to monitor corporate entities and reduces top managements' dependence on internal controls (Prechel 1997a:410). Even parent companies with adequate capital issue "tracking stock" in their subsidiary corporations to monitor the performance of product lines or product groups. After General Motors acquired Electronic Data Systems (EDS) in the mid-1980s, it issued stock in EDS for this purpose. Similarly, preceding DuPont's strategy to expand its life-sciences business entity it issued "tracking stock" to separate out the performance (e.g., stock value) of this product line from its others. If subsidiary corporations' profits or stock values begin to drop below the standards set by the parent company, top management in the parent company can take whatever action it deems appropriate, including selling all or part of the subsidiary corporation (Prechel 1997a:409). The MLSF was particularly advantageous in the 1980s, during a period of rapid corporate growth and increased complexity. Whereas the percentage of the *Fortune* 500 assets held by the largest fifty parent companies remained stable at 50 percent between 1958 and 1980, it increased to 62 percent by 1987 and remained at that level through 1993. Moreover, the largest firms grew at a much faster pace than the smallest fifty *Fortune* 500 firms during this same period. Whereas the largest fifty *Fortune* 500 firms held about twenty-seven times as many assets as the smallest of the *Fortune* 500 between 1958 and 1977, by 1988 the ratio had increased to 58 percent (Prechel and Boies 1998a:322–23).

The Case-Oriented Study

Historicizing the Contemporary Corporation

Capital-dependence theory suggests that although institutional arrangements (e.g., economic, political-legal) always affect corporations, the specific alignment of those institutions vary historically. This theoretical logic addresses a central problem in political and historical sociology: identifying the conditions under which classes mobilize and act on their shared interest (Tilly 1981; Prechel 1990:664). Like other historical phenomena, capital-accumulation opportunities and constraints are contingent. Neither the specific contradictions and crises in corporations' institutional environment nor the solutions are historically determined. Rather, solutions are effected by the historically specific institutional arrangements within which corporations are embedded. Explicit within capital-dependence theory is the assumption that constraints on capital accumulation are manifested in the corporation and that they elicit a response.

The Case

American Steel Company focused solely on steel manufacturing until the Great Depression when it merged with a large steel service and distribution corporation, creating a *wholly owned subsidiary:* a separate legal entity whose stock is wholly owned by another company (Allison et al. 1991; Prechel 1997b:161). The corporation grew by diversifying and expanding these two product lines. By the early 1980s, 63 percent of American Steel's revenues came from its integrated steel business, 24 percent from its service and distribution business, and the remaining 13 percent from a range of other product lines. In 1983, like many corporations, American Steel was a hybrid corporate form. American Steel set up this hybrid form in the 1930s when it organized steel manufacturing within the parent company, its service and distribution business as a subsidiary, and several steel and nonsteel business entities as subsidiaries. American Steel used its combination of raw material, steel manufacturing, and steel-consuming entities to establish a commodity chain that began with raw materials (e.g., coal, iron ore) and ended with large volume sales of its integrated steel products and smaller and more specialized sales of steel products in its steel service and distribution subsidiary.

The Decay Stage

After OPEC raised its oil prices in the 1970s the cost structure of high energy-dependent manufacturing industries rapidly increased. These added costs reduced

American Steel's cash flow and capacity to generate adequate capital to modernize its steel-making operations and compete in the global economy. Increasingly dependent on external capital markets, the central office created a new position—associate vice president of finance—which they filled with an executive recruited from the financial sector. In the late 1970s, this person was promoted to vice president of finance. He was the first person with a background in finance to hold this position. All previous vice presidents of finance had backgrounds in accounting. This event is important because it signified top management's realization that it was increasingly unable to generate capital internally, and that a top manager with expertise in finance would increase their capacity to access external capital markets.[4]

By the early 1980s, the institutional arrangements no longer ensured an adequate rate of return at American Steel. Global steel-making capability exceeded demand, and imported steel captured a larger share of the U.S. market, undermining the oligopolistic price-setting structure of the U.S. steel industry. Although American Steel's capability utilization rate remained high (i.e., 81 percent), its rate of return fell to 2.3 percent. During the 1981–1982 recession, when American Steel failed to realize a profit for the first time since the Great Depression, it eliminated quarterly dividends to preserve its liquidity position and ensure that it could meet its short-term financial obligations. In response to this crisis, the corporation create a team of five top executives to develop a strategy to address its crisis. The recently appointed vice president of finance was include on this team.

Between 1982 and 1983 its debt-to-capital ratio (i.e., debt as percent of total capitalization) increased from 35 percent to 38 percent. Also, in 1983, American Steel's liquidity position was a negative $1.6 million. Although its liquidity position improved in 1984, it dropped to a negative $48 million in 1985 and its debt-to-capital ratio increased to 43.9 percent. Additionally, 1985 was the fourth consecutive year that the company did not realize a profit. In response to its deteriorating financial position, the major rating agencies (e.g., Standard & Poor) downgraded American Steel's mortgage bond and commercial paper rating. This resulted in higher interest rates, increasing the cost of external financing. At the same time, stockholders pressured top management to take the necessary action to strengthen American Steel's financial position and to restore dividend payments, and to raise stock values.

Many of the problems at American Steel were manifested in the economy as a whole. By the mid-1970s, capital dependence increased within the industrial sector. Financial capitalists, who normally benefit from the industrial sector's capital dependence and high interest payments, become increasingly concerned. The rapid increase in debt, high cost of capital, and rising inflation had dramatically weakened the bond market (Greider 1989). Other capital markets (i.e., money, stock) experienced similar problems, undermining the capacity of finance capital to ensure an adequate rate of capital formation. By 1984, industrial corporations such as American Steel and organizations representing the industrial sector (e.g., Business Roundtable) began to mobilize politically, arguing that high interest rates were threatening the health of the economy. Financial capitalists argued that declining government revenues and rising public debt was a source of the problem. The decline in government revenues followed the *RA81*, which increased the federal debt and the government's dependence on external capital markets.

The Exploration Phase

Throughout the 1970s, the steel industry and other capitalist groups within the industrial sector mobilized politically to redefine state business policy to create more favorable institutional arrangements for corporations (chapter 7). Capitalist and state managers experimented with a range of business-policy changes. By the 1970s, the executive and judicial branches of the government began to adopt a probusiness ideology, easing antitrust enforcement and revising antitrust laws (Stearns and Allen 1996). A crucial aspect of the antitrust-law change included replacing the formula that triggered antitrust violations based on domestic market share to a formula based on global market share. This change in state business policy permitted the mergers and acquisition wave of the 1980s, raising the level of business concentration in many industries.

Although the tax credits and accelerated depreciation schedules increased cash flow into the industrial sector (chapter 7), a second, lesser known aspect of the *RA81* created additional mechanism to increase corporations' cash flow. These *leaseback arrangements*—developed by the Treasury Department working with business lobbyists (Birnbaum and Murray 1987)—allow an unprofitable corporation to lease capital investments (e.g., factories, computers) to a profitable corporation. The profitable corporation uses the tax write-offs (e.g., depreciation) from the equipment or facility and rents it back to the original owner who continues to use it (Prechel 1991:437). These institutional arrangements created an alternate form of capital formation by providing a way to move capital from one corporation to another so that both corporations benefited.

Although the cash-flow benefits of the ACRS were substantial, they did not eliminate American Steel's crisis. Thus, American Steel established elaborate lease-back arrangements permitted by these new institutional arrangements that:

> Ranged from modernization hardware on the . . . mill to computers, from forklifts to electronic office equipment, from overhead cranes to coal mining equipment and heavy-duty highway trucks—and the list goes on and on. (Corporate Document)

In one project alone, approximately $190 million was financed by lease-back arrangements. These financial arrangements allowed American Steel to reduce its dependence on external capital markets by improving its cash flow, while upgrading the quality of its manufacturing facilities.[5] As the chief financial officer (hereafter

CFO) stated: "Leasing has enabled us to obtain the use of top-flight equipment at a time when cash is scarce and [sic] it is virtually impossible to negotiate loans on affordable terms." Although these arrangements improved American Steel's long-term capital needs, they did not solve its cash-flow problems or restore profits. As a result, the value of American Steel's stock continued to drop and shareholders became increasingly critical of top management.

Initially, like many corporations, American Steel divested from product lines not connected to its core businesses. By 1983, American Steel sold seven wholly- or partly owned subsidiary corporations. Two criteria were used to make these decisions to disinvest: These "operations failed to meet the profit standard, or were judged to be strategically incompatible with the company's new" focus on the production and steel distribution of steel products less vulnerable to imports. The corporation also shut down several steel-related facilities and sold one steel-related subsidiary. The sale of subsidiaries between 1980 and 1986 raised approximately $275 million. The parent company's financial position was further strengthened by the *RA87*, which reinstated the investment tax credit, making the parent company eligible for a $50 million tax refund.

This structure, however, left the corporation vulnerable to future political and economic changes. On the one hand, there were limits on corporations' ability to control the political conditions that affected profits (e.g., tax credits, depreciation schedules, lease-back provisions). On the other, the move into fewer product lines makes corporations vulnerable to shifts in those markets. While disinvesting reduced the problem of managing a range of product lines, it did not overcome American Steel's larger problems of having (1) large capital investments in an industry with overcapacity and shrinking markets, and (2) a rigid organizational structure in a rapidly changing economy. As the CEO stated:

> [It is] risky to believe that the company's profitability can grow substantially based largely on a combination of steel manufacturing and steel distribution. It [is] important to restructure the company so that we have the *flexibility* of adding profitable businesses when those opportunities can be captured. (My emphasis)

To overcome short-and long-term capital-accumulation constraints, American Steel had to create a corporate form with (1) a structure capable of protecting the corporation's assets, and (2) the flexibility to take advantage of changing markets.

The *Tax Reform Act of 1986* (*TRA86*) provided a partial solution to American Steel's profitability crisis while protecting some of its assets from a possible bankruptcy. The aspect of the *TRA86* that fit American Steel's needs was the provision governing tax-free restructuring of existing assets that entail the redistribution of assets via stock within the corporate family. This provision allows corporations to distribute stock "of a newly created, or long-existing, subsidiary corporation to one or more of its shareholders" (Cavitch and Cavitch 1995:9–5). This type of corporate restructuring can take many forms including dividing one corporation into two or more separate corporations, and transferring capital via stocks to the new parent corporation and its new subsidiary corporations (for more detail see Cavitch and Cavitch 1995; Prechel 1997b). It entails the simultaneous creation of a subsidiary corporation and the distribution of stock; only the form of ownership changes. The new parent company owns the stock of the new subsidiary corporation versus the assets of a division. It is a tax-free means to transfer a business to shareholders—which may be the parent corporation or individuals—through stock sales.

These new institutional arrangements provided a solution to American Steel's capital dependence produced by its (1) growing debt-to-capital ratio, and (2) inability to generate adequate capital from its internal operations. Transforming to the MLSF also increased its organizational flexibility in a rapidly changing environment. Further, in the event of a failure (e.g., bankruptcy) of the corporation's steel-manufacturing business, the MLSF protected the parent company's other assets.

Restructuring the Central Office as a Parent Company

In the same year that Congress approved the *TRA86*, American Steel began to restructure its corporate form. During the first stage of restructuring its form, top management transformed American Steel's central office into a separate parent company, American Steel Holdings, Inc. The stock of American Steel Company—the "old" corporation—was transferred to the "new" parent holding company. The stockholders of American Steel Company (i.e., the "old" corporation) became the stockholders of American Steel Holdings, Inc.

Top management also created two separate holding-company subsidiaries through which it controlled its various business units (figure 9.3). One subsidiary holding company (American Steel) was created to hold the stock of the steel-manufacturing business. The second subsidiary holding company (i.e., American Steel-S/D) held the stock of American Steel's large steel service and distribution subsidiary. Before restructuring, the service and distribution subsidiary was a subsidiary of American Steel Company (i.e., the "old" corporation). Within the "new" company, the "old" service and distribution subsidiary became a second-level subsidiary owned and controlled by the parent company through its first-level subsidiary holding company (i.e., American Steel-S/D). This holding-company subsidiary structure also provided a corporate form through which the parent company could hold stock in other corporations.

The decision to restructure created a "new" parent company that was much more financially sound and flexible than the "old" corporation. The new institutional arrangements made it possible to transfer the long-term debt that the "old" company accumulated to the "new" subsidiary corporation (i.e., American Steel). That is, restructuring created a "new" parent company that owned all of the assets of the "old" corporation but was not legally responsible for its debt. Also, since

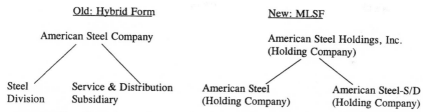

FIGURE 9.3 Transformation at American Steel to a multilayered subsidiary form, 1986. From Prechel 1997a.

this change creates a liability firewall neither the parent company nor its other subsidiaries were responsible for the debt of the "new" subsidiary.

By restructuring as a MLSF, American Steel (1) achieved its short-term goal of protecting the assets in its profitable businesses from the crisis in its steel-manufacturing business (2) protected the assets in its profitable businesses from future breakdowns in its other subsidiary corporations, and (3) created a corporate form that facilitated stock acquisition and financial control of other businesses.

Creating Internal Capital Markets to Reduce Dependence on
External Capital Markets

Restructuring its assets as subsidiary corporations created internal capital markets, which improved American Steel's self-financing capability. Restructuring to the MLSF entailed the public offering of 3,750,000 shares in its new first-level subsidiary holding company (i.e., American Steel). The total capital raised from the public was approximately $90.6 million and the parent company received over $85.6 million. Goldman Sachs was the underwriter and received over $3.98 million for underwriting the transaction. In addition, Goldman Sachs and Credit Suisse First Boston Corporation each agreed to purchase 429,750 shares in the newly formed subsidiary corporation, which gave these investment firms substantial ownership in the subsidiary corporation. These arrangements between industrial and financial capital are similar to those that occurred at the turn of the twentieth century where the underwriter had the option of buying shares in newly created subsidiary corporations.

In 1987, the parent corporation generated an additional $97 million by selling 2 million shares of its own preferred stock and $84 million by selling 3 million shares of a subsidiary's common stock. This decision to restructure and use public debt (i.e., equity financing) instead of private debt (i.e., financing from banks) resulted in a significant improvement in American Steel's cash flow. American Steel used much of this capital to redeem bonds, which reduced its annual interest payments by $16.9 million. By 1988, its debt-to-capital ratio declined to 27.6 percent from 43.9 percent in 1985. During that same period, its liquidity position changed from a negative $47.7 million to a positive $305.3 million (Corporate Documents).

In 1989, the parent company also used equity financing to raise the capital for its initial portion of a joint venture with a Japanese corporation by selling $185 million in preferred stock to that corporation. In total, American Steel sold 10 million stock shares after it restructured. These subsidiaries provided an internal capital market that increased the parent company's self-financing capacity and reduced its dependence on expensive capital from external capital markets.

The MLSF also provided the financial flexibility to transfer assets from the subsidiaries to the parent company. In 1994, when the profits of the subsidiary corporations improved, $225 million in dividends were transferred from the subsidiaries to the parent company. Top management used $147 million of this capital to buy back stock in its steel-manufacturing subsidiary. In 1995, the parent corporation purchased the $185 million of its preferred stocks that it sold to the Japanese corporation, which reduced its annual dividend payment on this preferred stock by $17.5 million. These stock buybacks simultaneously strengthened the parent company's financial position, improved its capacity to successfully issue stock in the future, and reduced shareholder input into strategic decisions thereby increasing top management's autonomy.

The MLSF also created a more clearly delineated managerial division of labor. By making a sharper distinction between the financial concerns of the enterprise as a whole and the operating concerns of the specific business units, this structural arrangement encouraged top management to focus more narrowly on financial management.

> The parent holding company no longer is an operating company. Thus the ongoing principle businesses are conducted by subsidiaries but *controlled* by a single [sic] publicly owned holding company. (Corporate document, my emphasis)

This structure allows top management to carry out the principle of

> [o]perating the corporation's businesses, including the steel manufacturing business and any additional businesses acquired by the [parent] holding company, on a more self-sufficient, independent economic basis. (Corporate document)

Transformation to the MLSF changed the legal and financial relationship between the parent company and the corporate entities. Within the MLSF the parent company became a separate corporation, as did the subsidiaries. The subsidiaries are owned and controlled by the parent company, and all or part of their stock can be liquidated to finance new or existing strategies. As the CEO put it:

> The new structure . . . facilitate[s] the entry into new businesses and the formation of joint ventures or other business combinations with third parties. It . . . also per-

mit[s] greater flexibility in the management and financing of new and existing business operations. (Corporate document)

Restructuring the Steel Subsidiary: From a Product Line to Product Groups

The next phase of restructuring included the reorganization of American Steel's integrated steel operations.[6] The new parent company restructured this broad product line into two, second-level divisions organized as product groups under the subsidiary holding company (American Steel) (figure 9.4).

One corporate entity (American Steel-Bar) manufacturers high-quality steel bars for the transportation, forging, and heavy-equipment industries and sells many of its products to the steel service and distribution industry. This product group competes in the same markets as minimills. The second corporate entity (American Steel-Sheet) manufacturers high-quality sheet steel (e.g., cold-rolled, coated products) for the automotive, appliance, office furniture, and steel service and distribution industries, and steel plate for the agriculture, rail, and construction industries. American Steel-Sheet's primary competitors are domestic and foreign integrated steel corporations. The restructuring of American Steel's steel-manufacturing business embedded these corporate entities into market niches where they directly compete with other firms manufacturing similar products. By separating this broad product line into product groups, the parent company can more closely monitor subsidiaries' performance and make strategic decisions (e.g., to exit those markets) based on these corporate entities' performance.

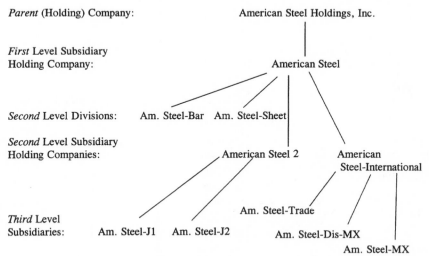

FIGURE 9.4 American Steel Holdings and its major corporate units, 1994. From Prechel 1997a.

Restructuring the Steel Service and Distribution Subsidiary through Equity Financing

Although American Steel's steel service and distribution subsidiary was already the largest in the industry, the parent company carried out a strategy to increase its market share in this growth industry. Little opposition existed to this strategy in the tolerant antitrust environment of the 1980s. This strategic change was preceded by a reconfiguration of this product line. Within its second-level subsidiary (American Steel-S/D-N), top management created three third-level divisions and organized them by geographic region (figure 9.5).

Despite failing to realize a profit throughout this period, American Steel was able to implement this strategy by raising capital through its successful initial public (stock) offering (IPO) in 1986. In that same year, American Steel purchased a large steel service and distribution company with operating facilities in most southern and several mid-Atlantic states. Top management organized this acquisition as a second-level subsidiary corporation (American Steel-S/D-S) under its first-level subsidiary holding company, American Steel S/D (figure 9.5). The parent company also purchased two smaller companies and organized one (American Steel-Metal) as a third-level subsidiary under American Steel-S/D-S, and the other as a division (American Steel-Coil) under American Steel-S/D-N. American Steel linked these corporate entities into its managerial process through a complex computer system, allowing central management to monitor and coordinate their operating activities. After these acquisitions, the combined revenues from this product

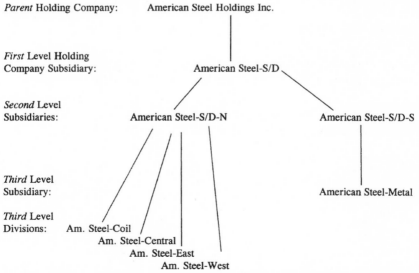

FIGURE 9.5 American Steel Holdings: Major service and distribution units, 1994. From Prechel 1997a.

line were more than twice the revenues of American Steel's next largest competitor in this market.

Moreover, the parent company implemented this strategy without changing the operating management of the acquired subsidiary corporations. Although top management in the parent company stated that the new subsidiary continued to be independently managed and operated, important differences exist. First, the parent company could require its steel service subsidiaries to purchase the products from its steel-manufacturing business. After American Steel gained ownership control of this link in the commodity chain, shipments from its steel manufacturing subsidiaries to the steel service and distribution industry increased from 26 (1981) to 32 (1991) percent. This ensured higher capability utilization rates in its steel business, increasing its potential to realize profits. The MLSF allowed the parent company to use subsidiaries to extend its commodity chain within a single organization without taking the ownership risks (e.g., responsibility for subsidiary debt). Although commodity chains exist within the MDF, the parent company is responsible for each corporate entity (e.g., debt) in this corporate form.

Second, the parent company designated one group of executives to concentrate on the strategic objectives of the parent company and a second group to monitor the corporate entities. In addition to making strategic decisions, the parent company retained the authority to set operating goals for all corporate entities, monitor their performance, and intervene if local management failed to achieve the goals established by the parent company. Transformation to the MLSF enhanced top management's control over the various corporate entities.

[This structure] provides greater flexibility in the financing and oversight of all [American Steel's] businesses, and positions corporate management to more effectively assess and support the performance of business units. (Corporate document)

These changes in corporate governance also sharpened the distinction between middle management's responsibility for making a profit in specific business activities and top management's responsibility for financial management. Middle managers have the independence to make tactical decisions, but the MLSF provides the managerial capacity to ensure that those decisions conform to the parent company's strategic agendas and goals. Together, market embeddedness and the new market-based governance structure of the MLSF increased top management's capacity to monitor members of its corporate family.

In 1996, the parent holding company continued to exploit the self-financing capability of this corporate form by recapitalizing the company through American Steel-S/D, a first-level subsidiary. As in 1986, 1987, and 1989, American Steel Holdings, Inc. (i.e., the parent company) used its subsidiaries as internal capital markets. The parent company sold 13 percent of American Steel-S/D's common stock, in an initial public offering, which raised $77.1 million for the parent company. In addition, recapitalization included the sale of $250 million of commercial notes by the subsidiary. Crucial to this recapitalization was the payment of $445.9 in dividends from the subsidiary to the parent company. American Steel used this capital to pay off the high-interest debt held by the parent company and the steel-manufacturing subsidiary.

In summary, in addition to raising capital through IPOs in subsidiary corporations, the MLSF provides the organizational capacity to transfer capital from the subsidiaries to the parent company. The company issued stocks and bonds in its more profitable subsidiary, transferred capital via a dividend payment to the parent company, and used the capital to repay high-interest debt owed by members of the corporate family. Through these recapitalization programs the parent company was able to reduce corporate family debt by $700 million, annual interest payments by $70 million, and long-term debt to total capitalization from 63 percent in 1992 to 50 percent, 47 percent, and 42 percent, respectively in 1995, 1996, 1997.

Following its most recent recapitalization, in March 1997 one of its large subsidiary holding companies (i.e., American Steel-S/D) established a $250 million credit line with the parent holding company. Interest paid to the parent company was set at market rates, and the terms of the loan restricted the amount of additional debt that the subsidiary was allowed to accumulate. The agreement with the parent also limited the amount that the subsidiary holding company could pay in dividends. Thus, the parent company retained ownership control over the subsidiary holding company and, through it, the assets that it acquired.

The subsidiary holding company used this credit line to pursue an acquisition strategy. In December 1997, American Steel-S/D acquired three more companies in the steel service and distribution product line. These companies were incorporated as wholly owned subsidiaries under American Steel-S/D. These acquisitions further extended the corporation's share of the steel service and distribution market and improved its access to international markets. After acquiring these companies, the company owned and operated more than seventy steel service and distribution facilities in North America, including twelve in Mexico. Through its acquisition strategy the company doubled its sales in this product line between 1986 and 1997.

Restructuring for Global Capitalism: Extension of American Steel's Commodity Chain

American Steel also used the MLSF to expand its steel business. In 1987, American Steel formed a second-level wholly-owned subsidiary holding company (American Steel2) (figure 9.4). The parent company also entered a joint venture (American Steel-J1) with a Japanese corporation to finance, construct, and operate a new steel-making facility. It organized this new product group as a separate, third-level subsidiary under American Steel2. In 1989, through American Steel2, the parent company entered a second joint-venture with the same Japanese corporation. Like the first joint venture, the parent company organized this new product group (American Steel-J2) as a separate, third-level subsidiary in its hierarchy of subsidiary corporations (figure 9.4). The parent company's initial investment was financed by the sale of $185 million of preferred stock (see above) to its Japanese partner in this joint venture.

This arrangement provided American Steel with the capital to construct a plant using the most advanced steel-finishing technology in the world. This $525 million joint venture finishes steel in a single one-third-mile-long continuous process. The fully automated mill includes material handling by robotic trucks programmed to pick up the finished spools of steel and computer-controlled cranes that place the finished steel in their storage locations. This entire continuous process to change hot-rolled (unfinished) steel into cold-rolled (finished) steel takes less than one hour. Convention mills require five steps and up to twelve days to complete the process.

Like expansion in the steel service and distribution product line, these joint ventures provided an additional link in American Steel's commodity chain by providing an outlet for steel produced in its other steel-making operations. These joint ventures also provide American Steel's Japanese partners with access to U.S. markets that bypass protectionist state business policy (chapter 7).

To reduce the effect of future domestic economic downturns, American Steel initiated a strategy to capture global steel markets. In 1994, it created a second-level holding company subsidiary (American Steel-International) and a third-level subsidiary (American Steel-Trade), and organized them under its first-level holding company subsidiary (American Steel) (figure 9.4). American Steel-International is a marketing subsidiary with joint ventures in China, India, and South Africa. American Steel-Trade buys and sells industrial products. A primary task of this subsidiary is to link the steel manufacturing and service subsidiaries to the global commodity chains by purchasing low-cost materials on the international market. Also, the parent company entered a joint venture with Mexico's largest steel producer creating American Steel-MX and established a steel distribution subsidiary in Mexico (American Steel-Dis-MX). These corporations were organized as third-level subsidiaries under American Steel-International (figure 9.4).

With its restructured and elaborate account-control system that centralized information on corporate entities (chapter 8), American Steel used the MLSF to further centralize decision-making authority. Within the old corporate form, American Steel's top management exercised control over its steel-producing operations. The remaining corporate entities, however, including the large steel-distribution subsidiary, operated independently. In the new MLSF, the top manager in each of

American Steel's corporate activities, including the much larger steel-distribution subsidiary, is the same person. The CEO of American Steel's parent holding company (i.e., American Steel Holdings, Inc.) is also the CEO of the first-level steel-producing subsidiary holding company (i.e., American Steel), the first-level steel-distribution subsidiary holding company (i.e., American Steel-S/D), and the second-level subsidiary holding company (i.e., American Steel-International). The MLSF created an organizational structure within which the top manager of American Steel's parent company is also the top manager of each of the first-level subsidiary corporations. The CEO has access to a wide range of information derived from the complex account-control system described in chapter 8 that allows him and members of his top managerial team and administrative staff to monitor the various corporate entities.

Selling the Integrated Steel Business

In March 1998, the parent company announced the pending sale of its wholly owned subsidiary, American Steel Company (i.e., the "old" corporation prior to restructuring), to Ispat International for $888 million in stock payments to American Steel Industries (i.e., the parent company), an additional $230.7 million in debt owed to the parent company, and $307.9 million owned to third parties. The total cost of the transaction was $1.43 billion. American Steel Company, a subsidiary of American Steel, will be incorporated as a subsidiary of Ispat. Ispat International is a member of the LNM Group based in the Netherlands, which has steel-manufacturing facilities in Kazakhstan and Indonesia. Ispat itself has steel-making operations in Canada, Germany, Ireland, Mexico, and Trinidad and marketing outlets in sixty countries. The acquisition will make the LNM Group the fourth largest steel producer in the world. Its membership in the LNM Group will provide access to global markets, allowing American Steel Company to operate at high capability utilization rates and achieve higher profits.

This transaction entails a complete exit of the parent company from the steel industry, which it entered over one hundred years ago (1890s) when many of the largest industrial corporations in the United States were created. The merger, which included a stock buyback by American Steel Industries (i.e., the parent company) of 25.5 million shares, was managed by investment banker Goldman Sachs.

The organizational flexibility of the MLSF makes this transaction relatively simple compared to selling or acquiring a division. Because American Steel Company is a subsidiary corporation—a legally separate entity—of Ispat, the managerial and accountings systems do not have to be compatible with those of the new parent company. The "new" Ispat subsidiary will retain the accounting systems, managerial systems, and managers of the "old" American Steel Industries subsidiary. Also, top management will remain the same. The president and chief executive officer of American Steel Industries will become the top manager of Ispat's North

American operations and the president and chief operating officer of American Steel Company will continue as the top manager of American Steel Company, Ispat. This transaction is an example of the financial flexibility of the MLSF. Little change occurred in the organizational structure of the subsidiary when ownership control was transferred from one parent company to another.

It is unlikely that the sale of American Steel Company will trigger an antitrust investigation under the probusiness ideology in the executive and judicial branches of the federal government. Both branches of the state began easing antitrust enforcement in the early 1980s. Further, during the exploration phase, the state replaced the formula that triggered antitrust violations based on domestic market share to a much more liberal formula based on global market share (see above).

Summary

This case study shows that rapid change occurred in one of the oldest U.S. corporations. Moreover, this corporation is in an industry known for a lack of innovation. However, confronted with severe capital dependence in an increasingly globalized and competitive economic environment, American Steel transformed its managerial process (chapter 8) and corporate form. American Steel created a parent company and restructured its large steel operation into a hierarchy of subsidiary corporations. The internal capital markets of the MLSF allowed the parent company to use equity financing, reducing its dependence on external capital markets. The embeddedness of subsidiaries in specific market niches provide additional measurements of subsidiaries' performance, mitigating the problem of central-office control of the MDF (Prechel 1997a:352–53). The MLSF also created liability firewalls, increased organizational flexibility, and enabled a more flexible system of financial management. There are several crucial dimensions of this change.

First, together with other large corporations American Steel mobilized politically to change the institutional arrangement within which the capital-accumulation process is organized. American Steel changed its corporate form after state business policy redefined the laws governing corporate restructuring. Further, the capital from its IPOs provided the resources to pursue an acquisition strategy.

Second, American Steel transformed its previous corporation organization into several legally separate subsidiary corporations, which embedded its corporate entities into their particular market niches. In addition to its internal monitoring system (chapter 8), American Steel used these market measurements to assess the performance of its subsidiary corporations and hold its managers responsible if they did not achieve standards set by the parent company.

Third, the MLSF reduced American Steel's dependence on external capital markets. American Steel's subsidiaries created internal capital markets that the parent company used to raise capital without taking on additional debt. Using subsidiaries as internal capital markets provided top management with more autonomy and flexibility in financing and managing its corporate family. American Steel used this capital to reduce debt and pursue an acquisition strategy. While all public corporations have this option, stock sales in the MLSF do not undermine top managerial autonomy to the same extent as in the MDF. Whereas selling stock in the MDF undermines top managerial autonomy over decisions by extending additional voting rights to stock owners, selling stock in a subsidiary only affects top management's autonomy in decisions concerning that subsidiary. It does not directly affect top management's autonomy to make decisions concerning the parent company or its remaining subsidiary corporations.

Fourth, the more flexible MLSF facilitated the implementation of an acquisition strategy without increasing American Steel's capital dependence. Capital became more expensive in the late 1970s and the consolidation strategies of the 1980s merger wave left corporations with high debt and costly interest payments. In contrast, corporate consolidation at American Steel in the late 1980s and early 1990s was financed with stock offerings, allowing it to keep its interest costs low and maintain its cash reserves. The more flexible MLSF provides an organizational structure through which the corporation implemented a strategy to shift its assets from one product line to another. In the early 1980s, before American Steel Industries changed to the MLSF, integrated steel accounted for 63 percent of the corporation's revenues. In the 1990s, the sale of the subsidiary holding company within which this product line is organized moved the parent company out of the steel-manufacturing business.

Fifth, state business policy governing the MLSF allowed top management to shift debt to the "new" subsidiary corporations. This left the parent company with less debt, strengthening its financial position and making its middle-level subsidiary management responsible for subsidiary debt. In this way, the MLSF provides the organizational capability to shift responsibility for the financial stability and strength of corporate entities from top to middle management, even though top management in the parent company retains control over capital investments and cash flows to those subsidiary corporations.

Sixth, while decentralizing responsibility to subsidiary managers, American steel centralized authority by assigning the same person to the top managerial position in each of the corporate entities in its new MLSF. It also established an administrative staff responsible to monitor subsidiary corporations' performance (also see Prechel 1997a:426). Top managerial control was further facilitated by the neo-Fordist controls (e.g., elaborate account controls, sophisticated computerized information processing systems), which provide top management with information to monitor corporate entities distributed throughout many geographic regions. Together, the MLSF and the new account controls centralized control over a range of spatially separated corporate entities. Together the account controls and market measurements on subsidiaries provide information on operating performance, which allows a few top managers to monitor a large and complex corporate family.

Seventh, within the MLSF the parent company becomes increasingly focused on financing activities. At American Steel, the parent company ensured that its two product lines had adequate capital to pursue their expansion, joint-venture, and acquisition strategies. It also operated as a direct financier. In addition to arranging for subsidiary financing through IPOs, the parent company loaned capital to its subsidiaries. When American Steel sold its steel product line the first-level subsidiary owed the parent company $230.7 million. Debt financing within the corporate family reduces total operating expenses by eliminating the cost of borrowing from external capital markets. Also, interest payments of subsidiaries to the parent company are sources of revenue. The parent company also charged its subsidiaries for financial and managerial services. The first-level steel service and distribution subsidiary was charged $5.5, $6.4, $6.8, and $7.4 million in 1997, 1996, 1995, and 1994 respectively, by the parent company for "services rendered." Thus, the MLSF denotes a change to more forms of financial management and control within the firm. The transformation of the institutional arrangements, of the managerial process, and of the corporate form to the MLSF in the late twentieth century accelerated the merging of banking functions with manufacturing functions (i.e., banking and industrial capital) that began with the nineteenth century holding company.

CHAPTER 10

Transformation to the Multilayered Subsidiary Form among the Largest Industrial Parent Companies

The 1880–1890s New Jersey laws of incorporation and the New Deal legislation in the 1930s represented important changes in corporations' institutional arrangements. During both of these historical periods, change in the state's institutional arrangements occurred in response to macroeconomic crises. The capitalist class mobilized politically to restructure the political-legal arrangements in an effort to advance their profit-making agenda. Change in the largest corporations occurred after a transformation in institutional arrangements. Similarly, change at American Steel in the 1980s followed economic crisis, and capitalists' capacity to mobilize politically and change crucial aspects of corporations' political-legal structure. A shift in the historical trajectory, however, occurs when a significant portion of social actors—corporations in this case—change. To detect whether the change at American Steel is typical of other corporations, the following examines the effect of variables identified in previous chapters on corporate form change in the one hundred largest industrial parent companies.

Corporate Characteristics and Strategies in the 1980s and 1990s

Many of the corporate characteristics, strategies, and behaviors described in the case-oriented study of American Steel are representative of other large corporations: profits declined, debt increased, mergers and acquisitions accelerated, and initial public offerings of stock skyrocketed. The rate of corporate profit declined sharply in the 1980s. Profits as percent of assets of the five hundred largest industrial firms declined from "approximately 6 percent in the 1960s to under 3 percent in the early 1990s" (Prechel and Boies 1998a:336). Also, some of the largest corporations merged with or acquired other corporations in the 1980s. Mergers and acquisitions reached a historic high point in 1988 when more than $240 billion in assets was transferred from one corporation to another (figure 10.1). Whether from mergers and acquisitions or other sources corporate debt escalated in the 1980s. Debt as percent of assets for the largest one hundred industrial corporations rose from 45 to 73 percent between 1981 and 1993 (Prechel, Boies, and Woods 1999). To reduce the cost of high dept payments, parent companies began to raise capital by selling subsidiaries' stock through IPOs. For example, after the *TRA86* was passed by Congress, Coca-Cola spun off Coca-Cola Enterprises in an initial public offering, which raised $1.5 billion for the parent company (*The Outlook* 1986). Between 1996 and 1998, corporations raised $123.5 billion through IPOs (for more detail see chapter 11).

Further, beginning in the 1970s, corporations engaged in more political strategies. One political strategy entailed a rapid increase in corporate-sponsored political action committee (PAC) contributions. PAC contributions increased from about $9.2 million in the 1977–1978 election cycle to $23.5 and $27.2 million in the 1985–86 and 1987–88 election cycles, respectively (figure 10.2).

Variable-Oriented Analysis

The following examines whether capital-dependence theory explains corporate-form change in the 1980s and early 1990s. The operationalization of capital-dependence theory suggests that institutional arrangements and corporate characteristics are sufficient conditions to produce a corporate-form change. Although industrial corporations dependence on external capital markets is an important basis of finance capital's power and capacity to coerce industrial corporations to change their behavior, corporations also have self-interests that affect their motives and behaviors. Capital-dependence theory suggests that long-term capital-accumulation constraints (e.g., shrinking markets, high debt, low profits) are sufficient conditions for corporate change. Corporations' social actions (i.e., corporate-form change) are based in their self-interests to create a better corporate form–environment fit (Prechel 1991:438) and desire to access valued resources through, for example, mergers and acquisitions.

Further, as shown in chapters 7 and 9, the continued weakening of the economy—including financial markets—produced capitalist class unity in the 1980s over policy initiatives designed to stimulate growth in the economy as a whole. Moreover, industrial capital's interest in creating internal capital markets (i.e., subsidiaries) is compatible with finance's capital's interests in a higher rate of return on their investments in industrial corporations (e.g., stocks, bonds). Capital from IPOs of subsidiaries' stock could be reinvested in ways to improve corporations'

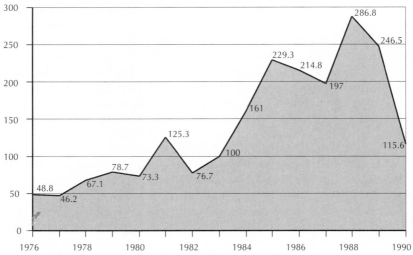

FIGURE 10.1 Total value of mergers and acquisitions in the U.S., 1976–1990, in 1992 billion dollars. *Source: Mergerstat.*

competitive position and rate of return on investment. Also, the massive revenues from underwriting corporate recapitalization—almost 5 percent at American Steel—became a major source of revenue for finance capital, creating an additional incentive for private investment banks and other financiers to support corporate-form change to the MLSF.

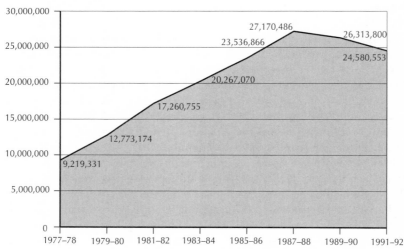

FIGURE 10.2 PAC receipts of the largest one hundred industrial parent companies, 1977–1992, in 1992 dollars. *Source:* U.S. Federal Election Commission, 1994.

The analysis tests whether the largest one hundred industrial parent companies transformed their form in the late 1980s and early 1990s. Although variable-oriented analyses are disadvantaged by the requirement to have many cases and few variables, I examine crucial variables that I identified in my case-oriented study (also see Prechel 1991). Four dimensions of capital-dependence theory (i.e., strategies and corporate characteristics) and a core concept of the new institutional theory are formulated as hypotheses.

Hypotheses

The first hypothesis suggests that debt dependence results in corporate-form change. By the late 1970s and early 1980s, existing strategies no longer ensured an adequate rate of return on investment. Using several measures, researchers have shown that this profitability crisis was part of a long-term trend that began in the 1940s (Dumenil, Glick, and Rangel 1987). Corporate strategies to improve their competitiveness (e.g., internal restructuring, mergers and acquisitions) required massive amounts of capital during a period when the economy was experiencing a capital shortage, high interest rates, and low rates of return on investment. Borrowing increased corporations' dependence on external capital markets, which resulted in a massive increase in corporate debt. Debt continued to increase throughout 1980s (Prechel, Boies, and Woods 1999), which increased corporations' operating costs (e.g., interest payments). To reduce their dependence on external capital markets, corporations change to the MLSF. Transforming divisions to subsidiaries provides a means to overcome corporations' dependence on external capital markets because the MLSF creates internal capital markets (Prechel 1997a:409, 423–24). Following this theoretical logic the first hypothesis (H1) states: *Firms with high debt are more likely to change to the MLSF.*

Second, capital-dependence theory suggests that as corporations' capacity to generate capital internally declines, they change to a form that provides a means to generate capital from other sources (e.g., stock sales). There are several reasons why low-profit firms prefer the MLSF. Once low-profit product lines or product groups are organized as subsidiaries they can be sold through a simple stock transaction. Further, declining profits and dependence on external capital markets are associated with the appointment of financial directors to corporate boards (Mizruchi and Stearns 1988, 1994). However, the appointment of financial directors undermines top managerial autonomy. Thus, top managers and the board of directors may prefer the MLSF, which they can use to generate capital internally through stock issues and avoid giving up autonomy to financiers. Thus, the second hypothesis suggests that low-profit firms change to the MLSF. Hypothesis two (H2) states: *Firms with low profits are more likely to change to the MLSF.*

Third, resource-dependence theory predicts that corporations set up merger strategies to absorb uncertainty (Pfeffer 1972). Several studies support this argument. At the turn of the century, when a high degree of uncertainty existed, corporations implemented horizontal merger and acquisition strategies to gain control over a larger share of the market (Haney 1920). During the 1960s and 1970s, corporate merger and acquisition strategies entailed political behavior to alleviate the threat of antitrust enforcement (Boies 1989). Research on the 1980s shows that merger and acquisition strategies were set up by the largest industrial corporations in response to increasingly competitive and global markets (Sanjal, Shleifer, and Vishny 1990; Prechel 1991; Davis, Dickmann, and Tinsley 1994). However, merger and acquisition strategies create management problems in the MDF. Reorganizing a large acquired corporation as a division or incorporating it into an existing division is complex, expensive, and time consuming. Moreover, large divisions that produce many products and perform many functions place tremendous burdens on internal monitoring mechanisms. The MLSF provides an organizational form that facilitates implementing merger and acquisition strategies (Prechel 1991:439). First, the MLSF alleviates the problem of bounded rationality by providing the organizational capability to create smaller and less complex corporate entities and by providing financial information to monitor subsidiaries performance (e.g., stock values, profits). Second, the MLSF allows parent companies to incorporate the acquired corporation as a subsidiary without changing the internal management structure of the new company or the parent company. Borden, a subsidiary of Kohlberg Kravis Roberts & Co. (KKR), agreed to acquire Corning's housewares business unit. Just as the sale of American Steel Company to Ispat entailed few managerial changes (chapter 9), the new Borden housewares subsidiary continued to be located near Corning Inc. and retained its original managers, including its top manager. Third, parent companies can swap their stock or the stock of their subsidiaries for an acquired corporation. That is, the parent company can self-finance their acquisitions with this internal source of capital, which allows them to set up a merger and acquisition strategy without becoming dependent on external capital markets. Although corporations may set up merger and acquisition strategies to reduce uncertainty, corporations use the MLSF to implement these strategies because it increases organizational flexibility and control while reducing capital dependence. The third hypothesis (H3) states: *Firms with larger dollar value of mergers and acquisitions are more likely to change to the MLSF.*

The fourth hypothesis suggests that corporate political behavior has an inverse effect on change to the MLSF. That is, corporations engage in political behavior to stabilize their environments, which reduces the need to change. Corporate political behavior can produce state business policy that mediates economic constraints in a range of ways including reducing corporate taxes, relaxing regulatory enforcement, and allocating defense contracts. That is, individual corporations pursue buffering strategies to eliminate dependence-based uncertainties (Palmer et al. 1993). Capitalists become most politically active when profits decline and the state has control over resources upon which corporate profits depend (Prechel 1990). Boies (1994) shows that firms with long-term material interest-based relationships with the federal government (e.g., defense contractors) are the most politically active. Individual corporations use speaking fees and PAC contributions to get key congressional leaders to bar the army from seeking competitive bids (Stubbing and Mendel 1986). This suggests that corporate political behavior stabilizes corporations' environments, which may reduce the need for change in corporate form. The fourth hypothesis (H4) states: *Politically active firms are less likely to change to the MLSF.*

Fifth, managers' background was included to test whether managers' characteristics effect change to the MLSF. The analaysis here shows that financial and family capitalists exercised their power in the 1920s to set up financial controls to monitor the efficient use of their capital (chapter 5). Dependent on capital from financial capitalists, industrial capitalists had little choice but to comply. Also, institutional investors pressured management to restructure in the 1980s (Unseem 1993). The new corporate form entails parent companies' financial management of its subsidiary corporations (see also Prechel 1991:439; 1997a:423). Thus, capital-dependence theory suggests that dependence on capital—a corporate characteristic versus an individual characteristic—explains the change to the MLSF (Prechel 1991:438–39; Prechel and Boies 1998a:350–51). In contrast, neo-institutional theory suggests that different conceptions of control emerge because groups of managers are professionalized in different ways (Fligstein 1990). This theory also suggests that managers' background (e.g., financial) is associated with corporate form change (Fligstein 1985). If managers' characteristics are associated with corporate form change, top managers with finance backgrounds should be related to change to the MLSF where added emphasis of financial management exists. The following hypothesis (H5) tests this dimension of neo-institutional theory: *Corporations whose top managers have financial and accounting backgrounds have a higher probability of changing to the MLSF.*

Research Design

The analysis examines factors accounting for corporate-form change during a period of changing institutional arrangements (1981–1993) (e.g., government business policy, economic globalization). It tests hypotheses using data on the largest one hundred publicly traded industrial firms in 1988. Like previous analyses, firms that were "acquired by other firms," filed for "bankruptcy," or were "restructured under private ownership between 1981 and 1993" were not included in the sample (Prechel and Boies 1998a:341). Firms that were subsidiaries of domestic or foreign firms (e.g., Shell Oil) were excluded from the sample because they do not meet the assumption of independent observation necessary for statistical analysis.

The analysis of change in corporate form uses a discrete time event history model. The discrete time model defines a case as corporate year, and uses logistical regression to analyze the data.[1] The discrete time model is easy to use and interpret and examines the effects of time-varying explanatory variables as well as explicit tests for the effects of time on the likelihood of the event (Allison 1984).[2]

Measurements

There are important differences between my data and that used in previous quantitative research on corporate form. First, the data used here cover the period between 1981 and 1993 when important changes occurred in corporations' political and economic institutional arrangements. Previous quantitative studies on corporate form examine change in the 1960s and 1970s (Fligstein 1985, 1990; Fligstein and Brantley 1992; Palmer et al. 1993). The data analyzed in these studies precede crucial changes in corporations' institutional arrangements.

Second, some researchers use *Moody's Manual of Industrials* to identify the presence of a legal holding company to decide whether the corporation operates through a subsidiary structure. If a legal holding company was not listed and a division vice president was listed, the corporation was assigned to the MDF category (Fligstein 1985:383, 1990:329). This procedure is problematic because "The holding company organization is not necessarily associated with firms that in legal terms are holding companies" (Rumelt 1974:38; also see Prechel 1997a:417). Thus, the measurement used in my study emphasizes *ownership control*, which directs researchers' attention toward how property rights define the legal, administrative, and financial relationships between parent companies and corporate entities. Also, researchers' classification schemes raise important questions. Some researchers acknowledge that data available during earlier periods were "reduced to crude levels of classification," that this may "invalidate" the study, and that "readers should proceed with healthy skepticism" (Fligstein 1985:382). As a result of these and other shortcomings, most studies fail to acknowledge that many of the largest industrial corporations had subsidiaries throughout the twentieth century. Although the largest one hundred industrial corporations averaged more than twenty-three domestic subsidiaries in 1981 (Prechel 1994a, 1997b:163), little attention was given to understanding why corporations organized their assets as subsidiaries (for exceptions see Rumelt 1974; Harris 1983; Prechel 1991).

Third, because systematic quantitative data on corporate form were not available prior to 1981 researchers were dependent on compiling this data from multiple sources (e.g., *Moody's Manual of Industrials*, case studies, newspapers) (Rumelt 1974; Fligstein 1985, 1990). Sources that provided quantitative data on divisions, subsidiaries, and especially levels of subsidiaries were not systematic in their reporting and are difficult to operationalize (e.g., *The Directory of Corporate Affiliations*). The data used in my study are from Dun & Bradstreet *America's Corporate*

Families: The Billion Dollar Directory, which does not have these shortcomings. The measurement of the dependent variable (i.e., corporate form) used here counts the number of divisions, domestic subsidiaries, and levels of subsidiaries.[3] Dun & Bradstreet compile these data from their *Business Information Reports*, telephone interviews, and corporations' annual reports. Dun & Bradstreet (1993) makes its page proofs available to companies for approval or correction. These data provide an accurate, standardized, and valid measurement of corporate form.

The analysis here overcomes previous measurement problems by using an actual count of the number of divisions and subsidiaries, collecting the data from a single source, eliminating judgements by the researcher, creating a conceptual definition of the corporate form, and computer assigning the empirical configuration of the corporation to the theoretical construct.

Variables and Data

The dependent variable for the discrete time model uses a dummy variable coded *one* in the year the firm became an MLSF and *zero* otherwise. A firm is defined as being a MLSF when it has "one or no divisions" and "one or more domestic subsidiary corporations at the second level" (Prechel 1997a:428). This operationalization captures both multiple subsidiaries and multiple levels of subsidiaries. All corporations with second-level subsidiaries have at least one first-level subsidiary. Explicit in this definition is the idea that the MLSF should be conceptualized as an *ideal type*, which serves as an abstraction to provide a means to aid in the description of the empirical level (Weber 1949:92–93; Hall 1963; Prechel 1990:650). The use of the ideal type is particularly useful when examining organizational change because it "aids in historicizing the corporation so that breaks from the past are more readily acknowledged" (Prechel 1997a:428). The MDF is operationalized as corporations with more than one division.

The data show that by 1981 all of the corporations in the sample that had two or more divisions also had multiple subsidiaries. Thus, if the same criteria were applied with the same level of rigor to the MDF (i.e., one or no subsidiaries and multiple divisions) as to the MLSF, there were no ideal type MDFs. Consequently, I refer to the contemporary MDF as a hybrid-MDF; corporations use both divisions and subsidiaries to organize their organizational entities. This operationalization of the dependent variable was used in previous analyses (Prechel 1997a:428, 1997b; Prechel and Boies 1998a; Prechel, Boies, and Woods 1999) because it is a conservative measure of corporate-form change. If any bias in the measure exists it is against showing that a corporation changed from the hybrid-MDF to the MLSF.

The model includes two control variables and five independent variables. The independent variables are dollar value of mergers and acquisitions, rate of return on equity, whether the firm sponsored a PAC during the 1980s, long-term debt as percent of assets, and CEO background. The control variables are the dollar value of a firm's assets and the year the company was first incorporated. Long-term debt, the total debt due after more than one year, divided by the firm's assets measures the firm's debt dependence. These data are from Compustat (items 4 and 9). The mean long-term debt as percent of assets for firms in the analysis was 41.8 percent for 1981–1986. Although some firms carried no long-term debt, others had significantly more debt (e.g., AMAX carried debt equal to 184 percent of its assets). (See appendix A for the descriptive statistics).

Profits are measured by a firm's rate of return on equity as reported in *Moody's Handbook of Common Stock*. The mean return on equity for the analysis was 13.95 percent. Chrysler had the highest average return at 33 percent. The poorest performing firm was AMAX with a rate of return of only 1.37 percent. Merger and acquisition data are from the United States Federal Trade Commission *Report on Mergers and Acquisitions* and *Mergers and Acquisitions*. Sara Lee made the largest transactions during this period with a total of $10.1 billion in acquisitions and mergers. Many firms made no transactions and the average firm made transactions of $830 million.

Firm political action is a dummy variable coded *one* if a firm sponsored a PAC with more than one dollar in receipts any time during 1981–1986 and *zero* otherwise.[4] Eighty-three percent of the firms in the analysis sponsored a PAC during this time. These data are from the *U.S. Federal Election Commission* (1994). Data on PAC receipts and expenditures are widely used in the literature on business political behavior (Clawson, Neustadtl, and Bearden 1986; Boies 1989; Grenzke 1989; Mizruchi 1992).

Data on manager's background are from Dun and Bradstreet *Reference Book on Corporate Management* (1982). This variable was operationalized by identifying the employment background of the CEO. CEOs that spend most of their careers in accounting and finance were coded as finance CEOs. CEOs with backgrounds in other areas were coded as other (*one* = accounting and finance background of CEO, *zero* = other background of CEOs). As shown in previous chapters, there are important differences in the conception of cost accounting and financial accounting that can affect managers' motives and behaviors. Whereas accounting managers are oriented toward identifying and controling costs, financial managers evaluate cash flows and pursue external sources of capital when internal cash flows are inadequate. However, I used this operationalization to test a core aspect of neoinstitutional theory that uses this variable to measure the financial conception of corporate control (Fligstein 1985, 1990; Fligstein and Brantley 1992). Also, because these functions were merged and confused in many corporations since the 1920s and 1930s (chapter 5) this is a reasonable operationalization of managers' background.

Firm size and age are included as control variables because several organizational theories consider them key variables. Size is measured by assets in millions of dollars and age was measured by the year the firm was first incorporated. Researchers disagree, however, on their relationship to change. Managerialism suggests that expansion without change reduces efficiency (Chandler 1962). In contrast, population ecology suggests that firm size contributes to organizational inertia, an impediment to change. Population ecology also argues that as firms age they rarely undergo rapid change (Hannan and Freeman 1984). These variables are included as controls because capital-dependence theory does not posit an explicit causal relationship between these organizational characteristics and corporate change. Capital-dependence theory, however, implicitly suggests that these variables are not impediments to change during crisis periods. The asset variable is from *Fortune* magazine and the age variable is from *Moody's Industrial Manual*.

In order to maximize the reliability of the independent and control variables mean values across a six-year period are used. Year of incorporation and the presence of a PAC are the two exceptions. Using the average of multiple years minimizes the effects of one or two aberrant years on the measures. Therefore, data for the six years prior to the event were used. Year of incorporation remains the same regardless of the year of event. The PAC data are based on data for three election cycles, 1981–82, 1983–84, and 1985–86. Annual data are not readily available for this measure.

Findings

There are two parts to the variable-oriented analysis. First, I present descriptive data on the change from the MDF to the MLSF. Second, I present the findings from the discrete time event history analysis that examines corporate-form change between 1981 and 1993. I selected 1981 through 1993 as the test period because crucial changes occurred in corporations' institutional arrangements during this period: the recessions in the early 1980s, the slow economic growth throughout the 1980s, increased globalization of the economy, the merger and acquisition movement of the 1980s, the increase in product-liability lawsuits, and the reform of state business policy governing corporate restructuring.

The following presents the data on the changes in the number of divisions, number of subsidiaries, and number of levels of subsidiaries to provide insight into the magnitude of corporate-form change during the test period. By 1981, twenty-three of the largest one hundred industrial corporations had no divisions. Corporations with no divisions in 1981, which include Anheuser-Busch, Caterpillar, H.J. Heinz, Ingersoll-Rand, Mobil, and Texas Instruments, represent several industries.

In contrast, every firm in the sample had one or more subsidiaries at the beginning of the test period. Only three corporations (i.e., Baxter International, Cooper Industries, Hewlett-Packard) had only 1 subsidiary in 1981. By 1993, these companies had 9, 34 and 26 subsidiary corporations, respectively. Although most of the one hundred largest industrial firms are transnational corporations, those with long-term experience operating in foreign countries—where assets must be organized as subsidiaries for legal reasons—also organized many of their domestic operations as subsidiaries in 1981. Chrysler, ITT, Sun Oil, Pepsico, WR Grace, and Beatrice had 80, 133, 95, 75, 78, 74 domestic subsidiaries in 1981, respectively. Although most petroleum companies have few or no divisions, analyses not shown here suggest little industry effect on change to the MLSF. The exception is the chemical industry where tort lawsuits for product liability became more prevalent in the 1980s (Prechel 1997a:415; Prechel and Boies 1998a). The organization of corporate assets as subsidiaries increased in all industries and in most corporations during this twelve-year period (table 10.1). The presence of subsidiaries in 1981 is consistent with previous research showing that corporations organized some of their assets as subsidiaries throughout much of the twentieth century (Rumelt 1974; Harris 1983; Prechel 1991).

The mean number of divisions in the largest industrial parent companies declined from 9 (1981) to 8 (1985) to 4 (1993) (figure 10.3). The opposite trend occurred among subsidiaries. The total number of subsidiary corporations under

TABLE 10.1 Domestic Subsidiary Change in Selected Corporations, 1981, 1993

Industry and Corporation	Subsidiaries in 1981	Subsidiaries in 1993	Industry and Corporation	Subsidiaries in 1981	Subsidiaries in 1993
Aerospace & Defense			*Oil*		
Boeing	9	11	Exxon	59	30
Lockheed	8	39	Mobil	63	74
			Texaco	9	73
Automobile*			Pennzoil	11	31
Chrysler	80	129			
General Motors	35	137	*Paper & Wood*		
			Scott Paper	6	22
Business Equipment			Weyerhaeuser	34	70
Hewlett-Packard	1	26			
IBM	5	14	*Pharmaceuticals*		
Xerox	15	58	Eli Lilly	7	21
			Merek	10	59
Chemical					
Dow Chemical	11	50	*Steel*		
DuPont	5	52	Bethlehem Steel	28	16
			Reynolds Metals	17	40
Food			USX	32	45
Archer Daniel Midland	13	41			
Conagra	7	110			
Heavy Equipment					
Caterpillar	4	27			
Deere	10	24			

* The very large number of domestic subsidiaries in the automobile industry exist, in part, because some automobile companies incorporate dealerships as subsidiaries.

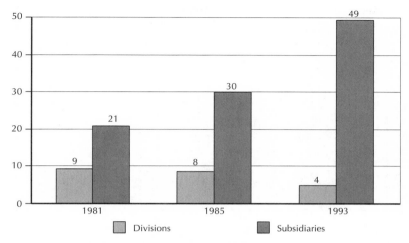

FIGURE 10.3 Change in the mean number of divisions and domestic subsidiaries in the one hundred largest U.S. industrial parent companies. *Source: American's Corporate Families,* Dun & Bradstreet

ownership control by the largest parent companies gradually increased from 21 to 30 between 1981 and 1985 and to 49 in 1993. These data show that the turbulent 1980s was a period of corporate transformation, and much of that change occurred after the *TRA86* and *RA87* were passed. (These calculations are based on available data, which include data on 90 or more of the largest one hundred companies in each year. Similar results were produced using slightly different samples [Prechel 1997a:428–29, 1997b:163–64; Prechel and Boies 1998a:346–47]).

Parent companies also restructured their corporate entities as a pyramid of subsidiary corporations. The mean number of subsidiaries in the organizational pyramid rapidly increased between 1981 and 1993 (figure 10.4). The mean number of first-level subsidiaries increased from 12.9 (1981) to 23.8 (1993). The largest parent companies also increased the mean number of second-level subsidiaries from 6.8 (1981) to 15.6 (1993) and the mean number of third-level subsidiaries from 1.6 (1981) to 6.6 (1993). Although no parent companies had fourth-level subsidiaries in 1981, the mean number at this level was 2.5 in 1993. These data show that the number of subsidiaries and layers of subsidiaries rapidly increased among the largest parent companies. (Similar results were produced using somewhat different samples [Prechel 1997a:428–29, 1997b:163–64; Prechel and Boies 1998a:346–47; Boies and Prechel 1998]). By 1996, numerous parent companies in different industries had four levels of subsidiary corporations, several had five levels of subsidiaries (e.g., Amoco, Atlantic Richfield, General Motors, Tenneco,

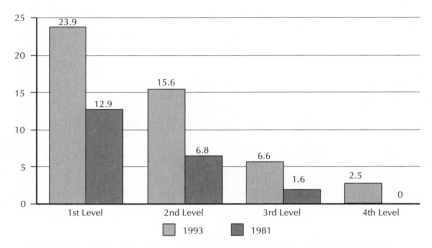

FIGURE 10.4 Change in the mean number in the top four layers of domestic subsidiary corporations in the one hundred largest industrial parent companies. *Source: America's Corporate Families*, Dun & Bradstreet.

Xerox Corporation), some had six levels (e.g., General Electric, Occidental Petroleum), and some had seven levels (e.g., Ford Motor Company, Pepsico).

In 1981, 75 percent of the largest one hundred industrial parent companies had MDFs (i.e., corporations with two or more divisions).[5] Also, in 1981, twenty-five of the largest one hundred industrial corporations were MLSF; they had one or no divisions and multiple subsidiaries and layers of subsidiaries. Between 1981 and 1993, 40 of the remaining 75 firms changed to the MLSF. Thus, by 1993, 65 of the 100 largest industrial corporations were MLSF. Change to the MLSF occurred at a more rapid rate than change to the MDF during the middle decades of the twentieth century, a period of relative economic stability.[6]

Because 25 of the one hundred firms in the sample changed to the MLSF prior to 1981 they are left-censored. Thirty-five firms are right-censored because they did not change to the MLSF by 1993. Eleven independent variables for change between years were created in the event history analysis to measure whether any of the years have an effect on change to MLSF. This results in 733 cases available for analyses. The most active period is 1991 to 1993 when more than 40 percent of the firms at risk changed their corporate form. Once a firm undergoes change it is removed from the analyses (since it is no longer at risk for change).

The first hypothesis, firms with higher levels of debt are more likely to change to the MLSF, is supported by the data (table 10.2). Higher levels of debt result in a substantially higher odds ratio of change. On the average a 1 percent increase in

TABLE 10.2 Discrete Time Model Predicting Change to MLSF with Year of Incorporation, Assets, Presence of Political Action Committee, Return on Equity, Long-Term Debt, Large Mergers and Acquisitions, and CEO's Financial Background, 1981–1993.

Independent Variables		
Capital Dependence		
Long-term debt	1.1131**[a]	(.0062)[b]
Return on equity	.0003	(.9899)
Mergers and acquisitions	.0009*	(.0412)
Presence of a PAC	− 1.9599***	(.0002)
Neo-Institutionalism		
CEO with accounting or financial background	.3675	(.5281)
Control Variables		
Assets	− .0460	(.0524)
Year of incorporation	− .0097	(.1456)
N		733
Overall Chi-square Score		60.801
Degrees of Freedom		18
Significance		.0001

a = Regression coefficient   b = Statistical significance   *$P<.05$ **$P<.01$ ***$P<.001$

long-term debt increases the odds ratio by 3 percent ($P=.0062$). The second hypothesis, corporate profits are likely to produce a change to the MLSF, was not supported ($P=.9899$). The third hypothesis, corporations that pursue mergers and acquisitions increase the likelihood of change to the MLSF, is supported. Acquirers of other firms are likely to change to the MLSF. On average a \$1 million increase in a firm's large acquisitions results in a .09 percent increase in the odds ratio ($P=.0412$). The fourth hypothesis, that the presence of a political action committee decreases the likelihood that a firm will change to the MLSF is also supported. Firms with a PAC reduced the odds of change by 85 percent ($P=.0002$).[7] The fifth hypothesis, CEO financial background is likely to result in a corporate form change is not supported ($P=.5281$). Neither of the control variables was statistically significant in this model ($P=.0524$ for assets and $P=.1456$ for age). However, assets was very close to the commonly accepted criteria for statistical significance. None of the dummy variables for the year were statistically discernible from zero.[8]

The findings provide strong support for capital-dependence theory. Debt, mergers and acquisitions, and firm political behaviors explain whether or not corporations change from the hybrid-MDF to the MLSF during a period of environmental turbulence. Although the restructuring of assets from divisions to subsidiaries entails a more advanced financial conception of control, the analysis does not support the neoinstitutional argument that a manager's background effects change to the MLSF. Analyses not presented here show that the effects for these variables are similar using different event history techniques and regression models using different samples and controlling for additional variables (Prechel 1994a; Prechel and Boies 1998b).

The event history analysis did not identify any single year as a statistically significant transformation year. This is expected for three reasons. First, there are many variables that contribute to variations in *when* a particular corporate-form transformation occurs. Corporate form change is a complex process and requires a significant degree of planning. The planning is affected by, for example, the degree of product line and product group diversification. Second, capital dependence varies across corporations. Those corporations that are more capital dependent are likely to implement change sooner than those that are less capital dependent. Third, and potentially most important, the conservative measurement of MLSF (i.e., one or no divisions and subsidiaries at the first and second levels) affects the date when corporations qualify as MLSFs.

Corporations changed from organizing their assets as divisions to organizing their assets in a hierarchy of subsidiary corporations. Fifty three percent (i.e., forty of seventy-five) of the corporations that were not MLSF at the beginning of the period of rapid change in corporations' environment (i.e., early 1980s) changed to the MLSF by 1993. These corporations changed from having multiple divisions to having one or no divisions and multiple subsidiaries and multiple levels of subsidiaries. Moreover, the negative relationship between corporate change and size at $P = .0524$ is important. This suggests that when capital dependence increases corporations change despite organizational inertia.

The findings presented here are consistent with the case-oriented study in the previous chapter. The one exception is the temporal ordering between merger and acquisition strategies and corporate-form change. The variable-oriented study suggests that mergers and acquisitions effect corporate-form change. In contrast, American Steel changed its form before it carried out an acquisition strategy. This difference may be due to the fact that American Steel underwent a much more severe crisis than most corporations. By the mid-1980s, its debt-to-equity ratio increased, its liquidity position declined, and it did not realize a profit for four consecutive years. American Steel's capital shortage restricted its capacity to set up a merger and acquisition strategy. It changed to the MLSF to create internal capital markets, improve its cash flow, and mitigate its liquidity crisis. Once it achieved these goals, American Steel pursued an acquisition strategy.

Discussion

Findings show that the largest industrial corporations in the United States, many of which are also the oldest, are changing to the MLSF. Parent companies are restructuring their corporate family into a hierarchy of subsidiary corporations.

Several measurements show that the MDF is in decline among the largest industrial corporations and the MLSF is becoming more widespread. Corporations pursued internal-oriented strategies and external-oriented strategies. These strategies affected whether or not corporations changed to the MLSF.

Corporations' internal-oriented strategies included pursuing mergers and acquisitions and taking on debt. These strategies had positive effects on change from the MDF to the MLSF. Although some corporations began to set up subsidiaries after the 1969 antitrust decision by the Department of Justice (p.129), the corporate tax law changes and the relaxed enforcement of antitrust policies in the 1980s made it less risky and less costly for corporations to set up merger and acquisition strategies. The likelihood of triggering an antitrust violation declined (chapter 7) and corporations could make these transactions through stock swaps or use capital raised through IPOs. The self-financing capability of the MLSF (e.g., using stock to finance mergers and acquisition) reduces dependence on external capital markets (Prechel 1991:439; Prechel 1997a:409). Despite this advantage of the MLSF, the 1980s merger and acquisition wave and other corporate strategies produced a tremendous growth in corporate debt. Parent companies with large long-term debt, whether emerging from mergers and acquisitions or other sources, were more likely to change to the MLSF. The self-financing capability of internal capital markets of the MLSF aids in containing corporate debt.

Although the rate of return on equity did not have the expected effect, this finding is consistent with previous research showing that declining profits do not have an effect on corporate form change (Palmer et al. 1993; Prechel and Boies 1998a). This finding suggests that this widely used measurement of corporations' success is less important than other political and economic corporate characteristics.

External-oriented political strategies to control their environment through political activity had, as predicted, negative effects on change to the MLSF. In response to economic constraints, many corporations mobilized politically and pursued an external-oriented strategy in the late 1970s and 1980s to change state business policy. Their political strategy included a rapid increase in PAC contributions (figure 10.2). The analysis shows that firms pursuing political strategies to improve their organization-environment fit are *less* likely to make internal changes. Even when controlling for the widely accepted explanation for why corporations do not change (i.e., inertia measured by age and size) (Hannan and Freeman 1984), politically active corporations are significantly less likely to undergo change. This moves beyond previous quantitative research, which provides little or no support for the argument that a relationship exists between political variables and corporate behavior. Moreover, this analysis challenges researchers who argue that corporations receive few tangible returns from their political action (Grenzke 1989). The PAC variable shows that corporate political behavior reduces corporations' need to change their form.[9] Specifically, corporations may engage in political activity to stabilize their environments or buffer themselves from their environment, thereby reducing the need to undergo change.

Cooperation between industrial and financial capitalist class segments was an essential component of this corporate form change. Core aspects of corporate restructuring described here and in chapter 9 (e.g., mergers and acquisitions, IPOs) were financed by investment firms. The lead underwriter establishes the price of the IPO and arranges the financing, which includes determining how many shares participating investment firms are allowed to sell. Underwriting these dimensions of corporate restructuring brought about a massive increase in the size and wealth of investment firms. Morgan Stanley, a subsidiary created from the J. P. Morgan empire, had $7 million in capital and employed 110 people in 1962. In 1995, after it merged with Dean Witter, this investment firm employed 10,000 people and had $12 billion in capital (Chernow 1997). In 1996 and 1997, Morgan Stanley Dean Witter received fees of $1.813 billion for underwriting stocks and bonds. Goldman Sachs, who employs 16,500 people, received $2.385 billion in fees in 1996 and 1997. Merrill Lynch, the largest underwriter in those years, received almost $2.704 billion in fees. In 1996 and 1997 alone, the largest ten underwriters in the United States received more than $13.445 billion in fees (*Wall Street Journal* 1998). These revenues do not include the profits from the sale of shares the investment firms are allowed to purchase and sell for underwriting corporate restructuring.

Conclusion

This analysis provides an important modification to traditional contingency theory, which argues that corporations in turbulent environments change their form. The analysis here shows that corporations that are not politically active change in response to rapidly changing environments. Politically active corporations, however, are less likely to change, which suggests that these firms pursue strategies to stabilize their environments or buffer themselves from their environment. Moreover, contingency theory does not account for the capacity of corporations to redefine their institutional arrangements. Contingency and other organizational theories fail to explain corporate political behavior because they broadly conceptualize environmental uncertainty and turbulence, and then argue that organizations change in response to environments with those characteristics. In contrast, capital-dependence theory provides a more precise conception of the relationship between corporations and their environments, and shows that corporations mobilize politically and change their environments. (Also see chapters 4 and 7.)

This study does not support the neoinstitutional argument that a top manager's background is a cause of corporate change. Despite the added need for financial expertise in the MLSF, where the parent company engages in financial management of its subsidiaries, a CEO's financial background did not effect change to the MLSF.[10] Given the emphasis on financial control beginning in the 1920s (chapter 5) and the emphasis on financial flexibility in the MLSF, however, it would be inappropriate to conclude that finance-based management is unimportant. Capital-dependence theory suggests that corporate structural characteristics (i.e., debt, mergers and acquisitions) versus individual characteristics (i.e., manager's background) explains this shift in the form of financial control over corporate entities. Capital-dependence theory is also confirmed by the actions of top-level decision makers in the case-oriented study (chapter 9). By the early 1970s, nonfinancial managers at American Steel recognized the need for more managerial expertise in finance. In response, top management hired a person from the financial sector whom they quickly promoted to vice president of finance (chapter 9).

The analysis shows that corporate-form change is occurring in the largest industrial corporations. Capital-dependence theory explains the relationship between corporations' internal-oriented and external-oriented strategies and corporate-form change. The model used here shows that corporate characteristics—long-term debt, the magnitude of their merger and acquisition activity, and the presence of PACs—explain why some firms change to the MLSF and others do not.

CHAPTER 11

Conclusion: Historical Transitions and Corporate Transformations

The analysis here encompasses four basic arguments. First, corporations' behavior is affected by their institutional arrangements. Second, during historical periods when dependence on external capital markets increases, corporations restructure their form and extend formal control over more spheres of the labor and managerial processes. Third, when institutional arrangements no longer provide the conditions necessary to ensure an acceptable rate of return on investment, capitalists mobilize politically to redefine their institutional arrangements. Fourth, the historically specific form of the emergent corporation and its institutional arrangements are dependent on the options available to social actors, the relative power of social actors engaged in pursuing valued resources, and the coalitions that emerge among powerful social actors.

Capital dependence theory focuses on historical transitions—radical shifts or turning points in historical trajectories—to explain rapid change. The theory captures the dynamic process whereby corporate transformations occur in response to historical transitions that are manifested as contradictions and incompatibilities among levels of the social structure. Change in the corporate form (i.e., corporate entities and relationships among them) occurs at a more rapid rate during historical periods when the social structure no longer establishes the conditions for an adequate rate of capital accumulation. To mitigate *meso-macro* contradictions (i.e., incompatibilities between the corporate form and the institutional arrangements), big business engages in political behavior to transform the institutional arrangements, pursues alternate corporate strategies, and transforms the corporation (table 1.2). The analysis shows that the historical transitions (i.e., decay-exploration stage) examined here produced three distinct corporate forms: the holding company, the multidivisional form (MDF), and the multilayered subsidiary form (MLSF). Among the most important differences in these corporate forms are the basis of ownership control, flexibility of the structure, and self-financing capability.

Similar to corporate-form change, managerial-process change is not an evolutionary, incremental process. Rather, the application of formal rationality proceeds at a more rapid rate following periods of crisis. Change in the managerial process occurs in response to *micro-meso* contradictions: situations in which the managerial process, which provides incentives to ensure that the "proper decision" is made, is incompatible with the corporate structure and agenda (Table 1.2). Formally rational controls are implemented to advance coordination and control by elaborating managerial controls that centralize authority over more spheres of social action. The analysis shows that the rationalization of the labor and managerial processes and the attempt to predict and control social action at the micro level (e.g., decisions) are inseparable from macro political and economic processes.

Controls are manifested in different ways at each historical transition. However, they always incorporated central dimensions of *scientific management*: measurement, quantification, standardization, and the separation of conception from execution. Although the scientific management of managers proceeded at a slower rate than the scientific management of workers—especially the separation of conception from execution—it also entailed measurement and quantification. The distinct forms of scientific management include Taylorism, Fordism, and neo-Fordism. Contradictions emerge because the administrative logic is manifested as corporate structures to ensure stability and control while the logic of capital accumulation entails change. During periods of rapid change, this contradiction emerges as crisis and undermines corporations' substantively rational goals. Further, formally rational controls create incentive structures that undermine organizational efficiency. Formal rationality is implemented not only because it potentially improves efficiency, but because it has become incorporated into the culture of capitalism and legitimates control over the labor and managerial processes. As such, the ideology of scientific management has become institutionalized; it is the grid through which capitalists and their managers perceive, understand, and search for the solutions to problems.

Three Historical Transitions and Corporate Transformations

Decay-Exploration I, 1870s to the late 1890s

The Taylorist stage of work organization—using scientific principles to design work activities—was set up in the late nineteenth century following a series of recessions and depressions that constrained profit making. To exercise more precise control over their larger and increasingly complex manufacturing processes, capitalists embraced Taylorism and the subsequent bureaucratization of the work-place. Two conditions affected this transformation. As nineteenth-century enter-prises expanded, businesses began to mass produce several products that con-tained many input costs. This change created a situation where markets no longer provided information to determine the profitability of each product. Although the use of skilled workers as subcontractors who understood product costs was an effec-tive mode of work organization, capitalists were not satisfied with this arrangement (Clawson 1980). Although capitalists assumed most of the financial risk, because of their limited knowledge of manufacturing costs, they were at a disadvantage when bargaining with subcontractors.

In response, capitalists experimented with two forms of scientific manage-ment. They implemented Taylor's system to collect information from workers and transmitted it from the shop floor to a central office where engineer-managers ex-amined and used this information to specify work tasks. Crucial to Taylorism was the standardization of the labor process and the reduction of workers' capacity to make independent decisions. Capitalists also employed engineer-managers to de-sign and develop information-gathering systems to control the managerial process by tracking the flow of materials and labor costs. These engineer-managers quickly developed sophisticated account-control systems that predicted the rates at which material and labor were to be consumed in the manufacturing process (Johnson and Kaplan 1991). By the 1880s, many textile, steel, and metal-working companies had information gathering systems capable of collecting product—cost data on shop-floor activities.

Despite these advances, the large vertically integrated holding companies formed during the great merger wave (i.e., 1897–1903), for whom these account controls based on product costs would be most useful, did not implement them. Instead, class segment politics defined the controls corporations set up. Pressured by financiers—upon whom industrial capitalists depended to finance their con-solidation strategies—corporations set up financial accounting systems designed to evaluate the use of capital. As a result, by the 1920s, controls that identified product costs were replaced with financial controls. Financial controls became the primary means to control the managerial process for the middle decades of the twentieth century.

Throughout this period, the federal government had comparatively little or-ganizational capacity to advance an economic agenda. Nineteenth-century Feder-alism designated authority over business enterprises to regional states who exer-cised autonomy in defining the parameters of business activity. Although the Sherman Antitrust Act (1890) began to shift authority to the federal government, regional states continued to control crucial aspects of business policy. These insti-tutional arrangements allowed business enterprises to circumvent federal antitrust laws. By the time that the federal government passed the Sherman Antitrust Act, pressured by big business, regional states redefined their policies and provided business with a wide range of property rights. These new institutional arrangements allowed business consolidation through the holding-company form. These policies were an outcome of historically specific institutional arrangements. Whereas Federalism granted the right to govern business activity to regional states, dependent on capital from business enterprises during a period of economic decline (i.e., 1880s recessions and depressions), regional states (initially New Jersey) established laws of incorporation to generate revenues. Competition for business revenues initiated a "race to the bottom" among regional states (e.g., Delaware), which resulted in policies that eliminated many constraints on business behavior by extending to them property rights previously reserved for individuals (e.g., stock ownership in other corporations).

In contrast to the loosely coupled pools, agreements, and trusts, regional states' laws of incorporation provided business with property rights and legal authority over members of its "corporate family." The holding company offered two advantages. First, the holding company became the centralized administrative unit with ownership control over previous loosely coupled business units. This more tightly coupled form of business organization allowed the parent holding company to coordinate market strategy among "corporate family" members. Second, this corporate form made it possible to establish ownership control while owning a smaller portion of "corporate family" members' assets.

After the initial consolidation occurred, corporations pursued vertical integration strategies that entailed both backward and forward integration. Corporations absorbed suppliers and raw material producers as well as distributors and consumers. A crucial organizational trait of the holding-company form was its capacity to permit new subsidiary corporations to continue to operate as they did before the merger or acquisition. Most subsidiary corporations retained the same management as when they were independent businesses. In many cases, only ownership changed and the previous owners became the top managers of the subsidiary corporation.

Capitalists' consolidation strategies came under scrutiny when corporations began to use the holding-company form to establish pyramided holding companies (chapter 4). As they understood the implications of the holding company, critics began to expose the abuses of this corporate form. In response to pressure from political coalitions and the spread of anti–big business sentiment, state managers passed Section 7 of the Clayton Act (1914) which prohibited corporations from acquiring subsidiaries through stock. These new institutional arrangements slowed corporate consolidation, now consolidation required that corporations acquire all of the assets of other firms.

Decay-Exploration II, 1920s–1930s

Throughout the early twentieth century, industrial consolidation, increased size, and the implementation of Taylorism (i.e., specifying work tasks) and later Fordism (i.e., bringing work to the worker) produced taller managerial hierarchies. As corporations became more complex, their capacity to control costs deteriorated. The financial stability of the corporation was further threatened by changing institutional arrangements from 1910 through the 1920s. Economic depression and the end to World War I resulted in lower capability utilization rates and reduced capital investment. Productivity declined in the mid-1920s, which increased business failure rates.

Corporations most dependent on a war economy, such as General Motors and DuPont, were among the first to experience crisis. The end of the war and the depression of the 1920s caused a sharp decrease in demand for vehicles and explosives. The crisis motivated capitalists to develop centralized financial controls to better evaluate corporate entities. Return on investment (ROI) became the basis of financial control. Pressured by financiers, both DuPont Company and General Motors restructured their product lines as divisions to evaluate the efficient use of capital. To extend their control over operating management, the corporations set up budget controls.

Although these financial controls were designed to assess the efficient use of capital in corporate entities, capitalists and top managers began to use them to evaluate middle managers' capacity to control operating costs. Two critical flaws exist in this approach. First, financial controls—which aggregated cost data—provided little information on individual product costs. Second, operating unit financial controls (e.g., budgets, ROI) created an incentive structure that encouraged operating managers to focus on lowering costs in their area of responsibility. Over time, this incentive structure created substantively rational goals within operating units to achieve budgetary and ROI targets. These controls were irrational, however, when evaluated in terms of corporate substantive goal rationality. Financial controls produced decisions in manufacturing units that opposed corporations' substantive goal to lower total product costs: lower manufacturing costs in one corporate unit sometimes produced higher manufacturing costs in a downstream unit.

By 1929, corporations' economic conditions worsened and the Great Depression resulted in bankruptcies and massive unemployment. This breakdown in institutional arrangements was due, in part, to the overcapitalization of corporations' assets. The subsequent exploration phrase created new institutional arrangements. New Deal policies further deinstitutionalized the holding company. To discourage abusive practices (e.g., under capitalization, establishing ownership with a small portion of assets), the federal government created disincentives to organize as holding companies by taxing capital transfers among parent companies and their subsidiary corporations. These institutional arrangements had profound effects on the corporate form. Many corporations restructured existing subsidiaries as divisions and incorporated mergers and acquisitions as divisions because no tax existed on capital transfers within a single corporation. Although thirty-one of the largest one hundred corporations were organized as holding companies in 1919, only five corporations remained organized under this form in 1948 (Fligstein 1990). This number remained relatively stable through 1979. Many corporations retained some subsidiaries (Rumelt 1974; Harris 1983), but they operated relatively independently of the parent company (Prechel 1991:430).

Although the New Deal placed some limits on big business, these capitalists mobilized politically and blocked legislation to constrain their behavior (Levine 1988). Also, organizations such as the American Liberty League employed ideological arguments (e.g., creeping socialism) to oppose working-class agenda. Like the political process that created the turn-of-the-century holding company, members of the business community had direct influence over state business policy. President Roosevelt appointed business leaders (e.g., Lammont DuPont) to his business advisory committee, which drafted legislation that later became the National Industrial Recovery Act (NIRA) (McNamee 1983). The new institutional arrangements and the steady economic growth during World War II, the Korean War, and the postwar period created conditions that ensured steady economic growth.

Throughout the middle decades of the twentieth century, financial control thwarted managers' capacity to make informed product-cost decisions as corporations' size increased. Account controls changed incrementally during this period of high capability utilization rates and profit making. Also, many corporations maintained a high price-earning ratio (i.e., P/E), which provided shareholders with high dividend yields (Lazonick 1991). However, this reduced the capital available for reinvestment. During this same period, European and Japanese corporations were rebuilding their manufacturing facilities destroyed in World War II. Also, by the 1970s, several newly industrialized countries (NICs) had developed new manufacturing facilities.

Decay-Exploration III, 1970s–1990

Throughout the 1950s and 1960s, U.S. corporations became more complex by manufacturing more product lines, product groups, and individual products. Big business gave little attention to rising manufacturing costs because the high capability utilization rate and oligopolistic price-setting practices ensured an adequate return on investment. Moreover, the financial conception of control did not provide realistic measures of product cost. Thus, managers were unable to detect changes in the cost of manufacturing individual products or product groups. By the 1970s, corporations in several countries were capable of manufacturing high-quality products at lower cost than U.S. corporations. When global production capability exceeded consumption during the early 1980s foreign corporations began to target the large U.S. markets.[1] These conditions were manifest in corporations as declining profits, reduced cash flow, and an inability to compete.

To improve operating managers' capacity to make cost-efficient decisions, corporations restructured their managerial processes by incorporating neo-Fordist controls. Corporations disaggregated cost data and set up flexible computer technologies to identify costs, monitor the decision-making process, and improve product quality. The largest corporations pressured suppliers in their respective commodity chains to introduce similar controls because the quality of the materials they purchased affected their product quality and manufacturing costs.

Although neo-Fordism shares some important characteristics with early stages of scientific management (e.g., measurement, quantification, standardization, centralization), it also entails a decisive break from Taylorism and Fordism. In addition to eliminating many working-class jobs, neo-Fordism had a profound effect on traditional middle-class occupations. In the past, middle management had a great deal of decision-making discretion, authority, and job security. In the 1980s and 1990s, however, corporations standardized the decision-making process and programmed computers to make adjustments in the manufacturing process that were previously done by operating managers. These changes eliminated many information-processing activities of managers, which made it possible to flatten the managerial hierarchy and reduce the ranks of lower- and middle-level management.

Neo-Fordism constitutes a third historical transition in the spatial separation of conception from execution. Experts in decision centers distribute information to define the premise of operating decisions. These controls over the managerial process separated conception from execution to increase the predictability of the hundreds of managers who participated in the decision-making process. Centralization of control over the managerial process increased surveillance and monitoring of operating managers to detect whether their decisions adhered to parameters established at a higher level in the corporation. The application of scientific management principles in the contemporary era moves beyond the tall hierarchal and rigid, rule-based managerial system that characterized Taylorism and Fordism. Neo-Fordist decision-making controls rapidly process, change, and transmit decision-making information. These controls also tightly couple the corporation while increasing its responsiveness and flexibility. As in the past, rationalization in the 1980s and 1990s increased corporations' capacity to centralize authority. With the aid of neo-Fordist account controls and computer technology, the top manager of the parent company organized as a MLSF can also be the top manager of several members of the corporate family (i.e., subsidiary corporations). As at American Steel (chapter 9), after Amoco Corporation restructured in 1992, the same person became the president of several of Amoco's subsidiary corporations (Prechel and Boies 1998a).

Corporations also pursued political strategies to realign their institutional arrangements, initiating a new phase of political capitalism. Corporate political behavior produced massive tax breaks for industrial corporations, relaxed antitrust enforcement, and created the conditions for massive industrial consolidation. Appointed state managers in the Reagan Administration including Treasury Secretary James Baker, Attorney General Edwin Meese, and Commerce Secretary Malcolm Baldridge endorsed corporations' argument for expansion to realized economies of scale. They even argued for eliminating parts of the Clayton Act that prohibited mergers and acquisitions when "the effect of such acquisition may be substantially to lessen competition, or tend to create monopoly" (*Fortune* 1985). Commerce Secretary Malcolm Baldridge warned that antitrust laws obstructed U.S. competitiveness abroad and recommended the repeal of Section 7 of the Clayton Act. State managers proposed to block mergers and acquisitions only when there was a "significant probability" that the transactions would create a monopoly (Plastic World 1986).

This probusiness ideology echoed Roosevelt's 1930 New Deal argument: "big was not bad." Big business and their supporters maintained that antitrust decisions should be based on whether the consolidation would result in more effective competition (*Fortune* 1985). Within this ideological climate William F. Baxter, President Reagan's first Justice Department antitrust chief, rewrote the antitrust guidelines to raise the level of market concentration that triggered a Justice Department challenge to conglomerate mergers, vertical combinations between suppliers and customers, and horizontal mergers between competitors (also see Stearns and Allan 1996).

Relaxed antitrust enforcement and the mid-1980s tax-free corporate restructuring policies resulted in corporate consolidations such as Raytheon's $9.5 billion acquisition of Hughes from General Motors. Not only did these state business policies create institutional arrangements that allowed industry consolidation, but they created incentives for product-related mergers and acquisitions. Under the *TRA86*, in order for an acquisition to qualify for tax-free corporate reorganization the acquisition must be in the same or a related product line as the existing business (Prentice-Hall 1987; Prechel 1997b:157). The Federal Reserve Bank's policy to lower interest rates increased capital formation by creating incentives to invest in corporate securities (e.g., stocks, bonds). Within these institutional arrangements industrial corporations restructured divisions and subsidiaries tax-free and used the capital from subsidiaries' IPOs to finance its modernization and merger and acquisition strategies.

While the new political-legal institutional arrangements allow corporations to expand their core businesses and market shares through mergers and acquisitions, the MLSF allows parent companies to establish ownership control by owning just over 50 percent of subsidiaries' stock. Particularly important are the added financial benefits of the MLSF. Through its subsidiary structure the MLSF creates internal capital markets, reducing parent companies' dependence on external capital markets.

Corporations are using the MLSF to establish financial structures similar to the late-nineteenth- and early-twentieth-century pyramided holding company. This financial structure makes it possible to establish ownership control over an extensive network of subsidiary corporations with less capital investment than with the MDF. In addition to the subsidiaries where parent companies have established ownership control, many parent companies own less than 50 percent of the voting stock in subsidiaries, but enough to effectively control their management. As a result, the Financial Accounting Standard Board (FASB) is considering a change that requires parent companies to include subsidiaries in their consolidated financial statements that they effectively control. Currently, the FASB requires that parent companies include only those subsidiaries in which they own more than 50 percent of the stock.

The MLSF can be used to create a network of subsidiaries that compete with other corporations in their market niche, which may include other subsidiaries controlled by a single parent company. In this way, the MLSF is a sharp break from previous corporate forms. Organizing its operating units as subsidiaries allows the parent company to gain control over a large share of the market and thereby reduce competition, while retaining the monitoring mechanisms of the market by embedding its subsidiaries in it. Also, ownership control over several subsidiaries competing in the same market niche gives parent companies the capacity to coordinate their strategies. In the MLSF, the parent company can set policy on expansion of production capability within each subsidiary. This social structure reduces the probability of expanding production capability beyond the market's consumption capability, which is more likely to occur when each corporation makes an independent decision. The MLSF can also be used to make subsidiaries compete with one another, which may encourage efficiency-enhancing decisions or pressure subsidiary managers to extract more labor from workers.

Further, if the parent company is not satisfied with a subsidiary's performance, it can sell the business unit though a simple stock transaction, and use the capital to acquire another firm that, for example, is more profitable or represents a better fit with the parent company's agenda (Prechel 1997a:433). Also, parent companies can couple (e.g., acquire, merge) other firms without being concerned with the compatibility of the managerial processes because subsidiary corporations are legally separate entities. Further, the MLSF allows corporations to be more responsive to their changing institutional arrangements by allowing parts of the corporation to persist and evolve semi-independently of each other.

Industrial Consolidation

Changes in state business policy and the probusiness ideology than emerged in the Reagan administration created state structures that facilitated consolidation among large transnational corporations in the 1980s. These include, for example, Gulf Oil and Chevron, Esmark with Beatrice, Texaco's $10.1 billion acquisition of Getty Oil, and Toyota's (the world's largest importer of small cars into the United States) partnership with General Motors (the world's largest automobile manufacturer).

Although the 1980s merger movement signified a massive consolidation of capital (figure 10.1), state and corporate structures provided the basis of the much larger 1990s merger movement when consolidation occurred in already high concentrated industries. Consolidation in the defense industry reduced the number of principal corporations in this industry to three. The first defense-industry consolidation resulted in a series of mergers and acquisitions that produced the $30 billion Lockheed Martin Corporation. In 1993, Lockheed Corporation acquired General Dynamics' military aircraft business unit for $1.5 billion. Also, in 1993, Loral Corporation acquired IBM's federal systems division. In 1994, Lockheed Corporation and Martin Marietta Corporation merged in a $10 billion deal. In 1996, Lockheed acquired most of Loral Corporation for more than $9 billion. The second defense-industry consolidation is well beyond the size of the Lockheed Martin Corporation. In 1996, Boeing Company acquired Rockwell International Corporation's defense business for $3.2 billion and merged with McDonnell Douglas Corporation in a deal valued at $13.3 billion. The Boeing-McDonnell Douglas transaction created the world's largest commercial jet and military aircraft manufacturer. The third major corporate consolidation in this industry was created through Raytheon Corporation's $3 billion acquisition of Texas Instruments' defense holdings and its $9.5 billion dollar acquisition of GM's Hughes Electronics Corporation's defense operation. The consolidation of Hughes, Raytheon, and Texas Instruments produced a corporation that controls virtually all U.S. air-to-air missile production.

Despite record profits, the consolidation of giant corporations was endorsed by top-level state managers in the Clinton administration. Although Boeing Corporation controlled 60 to 70 percent of the world market for manufacturing large aircraft (i.e., more than one hundred passengers), Defense Secretary William Perry argued that the Boeing-McDonnell Douglas consolidation is the kind of change needed in the defense industry. When the European Commission opposed the merger, President Clinton threatened a trade stand-off. Within days of Clinton's threat the European Commission approved the merger. Despite opposition from the European Commission, Boeing retained its long-term orders—valued at $16.9 billion—with Continental Airlines, Delta Airlines, and AMR

Corporation's subsidiary American Airlines. These agreements constitute a near-monopoly in the commercial aircraft industry.

Corporate consolidation that began in the mid-1990s dwarfed the 1980s merger wave. The mergers in 1998 alone representing a transfer of more than $1 trillion from one corporation to another. By contrast, the merger wave of the entire decade of the 1980s was approximately $1.7 trillion (figure 11.1).[2] Corporate strategies in the 1980s and 1990s had an important effect on industry consolidation, and the degree to which the largest industrial corporations exercised ownership control over other large corporations.

Moreover, state business policy governing corporate restructuring allowed many of these capital transfers to occur tax-free. General Motor's spinoff of Electronic Data Systems (EDS)—valued at $22.31 billion—was tax-free. WR Grace's tax-free spin-off of National Medical Care Inc. yielded approximately $2.3 billion in cash and between $1.3 and $1.6 billion in stock. Estimates suggest that if WR Grace had not transformed this corporate entity from a division to a subsidiary prior to the transaction, its tax bill would have been between $850 million and $1 billion (Forest, Anderson, Burns, and DeGeorge 1995). Using a similar strategy, ITT broke up its $25 billion conglomerate by restructuring its corporate entities as subsidiary corporations and spinning them off to shareholders. Since mergers can be accomplished by stock exchanges, many mergers are also tax free under this business policy. In 1995, the Federal Trade Commission approved the $6.8 billion tax-free merger—via stock transfer—of Kimberly-Clark and Scott Paper Co. In 1997, PepsiCo Inc. announced a tax-free plan to spin off its $10 billion fast-food business (e.g., Kentucky Fried Chicken, Pizza Hut, Taco Bell). The parent company will receive $4.5 billion from the newly created company. Transactions that do not qualify under the *TRA86* frequently qualify as tax free under the thirty-year-old Morris Trust provision. The *Morris Trust* ruling in 1966 specified a set of provisions allowing the tax-free distribution of assets through a stock spin-off.

In addition, 1970s, 1980s and 1990s state business policy lowered capital gains tax rates, which further reduced corporate taxes. A large portion of annual capital gains are accrued by parent companies who own the stock of subsidiary corporations. Also, revenues from the sale of a subsidiary through a stock sale are treated as capital gains, which is taxed at a lower rate than the minimum corporate tax rate required of an asset sale (i.e., division) (see Prechel 1997b:158). These institutional arrangements reduced government revenues from corporations and shifted the tax burden to individuals.

Class-based politics of the 1970s and 1980s redefined the institutional arrangements that made the excess of the 1990s possible. The end of the twentieth century is characterized by the expansion of the largest corporations, rising stock values, increased income and wealth inequality, and an increasingly politically powerful corporate class.

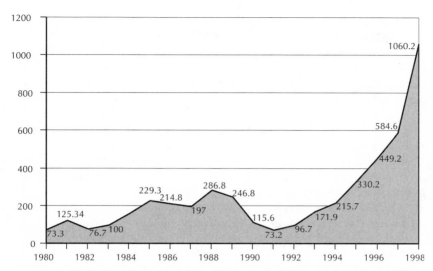

FIGURE 11.1 Total value of mergers and acquisitions in the U.S., 1980–1998 in 1992 billion dollars. *Source: Mergerstat.*

Finance Capital

Like corporate consolidation through the holding company at the turn to the twentieth century, corporate transformation to the MLSF was underwritten by large investment firms. Although capitalist class segments frequently disagree, like during previous crisis periods, class segment politics receded and a unified capitalist class used its formal organizational capacities and informal networks to ensure long-term economic stability. In the 1970s, capitalists began to develop a unified class consciousness oriented toward overcoming constraints in the economy as a whole. Diverse capitalist interests such as the National Association of Manufacturers (NAM), the Business Roundtable, the American Council on Capital Formation, the U.S. Chamber of Commerce, and the Conference Board organized politically to develop a unified capitalist agenda (Vogel 1989; Akard 1992). Their unified political behavior influenced a range of state business policies (chapter 7) including the *TRA86* and *RA87* allowing tax-free corporate restructuring via stock transactions.

Several historical conditions provided incentives that encouraged financial capital to aid industrial corporations' change to the MLSF. First, in the late 1970s and early 1980s, capital shortages and high debt threatened economic stability. Second, the largest one hundred industrial corporations increased in size (Prechel and Boies 1998a:322–23). As the largest corporations increased in size, each became increasingly important to economic stability. Pending bankruptcy of large corporations also generated concerns among state managers who provided loans to bailout corporations in the past (e.g., Chrysler Corporation). Third, investment bankers and other financial firms had significant capital investments in industrial corporations. By the 1980s, a weakened industrial sector characterized by low dividend payments and declining stock values was beginning to negatively affect financial corporations' earnings. Fourth, restructuring in the industrial sector provided profit-making opportunities for finance capital, which included underwriter fees and the option to purchase stock at a price negotiated before the stock is offered to the public. Fifth, by the early 1980s, it was clear that the high interest rates of the 1970s were impediments on capital formation and economic growth.

In short, financiers' dependence on industrial capital created incentives to use their political power, organizational capacities, and formal and informal networks to strengthen industrial capital. The response of capital markets to the 1990s crises in Asian countries, especially those with large economies like Japan, produced similar behavior. Financial capital pumped large amounts of capital into industrial corporations in an effort to create economic stability.

Investment bankers benefited substantially from underwriting corporate restructuring and recapitalization. Disclosure fees, which is the capital paid to investment firms for marketing new stocks and bonds, became a primary source of revenue for investment firms (chapter 10). Although disclosure fees are only one source of financial firms' revenue, they were more than the entire 1998 revenue in large industrial corporations such as Dana, Eli Lilly, Honeywell, and Whirlpool. Moreover, like at the turn of the twentieth century, a very few investment bankers underwrite these transactions. The revenues of the top three underwriters—Merrill Lynch, Morgan Stanley Dean Witter, and Goldman Sachs—for 1998 was $3.825 billion or 43.4 percent of the total. U.S. investment firms are also the primary underwriters of global consolidation. In 1998, Goldman Sachs underwrote 38.2 percent of the worldwide mergers and acquisitions entailing transactions of $960 billion. Many consolidations and virtually all of the largest consolidations occur through stock swaps (e.g., Exxon-Mobil, British Petroleum-Amoco, Daimler-Benz-Chrysler).

Several researchers argue that a coalition of banks exercises hegemonic power over corporations and conclude that when the business community is dependent on financiers for capital they exercise power over corporations (Herman 1981; Mintz and Schwartz 1985; Palmer, Friedland, and Singh 1986; Stearns and Mizruchi 1986; Mizruchi and Stearns 1994). An extension of this thesis might suggest that financiers would oppose change to the MLSF because the capacity of industrial corporations to issue stock would reduce financiers' control over them. However, the analysis here suggests that during the late twentieth century, change to the MLSF is advantageous for financial capital. In addition to the profit-making opportunities for financial firms described above, industrial corporations remain dependent on financial firms for underwriting future transactions. Moreover, underwriters frequently obtain large blocks of corporate stock, which creates the basis for revenues (e.g., dividend payments) and continued or increased capacity to exercise control over industrial firms.

Fast and Flexible Capitalism: The Deregulated Corporation

By the mid-1990s, crucial aspects of the antitrust laws were rewritten or not enforced, most of the key provisions of the Glass-Steagall Act were gutted, and the New Deal legislation restricting the transfer of capital via stock was replaced by new legislation that broadened corporations' rights concerning stock transactions. Within these institutional arrangements the MLSF emerged and is becoming the organizational form to consolidate corporations and transfer capital, technology, and resources from one part of the globe to another. Mergers in the late 1990s are creating transatlantic giant corporations. These corporations are pursuing merger and acquisition strategies to capture domestic and global markets.

The merger of Germany's largest industrial corporation Daimler-Benz and Chrysler Corporation in late 1998, the third largest U.S. automaker, constitutes one of the largest corporate consolidations in history. The merger occurred as a stock swap valued at approximately $38 billion. The estimated combined revenue of the new corporation is $130 billion with more than 420,000 employees. Less than two months after the Daimler-Benz and Chrysler deal Volvo agreed to be acquired by Ford Motor Company for $6.47 billion, which further consolidated the automobile industry. The acquisition of Amoco Corporation by British Petroleum for $48.2 billion will create the second largest petroleum company in the world behind Royal Dutch/Shell. The new corporation will be larger than Exxon and over twice the size of Mobil, the fourth largest oil corporation. However, the subsequent merger of Exxon and Mobil, the third and eighth largest U.S. corporations (ranked by sales), created the largest energy company in the world. A merger between these transnational parent companies and their subsidiaries in more than one hundred countries will reunite companies that were formerly part of John D. Rockefeller's Standard Oil Trust, which was broken up in 1911 for violation of the Sherman Antitrust Act. Mobil and Exxon were formerly Standard Oil of New York and Standard Oil of New Jersey, respectively. The new company (Exxon-Mobil) will have revenues of $203 billion, bypassing General Motors as the largest U.S. company and Royal Dutch/Shell as the largest petroleum company in the world. Mergers of similar magnitude are occurring in other economic sectors (banking, telecommunications).

The flexible structure and self-financing capability of the MLSF increases corporations' capacity to pursue a range of consolidation strategies. The practice of using subsidiary corporations as internal capital markets is increasing as companies use stock offerings instead of debt financing. IPOs allow parent companies to "unlock some of the true value" in the subsidiaries (*Wall Street Journal* 1996).

AT&T's IPO that accompanied the spin-off of its telecommunications-equipment operations as a subsidiary corporation (i.e., Lucent) netted the parent company more than $3 billion. By 1995, "IPOs dwarf[ed] anything seen in the past quarter century; the Standard & Poor new-issue index [was] up by 535 percent" since 1990 (Farrell, Rebello, and Hof 1995). In October 1996, 105 companies raised $6.2 billion in IPOs. In the first quarter of 1996, IPOs constituted a third of the total common stocks issued, and the total IPOs for the year raised $50 billion. Although many IPOs are relatively small, the largest parent companies also issue IPOs in their large subsidiaries. In 1998, DuPont's IPO of Conoco, previously a wholly owned subsidiary, netted approximately $4.4 billion. CBS Corporation's IPO in its subsidiary, Infinity Broadcasting Corporation, generated $2.9 billion and News Corporation's IPO of Fox Entertainment Group raised $2.8 billion. Also, General Motor's IPO of 15 to 19 percent of its automobile-parts subsidiary, Delphi, is expected to yield $1.5 billion.

The MLSF improves parent companies' flexibility in financial management by allowing top management to (1) use the capital from IPOs for expansion, funding acquisitions, and reducing debt (2) repurchase subsidiary stocks when the parent company's cash flow increases, and (3) transfer the capital obtained from dividend payments or IPOs in some subsidiaries to other subsidiaries anywhere in the global economy. In the mid-1990s, RJR Nabisco Holdings sold 20 percent of Nabisco stock and used the capital to reduce the parent company's debt (*Wall Street Journal* 1995c). Moreover, when parent companies' liquidity position improves, they can buy back their stock. IBM took advantage of this flexible financial structure in the 1980s and 1990s. To limit its dependence on external capital markets when its cash flow declined in the 1980s, IBM sold stock to meet its short-term capital needs. When IBM's cash flow increased in the mid-1990s, it initiated two stock buybacks valued at $5.5 billion and $2.5 billion (*Wall Street Journal* 1995b).

The transfer of capital into corporations and the recapitalization of firms were facilitated by lower interest rates and tax-deferred retirement programs. The historic low rate of return from saving accounts and rapid stock growth created incentives for individuals to invest their retirement and other savings into corporate securities. The subsequent influx of capital into the stock market provided much of the capital needed to recapitalize corporations. Between 1980 and 1999, the portion of households owning shares in mutual funds increased from 6 to 40 percent. To stimulate further growth in financial markets, finance capital is pressuring state managers to change social safety-net policies so that individuals can invest their Social Security Insurance contributions into the stock market. To advance this agenda politically, during the 1998 election cycle, the securities and investment industry became the largest contributor (i.e., more than $9 million) of unregulated "soft money" to the Republican Party.

The massive capital flows into stock since the mid-1980s and rapid increase in corporate stock values raises a vexing question: Do corporate stock values accurately represent their assets? While there is no clear answer to this question, the processes of determining stock values raise questions about corporate recapitalization. Stock prices are based on "what the market will bear." Investment bankers (e.g., Stanley Morgan Dean Witter; Goldman Sachs) set the value for IPOs, and the stock market determines whether these stocks are sold at that price. However, this is a highly speculative process. Many IPOs do not sell at this price and others increase in price within a few days of issuance. Also, stock prices are driven up as corporations competing with one another to gain market share. Following Hilton Hotel's bid to take over International Telephone and Telegraph (ITT) in January 1997, ITT's stock increased from less than $45 to more than $60 per share by March 1997. After ITT announced a restructuring plan, its stock increased by an additional 7 percent to over $66 per share. Hilton's next bid was for $6.5 billion or $55 per share. Then, in mid-November, Starwood Lodging offered $85 per share or $10.2 billion for ITT. The price of ITT's stock almost doubled from less than $45 to $85 per share from March 1997 to November 1997. This rapid increase in stock value suggests that stock values are not determined by rational analysis of corporate assets, but by competition among corporations pursuing consolidation strategies.[3]

Although capitalist and state managers established a complex of institutional arrangements intended to avoid events similar to those that preceded the stock market crash in the 1920s and 1930s, it is not clear that these institutional arrangements adequately ensure against overcapitalization. Contemporary capital structures are similar to those preceding the Great Depression. The MLSF is a variation on the holding company/subsidiary form with few limits on capitalization. Because most of the restrictions on the use of capital under the Glass Steagall Act have been eliminated, if a failure occurs, like in the 1930s, the financial losses will not be limited to the capitalist class. Overcapitalization will adversely affect a large proportion of the working and middle classes who invested their savings for retirement in stock and bond funds.[4]

Implications for Organizational Theory

The theoretical framework here entails a break from prevailing organizational theories. Beginning in the 1950s, the dominant trend in organizational theory has been to develop all-encompassing grand theories of organizations. These theories explicitly or implicitly purport to explain all kinds of organizational behavior (e.g., change, stability) in all kinds of organizations (e.g., large corporations, small companies, museums, newspapers, restaurants). This approach has produced a range of organizational theories with widely different explanations for the same phenomena. Although some sociologists advocate developing theories of the middle range, this would be a mistake because the problem is not intrinsic to grand theories. Rather, the problem is in the failure of organizational theorists to include scope statements that define the parameters of the theory's generalizability. In an effort to move beyond these shortcomings, capital-dependence theory includes two scope statements. In its current form, the theory limits analysis to (1) rapid organizational change in (2) the largest industrial corporations.

Using the theoretical framework elaborated in capital-dependence theory, the analysis here attempts to fill three gaps in the organizational literature. First, I theorized the relationship between the corporation and the state. Capital-dependence theory identifies the historical conditions when capitalists mobilize politically to change the social structure in which corporations are embedded. Second, I examined internal organization processes (e.g., account controls, decision making) and connect them to changes in corporations' institutional arrangements. Third, I examined multiple levels of analysis over an extended time period to explain the relationship between historical transitions and corporate transformations.

Capital-dependence theory focuses on the dynamic features of corporations to explain change in turbulent environments. The theory identifies (1) the historical conditions when change occurs (2) the irrational and contradictory aspects of corporations, and (3) disequilibria among levels of the social structure. During each historical transition examined here, transformation occurred in state business policy, the corporate form, and the managerial process. The theory demonstrates that micro-level process cannot be separated from the historical processes that contribute to the rationalization of corporations and their institutional arrangements.

Contingency Theory

The analysis here suggests that understanding contemporary controls over the labor and managerial process requires a reconceptualization of the relationships among flexibility, coupling, and centralization-decentralization. Traditional contingency theory argues that tightly coupled organizations are less flexible. Also, it argues that when the environment is rapidly changing, decentralization of decision making and authority will occur in order to increase organizational flexibility (Burns and Stalker 1961; Lawrence and Lorsch 1967; Thompson 1967). This decentralization is characterized by informal coordination and control of the manufacturing process.

Although contingency theory aids in our understanding of organizations, it cannot explain recent change in the managerial process because it treats authority and responsibility as a single variable and then assumes that they covary. In the contemporary era, neo-Fordist controls are used to tightly couple corporate units by *centralizing authority* while *decentralizing responsibility:* holding lower-level managers accountable for implementing the proper decision made at a higher level in the organizational hierarchy (Prechel 1994b). In this way, corporations increase organizational flexibility and responsiveness by tightly coupling their parts. A contemporary parent company organized as a MLSF can designate one group of executives to monitor its subsidiaries, set their financial goals, monitor their performance, and intervene if local management does not achieve those goals. Besides monitoring market performance, complex computer networks allow parent companies to monitor the activities of their operating managers.

Although this arrangement tightly couples subsidiaries to the parent company, a financial disturbance in a subsidiary does not reverberate throughout the corporation. The liability firewall aids in confining an economic breakdown to the subsidiary where it occurs, limiting financial risk and liability to the parent company. In contrast to previous tightly coupled organizations that lacked flexibility and responsiveness to their environments, neo-Fordist controls in the MLSF create a flexible structure. A parent company with an MLSF has the flexibility to allow subsidiary corporations the autonomy to respond to changing market conditions, while monitoring subsidiary managers to determine if they adhere to the parent company's agenda.

Centralization and decentralization in the contemporary corporation should not be understood as fixed categories, but as variables to be examined. In the past, researchers have associated the degree of centralization and decentralization with a particular corporate form (e.g., centralization in the unitary functional form, extreme decentralization in the holding company, decentralization in the MDF). Rather than adhering to rigid concepts that describe previous organizational phenomena, centralization in the MLSF should be considered at one end of a continuum, with decentralization at the other. The corporation can move along this continuum as conditions change. The MLSF provides the parent company with the flexibility to allow subsidiary corporations to operate autonomously or to monitor them closely. As long as subsidiary corporations contribute to the parent company's agenda, the parent company may not interfere with local managers, providing the impression of local managers' autonomy in subsidiary operations. The key issues when considering centralization and decentralization in the MLSF include identifying the conditions under which top managers decide to centralize control over their corporate family, and the conditions under which they decide to allow members of their corporate family to operate autonomously.

Managerial and Transaction Cost Theories

The findings here posit several challenges to efficiency arguments. Studies show that top mamagement did not have the kind of information to determine whether middle managers economized on costs when the MDF prevailed during the middle decades of the twentieth century (e.g., Johnson and Kaplan 1991; Prechel 1991; Ralf and Temin 1991; Temin 1991). The financial conception of controls used in most large corporations did not provide operating managers with the information necessary to understand product costs. Although financial controls may have been useful to make financial decisions (e.g., capital allocation), they did not ensure cost efficiency. Moreover, financial controls created an incentive system that encouraged operating managers to make decisions that, in some cases, undermined efficiency.

A problem with efficiency arguments is they assert rather than test their core argument. Survival and profit making are not equivalent to making cost-efficient transactions. Profits are affected by a wide range of variables. Oligopolistic structures can create conditions that improve the probability of corporations' survival by reducing competition through controlling production capability and setting prices. Further, state business policies (e.g., tax credits, accelerated depreciation allowances) improve corporations' cash flow and capacity to make a profit and survive. Moreover, many corporations do not conform to the image of the MDF presented by efficiency arguments. Instead, top managers tolerate opportunism to preserve cooperation and consent (Burawoy 1979; Best 1990; Lazonick 1991; Freeland 1996).

A proper test of transaction cost arguments—whether decisions are efficient—entails examining the data used by decision makers and determining whether these data provide the kind of information to take cost considerations into account. Throughout the middle decades of the twentieth century many operating managers did not have individual product data. In the absence of accurate cost data, there are no valid criteria to determine whether cost-efficient decisions were made. Further, if a corporate form failed to survive, these perspectives assume that the firm was inefficient and this inefficiency was caused by the self-optimizing behavior of individuals and the failure of contracts to contain that behavior. This points to another problem with efficiency arguments. Their assumptions preclude an analysis of whether spot contracts produce irrational and inefficiency behaviors when evaluated in terms of corporations' profit-making goals. As shown in chapters 5 and 6, financial controls created incentive structures that encouraged inefficient decision making.

Coporate transformation to the MLSF raises important questions about the explanatory power of efficiency arguments. If the managerial hierarchies in the MDF were more efficient because they internalized market functions, why did the parent companies restructure more of their divisions as subsidiaries—embedding corporate entities in the market—after oligopolistic market structures began to break down and competition increased?

TCA's insistence on rigid ahistorical neoclassical economic assumptions precludes analyses of issues central to understanding managers' behavior. It does not direct researchers' attention toward the incentives that effect social action. As a result, TCA theorists fail to examine alternate propositions, which include (1) whether corporate systems of control are set up to advance the interest of powerful social actors, and (2) whether the incentive structures that emerge from corporate control systems have the intended effect on social action (e.g., managers' decisions). Rigid theoretical assumptions result in insufficient depth of analysis and an unrealistic image of the effects of controls on managers' behavior. Efficiency arguments fail to acknowledge that the financial conception of control was institutionalized by powerful social actors to measures the flow of capital and return on investment, not costs. While the financial conception of control may be able to determine which organizational units used their capital more efficiently than others, it does not provide information on whether individual products or product groups were manufactured cost efficiently. Aggregated financial data distorted product costs and created incentive structures that undermine cost efficiency.

Further, financial controls are time-dependent measurements (e.g., annual, quarterly, monthly) of performance in a constantly changing market. Although financial statements provide insights into corporations' financial strengths at one point in time compared to a previous point in time, they do not provide the kind of information that markets do. At best, these account controls provide a snapshot of a historical process.[5] Thus, it is misleading to assume that the MDF is a "quasi" or "miniature" market (Williamson 1975). Financial controls transformed data in such a way that it provided incentives that were in sharp contrast to market-based incentives. Financial controls were based on aggregated product cost data, which distorted information derived from the market.

Neoinstitutional Theory

The framework elaborated here differs in several ways from the neoinstitutional model. One important difference is capital-dependence theory explicity theorizes a relationship between change and social action. Capital-dependence theory draws from a long tradition in economic sociology that emerged from institutional economics (e.g., Veblen), and Marxian, Weberian, and the old institutional sociology (e.g., Selznick). These theoretical traditions identify social actors (e.g., capitalists, absentee owners, community leaders) and examine how they exercise power. Capital-dependence theory incorporates a "strong" conception of social actors, which is in contrast to diffusion assumptions in neoinstitutional theory that has, at best, "weak" social actors. Stinchcombe (1997) points out that neoinstitutionalism is based on assumptions that reproduce the flaws of Durkheimian sociology where collective representations and social processes exist without social actors. The following assesses the capacity of the key theoretical concepts that neoinstitutional theorists use to explain change. I show that the conceptual framework elaborated in neoinstitutional theory may explain stability or gradual incremental changes. However, it has less capacity to explain historical transitions and corporate transformations.

Mimetic behavior did not contribute to the spread of the public holding company in the late nineteenth and early twentieth centuries. Variations on the holding company/subsidiary form existed prior to the adoption of this form during both historical periods. In the second half of the nineteenth century, several business enterprises were incorporated as holding companies under the auspices of special legislative acts in regional states that provided property rights to use this form. The corporate form was legitimized, but most business enterprises did not use it. Capitalists were unwilling to risk the public scrutiny that could occur during the process of obtaining a special legislative charter to restructure as a holding company. Also, the business enterprise did not change in response to coercive pressures from the state. To the contrary, big business placed coercive pressure on the state to change business policy so that they could incorporate as holding companies. Business enterprises changed in mass after regional states passed laws of incorporation that allowed corporations to change to this form without requiring them to make information on their financial holdings available to the public.

Similarly, most contemporary corporations were aware of the holding company/subsidiary form since the late twentieth century. This form was considered a legitimate way to organize assets and several of the largest U.S. industrial corporations had holding companies and subsidiaries at one point in their respective histories. Virtually all of the largest industrial corporations organized some of their assets as subsidiaries throughout the twentieth century. Also, most of these corporations owned foreign corporate entities that, for legal reasons, had to be organized as subsidiary corporations. Like change to the holding-company form in the late nineteenth century, change to the MLSF in the late twentieth century occurred after economic crises and capitalists' succeess in changing state business policy. The case- and variable-oriented analyses show that industrial corporations responded individually to these new institutional arrangements, not globally, as principles of diffusion and isomorphism predict. If mimetic behavior occurred, it did not occur because of the perceived legitimacy of the MLSF. Rather, like change to the nineteenth century holding company, change to the MLSF occurred when financial performance dropped and state policies created incentives to change.

The analysis here suggests that neoinstitutional theory places too much significance on mimetic behavior and coercive isomorphism to explain change to the MDF (Fligstein 1990). DuPont and General Motors established MDFs in the 1920s when capital shortages created crises. Other corporations began changing to the MDF following changes in state business policy that created incentives to not use the holding-company form. The policy shifts between 1911 and 1930 to restrict the use of stocks and to tax subsidiaries, however, was not the outcome of coercive isomorphism put in place by an autonomous state. Rather, policy change was the outcome of political pressure from the working, middle, and (small) capitalist classes and the state's own New Deal agendas to ensure economic stability and retain its legitimacy. When class-based politics reemerged in the 1970s and 1980s and eliminated many of the restrictions on the holding-company form, big business began to restructure as MLSFs, a corporate form that shares several characterisitics with the holding company (chapter 1).

Change in state business policy at each historical transition was the outcome of class-based political pressures that originated outside the state. Classes and capitalist subclass and class segments mobilized politically to change state business policy to advance their economic interests. At each historical juncture (i.e., 1880s, 1930s, 1980s), corporation changed their form in response to the political and economic institutional arrangements in which they were embedded that were defined, to a significant degree, by class-based politics. A problem with theories that assume state autonomy is that their theoretical parameters tend to exclude society-based phenomena. After society-based phenomena are defined away theoretically, empirical analysis tends to focus on the state. This narrow theoretical scope lessens the explanatory power of theory and distorts empirical processes. This is one reason why, in their current form, prevailing theories do not explain how organization forms are institutionalized or deinsitutionalized (DiMaggio 1988; Friedland and Alford 1991; Prechel 1994a; Hirsch 1997).

The analysis provides some support for the neoinstitutional argument that normative pressures affect the corporation. In particular, normative pressures appeared to be a powerful force of stability in the mid- to late twentieth century. Corporations continued to stress financial controls even though this control mechanism provided little data on product costs, and the incentive structure it produced undermined efficiency. Only after corporations' capital dependence increased and global competition threatened their survival did corporations revise their financial controls. Structural characteristics originating in the environment explain the emergence of financial controls in the 1920s and their transformation in the 1980s.

The conceptual framework of institutional theory views social actors as complying with prevailing concepts of appropriate behavior that are defined somewhere else in the social system. Within this framework elites and other powerful social actors who bring those events about become irrelevant. Neoinstitutional theory has been criticized for downplaying "structural and substance" variables such as resources, competition, and power and for reinterpreting them as providing "rituals and imagery" for the cultural framing of behavior (Hirsch 1997). Arthur Stinchcombe argues that as a result of these assumptions neoinstitutional theory is hampered by a narrowness that "guts . . . the causal process of institutional influences" (Stinchcombe 1997:6). It does not take into account, for example, how the structural contingencies of capitalist competition fail and are replaced by new institutional arrangements. Overtheorizing cultural diffusion and isomorphism and undertheorizing political behavior obfuscates the causal processes—social actors' efforts to change institutional constraints—that produce breaks from existing institutional arrangements.

Neoinstitutional Theory versus Power Structure Theory

For many years power-structure researchers have argued that a network of financiers exert control over corporations (Zeitlin 1980, 1989; Herman 1981; Mintz and Schwartz 1985; Mizruchi and Stearns 1988; Useem 1993). This position is being challenged by neoinstitutionalism, which elaborates a new version of managerialism claiming that conceptions of control explain corporate behavior. Neoinstitutionalism suggests that the dominant conception of control emerges from the diffusion of values and internal power struggles among managers with different backgrounds (e.g., manufacturing, sales, finance). Once established, conceptions of control create "totalizing world views that cause social actors to interpret every situation from a given perspective" (Fligstein 1990:10).

I suggest that these two arguments are not necessarily incompatible. However, there are two crucial obstacles to the resolution of this debate: (1) insufficient depth of (historical) analysis, and (2) failure to acknowledge that the theories are operating at different levels of analysis.[6] On the one hand, power-structure theory argues that financiers exercise control over the corporation. However, because the theory focuses on the environment-corporation relationship it gives little attention to internal organizational processes. On the other hand, neoinstitutional theory places a great deal of emphasis on internal power struggles among managers with different backgrounds as a basis of changing internal controls. The respective theories direct researchers' attention toward certain phenomena and preclude examination of the phenomena that would resolve the debate: the relationship between external and internal power structures.

The analysis here shows that external financiers in the corporate environment set up a financial conception of control in the 1920s. Financiers (e.g., initially the DuPont family) exercised ownership control over corporations, and management had little choice but to comply. After the financial conception of control was set up, it became the legitimate basis to evaluate corporations' strength. Financial management became increasingly important in the 1960s and 1970s as corporations expanded and became more complex. Financial control reached a historic high point in the 1980s and 1990s when parent companies began to create subsidiaries and engage in the financial management of them.

Power-structure theory correctly argues that external capital markets exercise control over corporations. However, because it does not focus on internal controls it does not capture the long-term effects of these external networks of power on changes that occur inside the corporation. Because neoinstitutional theory focuses on internal power struggles as the mechanism of change, it does not connect the origins of these internal controls to external sources of power.

In contrast to these theories, capital-dependence theory shows that external social actors exercised power to set up a financial conception of control to protect their economic interest. Financial controls became institutionalized (e.g., balance sheet, budgets, profit and loss statement) to protect family and finance capital's interest. That is, capital-dependence theory shows that internal controls are part of the rationalization process that cannot be disconnected from external social actors who exercise power to advance their interest, which includes their capacity to institutionalize and maintain their power even when it undermines efficiency.

Implications for State Theory

State-Centered versus Society-Centered Power

In the 1970s, some sociologists began to shift away from examining how class power affects the policy-formation process. Drawing from a long tradition in political science, these sociologists argued that states are autonomous (Skocpol 1980, 1985). Although advocates of this perspective suggest that state autonomy may come and go, they rarely demonstrated when states are not autonomous. Instead, the strong state autonomy assumption in the theory directs researchers to investigate how state structures affected policy outcomes. As a result, they fail to examine an alternate hypothesis: the effects of class-based power on the policy-formation process. Moreover, many of these studies are insufficiently historical to determine whether state autonomy varies over time.

In contrast, capital-dependence theory shows that state autonomy varies over time and is affected by a range of historical conditions including capitalist class unity. Also, the theory suggests that states are less autonomous when they are dependent on resources controlled by capitalists. When severe constraints on capital accumulation or crises emerge the capitalist class unifies and mobilizes politically to advance particular policies to resolve obstacles to their economic agenda. When corporations' capital dependence increased in the 1880s–1890s, 1930s, and 1970s–1980s, capitalists unified and mobilized politically to change state business policy. However, the particular alliances established among capitalists and the outcome of their political behavior were determined by how the conditions of capital accumulation affect respective class segments, and the relative power of competing classes (e.g., working class, small businesses, farmers).

The long-term consequences of political capitalism have produced state structures that are different from those in previous historical periods. Contemporary state structures extend the state's authority over more spheres of social and economic activity. This variation in state structures is important because: (1) it legitimizes state involvement in the economy, and (2) the existence of state structures provides a focal point for capitalists, and other groups, to direct their political efforts and exercise power over state agencies. That is, rather than providing a basis of state autonomy, once established, state structures provide capitalists with a legitimate political-legal apparatus within which to pursue their interests politically (Prechel 1990). The presence of state structures governing economic activity such as antidumping, antitrust, and international trade provide focal points for corporate-sponsored lobbyists to influence policy development, implementation, and enforcement.

Moreover, past policy initiatives become the basis of future political activity. For example, the depreciation schedules under the *RA81* were so lucrative some corporations could not use them all. To ensure that they could take advantage of these tax breaks corporations mobilized politically and pressured Congress to pass the lease-lend provision. This policy allowed corporations to sell their unused depreciation allowance to other corporations. Similarly, after the *TRA86* providing tax-free corporate restructuring provisions was passed, it became the base of future political activity, which resulted in legislation (e.g., the *RA87*) providing additional tax benefits to corporations.

Representative versus Bureaucratic State Structures

The expansion of state structures raises an important issue initially examined by Max Weber who drew the distinction between representative and bureaucratic state structures. Weber argued that once bureaucratic structures are established the authority of representative structures declines. Further, representative state structures become increasingly relegated to "negative politics" and exercising veto power while bureaucratic structures become increasingly influential over public policy (Weber 1978). Authority over important aspects of policy formation is allocated to appointed "experts" in the bureaucratic structure. Over time, elected state managers are increasingly relegated to approving or disapproving; exercising veto power over policies developed in the bureaucratic state structure.

This distinction between power derived from representative and bureaucratic state structures is particularly important in the contemporary era where appointed state managers carry out a great deal of policy formation and implementation. State managers in Federal Trade Commission were lobbied heavily by business interests during the late 1970s and early 1980s to redefine antitrust violations. After the criteria that initiated an antitrust investigation were redefined, corporations began to set up merger and acquisition strategies. Similarly, after Congress approved of the general guidelines defining the North American Free Trade Agreement (NAFTA), subsequently NAFTA policy formation occurred in the bureaucratic state structure. Congressional activity was limited to "negative politics" by, for example, exercising veto power over the "fast track" provision (Woods 1998).

Although state structures have expanded in the twentieth century and bureaucratic structures have control over more spheres of social and economic activity, it cannot be assumed that states are more autonomous. Bureaucratic state structures provide focal points for capitalists to advance their interests in an arena that is more removed from public scrutiny.

More Political Capitalism in the Late Twentieth Century

In response to the Watergate scandal in the 1970s, state managers implemented policies that expanded the means of legitimate political behavior by legalizing political action committees (PACs). PAC contributions steadily increased until after the 1987–1988 election cycle (Figure 10.2). During the 1980s, contribution limits began to rise. By 1988, corporations made hundreds of "soft money" donations of $100,000 or more (Clawson, Neustadtl, and Scott 1992). These contributions increased from approximately $37 million in the 1991–92 cycle to more than $260 million in the 1996–97 election cycle (Common Cause 1996). The primary function of PAC and "soft money" activity is not with policy initiatives. Rather, contributions to candidates and political parties are about access (Clawson et al. 1992). PACs and soft-money contributions are mechanisms to establish relations with state managers so that when issues crucial to corporate interests' emerge they have access to the state managers engaged in policy formation, implementation, and enforcement.

Thus, political capitalism in the 1990s must be understood as consisting of several interrelated strategies. A widely recognized form of political capitalism, but infrequently examined by researchers, is lobby activity. Whereas PACs provide access, once access is acquired, lobbyists present their policy position to state managers. Lobbying is done by professionals who work for organizations that subcontract with corporations and associations, or who work directly for organizations representing a political interest. These organizations and associations represent corporations, industries (e.g., American Iron and Steel Institute), and class segments (e.g., the Business Roundtable). Lobbyists present policy initiatives and policy positions to state managers on a wide range of issues (e.g., antitrust, subsidies, international trade). Although massive amounts of capital are funneled from corporations to state managers through PACs (figure 10.2), these donations are dwarfed by the amount spent on lobbying. In 1997 alone, the largest 509 corporations spent $323.8 million on lobby activities. The two largest spenders, Philip Morris and Bell Atlantic, spent more than $15 million each and General Motors, Boeing, and Pfizer spent more than $10 million each (Center for Responsive Politics 1997).

There are many ways in which contemporary forms of political capitalism benefit corporations. PAC benefits are not limited to favors manifested as political change: the passage of laws or policy initiatives. Corporations also benefit from PACs when state managers do not pass legislation or when they fail to enforce regulations that may undermine corporations' capacity to pursue their agenda. Important characteristics of class-based politics include the capacity of capitalists' to convince state managers to *not* act on certain social policy initiatives (e.g., national health insurance), and to *not* set up regulations (e.g., antitrust, environmental, workplace safety) that are enforceable.

Countervailing Power

As during the Progressive Era (early twentieth century) (Kolko 1963), little effective opposition to big business exists in the late twentieth century. This is in contrast to previous decay-exploration periods (late nineteenth century, the New Deal era) when regional states, farmers, labor unions, small businesses, and professionals constituted countervailing powers and exerted political pressure on the federal government. The political behavior of these social actors resulted in obstacles (e.g., Sherman Act, revisions to the Clayton Act, Glass Steagall Act) to corporate consolidation and other capitalists' agendas. Whereas the New Federalism of the late twentieth century provides business with additional bargaining power over regional states (Grant and Wallace 1994; Grant 1995), opposing political groups are largely ineffective in blocking big-business agendas. The absence of a countervailing power to big business raises an important question for political sociology: Why is there little effective opposition to policies that benefit big business in the late twentieth century?

One obstacle to developing a countervailing power to big business is the problem of public opinion. Information on most policy initiatives is presented to the public in such a way that the public is not well informed on the issues or they are influenced by particular interests. Recent estimates show that there are approximately 170,000 public-relations employees in the United States that attempt to manipulate the news to advance the interests of their clients (Korten 1995). Moreover, state managers themselves do not provide accurate information to the public. For example, the two most significant tax bills in the last two decades—*RA81* and *TRA86*—were presented to the public as policies that changed individual income-tax rates. Few citizens were aware that these policies contained provisions for massive corporate tax cuts. Also, individuals have little information that would help them understand that the increased national debt in the 1980s occurred to a large extent because state business policies dramatically reduced corporations' tax burden. Further, corporations gain support from the public because they have the power to set the ideological tone and parameters of public debate over policy initiatives. For example, beginning in the 1940s, the steel industry gained public support for government subsidies, in part, because they had the power and resources to set the parameters of the debate. They argued that a modern and competitive steel industry was necessary to ensure a strong national defense (Prechel 1990). Critics of policies that are presented as "in the national interest" are frequently met with ideological reproaches that are framed as unpatriotic or unsupportive of necessary national-defense initiatives.

Another contemporary development is that corporations' bargaining power with national and regional states has increased as they have become more flexible and mobile. While the mobility of capital has always provided advantages for capitalists, the organization of the largest corporations as MLSFs provides parent companies with increased mobility. Within the MLSF, corporations can shift production from one subsidiary to another, which frequently entails spatial relocation from one country, regional state, or municipality to another. When parent companies such as Exxon-Mobil, Ford, General Motors, General Electric, and Lockheed-Martin have production facilities in many locations they also have the option of relocating their production processes to those that provide the most favorable institutional arrangements. This implicit threat has a powerful effect on the political climate within which regional state managers—who are often held responsible for ensuring economic growth and stability—negotiate with corporations. In the New Federalism era, regional states and municipalities compete with one another for businesses. This has resulted in the contemporary "race to the bottom" among regional states and communities to attract business. Once a company is relocated, the implicit threat to relocate continues to give it power over state and local governments to create favorable institutional arrangements.

Political Capitalism and the Organizational State

The last 110 years have produced political-legal institutional arrangements that are increasingly engaged in and supportive of business activity. The analysis here identifies three core dimensions of *political capitalism*: (1) the capacity of capitalists to develop a coherent conception of the relationships between their economic goals and the policies necessary to achieve those goals (2) the capacity of competing capitalist class and subclass segments to agree on business policy, and (3) capitalists' capacity to exercise control over the state to ensure implementation of these policies.

Defining and redefining the political-legal arrangements within which capital accumulation occurs produced a *more prominent and less autonomous state*. A more prominent state is one that becomes more actively engaged in regulating the economy over time. A more prominent state is distinct from a more autonomous state. The contemporary state takes a more active role in advancing economic agenda, but this activity is less autonomous from the capitalist class in at least two ways. First, political capitalism has produced an elaborate state structure that is engaged in more spheres of economic activity to promote capitalists' agenda. By contrast, state structures (OSHA, EPA, NLRB) that promote working-class interests remain weak. Second, this state structure is important because it provides the means for capitalists to pursue their agenda and under some historical conditions, as was the case with the steel industry, successfully oppose the state. In short, the emergence and transformation of state business policy and state structures are important *not* because they ensure state autonomy, but rather because they establish the structural arrangements within which capitalists pursue their agendas.

Conclusion

The capital-dependence framework elaborated here connects the micro-level decision-making process to macro-level structures and processes (e.g., economic conditions, political structures, ideology) to explain change in the corporate form (i.e., meso level). The theoretical logic argues that change in the corporate form is historically contingent and occurs in response to long-term constraints on capital accumulation. This theoretical framework places social action at the center of the analysis, and maintains that social structures are the outcome of a dynamic process whereby social actors construct both the corporation and the institutional arrangements within which the corporation is embedded. Although constraints on capital accumulation require a response, the response is conditioned by the historically specific organizational structures (e.g., managerial process, corporate form) and institutional arrangements, which define the range of possible solutions. Although social change may be an orderly and evolutionary process during certain historical periods, social structures also contain irrationalities and contradictions that result in disequilibrium. During periods of severe capital dependence, irrationalities and contradictions emerge as crises and are resolved by attempts to realign internal corporate arrangements (e.g., the managerial process), corporate forms, institutional arrangements, and the relationship among these spheres of the social structure.

Although capitalists and state managers attempt to eliminate contradictions in the social structure, equilibrium is rarely achieved. Competing logics at different levels of the social structure produce incompatibilities. While macro-level economic conditions change, organizational structures and processes demand regularity and stability to ensure standardization of decisions and outputs (e.g., product). Standardization pressures exist because it is easier to predict costs when output (i.e., commodities) are similar, and because the output products from one corporation affect product costs and quality in downstream segments of the commodity chain. These inherently incompatible logics — change versus stability — between levels of the social structure produce contradictions that emerge as crises. Although these constraints generate a response by capitalists, the response is affected by historically specific conditions including the form of scientific management, the parameters of industrial capitalists' dependence on external capital markets, the parameters of the state's formal authority, capitalists' capacity to redefine state business policy, and prevailing ideologies.

Ideologies were used to legitimize existing social structures during periods of stability and to mobilize social actors to change the social structure during periods of crises. Distorted laissez-faire ideologies were used to justify regional state intervention in the economy in the late nineteenth and early twentieth centuries. Anti-big business ideologies during the 1930s mobilized groups inside and outside the state who supported New Deal business policies. In the 1970s and 1980s, pro-business ideologies were used to mobilize capitalists and to legitimate policies favorable to business. Also, corporate culture and scientific management ideologies were pivotal to the rationalization of the managerial process in the late twentieth century. Scientific management is an ideology, not simply a means to advance efficiency. Scientific management is incorporated into the culture of capitalism; it provides a "lens" through which managers perceive problems and conceptualize solutions.

Capital-dependence theory shows that the rationalization process is affected by historically specific conditions, and the capacity of social actors to mobilize politically to create new institutional arrangements. Market conditions are important *not only* because they effect corporate change directly, but also because market competition increases capitalist political behavior. State business policies affecting corporate-form change were the outcome of political struggles among classes and capitalist class and subclass segments. During each historical juncture when capital dependence increased, big business organized politically to create political-legal arrangements more conducive to profit-making. Corporate change is effected by the capacity of capitalists to develop a coherent conception of the relationship between their economic goals and the institutional arrangements necessary to advance those goals, the capacity of competing capitalist class and subclass segments to develop a unified political strategy, and capitalists' capacity to exercise control over the state to ensure implementation of policies that advance their agendas.

Capital-dependence theory contains a dynamic theoretical logic that accounts for historical variation in class-based political behavior, and directs researchers' attention toward social actors who organize politically to advance their interests. This theoretical framework identifies social actors (e.g., classes, class segments, subclass segments) who have control over valued resources and the social actors who are dependent on those resources. By focusing on how social actors construct institutional and organizational arrangements and linkages, the analysis here explains why the rate of social change varies over time, why the effects of specific variables change under different historical conditions, and how purposive social actors organize politically to effect social change.

Appendix

Descriptive Statistics for the Event History Analysis

	N	Minimum	Maximum	Mean	Standard deviation
Long-Term Debt	75	0	1.84	.4184	.4050
Return on Equity	75	1.37	33.05	13.9488	6.0641
Mergers and Acquisitions	75	0	10125	830.0503	1542.2847
Presence of a PAC	75	0	1	.83	.38
CEO with Financial and accounting Background	75	0	1	.09	.2929
Assets	75	870.52	65017.45	8488.2936	11131.2627
Year of Incorporation	75	1831	1988	1920.6	27.73
Time to the Event	75	3	13	10.7333	3.1594
Event Occurence	75	0	1	.52	.503
Valid N (listwise)	75				

Notes

Chapter 1. Capital Dependence, Historical Transitions, and Corporate Transformations

1. Although Kolko demonstrated that the legislation enacted during the Progressive Era established the foundation for the form of capitalism developed in the United States, he did not foresee the long-term effects of Progressive Era legislation on the concentration of wealth and economic power over time. Whereas the New Deal placed some limits on big business, by the 1990s most of the legislation passed during this period has been dismantled and economic power has become increasingly concentrated in large corporations. (I will return to this issue in chapter 11.)

2. Population ecology model maintains that older organizations will fail rather than change. Neo-institutional theory suggests that inertia limits rapid organizational change. This perspective stresses gradual diffusion of organizational types within a field (Fligstein 1990; Zucker 1991).

3. Like Chandler, both Harris (1983) and Rumelt (1974) use the administrative relationship to operationalize the corporate form. Fligstein (1985, 1990) uses some of Rumelt's classifications and assigns the MDF in other corporations when a division vice president exists.

4. Weber presents the Protestant-ethic thesis as an example of the manner in which such variations across time and space may have significant sociological consequences. Similarly, Weber shows how a different constellation of variables in China slowed the spread of capitalism (Kalberg 1994).

5. Findings from ahistorical methods are frequently falsified by changes in the relationships among variables across time (Miller and Friesen 1982). Even quantitative time-series regression and event-history analysis contain pre-theoretical and meta-methodological presuppositions that obscure the sudden or gradual temporal conditioning of structural relationships (Isaac and Griffin 1989).

6. Core industries include those that are central to the economy. The empirical form of core industries, however, vary over time. For example, the steel industry was central to economic growth in the early and middle decades of the twentieth century. Although the steel industry is still important, it is less central to the economy in the late twentieth century. Similarly, while the computer industry was not a central component of the early-twentieth-century economy, it is a core industry in the late twentieth century.

7. The historical method elaborated here does not draw the sharp distinction between theory and method common in quantitative research. This conceptual framework conforms to the perspective employed by the classical social theorists whose formulation of theoretical problems entailed the method to examine them.

Chapter 2.   The Federalist State and the Emergence of the Modern Corporation

1. *Holding companies* are corporate entities with small centralized administrative offices that control other corporations through ownership of their securities (Bonbright and Means 1932).

2. Throughout "state" refers to the national level and "regional state" refers to the local level (e.g., Kansas, Maryland, New York, Wisconsin).

3. Federalism is a form of government in which authority is distributed among a centralized national government and regional governments (e.g., United States). In contrast, many European countries have governments that centralize authority in a unitary parliamentary system.

4. Common laws are rules that have been developed from custom or judicial decisions without the aid of written legislation. These laws are used as a basis for later court decisions (Allison, Prentice, and Howell 1991).

5. In 1800, as few as one hundred business corporations existed in the United States (Haney 1920). In contrast, Massachusetts incorporated over seventy companies in 1837.

6. This is also the period when cost accounting became an important dimension of management.

7. *Fixed capital* is investment in such things as machinery, land, and buildings. *Variable capital* is investment in labor power (Mandel 1978).

8. Agreements and pools are frequently referred to as the same thing. Both fall under the broader category of a *federation*: consolidation alliances of separate organizations for mutual benefit. *Pools* establish a common fund to be divided among the members on some agreed-upon basis. The simple *agreement* does not include any collective control of output. Agreements were typical between 1865 and 1875. A more formal type of federation (i.e., pools) became widespread between 1875 and 1895 (Haney 1920).

9. This law was later incorporated into federal legislation. Congressional framers of the Transportation Act of 1920 considered complete fusion as a final outcome of consolidation in the railroad industry. Paragraph 2, section 5 of the revised Interstate Commerce Act allowed one railroad to purchase the stock of another (Bonbright and Means 1932).

10. A major promoter of the trust was Samuel Dodd, an attorney for Standard Oil, who developed and promoted the idea that resulted in the Standard Oil Trust (1880) (Heilbroner 1985).

11. Although the holding company was technically a legal mode of organizing assets prior to 1888 and some corporations pursued this option, most did not. As stated above, many corporations did not want their financial holdings, pooling agreements, and trust activities scrutinized by government officials or to become part of the public record.

12. The 1875 New Jersey law authorized corporations to purchase mines, factories, or other property necessary for their business. Stock issues, however, were restricted to the amount of the purchase. Moreover, the 1875 law did not provide corporations with the right to issue stock as a form of payment (New Jersey Laws, 1875 sec. 55 in Larcom 1937).

13. By 1935, twenty-nine states gave unlimited authority to corporations to acquire and hold stock (Larcom 1937).

14. The Interstate Commerce Act of 1887 established the Interstate Commerce Commission to regulate the railroads (Cochran and Miller 1966).

15. Soon after the laws of incorporation were passed, the Standard Oil Company of New

Jersey (i.e., successor of the Standard Oil Trust) was incorporated as a New Jersey holding company (1899). The new Standard Oil Company of New Jersey was formed to transfer the stock of the various corporations in the trust into a single corporation (Moody 1968; Nelson 1959).

16. Dill was also appointed as counsel to the committee that revised Canada's incorporation laws (see Seager and Gulick 1929; Kirkland 1967; Chandler 1977).

17. Laissez-faire ideology also influenced business policy at the federal level. For example, Congress funded the construction of the Central Pacific railroad, but obtained nothing in return (Thorelli 1955).

18. In 1927, the Delaware business policy was amended to authorize board members to modify the corporate charter by redefining the terms, conditions, and special rights of stockholders (Larcom 1937). By the early 1990s, almost one-half of the largest five hundred corporations and almost one-third of the corporations listed on the New York Stock Exchange were incorporated in Delaware, producing a major source of revenue for the state (Osterle 1991).

Chapter 3.   Restructuring the Business Enterprise to Obtain Market Control, 1890–1905

1. Banking entailed two basic activities. *Private investment bankers* issued and sold securities to the public. *Commercial banking* entailed taking deposits from individuals and paying a return in the form of interest. Prior to passage of New Deal banking legislation, through their affiliates bankers were allowed to engage in both activities, which allowed them to take individuals' deposits and use them to finance stock offerings.

2. By the early 1890s, many railroads were carrying first, second, and third mortgage bonds, and almost half of their gross revenues was paid to private bankers to cover interest payments (Roy 1991).

3. J. P. Morgan influenced the restructuring of the First National Bank (now Citicorp) of New York and a number of railroad companies (Oesterle 1991; Berle and Means 1991; Thorelli 1955).

4. Additional access to raw materials was achieved in an agreement with Rockefeller's Standard Oil in 1896 (Hogan 1971).

5. The American Steel & Wire Company was formed as a New Jersey corporation in 1899. By 1901, it controlled twenty-six subsidiary corporations. There were ten to twelve similar consolidations in 1900 (Haney 1920).

6. *Overcapitalization* occurs when corporations exaggerate the value of their assets. This occurs when the issued securities are more than the assets of the corporation. Overcapitalization is also referred to as "watered stock," indicating that the assets of the corporation are less than the market value of the stock (Haney 1920).

7. Some estimates show that it later controlled up to 80 percent of the steel industry (Moody 1968; Hogan 1971; Chandler 1977).

8. Also, investors preferred corporate securities to trust certificates. The first holding companies issued two kinds of stock: *preferred stock* based on earning capacity and secured by fixed assets, and the more speculative *common stock* based on anticipated growth in earnings resulting from the consolidation (Chandler 1977).

9. In some cases, arrangements had to be made to fund the debt of the merging companies.

10. The holding company structure also allowed corporations to circumvent regional state laws forbidding corporations from consolidating with, for example, a public utility or an investment bank (Bonbright and Means 1932). Although some regional

states allowed foreign corporations (i.e., those not incorporated in the regional state) to operate within their boundaries, the governments levied high taxes on these corporations. Thus, many business enterprises restructured as holding companies to avoid taxes (Douglas and Shanks 1929).

11. Little financial information on corporations was made available to the public until the mid-1930s.

12. The tax liability issue is complex, largely because state laws of incorporation vary (Bonbright and Means 1932).

13. Friedman (1977) uses this concept to explain how managers control workers. Burawoy's (1979) conception of "manufacturing consent" is similar.

Chapter 4.   The Rise and Demise of the Industrial Holding Company

1. Conflict between the railroads and farmers over issues related to property rights had a long history. One dimension of this conflict emerged when railroads successfully lobbied Congress to grant them prime agricultural land in the Midwest. This forced farmers to purchase land from the railroads, frequently at inflated prices (McNall 1988).

2. However, the Sherman Antitrust Act became an effective instrument to fight labor organization, which was an important consideration among capitalists who reversed their initial opposition to the law (Cochran and Miller 1942; Heilbroner 1985).

3. Under Section 11 of the Clayton Act, Congress delegated authority to enforce Section 7 to the Federal Trade Commission (FTC), the Federal Reserve Board, and the Interstate Commerce Commission. However, until 1950 when Section 7 was revised, the FTC was the primary enforcement agency.

4. Although the FTC explored approximately seven hundred corporate acquisitions between 1927 and 1950, it only issued thirty-one complaints and blocked four consolidations (Federal Trade Commission, 1927–1950).

5. When the economy was weak, arguments for tariffs emerged. When the economy was strong, criticisms against tariffs emerged. After the 1893 depression, when overproduction and underconsumption characterized the economy and prices dropped to historic lows, Republicans asserted that tariffs were necessary to ensure high wages. However, the support for protectionism declined when the domestic economy improved. In fact, state managers (e.g., Congress, President McKinley) reconsidered the Dingley Tariffs that protected U.S. industries from European imports. Changes in tariff laws had little effect on some industries. For example, by the early twentieth century, the Department of War established arrangements with the steel industry that included cost sharing to construct steel-making facilities and substantial government contracts to purchase steel.

6. *Selling short* is a speculative technique employed with the expectation of a drop in stock price. Selling short entails borrowing stock, selling that stock, waiting for the price to drop, and then paying the lower price for the stock after it drops. This practice can result in high profits on stock sales (Rosenberg 1978).

7. Investment bankers held a large amount of stock in industrial corporations that they reorganized and financed, which allowed them to demand representation on the board of directors. At one point, one of J. P. Morgan's partners sat on the board of directors of fifty-nine companies (Chernow 1997).

8. The previous 5 percent dividend tax was repealed with Prohibition. The capital-stock /excess-profits tax was set to end in 1934 (Paul 1954; Leff 1984).

9. Also in 1947, 66 percent of the steel in the United States was shipped by the eight largest companies and by 1958 they accounted for 70 percent of all steel shipments (U.S. Census of Manufacturers 1972, volume 1, table 5; Barnett and Schorsch 1983).

Chapter 5.   From Product Cost Controls to the Financial Conception of Control

1. The following draws from the excellent study by Johnson and Kaplan (1991).
2. *Variable costs* include the portion of expenses that change in direct proportion to change in output. *Fixed costs* include the minimum cost to operate a production facility (e.g., rent). Many accounting systems assume that fixed costs are unaffected by increases or decreases in output (for more detail see Johnson and Kaplan 1991).

Chapter 6.   The Management of Managers at American Steel, 1920–1970s

1. Like the analysis here, the new institutional theory in sociology is critical of efficiency arguments. This perspective suggests that efficiency does not entail "profit maximizing or even satisficing actions" (Fligstein 1990:18). Rather, efficiency is associated with growth, profit making, and survival (Fligstein 1992:358, 373; also see Roy 1997).
2. The analysis focuses solely on technical efficiency and does not make assumptions about the capacity of the corporation to use societal resources efficiently or whether efficiency is increased at the expense of reducing workers' wages.
3. In previous publications, I referred to this corporation as Taggert Steel Corporation.
4. Centralization of functional activities occurred in several industries in the middle of the twentieth century (e.g., steel, metal, electrical apparatus, power machinery, construction equipment) because fabricated shapes and forms made to customer specification entailed coordination between sales and manufacturing (Chandler 1962).
5. Gross cash flow averaged over $32 billion between 1960 and 1975, an all time high for the industry (Acs 1984; American Iron and Steel Institute, various years).
6. Fligstein (1990) argues that after the Celler-Kefauver Amendment (1950), conglomerates were immune from antitrust legislation.
7. In June 1970, the Justice Department stipulated certain other conditions. In order to retain its 81 percent interest in J&L, LTV had to relinquish its wholly owned cable and wire subsidiary, Okonite Company, and its 55.4 percent interest in Braniff Airways (Hogan 1972).
8. During the height of the diversification years (1969–1971), the corporation's dividend-payout ratio averaged 74 percent.
9. Although some researchers suggest that the relationship between evaluation and authority is important (Scott, Dornbush, Bushing, and Laing 1967), little attention is given to how mechanisms to evaluate managers affect their motives and behavior.

Chapter 7.   Changing Economic Conditions and Corporate Political Behavior, 1940–1985

1. Although these researchers acknowledge that state autonomy varies (Skocpol 1985), they fail to identify the basis of this variation or rely on psychological arguments. For example, Block (1977) argues that confidence of big business declines during depres-

sions and postwar construction when managers pay less attention to business opinion and are responsive to popular pressure. During these periods, the state expands its power.

2. I thank Robert Antonio for bringing this important point to my attention.

3. *Structure* includes the formal procedural rules, compliance procedures, and standard operating procedures that define the relationship among organizational units, and between the organization and its environment.

4. Other formulations view the state as a complex of organizations and attribute independence to parts of the state apparatus (Skocpol 1985).

5. The analysis focuses on the integrated steel industry, which manufactures steel from raw materials (e.g., limestone, coal, iron ore). In contrast, minimills produce steel from scrap and, therefore, have significantly lower capital investments, a different social organization of production, and a narrower product line and market niche. As a result, they have different political and economic requirements and concrete interests.

6. The steel industry invested this capital and between 1952 and 1960 the industry's production capability increased from 109 to 149 million tons (American Iron and Steel Institute 1960).

7. The cost of shipping ore from Brazil to Japan dropped by 60 percent from 1957 to 1968 (Crandall 1981; Walter 1983). The effects of changes in raw material prices, shipping costs, and technology lowered the cost of producing steel in Japan by approximately $25 a net finished ton from 1957 to 1967 (Crandall 1981). Moreover, wages in the United States were higher than in Japan (Goldberg 1986).

8. The federal government viewed higher steel prices as inflationary, and monitored steel wage and price increases throughout the 1960s. In 1962, a major confrontation occurred between President Kennedy and the steel industry over price increases (*Congressional Quarterly Almanac* 1962). During the 1968 labor negotiations President Johnson pressured the steel industry and the USW to keep wage and price increases at a minimum (U.S. Federal Trade Commission 1977).

9. By 1971, the accelerated depreciation allowances defined by the Revenue Tax Act of 1962 were eliminated.

10. Finance capital had become much more diversified than in the early 20th century when its capital-accumulation agenda was more closely tied to the industrial sector.

11. The Trade Agreements Act of 1979 also transferred the authority over protectionism from the Treasury to the Commerce Department because of the perception in Congress that it was a more effective enforcement unit.

12. The business community's targets also included organized labor (e.g., the Humphrey-Hawkins bill), consumer protection, OSHA, the Federal Trade Commission, energy, the environment, and economic deregulation (Vogel 1989; Akard 1996).

13. By 1983, imports and exports accounted for almost 25 percent of the GNP (Heilbroner 1985).

14. Although this legislation required steel corporations to reinvest into steel operations (U.S. Congress 1984), the amount was not defined and a mechanism to monitor the rate of reinvestment was not established.

15. Economic analysis of international steel trade suggests that between 1976 and 1983 import relief for steel was not warranted (Grossman 1986).

16. These changes in business policy were the result of concerted lobbying by a big-business coalition and a concern among state managers in several agencies that a weak manufacturing sector would undermine economic stability. The federal government, however, did not control how the steel industry disbursed these resources. For exam-

ple, after tax breaks were distributed under the Revenue Act of 1981, the U.S. Steel Corporation purchased Marathon Oil.

Chapter 8. Transformation of the Managerial Process, 1980s

1. I use the term neo-Fordist (versus post-Fordist) because this form of control has continuity with previous forms of control. Whereas Fordism employs technology to control the labor process, neo-Fordism uses many of the same techniques (e.g., rational calculation) to control the managerial process.
2. Weber appears to narrowly consider the application of rational calculation to workers' performances. However, Weber's theoretical framework predicts the extension of rational calculation throughout the capitalist enterprise, which is consistent with my hypothesis that rational calculation of work performances is extended to the managerial process in the late twentieth century.
3. See Stinchcombe (1990) for another sociological treatment of the use of information in decision making.
4. Frederick Taylor coined the term "need to know" basis in an attempt to demonstrate the efficiencies of scientific management. Research has shown that—during an earlier historical period—corporations centralized information and redistributed that information on a "need to know basis" to control the labor process (Braverman 1974; Edwards 1979; Clawson 1980).
5. Efficiency refers to the corporation's capacity to control costs. Effectiveness refers to the corporation's capacity to realize its goals (e.g., profits, product quality).
6. Estimates indicate that integrated steel created 10 percent of total particulate emissions and one-third of industrial waste discharge (Russell and Vaughan 1976). Therefore, the steel industry was a primary target for reducing industrial pollution in the 1970s.
7. Steel intensity is the ratio of steel's share of the GNP. Whereas early industrial development used steel for roads, bridges, railroads, and port facilities, mature economies require less infrastructure investment.
8. Minimills produce carbon steel with electric furnaces by melting scrap metal, eliminating fixed capital investment in raw materials, coke ovens, and blast furnaces.
9. A cost point is a cost that can be identified. Cost points range from the energy necessary to operate a blast furnace at a certain temperature over a specific time period to the labor cost to move finished steel from one location to another.
10. This is the dimension of the account-control system stressed by A. H. Church in the early twentieth century.
11. This does not include the capital investment in raw materials and finished inventories.
12. American Steel's strategy to manufacture consent included forms of *welfare capitalism* such as community tutoring, college tuition programs for employees' children, and housing, athletic, and education programs for employees.
13. American Steel's net loss declined from 4.2 percent in 1982 to 1.2 percent in 1984. The change, however, was due to the upturn in the recession and the subsequent increase in capability utilization rates from 55.6 percent in 1982 to 69.7 percent in 1984 (corporate documents).
14. Continuous processing lowers cost by reducing capital investments in unfinished inventories and by cutting expenditures on the energy necessary to reheat and roll the

unfinished steel. By the 1990s, American Steel *continuously cast* each product, enabling a bloom or slab to be made directly from molten steel avoiding separate reheating and rolling processes.

15. Although researchers have advanced our understanding of global commodity chains (Gereffi and Korzeniewicz 1994), little research exists on how commodity chains affect corporate change.

16. After failing to convince U.S. manufacturers to implement SQC in the 1950s, Edward Deming went to Japan where this technique was incorporated into manufacturing and became the primary technical means of ensuring product quality. In fact, the Japanese established a Deming Award to encourage manufacturers to develop and implement SQC (Cole 1979).

17. Similar changes occurred in British and German steel companies (Morris, Blyton, Bacon and Franz 1992).

18. Although production managers now have less authority, it cannot be assumed that their new tasks require fewer skills. The more technical nature of contemporary manufacturing suggests that skill requirements may be greater. Skill is an issue that must be addressed elsewhere.

Chapter 9. Changing Institutional Arrangements and Transformation to the Multilayered Subsidiary Form

1. Although the *TRA86* was presented to the public as closing special corporate tax loopholes (e.g., real estate), it preserved tax loopholes enjoyed by, for example, the oil industry (Birnbaum and Murray 1987).

2. Although the corporate debt increase is frequently attributed to leveraged buyouts and takeovers by wealthy investors, this represents only a portion of the total corporate debt.

3. Internal capital markets are distinct from Williamson's (1975:143–45) conception of the firm as a "miniature capital market," which functions as an "internal control apparatus" by manipulating the incentive structure, internal audits, and cash-flow allocation.

4. Most financial corporations were organized as holding companies with subsidiaries throughout the twentieth century, and executives in the financial sector were familiar with this corporate form.

5. Other examples include Ford's sale of its $1 billion tax break to IBM for a reported $100 to $200 million. Other corporations engaged in the sale of tax through the leaseback arrangement include Occidental Petroleum, LTV, Global Marine, and Chicago and North Western (Birnbaum and Murray 1987).

6. To limit the complexity in presenting this corporate transformation, some of the smaller subsidiaries are not discussed.

Chapter 10. Transformation to the Multilayered Subsidiary Form among the Largest Industrial Parent Companies

1. Central to the study of event histories is the concept of a "risk set," the set of cases that are at risk of encountering the event of interest (Allison 1984). In each year of the event history some cases will encounter the event and can no longer be at risk for the event. Thus, for each period (in this analysis a year) in which events occur fewer cases are

part of the risk set in the following years. The data set constructed for discrete time event history analysis has as its unit of analysis the case period (here corporate year) with the cases that change no longer contributing information to the analysis in the periods following the change. The analysis presented here examines the risk of change in corporate form from year to year (e.g., change from 1981 to 1982, 1982–1983). The dependent variable is a dummy coded "1" in the year change was observed.

2. The equation for a discrete time model with two explanatory variables can be written as:

$$\frac{log P(t)}{1 - P(t)} = a(t) + b_1 x_1 + b_2 x_2(t)$$

where $P(t)$ is the hazard rate, and $a(t)$ can refer to any variation in the hazard across time. This is made possible by including dummy variables in the logistical regression for each of the periods in the model (with one excluded period) (Allison 1984).

3. The analysis includes only domestic subsidiaries.

4. A dummy variable was used because the theory suggests that the presence of a PAC is a mechanism to pursue an external-oriented strategy. Non-linear (i.e., natural log) transformations of PAC receipts produced similar results.

5. This is roughly consistent with Fligstein's (1985) analysis which shows that 84.2 percent of the largest corporations were organized as MDFs in 1979. Fligsten's slightly higher percentage of MDF is probably due to differences in the sample, measurement, year, and data source.

6. The most rapid period of change to the MDF was between 1948 and 1959 when the annual average rates of change were 2.91 corporations or 3.6 percent of corporations at risk of change (Fligstein 1990; also see Rumelt 1974). In contrast, the annual average rates of change to the MLSF between 1981 and 1983 were 3.33 corporations or 4.4 percent of corporations at risk.

7. Several models were tested to ensure that the PAC findings were not spurious. These models included other variables such as chemical, oil, and defense industry and several interactions with PACs and industry. Variables tested in other models that had no significant effect on the PAC variable include operating profit margin, working capital, and earning per share. Since none of these variables had an effect, they were not included in the model presented here. Instead, I present the most parsimonious theory driven model.

8. The coefficients for the dummy variables for year and their probability values for the Wald statistics (in parenthesis) are 1983: 7.3089 (.6857); 1984: 6.6869 (.7122); 1985: 7.1847 (.6918); 1986: 6.7742 (.7087); 1987: 6.9070 (.7032); 1988: 7.7651 (.6683); 1989: 7.4997 (.6791); 1990: .2348 (.9933); 1991: 9.1142 (.6150); 1992: 8.6152 (.6345); 1993: 8.5406 (.6375).

9. This relationship remains when controlling for a range of variables, including industry.

10. Other operationalizations of the variable were tested, but none were statistically significant.

Chapter 11. Conclusion: Historical Transitions and Corporate Transformations, 1880s–1990s

1. Karl Marx identified overproduction and underconsumption as one of the fundamental contradictions of capitalism: the tendency for production capability to advance at a faster rate than consumption.

2. These values are adjusted using implicit price deflator in 1992 dollars.

3. The increase from $45 to $85 per share constitutes an almost $5 billion increase in total value.

4. Resistance to the early-twentieth-century holding company emerged, in part, because of its capacity to disguise ownership control by not attaching the parent company's name to its subsidiary corporations. Members of Congress (i.e., Senator LaFollette) unsuccessfully attempted to require corporations to identify the public subsidiary corporations over which they had ownership-control. Although state business policy always allowed corporations to conceal parent companies' identity, the extensiveness of ownership control within the MLSF is far beyond that of previous corporate structures. The largest corporations are acquiring ownership control of other giant corporations and leaving the consumer with the understanding that these are independently owned and operated corporations when they are not.

5. In contrast, market measurements (e.g., stock price, price-earning ratio) are available on a daily basis.

6. For discussions of the issues in this debate see Palmer, Barber, Zhou, and Soysal (1995a, 1995b) and Fligstein (1995).

References

Abbott, Andrew. 1991. "Causality and Contingency." Paper presented at the annual meeting of the American Sociological Association, Cincinnati, Ohio.

———. 1992. "From Causes to Events." *Sociological Methods and Research* 20:428:255.

———. 1997. "On the Concept of Turning Point." *Comparative Social Research* 16:85–106.

Acs, Zoltan. 1984. *Changing Structure of the U.S. Economy.* New York: Praeger.

Aglietta, Michel. 1979. *A Theory of Capitalist Regulation.* London: New Left Books.

Akard, Patrick. 1992. "Corporate Mobilization and Political Power: The Transformation of U.S. Economic Policy in the 1970s." *American Sociological Review* 57:597–615.

———. 1996. "The Political Origins of 'Supply-Side' Economic Policy." *Political Power and Social Theory* 10:95–148.

Allison, John, Robert Prentice, and Rate Howell. 1991. *Business Law.* Chicago, IL: The Dryden Press.

Allison, Paul. 1984. *Event History Analysis: Regression for Longitudinal Event Data.* Beverly Hills, CA: Sage Publications.

American Iron and Steel Institute. 1940–1988. *Annual Statistical Report.* New York: AISI.

———. 1947. "Address of the President." Yearbook. New York: AISI.

Antonio, Robert. 1979. "The Contradiction of Domination and Production in Bureaucracy." *American Sociological Review* 44:895–912.

Armitage, Howard, and Anthony Atkinson. 1990. *Choice of Productivity Measurements in Organizations.* Hamilton, Ontario: Society of Management Accountants of Canada.

Bacas, Harry. 1986. "New Directions in Liability Laws." *Nation's Business,* February 28.

Bannock, Donald, R. E. Baxter, and Ray Rees. 1978. *The Penguin Dictionary of Economics.* New York: Penguin Books.

Baran, Paul, and Paul Sweezy. 1966. *Monopoly Capital.* New York: Monthly Review Press.

Barnet, Richard, and John Cavanagh. 1995. *Global Dreams: Imperial Corporations and the New World Order.* New York: Simon & Schuster.

Barnett, Donald, and Louis Schorsch. 1983. *Steel Upheaval in a Basic Industry.* Cambridge, MA: Ballinger.

Beetham, David. 1987. *Bureaucracy.* Minneapolis, MI: University of Minnesota Press.

Benson, Kenneth. 1977. "Organizations: A Dialectical View." *Administrative Science Quarterly* 20:229–49.

Berg, Ivar, and Mayer Zald. 1978. "Business and Society." *Annual Review of Sociology* 4:115–43.

Berle, Adolf, and Gardiner Means. [1932] 1991. *The Modern Corporation and Private Property.* New Brunswick, NJ: Transaction Publishers.

Bernstein, Meyer. 1975. "The Trade Policy of the United Steelworkers of America." Pp. 229–84 in *Toward a New World Trade Policy,* edited by C. Fred Bergsten. Lexington, MA: Lexington Books.

Best, Michael. 1990. *The New Competition.* Cambridge, MA: Harvard University Press.

Birnbaum, Jeffrey, and Alan Murray. 1987. *Showdown at Gucci Gulch*. New York: Vintage Books.

Block, Fred. 1977. "The Ruling Class Does Not Rule." *Socialists Review* 7:6–28.

Boies, John. 1989. "Money, Business and the State." *American Sociological Review* 54:821–33.

———. 1994. *Buying for Armageddon*. ASA Rose Monograph Series. New Brunswick, NJ: Rutgers University Press.

Boies, John, and Harland Prechel. 1998. "Capital Dependence, Business Political Action, and Change in the Corporate Form." Annual meeting of the American Sociological Association, San Francisco, CA.

Bonbright, James, and Gardiner Means. 1932. *The Holding Company*. New York: McGraw-Hill.

Bowles, Samuel, and Richard Edwards. 1985. *Understanding Capitalism*. New York: Harper & Row.

Bowles, Samuel, David Gordon, and Thomas Weisskopf. 1983. *Beyond the Wasteland*. New York: Anchor Press.

Braverman, Harry. 1974. *Labor and Monopoly Capital: The Degradation of Work in the Twentieth Century*. New York: Monthly Review Press.

Broude, Henry. 1963. *Steel Decisions and the National Economy*. New Haven, CT: Yale University Press.

Burawoy, Michael. 1979. *Manufacturing Consent*. Chicago, IL: University of Chicago Press.

———. 1985. *The Politics of Production: Factory Regimes under Capitalism and Socialism*. London: Verso-New Left Books.

Burk, James. 1988. *Values in the Marketplace*. New York: W. de Gruyter.

Burns, Tom, and G. Stalker. 1961. *The Management of Innovation*. London: Tavistock.

Burris, Beverly. 1993. *Technocracy at Work*. Albany, NY: State University of New York Press.

Campbell, E. G. 1938. *The Reorganization of the American Railroad System, 1893–1900*. New York: Columbia University Press.

Carosso, Vincent. 1970. *Investment Banking in America: A History*. Cambridge, MA: Harvard University Press.

Carter, R. 1985. *Capitalism, Class Conflict, and the New Middle Class*. London: Routledge and Kegan Paul.

Cavitch, Zolman, and Matthew Cavitch. 1995. *Tax Planning for Corporations and Shareholders*, 2d ed. New York: Matthew Bender.

Center for Responsive Politics. 1997. Washington, D.C.

Chandler, Alfred, D. Jr. 1962. *Strategy and Structure*. Cambridge, MA: The MIT Press.

———. 1977. *The Visible Hand*. Cambridge, MA: Belknap-Harvard University Press.

———. 1990. *Scale and Scope*. Cambridge, MA: Belknap-Harvard University Press.

Chandler, Alfred, D. Jr. and Stephen Salsburg. 1971. *Pierre S. DuPont and the Making of the Modern Corporation*. New York: Harper & Row.

Chernow, Ron. 1997. *The Death of the Banker*. New York: Vintage Books.

Child, John. 1972. "Organization Structure and Strategies of Control: A Replication of the Aston Study." *Administrative Science Quarterly* 17:163–77.

———. 1984. *Organization*. London: Harper & Row.

Church, Alexander Hamilton. 1914. *The Science and Practice of Management*. New York: The Engineering Magazine Co.

Clark, Maurice J. 1923. *Studies in the Economics of Overhead Costs*. Chicago, IL: University of Chicago Press.

Clawson, Dan. 1980. *Bureaucracy and the Labor Process*. New York: Monthly Review.

Clawson, Dan, and Alan Neustadtl. 1989. "Interlocks, PACs, and Corporate Conservatism." *American Journal of Sociology* 94:749–73.

Clawson, Dan, Alan Neustadtl, and James Bearden. 1986. "The Logic of Business Unity." *American Sociological Review* 51:797–811.

Clawson, Dan, Alan Neustadtl, and Denise Scott. 1992. *Money Talks: Corporate PACs and Political Influence.* New York: Basic Books.

Cochran, Thomas. 1957. *The American Business System.* New York: Harper Torchbooks.

———. 1966. "The New Business Environment." Pp. 272–82 in *Views of American Economic Growth: The Industrial Era.* New York: McGraw-Hill.

Cochran, Thomas, and William Miller. 1942. *The Age of Enterprise.* New York: Macmillan.

———. 1966. "The Business of Politics." Pp. 3–14 in *Views of American Economic Growth: The Industrial Era.* New York: McGraw-Hill.

Coffee, John, Jr. 1988. "Shareholders Versus Managers." Pp. 194–210 in *Knights, Raiders and Targets,* edited by John Coffee, Louis Lowenstein, and Susan Rose-Ackerman. New York: Oxford University Press.

Cole, Robert. 1979. *Work, Mobility and Participation.* Berkeley, CA: University of California Press.

Coleman, James. 1986. *Foundations of Social Theory.* Cambridge, MA: Harvard University Press.

Collins, Randall. 1988. *Theoretical Sociology.* San Diego, CA: Harcourt Brace Jovanovich.

Common Cause. 1996. "'96 Soft Money to Democrats & Republicans Double Amount Raised During Same Period in '92; Soft Money Tops $83 Million in First 15 Months of Election Cycle." Press Release, May 1996.

Compustat. 1980–1990. New York: Standard and Poor's.

Congressional Quarterly Almanac. 1961. Washington, DC: Congressional Quarterly, Inc.

———. 1962. Washington, DC: Congressional Quarterly, Inc.

———. 1979. Washington, DC: Congressional Quarterly, Inc.

Congressional Quarterly Weekly Report. 1962. Washington, DC: Congressional Quarterly, Inc., October 27.

———. 1968. Washington, DC: Congressional Quarterly, Inc., February 2.

———. 1974. Washington, DC: Congressional Quarterly, Inc., December 28.

———. 1977. Washington, DC: Congressional Quarterly, Inc., November 19.

———. 1981a. Washington, DC: Congressional Quarterly, Inc., March 7.

———. 1981b. Washington, DC: Congressional Quarterly, Inc., August 8.

———. 1986. Washington, DC: Congressional Quarterly, Inc. July 26.

———. 1989. Washington, DC: Congressional Quarterly, Inc., March 25.

Congressional Record. 1982. H 8388, October 1.

Crandall, Robert. 1981. *The U.S. Steel Industry in Recurrent Crisis.* Washington, DC: The Brookings Institute.

Cutler, Antony, Barry Hindess, Paul Hirst, and Athar Hussain. 1978. *Marx's Capital and Capitalism Today.* Vol. 2. London: Routledge and Kegan Paul.

Davis, Gerald, Kristina Diekmann, and Catherine Tinsley. 1994. "The Decline and Fall of the Conglomerate Firm in the 1980s." *American Sociological Review* 59:547–70.

DeLong, J. Bradford. 1991. "Did J. P. Morgan's Men Add Value?" Pp. 205–36 in *Inside the Business Enterprise,* edited by Peter Temin. Chicago, IL: The University of Chicago Press.

Deming, W. Edward. 1969. "Statistical Control of Quality in Japan." Paper presented at the International Conference on Quality Control, Tokyo, Japan.

Dewing, Arthur. 1941. *The Financial Policies of Corporations.* New York: The Ronald Press Company.

DiDonato, Donna, Davita Glasberg, Silfen Mintz, Michael Schwartz. 1988. "Theories of Corporate Interlocks." *Research in the Sociology of Organizations* 6:135–57.

DiMaggio, Paul. 1988. "Interests and Agency in Institutional Theory." Pp. 3–22 in *Institutional Patterns and Organizations*, edited by Lynn Zucker. Cambridge, MA: Ballinger.

Dobbin, Frank. 1994. *Forging Industrial Policy.* Cambridge: Cambridge University Press.

Domhoff, William. 1987. "The Wagner Act and Theories of the State." *Political Power and Social Theory* 6. Greenwich, CT: JAI Press.

———. 1979. *The Powers That Be.* New York: Vintage Books.

Dornbusch, Stanford, and W. Richard Scott. 1975. *Evaluation and the Exercise of Authority.* San Francisco, CA: Jossey-Bass.

Douglas, William, and Carrol Shanks, 1929. "Institutions from Liability through Subsidiary Corporations." *Yale Law Journal* 39:193–318.

Drucker, Peter. 1976. *The Unseen Revolution.* New York: Harper & Row.

———. 1990. "The Emerging Theory of Manufacturing." *Harvard Business Review* (May-June): 94–103.

Dumenil, G. M. Glick, and J. Rangel. 1987. "The Rate of Profit in the United States." *Cambridge Journal of Economics* 11:331–59.

Dun and Bradstreet. 1981–1994. *America's Corporate Families: Billion Dollar Directory.* Parsippany, NJ: Dun & Bradstreet.

———.1982. *Reference Book on Corporate Management.* Parsippany, NJ: Dun & Bradstreet.

Eckes, Alfred. 1995. *Opening America's Market.* Chapel Hill, NC: University of North Carolina Press.

Edwards, Richard. 1979. *Contested Terrain.* New York: Basic Books.

Eichner, Alfred. 1969. *The Emergence of Oligopoly.* Baltimore, MD: John Hopkins Press.

Elnicki, Richard. 1971. "The Genesis of Management Accounting." *Management Accounting*, April 16.

Engineering News Record. 1986. "Cleanup Firms Cover Their Assets." March 6. New York: Harper.

Farrell, Christopher, Kathy Rebello, Robert Hof. 1995. "The Boom in IPOs." *Business Week*, December 18:64–72.

Fligstein, Neil. 1985."The Spread of the Multidivisional Form among Large Firms, 1919–1979." *American Sociological Review* 50:377–91.

———. 1987. "Intraorganizational Power Struggles: Rise of Financial Personnel to Top Leadership in Large Corporations, 1919–1979." *American Sociological Review*, 52:44–58.

———. 1990. *The Transformation of Corporate Control.* Cambridge, MA: Harvard University Press.

———. 1995. "Networks of Power of the Financial Conception of Control?" *American Sociological Review* 60:500–503.

Fligstein, Neil, and Peter Brantley. 1992. "Bank Control, Owner Control, or Organizational Dynamics." *American Journal of Sociology* 98:280–307.

Forbes. 1984. "Taking It To The Courts." January 2.

———. 1985. October 14, p. 31.

Forest, Stephanie Anderson, Greg Burns, and Gail DeGeorge. 1995. "The Whirlwind Breaking up Companies." *Business Week*, August 14:44.

Fortune. 1966. "Steel is Rebuilding for a New Era." October.

Freeland, Robert. 1996. "The Myth of the M-Form? Governance, Consent, and Organizational Change." *American Journal of Sociology* 102:483–526.

Freidman, Milton. 1963. *Monetary History of the United States, 1867–1960.* Princeton, NJ: Princeton University Press.

Friedland, Roger, and Robert Alford. 1991. "Bringing Society Back In." Pp. 232–58 in *The New Institutionalism in Organizational Analysis*, edited by Walter Powell and Paul Di-Maggio. Chicago, IL: University of Chicago Press.

Friedman, Andrew. 1977. *Industry and Labour: Class Struggle at Work and Monopoly Capitalism*. New York: Macmillan.

Fusfield, Daniel. 1958. "Joint Subsidiaries in the Iron and Steel Industry." *American Economic Review* 48:578–87.

Galbraith Kenneth. 1967. *The New Industrial State*. New York: New American Library.

Galaskiewicz, Joseph. 1985. "Interorganizational Relations." *Annual Review of Sociology* 11:281–304. Palo Alto, CA: Annual Reviews.

Gereffi, Gary, and Miguel Korzeniewicz. 1994. *Commodity Chains and Global Capitalism*. Westport, CT: Greenwood Press.

Giddens, Anthony. 1979. *Central Problems in Social Theory*. Berkeley, CA: University of California Press.

Goldberg, Walter. 1986. *Ailing Steel: The Transoceanic Quarrel*. New York: St. Martin's Press.

Gordon, Colin. 1994. *New Deals: Business, Labor, and Politics in America, 1920–1935*. Cambridge: Cambridge University Press.

Gordon, David. 1980. "Stages of Accumulation and Long Economic Cycles." Pp. 19–45 in *Processes of the World System*, edited by Terrance Hopkins and Immanuel Wallerstein. Beverly Hills, CA: Sage.

Gordon, David, Richard Edwards, and Michael Reich. 1982. *Segmented Work, Divided Workers: The Historical Transformation of Labor in the United States*. Cambridge: Cambridge University Press.

Gordon, Robert. 1945. *Business Leadership in Large Corporations*. Washington, DC: Brookings Institute.

Grandy, Christopher. 1993. *New Jersey and the Fiscal Origins of Modern American Corporation Law*. New York: Garland.

Granovetter, Mark. 1993. "The Nature of Economic Relationships." Pp. 2–41 in *Explorations in Economic Sociology*, edited by Richard Swedberg. New York: Russell Sage Foundation.

Grant, Don Sherman II. 1995. "The Political Economy of Business Failures across the American States, 1970–1985." *American Review of Sociology* 60:851–87.

Grant, Don Sherman II, and Michael Wallace. 1994. "The Political Economy of Manufacturing Growth and Decline across the American States, 1970–1985." *Social Forces* 73:33–63.

Greider, William. 1982. *The Education of David Stockman and Other Americans*. New York: E.P. Dutton.

———. 1989. *Secrets of the Temple*. New York: Simon & Schuster.

Grenzke, Janet M. 1989. "PACs and the Congressional Supermarket: The Currency is Complex." *American Journal of Political Science* 33:1–24.

Grossman, Gene. 1986. "Imports as a Cause of Injury: The Case of the U.S. Steel Industry." *Journal of International Economics* 20:201–23.

Hage, Jerald, and Michael Aiken. 1969. "Routine Technology, Social Structure, and Organizational Goals." *Administrative Science Quarterly* 14:366–76.

———. 1970 *Social Change in Complex Organizations*. New York: Random House.

Hall, Richard. 1963. "On the Concept of Bureaucracy." *American Journal of Sociology* 69:32–40.

———. 1987. 1991. *Organizations: Structures, Processes, and Outcomes*. 4th and 5th eds. New York: Prentice-Hall.

Hamilton, Gary, and Nicole Woolsey Biggart. 1988. "Market, Culture, and Authority: A Comparative Analysis of Management and Organization in the Far East." *American Journal of Sociology* 94:S52-S94.

Haney, Lewis. 1920. *Business Organization and Combination*. New York: Macmillan Company.

Hannan Michael, and John Freeman. 1984. "Structural Inertia and Organizational Change." *American Sociological Review* 49:149–64.

Harris, Barry. 1983. *Organization: The Effect of Large Corporations*. Ann Arbor, MI: University of Michigan Press.

Harrison, Bennett, and Barry Bluestone. 1988. *The Great U-Turn*. New York: Basic Books.

Hartz, Louis. 1948. *Economic Policy and Democratic Thought*. Cambridge MA: Harvard University Press.

Heilbroner, Robert. 1985. *The Making of Economic Society*. Englewood Cliffs, NJ: Prentice-Hall.

Herman, Edward. 1981. *Corporate Control, Corporate Power*. Cambridge: Cambridge University Press.

Hernes, Gudmund. 1976. "Structural Change in Social Progress." *American Journal of Sociology* 82:513–47.

Hessen, Robert. 1975. *Steel Titan*. New York: Oxford University Press.

Heydebrand, Wolf. 1977. "Organizational Contradictions in Public Bureaucracies." *The Sociological Quarterly*, 18:85–109.

———. 1985. "Technarchy and Neo-Corporatism." *Current Perspectives in Social Theory* 6:71–128.

Hirsch, Paul. 1997. "Sociology without Social Structure: Neoinstitutional Theory Meets Brave New World." *American Journal of Sociology* 102:1,702–1,723.

Hogan, William. 1971. *Economic History of the Iron and Steel Industry in the United States*. Lexington, MA: Lexington Books.

———. 1972. *The 1970s: Critical Years for Steel*. Lexington, MA: Lexington Books.

———. 1983. *World Steel in the 1980s: A Case of Survival*. Lexington, MA: Lexington Books.

International Trade Commission. 1984. "Carbon and Certain Alloy Steel Products." Publication 1553. Washington, DC: U.S. International Trade Commission.

Isaac, Larry, and Larry Griffin. 1989. "Ahistoricism in Time-Series Analysis of Historical Processes." *American Sociological Review* 54:873–90.

Iron Age. 1941. "Steel Industry Taxes $210 Million in '40, Earnings $260 Millions." 3 April.

———. 1976. "Why Specialty Steel Won its Case for Quotas." 19 July.

James, David, and Michael Soref. 1981. "Managerial Theory: Unmaking of the Corporate President." *American Sociological Review* 46:1–18.

Janoski, Thomas, Christa McGill, and Vanessa Tinsley. 1997. "Making Institutions Dynamic in Cross-national Research." *Comparative Social Research* 16:227–68.

Jensen, Michael. 1984. "Takeovers: Folklore and Science." *Harvard Business Review*, November–December:109–21.

Jessop, Bob. 1982. *The Capitalist State*. New York: New York University Press.

Johnson, H. Thomas. 1991. "Managing by Remote Control. Pp. 41–70 in *Inside the Business Enterprise: Historical Perspectives on the Use of Information*, edited by Peter Temin. Chicago, IL: The University of Chicago Press.

Johnson, H. Thomas, and Robert Kaplan. 1991. *Relevance Lost: The Rise and Fall of Management Accounting*. Boston, MA: Harvard Business School Press.

Jones, Eliot. [1921] 1926. *The Trust Problem in the United States*. New York: Macmillan Company.

Jones, Kent. 1986. *Politics vs. Economics in World Steel Trade*. London: Allen & Unwin.

Josephson, Mathew. [1932] 1962. *The Robber Barons*. New York: Harcourt Brace.

Kalberg, Stephen. 1983. "Max Weber's Universal-Historical Architectonic of Economically Oriented Action." *Current Perspectives in Social Theory* 4:253–88.

_____. 1994. *Max Weber's Comparative-Historical Sociology*. Chicago, IL: University of Chicago Press.

Kanter, Rosabeth Moss. 1989. *When Giants Learn to Dance*. New York: Simon & Schuster.

Kaplan, Robert. 1982. *Advanced Management Accounting*. Englewood Cliffs, NJ: Prentice-Hall.

Keasbey, Edward. 1899. "New Jersey and the Trusts." *New Jersey Law Journal* 22:357–68.

Keller, Morton. 1990. *Regulating a New Economy, 1900–1933*. Cambridge, MA: Harvard University Press.

Kirkland, Edward. 1967. *Industry Comes of Age*. Chicago, IL: Quadrangle Books.

Kolko, Gabriel. 1963. *The Triumph of Conservativism*. Glenco, IL: The Free Press.

_____. 1984. *Main Currents in Modern American History*. New York: Pantheon Books.

Kondratieff, N. D. 1935. "The Long Waves in Economic Life." *Review of Economic Statistics* 17(6):105–15.

Korten, David. 1995. *When Corporations Rule the World*. West Hartford, CT: Kumarian Press.

Kotz, David. 1994. "Interpreting the Social Structure of Accumulation." Pp. 50–71 in *Social Structures of Accumulation*, edited by Kotz, David, Terrence McDonough, and Michael Reich. Cambridge: Cambridge University Press.

Kotz, David, Terrence McDonough, and Michael Reich. 1994. *Social Structures of Accumulation*. Cambridge: Cambridge University Press.

Kudla, Ronald, and Thomas McInish. 1984. *Corporate Spin-offs*. Westport, CT: Quorum Books.

Lamoreaux, Naomi. 1985. *The Great Merger Movement in American Business, 1899–1904*. New York: Cambridge University Press.

Larcom, Russell. 1937. *The Delaware Corporation*. Baltimore, MD: John Hopkins Press.

Laumann, Edward, and David Knoke. 1987. *The Organizational State*. Madison, WI: University of Wisconsin Press.

Lawrence, Paul, and Jay Lorsch. 1967. *Organizations and Environment*. Boston, MA: Graduate School Business Administration, Harvard University.

Lazonick, William. 1991. *Business Organization and the Myth of the Market Economy*. Cambridge: Cambridge University Press.

LeBaron, Dean, and Lawrence Speidel. 1987. "Why are the Parts Worth More Than the Sum? 'Chop Shop,' a Corporate Valuation Model." Pp. 78–101 in *The Merger Boom*, edited by L. E. Browne and E. S. Rosengren. Boston, MA: Federal Reserve Bank of Boston.

Leff, Mark. 1984. *The Limits of Symbolic Reform: The New Deal and Taxation, 1933–1939*. Cambridge: Cambridge University Press.

Levenstein, Margaret. 1991. "The Use of Cost Measures: The Dow Chemical Company, 1890–1914." Pp. 71–116 in *Inside the Business Enterprise*, edited by Peter Temin. Chicago, IL: The University of Chicago Press.

Levine, Michael. 1985. *Inside International Trade Policy Formulation*. New York: Praeger.

Levine, Rhonda. 1988. *Class Struggle and the New Deal*. Lawrence, KS: University of Kansas Press.

Livesay, Harold. 1975. *Andrew Carnegie and the Rise of Big Business*. Boston, MA: Little, Brown.

Maher, Michael, Clyde Stickney, Roman Weil, and Sidney Davidson. 1991. *Managerial Accounting*. San Diego, CA: Harcourt Brace Jovanovich.

Mandel, Ernest. 1978. *Late Capitalism*. London: Verso.

March, James, and Johan Olsen. 1984. "The New Institutionalism: Organizational Factors in Political Life." *American Political Science Review* 78:734–49.

_____. 1989. *Rediscovering Institutions: The Organizational Basis of Politics*. New York: The Free Press.

Martin, David. 1959. *Mergers and the Clayton Act*. Berkeley, CA: University of California Press.

Markovsky, Barry, David Willer, and Travis Patton. 1988 "Power Relations in Exchange Networks." *American Sociological Review* 53:220–36.

Marx, Karl. [1867] 1977. *Capital*. Volume 1. New York: Vintage Books.

_____. [1893] 1981. *Capital*, Volume 2. New York: Vintage Books.

McDonough, Terrence. 1994. Pp. 72–84 in *Social Structures of Accumulation*, edited by Kotz, David, Terrence McDonough, and Michael Reich. Cambridge: Cambridge University Press.

McIntyre, Robert, and Dean Tipps. 1983. *Inequality and Decline*. Washington, DC: Center on Budget and Policy Priorities.

McNall, Scott. 1988. *The Road to Rebellion: Class Formation and Kansas Populism, 1860–1900*. Chicago, IL: University of Chicago Press.

McNamee, Stephen. 1983. "DuPont State Linkages: A Sociohistorical Case Study." *Organizational Studies* 4:201–18

McNeil, Kenneth. 1978. "Understanding Organizational Power: Building on the Weberian Legacy." *Administrative Science Quarterly* 23:65–90.

Mead, George Herbert. 1931. *The Philosophy of the Present*. Chicago, IL: University of Chicago Press.

Mergers and Acquisitions. 1976–1998. "More Than 30 Years of M&A Activity." Washington DC: Mergers and Acquisitions, Inc.

Mergerstat. 1980–1990. *Mergerstat Review*. Merrill Lynch Business, Brokerage and Valuation. Schaumburg, IL.

Meyer, John and Brian Rowan. 1977. "Institutionalized Organizations: Formal Structure as Myth and Ceremony." *American Journal of Sociology*, 83:340–363.

Miliband, Ralph. 1969. *The State in Capitalist Society*. New York: Basic Books.

Miller, Danny, and Peter Friesen. 1982. "The Longitudinal Analysis of Organizations." *Management Science* 28:1,013–1,034.

Mintz, Beth, and Michael Schwartz. 1985. *The Structure of Power in American Business*. Chicago, IL: University of Chicago Press.

Mintzberg, Henry. 1979. *The Structuring of Organizations*. Englewood Cliffs, NJ: Prentice-Hall.

Mizruchi, Mark. 1989. "Similarity of Political Behavior among Large American Corporations." *American Journal of Sociology*, 95:401–24.

_____. 1992. *The Structure of Corporate Political Action*. Cambridge, MA: Harvard University Press.

Mizruchi, Mark, and Linda Brewster Stearns. 1988. "A Longitudinal Study of the Formation of Interlocking Directorates." *Administrative Science Quarterly*, 33:194–210.

_____. 1994. "A Longitudinal Study of Borrowing by Large American Corporations." *Administrative Science Quarterly* 39:118–40.

Moody, John. [1904] 1968. *The Truth about Trusts*. New York: Greenwood Press.

Moody's. 1960–1988. *Moody's Handbook of Common Stock*. New York: Dun & Bradstreet.

_____. 1981–1993. *Moody's Industrial Manual*. New York: Dun & Bradstreet.

Moore, Barrington. 1966. *Social Origins of Dictatorship and Democracy*. Boston, MA: Beacon Press.

Morris, Jonathan, Paul Blyton, Nick Bacon, and Hans-Werner Franz. 1992. "Beyond Survival: The Implementation of New Forms of Work Organization in the UK and German Steel Industries." *The International Journal of Human Resource Management* 3:307–29.

Moskowitz Daniel, and Rich Laurie. 1986. "The Chemical Industry Fights for Tort Reform." *Chemical Week* 19:76–78.

Mueller, Willard. 1970. *Primer on Monopoly and Competition*. New York: Random House.

National Association of Manufacturers. 1941. *The Iron and Steel Industry in the Defense Economy*. New York: National Association of Manufacturers.

Neale, A. D. and D. G. Goyder. 1980. *The Antitrust Laws of the United States of America*. (3d ed.) Cambridge: Cambridge University Press.

Nelson, Daniel. 1975. *Managers and Workers*. Madison, WI: University of Wisconsin Press.

Nelson, Ralph. 1959. *Merger Movements in American History*. Princeton, NJ: Princeton University Press.

Nevins, Allan. 1953. *Study in Power: John D. Rockefeller, Industrialist and Philanthropist*. 2 vols. New York: Charles Scribner's Sons.

New York Times. 1888. October 9.

———. 1989. June 28, p. D5.

Noble, David. 1977. *American by Design*. New York: Alfred A. Knopf.

O'Connor, James. 1973. *Fiscal Crisis of the State*. New York: St. Martin's Press.

Offe, Claus. 1975. "The Theory of the Capitalist State and the Problem of Policy Formation." Pp. 125–44 in *Stress and Contradiction in Modern Capitalism*, edited by Leon Lindberg, Robert Alford, Colin Crouch, and Claus Offe. Lexington, MA: D.C. Heath and Company.

Offe, Claus, and Volker Ronge. 1975. "Theses on the Theory of the State." *New German Critique* 6:139–47

Offe, Claus, and Helmut Wiesenthal. 1980. "Two Logics of Collective Action." *Political Power and Social Theory* 1:67–115.

Osterle, Dale. 1991. *The Law of Mergers, Acquisitions, and Reorganizations*. St. Paul, Minn: West Publishing Co.

Palmer, Donald, Brad Barber, Xuenguang Zhou, and Yasemin Soysal. 1995a. "The Friendly and Predatory Acquisitions of Large U.S. Corporations in the 1960s." *American Sociological Review* 60:469–99.

———. 1995b. "The Financial Conception of Control: 'The Theory That Ate New York?'" *American Sociological Review* 60:504–508.

Palmer, Donald, Roger Friedland, and Jitendra Singh. 1986. "The Ties That Bind." *American Sociological Review* 51:781–96.

Palmer, Donald., P. Devereaux Jennings, and Xueguong Zhou. 1993. "Late Adopting of the Multidivisional Form by Large U.S. Corporations." *Administrative Science Quarterly* 38:100–131.

Paul, Randolph. 1954. *Taxation in the United States*. Boston, MA: Little, Brown and Company.

Perrow, Charles. 1986. *Complex Organizations*. New York: Random House.

Pfeffer, Jeffrey. 1972. "Merger as a Response to Organizational Interdependence." *Administrative Science Quarterly* 17:382–392.

Pfeffer, Jeffrey, and Huseyin Leblebici. 1973. "The Effect of Competition on Some Dimensions of Organizational Structure." *Social Forces* 52:268–79.

Pfeffer, Jeffrey, and Gerald Salancik. 1978. *The External Control of Organizations: A Resource Dependence Perspective*. New York: Harper & Row.

Piore, Michael, and Charles Sabel. 1984. *The Second Industrial Divide*. New York: Basic Books.

Plastic World, 1986, April.

Porter, Michael. 1987. "From Competitive Advantage to Corporate Strategy." *Harvard Business Review* 65(3):43–59.

Poulantzas, Nicos. [1974] 1978. *Classes in Contemporary Capitalism*. London: Verso.

Prechel, Harland. 1990. "Steel and the State." *American Sociological Review* 55:648–68.

———. 1991. "Irrationality and Contradiction in Organizational Change: Transformations in the Corporate Form of a U.S. Steel Corporation." *The Sociological Quarterly* 32 (August).

———. 1994a. "Restructuring the Corporate Form: The Emerging Multisubsidiary Form." Unfunded National Science Foundation grant proposal no. RF-94–1793.

———. 1994b. "Economic Crisis and the Centralization of Control over the Managerial Process: Corporate Restructuring and Neo-Fordist Decision Making." *American Sociological Review* 59:723–45.

———. 1997a. "Corporate Transformation to the Multilayered Subsidiary Form: Changing Economic Conditions and State Business Policy." *Sociological Forum* 12:405–439.

———. 1997b. "Corporate Form and the State: Business Policy and Change from the Multidivisional to the Multilayered Subsidiary Form." *Sociological Inquiry* 67:151–74.

Prechel, Harland, and John Boies. 1998a. "Capital Dependence, Financial Risk, and Change from the Multidivisional to the Multilayered Subsidiary Form." *Sociological Forum* 13:321–362.

———. 1998b. "Capital Dependence, Business Political Behavior, and Change in the Corporate Form." Paper presented at the American Sociological Association annual meeting, August, San Francisco, CA.

Prechel, Harland, John Boies, and Tim Woods. 1999. "Debt, Mergers and Acquisitions: Changing Institutional Arrangements and Transformation to the Multilayered Subsidiary Form." *Social Science Quarterly* 80:115–135.

Prentice-Hall. 1987. *Prentice-Hall 1987 Federal Tax Handbook*. Paramus, NJ: Prentice-Hall.

Quadagno, Jill. 1992. "Social Movements and State Transformation: Labor Unions and Racial Conflict in the War on Poverty." *American Sociological Review* 57:616–34.

Rae, John. 1984. *The American Automobile Industry*. Boston, MA: G.K. Hall & Company.

Raff, Daniel, and Peter Temin. 1991. "Business History and Recent Economic Theory." Pp. 71–116 in *Inside the Business Enterprise*, edited by Peter Temin. Chicago, IL: The University of Chicago Press.

Ragin, Charles. 1992. "Introduction: Cases of 'What is a Case?'" Pp. 1–19 in *What is a Case?* Cambridge: Cambridge University Press.

———. 1997. "Turning the Tables: How Case-Oriented Research Challenges Variable-Oriented Research." *Comparative Social Research*, 16:27–42.

Ranson, Stewart, Bob Hining, and Royster Greenwood. 1980. "The Structuring of Organizational Structures." *Administrative Science Quarterly* 25:1–17.

Ripley, William. 1905. *Trusts, Pools, and Corporations*. Boston, MA: Ginn & Co.

Ritzer, George. 1989. "The Permanently New Economy: The Case for Reviving Economic Sociology." *Work and Occupations* 16:243–72.

Reagan, Ronald. 1984. "Steel Import Relief Determination" (Memorandum for the U.S. Trade Representative), 18 September.

Roe, Mark. 1994. *Strong Managers, Weak Owners*. Princeton, NJ: Princeton University Press.

Roosevelt, Theodore. 1913. *An Autobiography*. New York: Scribner's.

Rosenberg, Jerry. 1978. *Dictionary of Business and Management*. New York: John Wiley & Sons.

Roy, William. 1991. "The Organization of the Corporate Class Segment of the U.S. Capitalist

Class at the Turn of This Century." Pp. 139–64 in *Bringing Class Back In*, edited by Scott McNall. Boulder, Co. Westview Press.

———. 1997. *Socializing Capital: The Rise of the Large Industrial Corporation in America*. Princeton, NJ: Princeton University Press.

Rueschemeyer, Dietrich, and Peter B. Evans. 1985. "The State and Economic Transformation: Toward an Analysis of the Conditions Underlying Effective Intervention." Pp. 44–77 in *Bringing the State Back In*, edited by Peter Evans, Dietrich Rueschemeyer, and Theda Skocpol. Cambridge: Cambridge University Press.

Rueschemeyer, Dietrich, and John Stephens. 1997. "Comparing Historical Sequences: A Powerful Tool for Causal Analysis." *Comparative Social Research* 16:55–72.

Rumelt, Richard. 1974. *Strategy, Structure, and Economic Performance*. Chicago, IL: Rand McNally.

Russell, Clifford, and William Vaughn. 1976. *Steel Production: Process, Products and Residuals*. Baltimore, MD: Resources of the Future and Johns Hopkins University Press.

Sanjai, Bhagat, Andrei Shleifer, and Robert Vishny. 1990. "Hostile Takeovers in the 1980s: The Return to Corporate Specialization." Pp. 1–72 *Brookings Papers on Economic Activity*, edited by Martin Baily and Clifford Winston. Washington, DC: Brookings Institution.

Scheiber, Harry. 1975. "Federalism and the American Economic Order, 1789–1910." *Law and Society Review* 10:51–111.

Scheuerman, William. 1986. *The Steel Crisis: The Economics of Politics of a Declining Industry*. New York: Praeger.

Schiff, Jonathan. 1986. "An Unusual Financing Source." *Management Accounting* (October):42–45.

Schugaret, Gary, James Benjamin, Arthur Francia, and Robert Strawser. 1994. *Survey of Financial Accounting*. Houston, TX: Dame Publications.

Schumpeter, Joseph. [1939] 1964. *Business Cycles: A Theoretical, Historical, and Statistical Analysis of the Capitalist Process*. Abridged by Rinding Fels. New York: McGraw-Hill.

———. 1950. *Capitalism, Socialism and Democracy*. New York: Harper Torchbooks.

Scott, W. Richard, Sanford Dornbush, Brush Bushing, and James Laing. 1967. "Organizational Evaluation and Authority," *Administrative Science Quarterly*, 12:93–117.

Seager, Henry, and Charles Gulick. 1929. *Trust and the Corporation Problems*. New York: Harper & Bros.

Seligman, Joel. [1982] 1995. *The Transformation of Wall Street*. Boston, MA: Northeastern University Press.

Shaiken, Harley. 1984. *Work Transformed: Automation & Labor in the Computer Age*. New York: Holt, Reinhart & Winston.

Shewhart, Walter. 1931. *Economic Control of Quality of Manufactured Product*. New York, NY: Van Nostrand.

———. 1939. *Statistical Method from the Viewpoint of Quality Control*. Washington, D.C.: The Graduate School: The Department of Agriculture.

Shonfield, Andrew. 1965. *Modern Capitalism: The Changing Balance of Public and Private Power*. New York: Oxford University Press.

Silver, M. L. 1982. "The Structure of Craft Work: The Construction Industry." Pp. 232–52 in *Varieties of Work*, edited by P. L. Stewart and M. G. Cantor. Beverly Hills, CA: Sage.

Simon, Herbert. 1957. *Administrative Behavior*. 2d ed. New York: Macmillan.

Sklar, Martin. 1988. *The Corporate Reconstruction of American Capitalism, 1890–1916*. Cambridge: Cambridge University Press.

Skocpol, Theda. 1980. "Political Response to Capitalist Crisis: Neo-Marxist Theories of the State and the Case of the New Deal." *Politics and Society* 10:155–201.

_____. 1985. "Bringing the State Back In: Strategies of Analysis in Current Research." Pp. 3–43 in *Bringing the State Back In*, edited by Peter Evans, Dietrich Rueschemeyer, and Theda Skocpol. Cambridge: Cambridge University Press.

Smith, Vicki. 1990. *Managing in the Corporate Interest*. Berkeley, CA: The University of California.

Sobel, Robert. 1984. *The Age of Giant Corporations*. Green Press.

Sombart, Werner. 1953. "Medieval and Modern Commercial Enterprise." Pp. 25–40 in *Enterprise and Secular Change*, edited by Frederic C. Lane and Jelle Riemersma. Homewood, IL.: Irwin.

Staples, William. 1987. "Technology, Control, and the Social Organization of Work at a British Hardware Firm, 1791–1891." *American Journal of Sociology* 93:62–88.

Stearns, Linda Brewster and Kenneth Allan. 1996. "Economic Behavior in Institutional Environments: The Corporate Merger Wave of the 1980s." *American Sociological Review*, 61:699–718.

Stearns, Linda Brewster, and Mark Mizruchi. 1986. "Broken-Tie Reconstitution and the Functions of Interorganizational Interlocks." *Administrative Science Quarterly* 31:522–38.

Stevens, William. 1913. *Industrial Combinations and Trusts*. New York: Macmillan.

Stinchcombe, Arthur. 1965. "Social Structure and Organizations." Pp. 142–93 in *Handbook of Organizations*, edited by James March. Chicago, IL: Rand McNally.

_____. 1990. *Information and Organizations*. Berkeley, CA: University of California Press.

_____. 1997. "On the Virtues of the Old Institutionalism." *Annual Review of Sociology* 23:1–18.

Stockman, David. 1986. *The Triumph of Politics*. New York. Harper & Row.

Stubbing, Richard, and Richard Mendel. 1986. *The Defense Game: An Insider Explores the Astonishing Realities of America's Defense Establishment*. New York: Harper & Row.

Sweezy, Paul. 1970. *The Theory of Capitalist Development*. New York: Oxford University Press.

Taylor, Frederick. [1911] 1967. *The Principles of Scientific Management*. New York: W.W. Norton & Company.

Temin, Peter, ed. 1991. *Inside the Business Enterprise*. Chicago, IL: University of Chicago Press.

Tennant, Richard. 1950. *The American Cigarette Industry*. New Haven, CT: Yale University Press.

The Outlook. 1986. "Partial Spinoffs Enhance Shareholder Value." New York: Standard & Poors, November 12:483–485.

Thomas, Robert. 1994. *What Machines Can't Do*. Berkeley, CA: University of California Press.

Thompson, James. 1967. *Organization in Action*. New York: McGraw-Hill.

Thorelli, Hans. 1955. *The Federal Antitrust Policy*. Baltimore, MD: Johns Hopkins Press.

Tiffany, Paul. 1988. *The Decline of American Steel*. New York: Oxford University Press.

Tilly, Charles. 1981. *As Sociology Meets History*. New York: Academic.

Tower, Walter. 1941. "Address of the President." Pp. 28–42 in *Yearbook of American Iron and Steel Institute*. New York: American Iron and Steel Institute.

Tushman, Michael, and Elaine Romanelli. 1985. "Organizational Evolution." *Research in Organizational Behavior* 7:171–222.

Urofsky, Melvin. 1982. "Proposed Federal Incorporations in the Progressive Era." *The American Journal of Legal History* 26:160–83.

U.S. Bureau of Census. 1975. *Historical Statistics of the United States: Colonial Times to 1979*. Washington, DC: Government Printing Office.

U.S. Census of Manufacturers. 1972. Volume 1.

U.S. Congress. 1946. Senate, Surplus Property Subcommittee of the Committee on Military Affairs, "War-Plant Disposal: Acceptance of Bid of United States Steel Corporation for Geneva Steel Plant, Report Pursuant to S. Res. 129."

———. 1948. Senate, Hearings before the Special Committee to Study Problems of American Small Business. "Problems of American Small Business." 80th Congress, 2d Session.

———. 1950a. House of Representatives, Subcommittee on Study of Monopoly Power of the Committee on the Judiciary. "Study of Monopoly Power: Hearing." 81st Congress, 2nd Session.

———. 1950b. *Congressional Quarterly Almanac.* Washington D.C., p. 654.

———. 1961. House of Representatives, 87th Congress. 1st session: "Message from the President of the United States Relative of Our Federal Tax System." April 20. House Document No. 140.

———. 1962. Senate, Committee on Finance, Hearing, Revenue Act of 1962, 87th Congress, 2d Session, April.

———. 1968. Steel Imports, Staff Study of Senate Committee on Finance, Senate Document no. 107, 90th Congress.

———. 1973. House of Representatives, Committee on Ways and Means. Trade Reform Act of 1973. Hearing of HR 6767, 93rd Congress, 1st session, pp. 3,957–4,031.

———. 1977. House Ways and Means Committee on Trade, Hearing on World Steel Trade: Current Trends and Structural Problems, 95th Congress, September 30.

———. 1978. House of Representatives, Hearing before the Subcommittee on Trade of the Committee on Ways and Means. Reprint in Administration's Comprehensive Program for the Steel Industry. Originally titled "A Comprehensive Program for the Steel Industry," Report to the President Submitted by Anthony M. Soloman, Chairman Task Force, December 6, 1977.

———. 1984. "The Effects of Import Quotas on the Steel Industry." Congressional Budget Office.

U.S. Department of Commerce. 1960–1979. Statistical Abstract of the United States. Washington, DC: Government Printing Office.

———. 1965–1988. Quarterly Financial Reports for Manufacturing, Mining, & Trade Corporations. Washington. DC: Government Printing Office.

Useem, Michael. 1983. "The Corporate Community: Its Social Organization and the Rise of Business Political Activity in the United States and United Kingdom." In *Organizational Theory and Public Policy*, edited by Richard Hall and Robert Quinn. Beverly Hills, CA: Sage Publications.

———. 1993. *Executive Defense.* Cambridge, Cambridge University Press.

U.S. Federal Election Commission. 1994. *Campaign Expenditures in the United States, 1978–1992: Longitudinal Political Action Committee (PAC) Data [MRDF].* ICPSR version. Washington, DC Federal Election Commission [producer], Ann Arbor, MI: Interuniversity Consortium for Political and Social Research [distributor], 1995.

U.S. Federal Trade Commission. 1981. *Report on Mergers and Acquisitions.* Washington, DC: Government Printing Office.

U.S. Federal Trade Commission—Securities and Exchange Commission. 1950–1982. Quarterly Financial Reports for Manufacturing Corporations.

———. 1977. Staff Report on the United States Steel Industry and its International Rivals: Trends and Factors Determining International Competitiveness.

U.S. Office of Technological Assessment. 1981. Technology and Steel Industry Competitiveness. (June).

Veblen, Thorsten. [1923] 1967. *Absentee Ownership and Business Enterprise in Recent Times.* Boston, MA: Beacon Press.

Vogel, David. 1989. *Fluctuating Fortunes.* New York: Basic Books.

Wall Street Journal. 1995a. Junaruay 4, p. A2.

———. 1995b. July 26, p. B5.

———. 1995c. November 11, p. B1.

———. 1996. December 24, p. A3.

———. 1998. January 2, p. R38.

Walter, Ingo. 1983. "Structural Adjustment and Trade Policy in the International Steel Industry." Pp. 483–525 in *Trade Policy in the 1980s,* edited by William C. Cline. Washington, DC: Institute for International Economics.

War Production Board. 1945. "American Industry in War and Transition, 1940–1950." Document 27, July 20. Washington, DC: U.S. Government Printing Office.

Warriner, Charles. 1980. "Organizational Types." Unpublished paper. Lawrence, KS: University of Kansas.

———. 1984. *Organizations and Their Environments.* Greenwich, CT: JAI Press Inc.

Waters, Malcolm. 1990. "Interest and Procedural Norms in the Analysis of Collegiality." *American Journal of Sociology* 96:192–99.

Watkins, Myron. 1927. *Industrial Combinations and Public Policy.* Boston, MA: Houghton Mifflin.

Weber, Max. [1921] 1978. *Economy and Society.* Edited by Guenther Roth and Claus Wittich. Berkeley, CA: University of California Press.

———. 1946. *From Max Weber: Essays in Sociology.* Edited by Hans Girth and C. W. Mills. New York: Oxford University Press.

———. 1949. *The Methodology of the Social Sciences.* Translated and edited by Edward Shils and Henry Finch. New York: The Free Press.

———. 1958. *The Protestant Ethic and the Spirit of Capitalism.* New York, NY: Charles Scribner's Sons.

Weick, Karl. 1969. *The Social Psychology of Organizing.* Reading, MA: Addison-Wesley.

———. 1976. "Educational Organizations as Loosely Coupled Systems." *Administrative Science Quarterly* 21 (1):1–19.

Weitzel, William, and Ellen Jonsson. 1989. "Decline in Organizations: A Literature Integration and Extension." *Administrative Science Quarterly* 34:91–109.

Wiebe, Robert. 1967. *A Search for Order, 1877–1920.* New York: Wang.

Willens, Robert. 1988. "The Revenue Act of 1987." *Journal of Accountancy* (March):22–29.

Willer, David. 1986. "Vulnerability and the Location of Power Positions." *American Journal of Sociology* 92:441–48.

Williamson, Oliver. 1970. *Corporate Control and Business Behavior.* Englewood Cliffs, N.J.: Prentice-Hall.

———. 1975. *Markets and Hierarchies.* New York: The Free Press.

———. 1985. *The Economic Institutions of Capitalism.* New York: The Free Press.

Williamson, Oliver, and William Ouchi. 1981. "The Markets and Hierarchies and Visible Hand Perspectives." Pp. 347–370 in *Perspectives in Organizational Design and Behavior,* edited by Andrew Van de Ven and William Joyce. New York: John Wiley.

Wolfson, Martin. 1994. *Financial Crisis: Understanding the Postwar U. S. Experience,* second edition. Armonk, NY: M. E. Sharpe.

Wood, Robert. 1987. "General Utilities Repeal." *Mergers and Acquisitions* (January–February):44–47.

Woods, Tim. 1998. "Organizational State Structures and State Autonomy: Analyzing the

Fast Track to the NAFTA." Paper presented at the annual meeting of the American Sociological Association, San Francisco, CA.

Zammuto, Raymond, and Kim Cameron. 1985. "Environmental Decline and Organizational Response." *Research in Organizational Behavior* 7:223–62.

Zeitlin, Maurice. 1974. "Corporate Ownership and Corporate Control." *American Journal of Sociology* 79:1073–80.

_____. 1980. *Classes, Class Conflict, and the State.* Cambridge: Winthrop.

_____. 1984. *The Civil Wars in Chile (or the Bourgeois Revolutions That Never Were).* Princeton, NJ: Princeton University Press.

_____. 1989. *The Large Corporation and Contemporary Classes.* New Brunswick, NJ: Rutgers University Press.

Zeitlin, Maurice, W. Lawrence Neuman, and Richard Ratcliff. 1976. "Class Segments: Agrarian Property and Political Leadership in the Capitalist Class of Chile." *American Sociological Review* 41:1,006–29.

Zucker, Lynn. 1991. "The Role of Institutionalization in Cultural Persistence." Pp. 63–81 in *The New Institutionalism in Organizational Analysis,* edited by Powell, Walter and Paul DiMaggio. Chicago, IL: The University of Chicago Press.

Index